Beyond
the
Brain

SUNY Series in Transpersonal and Humanistic Psychology
Richard D. Mann and Jeanne B. Mann, Editors

Beyond the Brain

Birth, Death, and Transcendence in Psychotherapy

STANISLAV GROF

State University of New York Press

To Christina, Paul, and my mother Maria

Published by
State University of New York, Albany
© 1985 State University of New York
All rights reserved
Printed in the United States of America
For information, address State University of New York
Press, State University Plaza, Albany, N.Y., 12246

Library of Congress Cataloging in Publication Data

Grof, Stanislav, 1931–
Beyond the brain.
Bibliography: p.
Includes index.
1. Transpersonal psychotherapy. 2. Consciousness.
3. Subconsciousness. 4. Psychiatry—Philosophy.
I. Title.
RC489.T75G76   1985   616.89′14   85-14882
ISBN 0-87395-953-1
ISBN 0-87395-899-3 (pbk.)
10 9 8 7 6 5 4 3 2

Fig. 5 is reprinted with permission from Timothy Leary, *Politics of Ecstasy* (New York: G. P. Putnam's, 1965).

Fig. 6 is reprinted by permission from Michael Wenyon, *Understanding Holography* (New York: Arco Publishing).

Figs. 7 and 8 are reprinted with permission from J. Roubíček, *Experimental Psychoses* (Prague: Státní Zdravotnické Nakladatelstvi, 1961).

Figs. 17 and 21 are reprinted by permission from H. Giger, *Necronomicon* (Basel: Sphinx, 1977).

Figs. 18 and 19 are reprinted by permission from K. Seligman, *The History of Magic* (New York: Pantheon, 1948).

Fig. 20 is reprinted by permission from the Bodleian Library, Douce Portfolio W.7.7.

Contents

CHAPTER SIX

A New Understanding of The
Psychotherapeutic Process   336

CHAPTER SEVEN

New Perspectives in Psychotherapy and Self-Exploration 371

CHAPTER EIGHT

Epilogue: The Current Global Crisis and the
Future of Consciousness Evolution   405

Acknowledgments

This book is the product of an intensive and systematic search that has extended over a period of almost three decades. In all the stages of this long quest, the professional and personal dimensions were so intimately interwoven that they have merged into an inseparable amalgam. It has been a journey of personal transformation and self-discovery as much as a process of scientific exploration of uncharted territories of the human psyche.

Over the years, I have received inestimable help, encouragement, and inspiration from many people who have been important in my life, some as teachers, others as friends and fellow searchers, and a few in a combination of all these roles. It is impossible here to mention all of them by name. However, in several instances the contributions have been so outstanding that they deserve special notice.

Angeles Arrien, an anthropologist trained in the Basque mystical tradition, has been a true friend and a living example of how to integrate the feminine and masculine aspects of one's psyche and how to "walk the mystical path with practical feet."

Anne and Jim Armstrong have taught me much about the nature of a genuine psychic gift and about the evolutionary potential of transpersonal crises. Their excitement, enthusiasm, and courage in exploring the human psyche and the unknown provide a unique example of a shared adventure in consciousness.

Gregory Bateson, with whom I had the privilege to spend many hours of intense personal and intellectual interaction during the two and a half years before his death, when we both were scholars-in-residence at the Esalen Institute in California, was an important teacher and a special friend. His incisive critique of mechanistic thinking in science and his creative synthesis of cybernetics, information and systems theory, psychiatry, and anthropology have had a profound influence on my own development.

Joseph Campbell, brilliant thinker, master teacher, and a dear friend, has taught me invaluable lessons about the paramount relevance of mythology for psychiatry and our everyday life. His influence on my personal life has been equally profound.

Fritjof Capra's work has played a critical role in my own intellectual development and scientific quest. Reading his *Tao of Physics* gave me firm hope that the extraordinary observations from modern consciousness research could in the future be integrated into a new and comprehensive scientific world view. Our friendship over the years, and a rich exchange of information during the time he was writing *The Turning Point,* have been of great help for my work on the present book.

Michael and Sandra Harner, who belong to our most intimate circle of friends, have given me much support, encouragement, and opportunity for the sharing of unconventional observations and information. Michael, who combines the role of a respectable academician and an accomplished "white shaman," provides an important model and example for my own life.

Swami Muktananda Paramahansa, the late spiritual teacher and head of the Siddha Yoga lineage, with whom I have had much contact over the years, gave me the unique opportunity to observe and experience the powerful influence of a vital mystical tradition on human lives.

Ralph Metzner, who combines in a unique way solid scholarship, an inquisitive mind, and an adventurous spirit, has been an important friend and fellow searcher.

Rupert Sheldrake has been able to formulate with unusual clarity and incisiveness the limitations of mechanistic thinking in natural sciences that I have myself been aware of for many years. His work has helped me considerably to free myself from the straitjacket of the belief systems imposed on me by my professional training.

Anthony Sutich and Abraham Maslow, the two main initiators and founders of both humanistic and transpersonal psychology, were for me important sources of inspiration, giving a concrete form to some of my dreams and hopes concerning the future of psychology. It was an unforgettable experience to be with them at the cradle of the transpersonal movement.

Arthur Young's theory of process represents one of the most exciting concepts I have encountered during my intellectual life. My appreciation of it as a scientific metaparadigm of the future has been increasing rapidly as I become more intimately acquainted with it.

The discovery of the holonomic principles opened for me an entirely new world of possibilities for theoretical speculations and practical applications. My special thanks here belong to David Bohm, Karl Pribram, and Hugo Zucarelli.

My clinical work with psychedelics has played a critical role in instigating my lifelong interest in consciousness research and in generating the most important data discussed in this book. It would not have been possible without the epoch-making discoveries of Albert Hofmann. I would like to express here my deep gratitude for the profound influence that his work has had on my professional and personal life.

The stimulating atmosphere of the Esalen Institute and the natural beauty of the Big Sur coast have provided a unique setting for the work on this book. I would like to thank my Esalen friends, Dick and Chris Price, Michael and Dulce Murphy, and Rick and Heather Tarnas for their support over the years. In addition, Rick taught me much about the relationships between astronomical processes and the archetypal dynamics. Kathleen O'Shaughnessy deserves special thanks for her dedicated and sensitive help in the final typing of the manuscript.

My deepest thanks go to the immediate members of my family—my mother Maria, my brother Paul, and my wife Christina. They have carried the most immediate impact of the intellectual, psychological, philosophical, and spiritual roller coaster of my unconventional quest over the years. Christina, in particular, has been my closest friend and fellow searcher for many years, sharing both my personal and professional life. We have jointly developed and practiced the technique of holotropic therapy described in this book. I have learned from her own dramatic personal journey many lessons that only life can provide. She has also been the main inspiration for the Spiritual Emergency Network that we jointly launched in Big Sur, California.

Introduction

The following pages represent an attempt to condense into a single volume data from almost thirty years of research on nonordinary states of consciousness induced by psychedelic drugs and a variety of nonpharmacological methods. It is a document reflecting my efforts to organize and integrate in a comprehensive way a large number of observations that have for many years daily challenged my scientific belief system, as well as my common sense. In response to this avalanche of disturbing data, I have many times adjusted and readjusted my conceptual frameworks and patched them up with various ad hoc hypotheses, only to face the need to change them again.

In view of the difficulties I myself have had over the years in accepting the evidence presented in this book, I do not expect my readers to find it easy to believe much of the information I put forward, unless they themselves have had corresponding experiences, personally and in work with others. I hope those who belong to this category will welcome this evidence as independent confirmation of many of the issues they themselves have been struggling with. It has been exciting and encouraging for me over the years to come across reports of others, indicating that my quest was not as solitary as it has at times appeared.

As for readers who have not had such corresponding experiences, I am particularly interested in reaching those who are sufficiently open-minded to use the data I present as an incentive to conduct their own work aimed at confirming or refuting them. I do not expect anybody to accept the material in this book at face value; the technologies through which the experiences and observations discussed were obtained are described in sufficient detail to allow replication. The use of psychedelics, the most potent tool among these technologies, is, of course, associated these days with considerable political, legal, and administrative difficulty. However, the nondrug approaches described are readily available to anyone seriously interested in pursuing this avenue of research.

The data may also interest those researchers who have been studying the same or related phenomena in the context of other disciplines and with the use of other techniques and methodologies. Here belong, for example, anthropologists doing field research in aboriginal cultures and studying shamanic practices, rites of passage, and healing ceremonies; thanatologists exploring death and near-death experiences; therapists using various powerful experiential techniques of psychotherapy, body work, or nonauthoritative forms of hypnosis; scientists experimenting with laboratory mind-altering techniques, such as sensory isolation or overload, biofeedback techniques, holophonic sound or other sound technologies; psychiatrists working with patients experiencing acute nonordinary states of consciousness; parapsychologists researching extrasensory perception; and physicists interested in the nature of space and time and in the implications of quantum-relativistic physics for the understanding of the relationship between matter and consciousness.

My own difficulties in accepting these new observations without repeated, overwhelming evidence and, particularly, without first-hand personal experience, have shown me the futility of evaluating the data from consciousness research from the ivory tower of one's old belief systems. The history of science clearly demonstrates the short-sightedness of rejecting new observations and evidence just because they are incompatible with the existing world view or current scientific paradigm. The unwillingness of Galileo's contemporaries to look through his telescope, because they already knew there could not possibly be craters on the moon, is a prime example of the limitations of such an approach.

I believe that many of the problems discussed in the following pages are of such basic importance and general interest that the book could be of use for many intelligent lay persons who are not involved specifically in research in any of the areas mentioned. The issues that should be particularly relevant for general audiences are the new image of reality and of human nature; a scientific world view incorporating the mystical dimensions of existence; an alternative understanding of emotional and psychosomatic problems, including some psychotic states; a new strategy for therapy and self-exploration; and insights into the current global crisis. This book, in manuscript form, has already been helpful for many individuals experiencing episodes of nonordinary states of consciousness, providing for them a new conceptual framework and a new strategy.

When, in the early days of my psychedelic research, I approached my friends and immediate colleagues to share the new exciting observations, I learned an important lesson. It became painfully obvious that an honest and uncensored presentation of what I have seen would meet deep disbelief and suspicion and would entail a serious risk of professional disqualification and ridicule. From then on, the task has not been to find the best way of articulating and communicating the new realities in their totality, but to decide from one situation to another how much it was possible and reasonable to report, what metaphors and language to use, and how to relate the reported facts to the existing body of knowledge accepted by the scientific community.

During my first ten years of psychedelic research in Czechoslovakia, I found only a handful of friends and colleagues who were sufficiently open-minded to accept the entire spectrum of the new findings and consider seriously their scientific and philosophical implications. Although, in 1967, when I was leaving Czechoslovakia, there were more than forty research projects on the use of psychedelics, many of those involved tried to limit their clinical work and conceptual frameworks to the biographical level; they were avoiding the new observations, or attempting to explain them in traditional ways.

When I began lecturing about my European research in the United States, the circle of my like-minded colleagues increased

rapidly. Among these new friends were not only psychedelic researchers, but anthropologists, parapsychologists, neurophysiologists, and thanatologists, who shared with me a determined conceptual struggle to integrate the results of unconventional personal
and professional search and research with the philosophy of contemporary science. Many of them also had files of unpublished and
unpublishable data and observations, articles, and even manuscripts
that they did not dare to share with their Newtonian-Cartesian
colleagues or with the public. After my many years of professional
isolation, this was a very exciting and encouraging development.

In the late sixties, I made the acquaintance of a small group
of professionals, including Abraham Maslow, Anthony Sutich, and
James Fadiman, who shared my belief that the time was ripe for
launching a new movement in psychology, focusing on the study
of consciousness and recognizing the significance of the spiritual
dimensions of the psyche. After several meetings aimed at clarification of these new concepts, we decided to call this new orientation
"transpersonal psychology." This was soon followed by the launching of the *Journal of Transpersonal Psychology* and the Association
for Transpersonal Psychology.

Although it was very encouraging to find a sense of professional
identity—a rapidly growing group of like-minded colleagues sharing
the same understanding of psychology and psychiatry—this did not
completely solve my old problem of identity as a scientist. In spite
of the fact that transpersonal psychology had a certain inner cohesion and was to some extent comprehensive in itself, it was almost
completely isolated from mainstream science. Like my own world
view and belief system, it was vulnerable to accusations of being
irrational and unscientific, meaning, incompatible with common
sense and current scientific thinking.

This situation changed very rapidly during the first decade of
the Association of Transpersonal Psychology. It became clear that
the transpersonal orientation and perspective by far transcended
the narrow confines of psychiatry, psychology, and psychotherapy.
During this time, important links were made to revolutionary developments in other scientific disciplines—quantum-relativity physics, systems and information theory, study of dissipative structures,
brain research, parapsychology, holography, and holonomic thinking. More recently this has been complemented by new formulations

in biology, embryology, genetics, and the study of behavior, and by the development of holophonic technology.

Many of the pioneers of these new ways of thinking in science participated over the years as guest faculty members during the four-week experimental educational programs that my wife Christina and I have been conducting at the Esalen Institute, in Big Sur, California. In this context, I have been able to spend formal and informal time in fascinating interactions with Frank Barr, Gregory Bateson, Joseph Campbell, Fritjof Capra, Duane Elgin, David Finkelstein, Elmer and Alyce Green, Michael Harner, Stanley Krippner, Rupert Sheldrake, Saul-Paul Siraq, Russel Targ, Charles Tart, Arthur Young, and many others. I have also had the opportunity for some intimate time and information exchange with pioneers in transpersonal psychology—Angeles Arrien, Arthur Hastings, Jack Kornfield, Ralph Metzner, John Perry, June Singer, Richard Tarnas, Frances Vaughan, Roger Walsh, and Ken Wilber.

The contacts and interactions with a wide spectrum of unique and creative individuals, made possible by our four-week seminars at the institute, were the major source of inspiration for the International Transpersonal Association (ITA), which I launched, in 1978, jointly with Michael Murphy and Richard Price, the founders of the Esalen Institute. The ITA differed from the Association for Transpersonal Psychology in its explicit international and interdisciplinary emphasis. During the early years, when I functioned as ITA's first president, I had the opportunity to organize large international transpersonal conferences in Boston, Melbourne, and Bombay. These annual meetings of the ITA have attracted groups of unique speakers and large open-minded audiences and have helped to crystallize the theoretical formulations and consolidate the transpersonal movement.

At present, the new thinking in science seems to be rapidly gaining momentum. Although the fascinating individual developments have not yet been integrated into a coherent and comprehensive scientific paradigm replacing the mechanistic model of the universe, new pieces are being added to this impressive jigsaw puzzle at an unprecedented rate. It is my personal belief that it is extremely important for the future of science and possibly of our planet that these new developments win the acceptance of the scientific community. For this reason, I have not presented this material in a simplified and popularized version, which would have been the preference of many publishers with whom I negotiated. I felt a strong need to present the data from my consciousness research in the context of the revolutionary findings in the other disciplines mentioned above, which were so important for my own personal and professional development. The presentation of my own data is thus preceded by a chapter on the emerging paradigm, which summarizes the work of many other researchers and thinkers and sets the context for the rest of the book.

One of the deepest influences on my thinking was the discovery of holonomic principles, as exemplified by the work of Gottfried Wilhelm von Leibnitz, Jean Baptiste Fourier, Dennis Gabor, David Bohm, Karl Pribram, and Hugo Zucarelli. It was the recognition of the revolutionary alternatives to the mechanistic concept of the "mind contained in the brain," offered by holonomic thinking, that inspired the title of this book, *Beyond the Brain*.

CHAPTER ONE

The Nature of Reality: Dawning of a New Paradigm

In various sections of this book, important observations from diverse fields will be discussed—observations that cannot be accounted for and explained by mechanistic science and the traditional conceptual frameworks of psychiatry, psychology, anthropology, and medicine. Some of the new data are of such far-reaching significance that they indicate the need for a drastic revision of current understanding of human nature, and even the nature of reality. It seems, therefore, appropriate to start this book with an excursion into the philosophy of science by reviewing some modern ideas about the relationship between scientific theories and reality. Much of the resistance on the part of traditional scientists against the influx of new revolutionary data is based on a fundamental misunderstanding of the nature and function of scientific theories. In the last few decades, such philosophers and historians of science as Thomas Kuhn (1962), Philipp

Frank (1974), Karl Popper (1963; 1965), and Paul Feyerabend (1978) have brought much clarity into this area. The pioneering work of these thinkers deserves a brief review here.

Philosophy of Science
and the Role of Paradigms

Since the Industrial Revolution, Western science has achieved astounding successes and has become a powerful force, shaping the lives of millions of people. Its materialistic and mechanistic orientations have all but replaced theology and philosophy as guiding principles of human existence and transformed to an unimaginable degree the world we live in. The technological triumphs have been so remarkable that, until quite recently, very few individuals questioned the absolute authority of science in determining the basic strategies of life. The textbooks of various disciplines tend to describe the history of science as a linear development with a gradual accumulation of knowledge about the universe that culminates in the present state of affairs. Important figures in the development of scientific thinking are thus presented as contributors who have worked on the same set of problems and according to the same set of fixed rules that the most recent achievements have established as scientific. Each period of the history of scientific ideas and methods is seen as a logical step in a gradual approximation to an increasingly accurate description of the universe and to the ultimate truth about existence.

Detailed analysis of the history and philosophy of science reveals that this is a grossly distorted and romanticized image of the actual course of events. One can make a very powerful and convincing argument that the history of science is far from linear and that, in spite of their technological successes, scientific disciplines do not necessarily bring us closer to an ever more accurate description of reality. The most prominent representative of this heretical point of view is the physicist and historian of science, Thomas Kuhn. His study of the development of scientific theories and revolutions in science was first inspired by his observation of certain fundamental differences between the social and natural sciences. He was struck by the number and extent of disagreements among social scientists concerning the basic nature of legitimate problems and approaches. This situation seemed to contrast sharply with that of the natural sciences. Although it was unlikely that practitioners of astronomy, physics, and chemistry would have firmer and more definitive answers than psychologists, anthropologists, and sociologists, the former for some reason did not seem to get involved in serious controversies over fundamental problems. Exploring this obvious discrepancy further, Kuhn launched an intensive study of the history of science that, after fifteen years, led to the publication of his ground-breaking work, *The Structure of Scientific Revolutions* (1962).

In the course of this research it became increasingly evident that, from a historical perspective, even the development of the so-called hard sciences is far from smooth and unambiguous. The history of science is by no means a process of gradual accumulation of data and formulation of ever more accurate theories. Instead, it shows a clearly cyclical nature with specific stages and characteristic dynamics. This process is lawful, and the changes involved can be understood and even predicted; the central concept of Kuhn's theory, which makes this possible, is that of a paradigm. In the broadest sense, a *paradigm* can be defined as a constellation of beliefs, values, and techniques shared by the members of a given scientific community. Some paradigms are of a basic philosophical nature and are very general and encompassing, others govern scientific thinking in rather specific and circumscribed areas of research. A particular paradigm can thus be mandatory for all natural sciences; others for astronomy, physics, biochemistry, or molecular biology; yet others for such highly specialized and esoteric areas as the study of viruses or genetic engineering.[1]

A paradigm is as essential for science as are observation and experiment; adherence to specific paradigms is an absolutely indispensable prerequisite of any serious scientific endeavor. Reality is extremely complex and dealing with it in its totality is impossible. Science does not and cannot observe and take into consideration all the variables involved in a particular phenomenon, conduct all possible experiments, and perform all laboratory or clinical manipulations. The scientist must reduce the problem to a workable scale and his or her selection is guided by the leading paradigm of the time. Thus the scientist cannot avoid bringing a definite belief system into the area of study.

Scientific observations do not themselves clearly dictate unique and unambiguous solutions; no paradigm ever explains all available facts, and many different paradigms can theoretically account for the same set of data. Many factors determine which aspect of a complex phenomenon will be chosen and which of many conceivable experiments will be carried out or conducted first—accidents of investigation, basic education and specific training, prior experience in other fields, individual makeup, economic and political factors, and other variables. Observations and experiments can and must drastically reduce and restrict the range of acceptable scientific solutions; without this element, science would become science fiction. However, they cannot in and by themselves fully justify a particular interpretation or a belief system. It is thus, in principle, impossible to practice science without some set of a priori beliefs, fundamental metaphysical assumptions, and answers about the nature of reality and of human knowledge. However, the relative nature of any paradigm, no matter how advanced and convincingly articulated, should be clearly recognized and the scientist should not confuse it with the truth about reality.

According to Thomas Kuhn, paradigms play a crucial, complex, and ambiguous role in the history of science. Because of the above reasons, they are absolutely essential and indispensable for scientific progress. However, in certain stages of development they function as conceptual straitjackets that drastically interfere with the possibility of new discoveries and with the exploration of new areas of reality. In the history of science, the progressive and reactionary function of paradigms seems to oscillate in certain predictable patterns.

Early stages of most sciences, which Thomas Kuhn describes as "pre-paradigm periods," have been characterized by conceptual chaos and competition among a large number of divergent views of nature. None of these can be clearly discarded as incorrect, since they are all roughly compatible with observations and with the scientific method of the time. A simple, elegant and plausible conceptualization of the data that seems to account well for the majority of available observations, and also holds promise as a guideline for future explorations, emerges out of this situation as the dominant paradigm.

When a paradigm is accepted by the majority of the scientific community, it becomes the mandatory way of approaching problems. At this point, it also tends to be mistaken for an accurate description of reality instead of being seen as a useful map, a convenient approximation, and a model for organizing currently available data. This confusion of the map with the territory is characteristic for the history of science. The limited knowledge of nature that has existed in successive historical periods has been seen by the practitioners of science of those times as a comprehensive image of reality that was incomplete only in details. This observation is so striking that it would be easy for a historian to present the development of science as a history of errors and idiosyncrasies rather than as a systematic accumulation of information and a gradual approximation to ultimate truth.

Once a paradigm has been accepted, it becomes a powerful catalyst of scientific progress; in Kuhn's terminology, this stage is referred to as the "period of normal science." Most scientists spend all their time pursuing normal science; consequently, in the past, this particular aspect of scientific activity has become synonymous with science itself. Normal science is predicated on the assumption that the scientific community knows what the universe is like. The leading theory defines not only what the world is, but also what it is not; it determines what is possible, as well as what is in principle impossible. Thomas Kuhn describes research as "a strenuous and devoted effort to force nature into the conceptual boxes supplied by professional education." As long as the paradigm is taken for granted, only those problems will be considered legitimate that can be assumed to have solutions; this guarantees rapid success of normal science. Under these circumstances, the scientific community suppresses, often at a considerable cost, all novelties, because they are subversive to its basic commitments.

Paradigms have not only a cognitive, but also a normative influence; in addition to being statements about nature and reality, they also define the permissible problem field, determine the acceptable methods of approaching it, and set the standards of solution. Under the influence of a paradigm, all the fundamentals of science in a particular area become drastically redefined. Some problems that were seen as crucial might be declared irrelevant or unscientific, others are relegated to another discipline. Conversely, certain issues previously nonexistent or trivial may suddenly represent significant scientific factors or achievements. Even in areas where the old paradigm retains its validity, the understanding of the problems is not identical and requires translation and redefinition. Normal science based on the new paradigm is not only incompatible, but incommensurate with the practice governed by the previous one.

Normal science is essentially puzzle solving; its results are generally anticipated by the paradigm and it produces little novelty. The emphasis is on the way of achieving the results, and the objective is a further articulation of the leading paradigm, contributing to the scope and precision with which it can be applied. Normal research is, thus, cumulative, because scientists select only those problems that can be solved with conceptual and instrumental tools already in existence. Cumulative acquisition of fundamentally new knowledge under these circumstances is not only rare and unlikely, but improbable in principle. New discovery can appear only if the anticipations about nature and instruments based on the existing paradigm are failing. New theories cannot arise without destructive changes in the old beliefs about nature.

A really new and radical theory is never just an addition or increment to the existing knowledge. It changes basic rules, requires drastic revision or reformulation of the fundamental assumptions of prior theory, and involves re-evaluation of the existing facts and observations. According to Thomas Kuhn, only events of this nature represent true scientific revolutions. These can occur in certain limited fields of human knowledge or they can have a sweeping influence on a number of disciplines. The shifts from Aristotelian to Newtonian physics, or from Newtonian to Einsteinian physics, from the Ptolemaic geocentric system to the astronomy of Copernicus and Galileo, or from the phlogiston theory to Lavoisier's chemistry are salient examples of changes of this kind. Each of them required rejection of a widely accepted and honored scientific theory in favor of another that was in principle incompatible with it. They all resulted in a drastic redefinition of the problems available and important for scientific exploration. In addition, they also redefined what should be considered an admissible problem and what should be the standards of a legitimate solution of a problem. This led to a drastic transformation of scientific imagination; it is not an exaggeration to say that the very perception of the world itself changed as a result of their impact.

Thomas Kuhn noted that scientific revolutions are preceded and heralded by a period of conceptual chaos in which the normal practice of science gradually changes into what he calls "extraordinary science." Sooner or later, the everyday practice of normal science will necessarily lead to the discovery of anomalies. In many instances, certain pieces of equipment will fail to perform as anticipated by the paradigm, numerous observations accumulate that cannot be in any way accommodated by the existing belief system, or a problem that ought to be solved resists repeated efforts of prominent representatives of the profession.

As long as the paradigm exerts its spell on the scientific community, anomalies will not be sufficient to question the validity of basic assumptions. Initially, unexpected results tend to be labeled "bad research," since the range of possible results is clearly defined by the paradigm. When the results are confirmed by the repeated experiments, this can lead to a crisis in the field. However, even then scientists do not renounce the paradigm that has led them into crisis. Once a scientific theory has achieved the status of a paradigm, it will not be declared invalid unless viable alternative is available. Lack of congruence between the postulates of a paradigm and observations of the world is not sufficient. For some time the discrepancy will be seen as a problem that might eventually be solved by future modifications and articulations.

However, when, after a period of tedious and fruitless effort, the anomaly suddenly emerges as more than just another puzzle, the discipline involved enters a period of extraordinary science. The best minds in the field concentrate their attention on the problem. The criteria for research tend to loosen up, and the experimenters become more open-minded and willing to consider daring alternatives. At this time, competing formulations proliferate and become increasingly divergent. The discontent with the existing paradigm grows and is expressed more and more explicitly. Scientists are willing to take recourse to philosophy and debate over fundamental assumptions—a situation that is inconceivable during periods of normal research. Before and during scientific revolutions there are also deep debates over legitimate methods, problems, and standards. Under these circumstances, in a state of growing crisis, professional insecurity increases. The failure of old rules leads to an intense search for new ones.

During the transition, there is an overlap between the problems that can be solved by the old and by the new paradigms. This is not surprising since philosophers of science have repeatedly demonstrated that more than one theoretical construct is always applicable to a given set of data. Scientific revolutions are those noncumulative episodes in which an older paradigm is replaced in its entirety, or in part, by a new one that is incompatible with it. The choice between two competing paradigms cannot be made by the use of evaluative procedures of normal science. The latter are a direct outgrowth of the old paradigm that is at issue, and their validity is critically dependent on the outcome of the argument. The function of the paradigm is thus of necessity circular; it can persuade but not convince by logical or even probabilistic arguments.

The two competing schools have a serious problem of communication or language. They operate on the basis of different basic postulates, assumptions about reality, and definitions of elementary concepts. As a result, they will not even agree as to what the important problems are, their nature is, and what would constitute their solution. Their criteria of science are not the same, their arguments are paradigm-dependent, and meaningful confrontation is impossible without intelligent translation. Within the new paradigm, the old terms are drastically redefined and receive a totally new meaning; as a result, they will appear to be related to each other in a very different way. The communication across the conceptual divide is only partial and confusing. Entirely different meanings of such concepts as matter, space, and time in the Newtonian and Einsteinian models could be used here as characteristic examples. At some point, a value judgment will also enter the field, since different paradigms differ in terms of which problems they solve and which questions they leave unanswered. The criteria for assessing this situation lie entirely outside the scope of normal science.

A scientist who is practicing normal science is essentially a problem solver. He takes the paradigm for granted and has no interest in testing its validity. As a matter of fact, he or she has considerable investment in the preservation of its basic assumptions. In part this is based on understandable human motives, such as time and energy spent in past training or academic achievements closely linked with the exploitation of the paradigm at issue. However, the problem has much deeper roots and goes beyond human errors and emotional investment. It touches on the very nature of paradigms and their role for science.

An important part of this resistance is a deep reliance on the current paradigm as a true representation of reality and trust that it will ultimately solve all its problems. Thus, the resistance to the new paradigm is, in the last analysis, the very attitude that makes normal science possible. A scientist practicing normal science resembles a chess player whose problem-solving activity and capacity is critically dependent on a rigid set of rules. The objective of the game is to search for optimal solutions within the context of these a priori given rules; under these circumstances it would be absurd to consider questioning these rules, not to say changing them. The rules of the game are taken for granted in both instances, and they represent a necessary set of premises for the problem-solving activity. In science, novelty for its own sake is not desirable as it is in other creative fields.

Paradigm testing thus occurs only after persistent failure to solve an important puzzle has created a crisis and led to a competition of two rival paradigms. The new candidate for a paradigm has to meet certain important criteria to qualify. It must offer the solution to some crucial problems in areas where the old paradigm failed. In addition, the problem-solving capacity of its predecessor has to be preserved after the paradigm shift. It is also important for the new approach to promise additional problem solving in new areas. However, there are always losses as well as gains in scientific revolutions. The former are usually obscured and tacitly accepted, so long as progress is guaranteed.

Thus, Newtonian mechanics, unlike both the Aristotelian and Cartesian dynamics, did not explain the nature of the attractive forces between particles of matter, but simply took gravity for granted. This question was later addressed and answered by the general theory of relativity. Newton's opponents saw in his reliance upon innate forces a return to the Dark Ages. Similarly, Lavoisier's theory failed to answer the question why various metals are so much alike—one that had been successfully dealt with in the phlogiston theory. It was not until the twentieth century that science was again capable of tackling this issue. The opponents of Lavoisier also raised the objection that the rejection of "chemical principles" in favor of laboratory elements was a regression from established explanation to a mere name. Similarly, Einstein and other physicists opposed the dominant probabilistic interpretation of quantum physics.

The choice of the new paradigm does not occur in stages, step by step, under the inexorable impact of evidence and logic. It is an instant change, resembling psychological conversion or a shift in perception between figure and background, and it follows the all-or-none law. The scientists who embrace a new paradigm talk about an "Aha!" experience, sudden resolution, or a flash of illuminating intuition. The reasons why this happens are, obviously, rather complex. In addition to the paradigm's capacity to rectify the situation that has led the old paradigm into crisis, Kuhn mentions motives of an irrational nature, biographically determined idiosyncrasies, prior reputation or nationality of the originator, and others. Also, the aesthetic qualities of the paradigm can play an important role, such as its elegance, simplicity, and beauty.

There has been a tendency in science to see the consequences of a paradigm shift in terms of a new interpretation of earlier data. According to this view, observations are unambiguously determined by the nature of the objective world and of the perceptual apparatus. However, this view is itself paradigm-dependent and is one of the basic assumptions of the Cartesian approach to the world. The raw data of observation are far from representing pure perception; stimuli should not be confused with perceptions or sensations. The latter are conditioned by experience, education, language, and culture. Under certain circumstances, the same stimuli can lead to different perceptions, and different stimuli to the same perceptions. The former can be exemplified by ambiguous pictures inviting a radical switch of perceptual gestalt. The most famous of these are the pictures that can be perceived in two different ways—e.g. as a duck or a rabbit, or as an antique vase or two human profiles, respectively. A good example of the latter is a person with inverted lenses who learns to correct the image of the world. There is no neutral language of observation based on retinal imprints only. The understanding of the nature of stimuli, of the sensory organs, and of their mutual interrelations reflects the existing theory of perception and of the human mind.

Rather than interpreting reality in a new way, a scientist who accepts a new paradigm is like a person putting on inverted lenses. Seeing the same objects and constellations of objects, and being

Figure-ground reversal is shown in the familiar goblet/silhouetted faces, introduced by Edgar Rubin in 1915.

aware that this is so, he or she will find them thoroughly transformed, in essence and in many of their details. It is not an exaggeration to say that, when a paradigm changes, the world of the scientists changes with it. They use new instruments, look into new places, observe different things, and perceive even familiar objects in an entirely new light. According to Kuhn, this radical shift of perception can be compared to a sudden transportation to another planet. Scientific fact and paradigm cannot be separated with absolute clarity. The world of the scientist is changed quantitatively and qualitatively by new developments of either fact or theory.

The partisans of a revolutionary paradigm do not usually interpret the conceptual shift as a new, but ultimately relative, perception of reality. Once it occurs, there is a tendency to discard the old as wrong and welcome the new as accurate description. However, in a strict sense, none of the old theories were really wrong, so long as they were applied only to those phenomena that they could adequately explain. It was the generalization to other realms that was incorrect. Thus, according to Kuhn, old theories can be saved and maintained as correct when their range of application is restricted to only those phenomena and that precision of observation with which the experimental evidence in hand already deals. This implies that a scientist cannot speak "scientifically" and with authority about any phenomenon not already observed. Strictly speaking, it is not permissible to rely upon a paradigm whenever research enters a new area or seeks a degree of precision for which the theory offers no precedent. From this point of view, even the phlogiston theory could never have been disproved, had it not been generalized beyond the realm of phenomena that it could account for.

After a paradigm shift, the old theory can be seen in some sense as a special case of the new one, but it must be reformulated and transformed for that purpose. This revision can be undertaken only because the scientist can use the advantages of hindsight; it involves a change of the meaning of fundamental concepts. Thus, Newton's mechanics can be reinterpreted as a special case of Einstein's theory of relativity, and an explanation can be offered for its working within the limits of its applicability. Yet such basic concepts as space, time, and mass have been drastically changed and are not comparable. Newtonian mechanics maintains its validity, unless it claims applicability to high velocities or an unlimited accuracy of its descriptions and predictions. All historically significant theories showed congruence with the observed facts, even if only more or less. There is no conclusive answer on any level of scientific development whether, or to what degree, an individual theory corresponds accurately with the facts. However, it makes perfect sense to compare two paradigms and ask which of them better reflects the observed facts. In any case, paradigms should always be seen only as models, not as definitive descriptions of reality.

The acceptance of a new paradigm is seldom easy, since it depends on a variety of factors of emotional, political, and administrative nature and is not simply a matter of logical proof. Depending on the nature and scope of the paradigm, and on specific circumstances, it can take more than one generation before the new way of looking at the world is fully established in the scientific community. The statements of two great scientists provide illustrations. The first is a concluding passage of Charles Darwin's *Origin of Species* (1859): "Although I am fully convinced of the truth of the views given in this volume. . . . I by no means expect to convince experienced naturalists whose minds are stocked with a multitude of facts all viewed, during a long course of years, from a point of view directly opposite to mine. . . . But I look with confidence to the future—to young and rising naturalists who will be able to view both sides of the question with impartiality." Even stronger is Max Planck's comment in his *Scientific Autobiography* (1968): ". . . a new scientific truth does not triumph by convincing its opponents and making them see the light, but rather because its opponents eventually die, and a new generation grows up that is familiar with it."

Once the new paradigm is accepted and assimilated, its basic assumptions are incorporated into textbooks. Being sources of authority and pedagogical vehicles, these must be rewritten after each scientific revolution. By their very nature, they tend to disguise not only specifics, but also the very existence of the revolutions that produced them. Science is described as a series of individual discoveries and inventions that in their totality represent the modern body of knowledge. It thus appears that, from the very beginning, scientists have tried to achieve the objectives that are reflected in the latest paradigm. In their historical accounts, the texts tend to cover only those aspects of the work of individual scientists that can be seen as contributions to the contemporary point of view. Thus, in discussing Newton's mechanics, they do not mention the role Newton attributed to God, or his deep interest in astrology and alchemy, which were integral to his philosophy. Similarly, one does not read that Descartes' dualism of mind and body implied the existence of God. It is not usually mentioned in standard textbooks that many of the founders of modern physics, such as Einstein, Bohm, Heisenberg, Schroedinger, Bohr, and Oppenheimer not only found their work fully compatible with the mystical world view, but in a sense entered the mystical realms through their scientific pursuits. Once the textbooks are rewritten, science again appears to be a linear and cumulative enterprise, and the history of science seems to be characterized by gradual increments of knowledge. The role of human error and idiosyncrasy has been played down, and the cyclical dynamics of the paradigms with periodic shifts has been obscured. The field is prepared for secure practice of normal science, at least until the next accumulation of observations challenging the new paradigm.

Another important philosopher whose work is highly relevant in this connection is Philipp Frank. In his seminal work, *Philosophy of Science* (1974), he offered an incisive and detailed analysis of the relationship between observable facts and scientific theories. He succeeded in dispelling the myth that scientific theories can be logically derived from available facts and are unambiguously determined by observations of the phenomenal world. Using as historical examples the geometries of Euclid, Riemann, and Lobachevsky, Newton's mechanics, Einstein's theories of relativity and quantum physics, he provided remarkable insights into the nature and dynamics of scientific theories.

According to Frank, every scientific system is based on a small number of basic statements about reality, or axioms that are considered self-evident. The truth of the axioms is discovered, not by reasoning, but by direct intuition; they are products of the imaginative faculties of the mind rather than logic.[2] By the application of a strict logical process it is possible to derive from the axioms a system of other statements, or theorems. The resulting theoretical system is of a purely logical nature; it is self-validating and its truth is essentially independent of the physical occurrences in the world. The relationship between such a system and the empirical observations must be tested to assess the degree of its practical applicability and correspondence. For this purpose, the elements of the theory must be described by "operational definitions," in Bridgman's sense.[3] Only then can one determine the degree and limits of applicability of the theoretical system to material reality.

The intrinsic logical truth of Euclidean geometry, or of Newtonian mechanics, has not been destroyed by the discovery that their application to physical reality has specific limits. According to Frank, all hypotheses are essentially speculative. The difference between a purely philosophical hypothesis and a scientific one is that the latter can be tested. It is no longer important that a scientific theory appeals to common sense; this requirement was discarded by Galileo Galilei. It can be fantastic and absurd, as long as its testing can be done on the level of common experience.

Conversely, a direct statement about the nature of the universe that cannot be subjected to experimental testing is pure metaphysical speculation and not a scientific theory. Such statements as, "All existing things are of a material nature and there is no spiritual world," or, "Consciousness is a product of matter," clearly belong to this category, no matter how self-evident they might appear to common sense or to a mechanistic scientist.

The most radical criticism of scientific methodology and its current practices was formulated by Paul Feyerabend. In his explosive book, *Against Method: Outline of an Anarchistic Theory of Knowledge* (1978), he argued emphatically that science is not and cannot be governed by a system of firm, unchanging, and absolute principles. History provides unambiguous evidence that science is essentially an anarchistic enterprise. Violations of the basic epistemological rules have not been mere accidental events; throughout history they have been absolutely necessary for scientific progress. The most successful scientific inquiries have never proceeded according to the rational method. In the history of science in general, and in the time of great revolutions in particular, a more determined application of the canons of current scientific method would not have accelerated the development; it would have brought it to a standstill. The Copernican revolution and other essential developments in modern science have survived only because reason was frequently overruled in the past.

The so-called consistency condition, which demands that a new hypothesis agrees with accepted ones, is unreasonable and counterproductive. It eliminates a hypothesis not because it disagrees with facts, but because it is in conflict with another theory. As a result, it tends to protect and preserve the theory that is older, not the one that is better. Hypotheses contradicting well-established theories give us evidence that cannot be obtained in any other way. Facts and theories are more intimately connected than conventional science has assumed, and certain facts cannot be unearthed without the help of alternatives to the established theories.

When discussing questions of testing, it is imperative to use a whole set of overlapping, factually adequate, but mutually inconsistent theories. The invention of alternatives to the view at the center of a discussion constitutes an essential part of the empirical method. It is not sufficient to compare theories with observations and facts. Data obtained in the context of a particular conceptual system are not independent of the basic theoretical and philosophical assumptions of this system. A truly scientific comparison of two theories has to treat "facts" and "observations" in the context of the theory that is being tested.

Since the facts, observations, and even criteria for evaluation are "paradigm-bound," the most important formal properties of a theory are found by contrast, not by analysis. If the scientist wants to maximize the empirical content of the view he or she holds, it is mandatory to use pluralistic methodology—to introduce rival theories and compare ideas with ideas rather than with experience.

There is no idea or system of thought, however ancient or seemingly absurd, that is not capable of improving our knowledge. Thus, ancient spiritual systems and aboriginal myths appear strange and nonsensical only because their scientific content is either unknown or is distorted by anthropologists or philologists unfamiliar with the simplest physical, medical, or astronomical knowledge. In science, reason cannot be universal and the irrational cannot be entirely excluded. There is not a single interesting theory that agrees with all the facts in its domain. We find that all theories fail to reproduce certain quantitative results and that they are qualitatively incompetent to a surprising degree.

All methodologies, even the most obvious ones, have their limits. New theories are initially restricted to a fairly narrow domain of facts and are only slowly extended to other areas. The mode of this extension is rarely determined by the elements that constitute the content of its predecessors. The emerging conceptual apparatus of the new theory soon starts defining its own problems and problem areas. Many earlier questions, facts, and observations that make sense only in the abandoned context appear suddenly silly and irrelevant; they are either forgotten or pushed aside. And, conversely, a host of entirely new issues emerges as problems of critical importance.

The above discussion of scientific revolutions, of the dynamics of paradigms, and of the function of theories in science might leave the contemporary reader with the impression that the relevance of this work is primarily historical. It would be easy to assume that the last major conceptual upheaval took place in the early decades of this century, and that the next scientific revolution will occur some time in the remote future. To the contrary, the central message of this book is that Western science is approaching a paradigm shift of unprecedented proportions, one that will change our concepts of reality and of human nature, bridge the gap between ancient wisdom and modern science, and reconcile the difference between Eastern spirituality and Western pragmatism.

The Newtonian-Cartesian
Spell of Mechanistic Science

During the last three centuries, Western science has been dominated by the Newtonian-Cartesian paradigm, a system of thought based on the work of the British scientist Isaac Newton and the French philosopher René Descartes.[4] Using this model, physics has made astonishing progress, gaining great reputation among all the other disciplines. Its consistent use of mathematics, efficacy in problem solving, and successful application in various areas of everyday life have set standards for all of science. The ability to relate basic concepts and findings to the mechanistic model of the universe developed by Newtonian physics became an important criterion of scientific legitimacy in more complex and less developed fields, such as biology, medicine, psychology, psychiatry, anthropology, and sociology. Initially, this firm adherence to the mechanistic world view had a very positive impact on scientific progress in these disciplines. However, in the course of later development, the conceptual frameworks derived from the Newtonian-Cartesian paradigm lost their revolutionary power and became serious obstacles for scientific research and progress.

Since the beginning of the twentieth century, physics has undergone profound and radical changes, transcending the mechanistic world view and all the basic assumptions of the Newtonian-Cartesian paradigm. In the course of this extraordinary transformation, it has become quite complex, esoteric, and incomprehensible for most scientists outside the realm of physics. As a result, disciplines like medicine, psychology, and psychiatry have failed to adjust to these rapid changes and to assimilate them into their way of thinking. The world view long outdated in modern physics continues to be considered scientific in many other fields, to the detriment of future progress. Observations and data that are in conflict with the mechanistic model of the universe tend to be discarded or suppressed, and research projects that have no relevance for the dominant paradigm have no chance for funding. Parapsychology, alternative approaches to healing, psychedelic research, thanatology, and certain areas of anthropological fieldwork are salient examples.

During the last two decades, the antievolutionary and counterproductive nature of the old paradigm has become increasingly obvious, particularly in those scientific disciplines that study human beings. In psychology, psychiatry, and anthropology, the conceptual schisms have reached such a degree that these disciplines seem to be facing a deep crisis, comparable in scope to the crisis physics was facing at the time of the Michelson-Morley experiment. There is an urgent need for a fundamental paradigm shift that would make it possible to accommodate an ever-increasing influx of revolutionary data from various areas that are in irreconcilable conflict with the old models. Many researchers feel that the new paradigm should also make it possible to bridge the gap separating our traditional psychology and psychiatry from the profound wisdom of the ancient and Oriental systems of thought. Before discussing in detail the reasons for the forthcoming scientific revolution and the possible directions it may take, it is appropriate to describe the characteristic features of the old paradigm the adequacy of which is now being seriously questioned.

Newton's mechanistic universe is a universe of solid matter, made of atoms,[5] small and indestructible particles that constitute its fundamental building blocks. They are essentially passive and unchangeable; their mass and form always remain constant. Newton's most important contribution to the otherwise comparable model of the Greek atomists was a precise definition of the force acting between the particles. He referred to it as the force of gravity and established that it was directly proportionate to the masses involved and indirectly proportionate to the square of their distance. In Newton's system, gravity is a rather mysterious entity. It is seen as an intrinsic attribute of the bodies it acts upon; this action is exerted instantaneously over distance.

Another essential characteristic of the Newtonian universe is the three-dimensional space of classic Euclidean geometry, which is absolute, constant, and always at rest. The distinction between matter and empty space is clear and unambiguous. Similarly, time is absolute, autonomous, and independent of the material world; it shows a uniform and unchangeable flow from the past through the present to the future. According to Newton, all physical processes can be reduced to movements of material points that result from the force of gravity acting among them and causing their mutual attraction. Newton was able to describe the dynamics of these forces by means of the new mathematical approach of differential calculus that he had invented for the purpose.

The resulting image of the universe is of a gigantic and entirely deterministic clockwork. The particles move according to eternal and unchangeable laws, and the events and processes in the material world consist of chains of interdependent causes and effects. As a consequence, it should be possible—at least in principle—to reconstruct accurately any past situation in the universe or predict everything in its future with absolute certainty. Practically, this is never actually possible; however, this circumstance is explained by our inability to obtain detailed information about all the intricate variables involved in any particular situation. The theoretical feasibility of such an undertaking is never seriously questioned. As a basic metaphysical assumption, this represents an essential element of the mechanistic world view. Ilya Prigogine (1980) called this belief in unlimited predictability "the founding myth of classical science."

Another important influence in the philosophy and history of science during the last two centuries has been René Descartes, one of the greatest French philosophers. His most significant contribution to the leading paradigm was an extreme formulation of the absolute dualism between mind *(res cogitans)* and matter *(res extensa)*, resulting in a belief that the material world can be described objectively, without reference to the human observer. This concept was instrumental in the rapid development of the natural sciences and technology, but one of its ultimate consequences has been a serious neglect of a holistic approach to human beings, society, and life on this planet. In a sense, the Cartesian legacy proved to be a more recalcitrant element in Western science than the Newtonian mechanistic world view. Even Albert Einstein—a genius who undermined the foundations of Newtonian physics, formulated single-handedly the theories of relativity, and initiated quantum theory—was incapable of freeing himself from the spell of Cartesian dualism (Capra 1982).

Whenever we use the term "Newtonian-Cartesian paradigm," we should be aware that Western mechanistic science has skewed and distorted the legacy of these two great thinkers. For both Newton and Descartes, the concept of God was an essential element in their philosophies and world views. Newton was a deeply spiritual person who had great interest in astrology, occultism, and alchemy. In the words of his biographer, John Maynard Keynes (1951), he was the last of the great magicians, rather than the first great scientist. Newton believed that the universe was material in its nature, but he did not think its origin could be explained from material causes. According to him, it was God who had initially created the material particles, the forces between them, and the laws that govern their motions. The universe, having once been created, would continue to function as a machine and could be described and understood in those terms. Descartes also believed that the world existed objectively and independently of the human observer. For him, however, its objectivity was based on its constantly being perceived by God.

Western science subjected Newton and Descartes to the same treatment that Marx and Engels gave Hegel. While formulating the principles of dialectic and historical materialism, they dissected Hegel's phenomenology of the world spirit, keeping his dialectics but replacing spirit with matter. Similarly, conceptual thinking in many disciplines represents a direct logical extension of the Newtonian-Cartesian model, but the image of divine intelligence that was at the core of the speculations of these two great men disappeared from the picture. The consequential systematic and radical philosophical materialism became the new ideological foundation of the modern scientific world view.

In all its numerous ramifications and applications, the Newtonian-Cartesian model has proved extremely successful in a variety of areas. It provided a comprehensive explanation of the basic mechanics of the solar system and was effectively applied to the understanding of the continuous motion of fluids, the vibration of elastic bodies, and thermodynamics. It became the basis of, and the moving force behind, the remarkable progress of the natural sciences in the eighteenth and nineteenth centuries.

The disciplines that modeled themselves after Newton and Descartes have elaborated in detail an image of the universe as an immensely complex mechanical system, an assembly of passive and inert matter, developing with no participation of consciousness or creative intelligence. From the Big Bang through the initial expansion of the galaxies to the creation of the solar system and the early geophysical processes that created this planet, the cosmic evolution was allegedly governed solely by blind mechanical forces. According to this model, life originated in the primeval ocean, accidentally, as a result of random chemical reactions. Similarly, the cellular organization of organic matter and the evolution to higher life forms occurred quite mechanically, without participation of an intelligent principle, through random genetic mutations and a natural selection guaranteeing the survival of the fittest. This eventually resulted in a ramified phylogenetic system of hierarchically arranged species with increasing levels of complexity.

Then, somewhere very high in the Darwinian pedigree, a spectacular—and so far unexplainable—event occurred: the unconscious and inert matter became aware of itself and of the surrounding world. Although the mechanism involved in this miraculous event entirely escapes even the crudest attempts at scientific speculation, the correctness of this metaphysical assumption is taken for granted, and the solution of this problem is tacitly relegated to future research. Scientists do not even agree on the evolutionary stage at which consciousness appeared. However, the belief that consciousness is limited to living organisms and that it requires a highly developed central nervous system represents a fundamental postulate of the materialistic and mechanistic world view. Consciousness is seen as the product of highly organized matter—the central nervous system—and as an epiphenomenon of physiological processes in the brain.[6]

The belief that consciousness is the product of the brain is, of course, not entirely arbitrary. It is based on a vast mass of observations from clinical and experimental neurology and psychiatry that suggest close connections between various aspects of consciousness and physiological or pathological processes in the brain, such as traumas, tumors, or infections. For example, a brain contusion or a lack of oxygen supply can result in the loss of consciousness. A tumor or a trauma of the temporal lobe involve certain distortions of conscious processes that are distinct and different from those associated with prefrontal lesions. Infections of the brain or administration of certain drugs with psychoactive properties, such as hypnotics, stimulants, or psychedelics, are conducive to quite characteristic alterations of consciousness. Occasionally the changes in consciousness associated with neurological disorders are so specific that they can contribute to correct diagnosis. Moreover, successful neurosurgery or other medical interventions can be followed by distinct clinical improvement.

These observations demonstrate beyond any doubt that there is a close connection between consciousness and the brain. However, they do not necessarily prove that consciousness is produced by the brain. The logic of the conclusion that mechanistic science has drawn is highly problematic, and it is certainly possible to imagine theoretical systems that would interpret the existing data in an entirely different way. This can be illustrated by such a simple example as a television set. The quality of the picture and sound is critically dependent on proper functioning of all the components, and malfunction or destruction of some of them will create very specific distortions. A television mechanic can identify the malfunctioning component on the basis of the nature of the distortion and correct the problem by replacing or repairing the hardware in question. None of us would see this as a scientific proof that the program must therefore be generated in the television set, since television is a man-made system and its functioning is well known. Yet, this is precisely the kind of conclusion mechanistic science has drawn in regard to brain and consciousness. It is interesting in this connection that Wilder Penfield (the world-famous neurosurgeon who has conducted ground-breaking brain research and has made fundamental contributions to modern neurophysiology) expressed in his last book, *The Mystery of the Mind* (1976), which summarizes his life work, a deep doubt that consciousness is a product of the brain and can be explained in terms of cerebral anatomy and physiology.

According to materialistic science, individual organisms are essentially separate systems that can communicate with the external world and with each other only through their sensory organs; all these communications are mediated by known forms of energy. Mental processes are explained in terms of reactions of the organism to the environment, and of creative recombinations of previous sensory input acquired in the course of the individual's present lifetime and stored in the brain in the form of engrams. Here materialistic psychology uses the credo of the British empiricist school, expressed succinctly by John Locke (1823): *"Nihil est in intellectu quod non antea fuerit in sensu."* ("There is nothing in the intellect that had not first been processed through the senses.")

Because of the linear nature of time, past events are irretrievably lost, unless they are recorded in specific memory systems. Memories of any kind, then, require a specific material substrate—the cells of the central nervous system or the physiochemical code of the genes. Memories of events from the individual's lifetime are stored in the memory banks of the central nervous system. Psychiatry has accepted the overwhelming clinical evidence that, in humans, these memories can be not only consciously retrieved, but also under certain circumstances, actually relived in a vivid and complex way. The only conceivable substrate for the transfer of ancestral and phylogenetic information is the physiochemical code of the DNA and RNA molecules. The present medical model recognizes the possibility of such transmission for the information concerning the mechanics of embryological development, constitutional factors, hereditary dispositions, parental characteristics or talents, and similar phenomena, but certainly not for complex memories of specific events preceding the individual's conception.

Under the influence of the Freudian model, mainstream psychiatry and psychotherapy have accepted the notion that the newborn child is a *tabula rasa* ("blank or erased tablet") whose development is entirely determined by the sequences of childhood experiences. Contemporary medical theory denies the possibility that the experience of biological birth is recorded in the child's memory; the usual reason given for this in medical handbooks is the immaturity of the cerebral cortex of the newborn (incomplete myelinization of the sheaths of the cerebral neurons). The only prenatal influences generally recognized in developmental speculations of psychiatrists and psychologists are heredity, vague constitutional factors, physical damage to the organism, and, possibly, differences in the relative strength of various instincts.

According to materialistic psychology, access to any new information is possible only through direct sensory input, and by recombining old data or combining them with new sensory input. Mechanistic science tries to explain even such phenomena as human intelligence, art, religion, ethics, and science itself as products of material processes in the brain. The probability that human intelligence developed all the way from the chemical ooze of the primeval ocean solely through sequences of random mechanical processes has been recently aptly compared to the probability of a tornado blowing through a gigantic junkyard and assembling by accident a 747 jumbo jet. This highly improbable assumption is a metaphysical statement that cannot be proved by existing scientific methods. Far from being a scientific piece of information—as its proponents so fiercely maintain—it is, in the present state of knowledge, little more than one of the leading myths of Western science.

Mechanistic science has had many decades of practice in defending its belief systems by labeling every major departure from perceptual and conceptual congruence with the Newtonian-Cartesian model as "psychosis" and all research generating incompatible data as "bad science." This strategy has probably had the most immediate deleterious effects on the theory and practice of psychiatry. Contemporary psychiatric theory cannot adequately account for a wide range of phenomena that lie beyond the biographical realm of the unconscious, such as the perinatal and transpersonal experiences that are discussed in detail in this book.

Since intimate knowledge of transbiographical experiential realms is absolutely essential for a genuine understanding of most of the problems psychiatry deals with, this situation has serious consequences. In particular, a deeper understanding of the psychotic process is virtually impossible without acknowledging the transpersonal dimensions of the psyche. Thus, the existing explanations either offer superficial and unconvincing psychodynamic interpretations, reducing the problems involved to biographical factors from early childhood, or postulate unknown biochemical factors to account for distortions of "objective reality" and other bizarre and incomprehensible manifestations.

The explanatory weakness of the old paradigm is even more obvious in regard to important sociocultural phenomena, such as shamanism, religion, mysticism, rites of passage, ancient mysteries, and healing ceremonies of various pre-industrial cultures. The present tendency to reduce mystical experiences and spiritual life to culturally accepted, quasi-psychotic states, primitive superstition, or unresolved conflicts and dependencies from childhood reveals a grave misunderstanding of their real nature. Freud's attempt to equate religion with obsessive compulsive neurosis might at best be considered relevant in relation to one aspect of religion—the performance of rituals. However, it misses entirely the critical significance of first-hand visionary experiences of alternate realities for the development of all great religions. Equally dubious are the numerous theories inspired by psychoanalysis that try to explain historical events of apocalyptic proportions (such as wars, bloody revolutions, genocide, and totalitarian systems) as the result of childhood traumas and other biographical events of the persons involved.

The lack of explanatory power of the old models represents only one aspect of their negative role in psychiatry. They also exert a strong inhibiting effect on open-minded exploration of new observations and areas that appear to be incompatible with their basic assumptions about reality. This can be illustrated by the reluctance of mainstream psychology and psychiatry to accept an avalanche of data coming from many diverse sources, such as the practice of Jungian analysis and the new experiential psychotherapies, study of death experiences and near-death phenomena, psychedelic research, modern parapsychological studies, and reports of "visionary anthropologists."

Rigid adherence to the Newtonian-Cartesian paradigm has had particularly detrimental consequences for the practice of psychiatry and psychotherapy. It is largely responsible for the inappropriate application of the medical model to areas of psychiatry that deal with problems of living, rather than diseases. The image of the universe created by Western science is a pragmatically useful construct that helps to organize presently available observations and data. However, it has been generally mistaken for an accurate and comprehensive description of reality. As a result of this epistemological error, perceptual and cognitive congruence with the Newtonian-Cartesian world view is considered essential for mental health and normalcy.

Major deviations from this "accurate perception of reality" are then seen as indications of serious psychopathology, reflecting disorder or impairment of the sensory organs and the central nervous system, a medical condition, or a disease. In this context, nonordinary states of consciousness, with a few exceptions, are generally considered to be symptomatic of mental disorders. The very term "altered states of consciousness" clearly suggests that they represent distortions or bastardized versions of the correct perception of "objective reality." Under these circumstances it would appear absurd to presume that such altered states have any ontological or gnoseological relevance. It would be equally unlikely to believe that these unusual states of mind, which are essentially pathological, could have any intrinsic therapeutic potential. Thus, the prevailing orientation in psychiatric therapy is to eliminate symptoms and unusual phenomena of any kind, and to return the individual to agreed-upon perceptions and experiences of the world.

Conceptual Challenges from
Modern Consciousness Research

All through the history of modern science, generations of
investigators have pursued with great enthusiasm and determination
the various avenues of research offered by the Newtonian-Cartesian
paradigm, readily discarding concepts and observations that would
have questioned some of the basic philosophical assumptions shared
by the scientific community. Most scientists have been so thoroughly
programmed by their education or so impressed and carried away
by their pragmatic successes that they have taken their model
literally as an accurate and exhaustive description of reality. In this
atmosphere, countless observations from various fields have been
systematically discarded, suppressed, or even ridiculed on the basis
of their incompatibility with the mechanistic and reductionistic
thinking that for many became synonymous with a scientific approach.

For a long time the successes of this endeavor were so striking
that they overshadowed the practical and theoretical failures. In
the atmosphere of the rapidly developing crisis in the world that
accompanies precipitate scientific progress, it has become increasingly difficult to maintain this position. It is quite clear that the
old scientific models cannot provide satisfactory solutions to the
human problems we are facing individually, socially, internationally,
and on a global scale. Many prominent scientists have voiced in
different ways a growing suspicion that the mechanistic world view
of Western science has actually substantially contributed to the
present crisis, if not generated it.

A paradigm is more than simply a useful theoretical model for
science; its philosophy actually shapes the world by its indirect
influence on individuals and society. Newtonian-Cartesian science
has created a very negative image of human beings, depicting them
as biological machines driven by instinctual impulses of a bestial
nature. It has no genuine recognition of higher values, such as
spiritual awareness, feelings of love, aesthetic needs, or sense of
justice. All these are seen as derivatives of base instincts, or compromises essentially alien to human nature. This image endorses
individualism, egoistic emphasis, competition, and the principle of
"survival of the fittest" as natural and essentially healthy tendencies.

Materialistic science, blinded by its model of the world as a conglomerate of mechanically interacting separate units, has been unable to recognize the value and vital importance of cooperation, synergy, and ecological concerns.

The stupendous technical achievements of this science, which have the potential for solving most of the material problems that plague humanity, have backfired. Their success has created a world in which its greatest triumphs—nuclear energy, space-age rocketry, cybernetics, lasers, computers and other electronic gadgets, and the miracles of modern chemistry and bacteriology—have turned into a vital danger and a living nightmare. As a result, we have a world divided politically and ideologically, which is critically threatened by economic crises, industrial pollution and the specter of nuclear war. In view of this situation, more and more people are questioning the usefulness of precipitate technological progress that is not harnessed and controlled by emotionally mature individuals and a species sufficiently evolved to handle constructively the powerful tools it has created.

As the economic, sociopolitical, and ecological situation in the world deteriorates, more and more individuals seem to be giving up the strategy of one-sided manipulation and control of the material world and turning within themselves for answers. There is a growing interest in the evolution of consciousness as a possible alternative to global destruction. It is manifested in the increasing popularity of meditation or other ancient and Oriental spiritual practices, experiential psychotherapies, as well as clinical and laboratory research into consciousness. These activities have brought to a new focus the fact that traditional paradigms are unable to account for and accommodate a vast number of seriously challenging observations from many different areas and sources.

In their totality, these data are of critical importance; they indicate an urgent need for a drastic revision of our fundamental concepts of human nature and the nature of reality. Many open-minded scientists and mental health professionals have been aware of the abysmal gap between contemporary psychology and psychiatry and the great ancient or Oriental spiritual traditions, such as the various forms of yoga, Kashmir Shaivism, Tibetan Vajrayana, Taoism, Zen Buddhism, Sufism, Kabbalah, or alchemy. The wealth of profound knowledge about the human psyche and consciousness accumulated within these systems over centuries, or even millenia, has not been adequately acknowledged, explored, and integrated by Western science.

Similarly, anthropologists conducting field research in non-Western cultures have been reporting for decades a variety of phenomena for which traditional conceptual frameworks offer only superficial and unconvincing explanations, or no explanations at all. Although many extraordinary, culture-bound observations have been repeatedly described in well-documented studies, they tend to be discarded or interpreted in terms of primitive belief, superstition, or individual and group psychopathology. We can mention in this connection shamanic experiences and practices, trance states, fire walking, aboriginal rituals, spiritual healing practices, or the development of various paranormal abilities by individuals and entire social groups. This situation is far more complicated than might appear on the surface. Informal and confidential contact with anthropologists has convinced me that many of them have decided not to report certain aspects of their field experiences for fear they would be ridiculed or ostracized by their Newtonian-Cartesian colleagues and would endanger their professional image.

The conceptual inadequacies and failures of the old paradigm are not limited to data from exotic cultures. Equally serious challenges have emerged from Western clinical and laboratory research. Experiments with hypnosis, sensory isolation and overload, voluntary control of internal states, biofeedback, and acupuncture have cast new light on many ancient and Oriental practices, but they have generated more conceptual problems than satisfactory answers. Psychedelic research clarified in one way many previously puzzling historical and anthropological data concerning shamanism, mystery cults, rites of passage, healing ceremonies, and paranormal phenomena involving the use of sacred plants. However, at the same time, it validated much of the ancient, aboriginal and Oriental knowledge about consciousness and undermined some of the basic philosophical assumptions of mechanistic science. As will be discussed later, the experimentation with psychedelic drugs has shattered the conventional understanding of psychotherapy, the traditional models of the psyche, the image of human nature, and even basic beliefs about the nature of reality.

The observations from psychedelic research are in no way limited to the use of psychoactive substances; essentially the same experiences have been reported from modern nondrug psychotherapies and body work, such as Jungian analysis, psychosynthesis, various neo-Reichian approaches, Gestalt practice, modified forms of primal therapy, guided imagery with music, Rolfing, various techniques of rebirthing, past life regression, and auditing in scientology. The technique of holonomic integration or holotropic therapy, developed by my wife, Christina, and myself, a nondrug approach combining controlled breathing, evocative music, and focused body work, can induce a wide spectrum of experiences that practically coincides with the spectrum of psychedelic experience. This technique is described in chapter 7.

Another important source of information challenging the established paradigms of mechanistic science is modern parapsychological research. It has become increasingly difficult to ignore and deny a priori data from many methodologically sound and carefully conducted experiments on the sole basis of their incompatibility with the traditional belief system. Respectable scientists with good credentials, such as Joseph Banks Rhine, Gardner Murphy, Jules Eisenbud, Stanley Krippner, Charles Tart, Elmer and Alyce Green, Arthur Hastings, Russell Targ, and Harold Puthoff, have accumulated evidence on the existence of telepathy, clairvoyance, astral projection, remote viewing, psychic diagnosis and healing, or psychokinesis that might provide important clues for a new understanding of reality. It is interesting that many modern physicists familiar with quantum-relativistic physics seem to show a generally more serious interest in paranormal phenomena than do traditional psychiatrists and psychologists. We should also mention here the fascinating data from the field of thanatology, suggesting among other things that clinically dead persons can frequently accurately perceive the situation in their surroundings from vantage points that would not be available to them even in a fully conscious state.

Instead of discussing all these topics in a synoptic and comprehensive way, I will focus in what follows on the observations from psychedelic research, particularly from LSD psychotherapy. I have chosen this approach, after some consideration, for several important reasons. Most researchers studying the effects of psychedelics have come to the conclusion that these drugs can best be viewed as amplifiers or catalysts of mental processes. Instead of inducing drug-specific states, they seem to activate pre-existing matrices or potentials of the human mind. The individual who ingests them does not experience a "toxic psychosis" essentially unrelated to how the psyche functions under normal circumstances; instead, he or she takes a fantastic inner journey into the unconscious and superconscious mind. These drugs thus reveal, and make available for direct observation, a wide range of otherwise hidden phenomena that represent intrinsic capacities of the human mind and play an important role in normal mental dynamics.

Since the psychedelic spectrum covers the entire range of experiences that are humanly possible, it includes all the phenomena occurring in nondrug contexts mentioned earlier—in aboriginal ceremonies, various spiritual practices, experiential psychotherapies, modern laboratory techniques, parapsychological research, and in biological emergencies or near-death situations. At the same time, the amplifying and catalyzing effects of psychedelics make it possible to induce unusual states of consciousness of extraordinary intensity and clarity under controlled conditions and with great consistency. This fact represents a considerable advantage for the researcher and makes psychedelic phenomena particularly suitable for systematic study.

The most important and obvious reason for limiting this discussion to the field of psychedelic research is my long-term scientific interest in the subject. Having conducted several thousand sessions with LSD and other mind-altering substances, and having myself experienced many psychedelic states, I have a degree of expertise concerning drug-induced phenomena that I lack in regard to the other types of related experiences. Since 1954, when I first became interested in and familiar with psychedelic drugs, I have personally guided more than 3,000 sessions with LSD and have had access to more than 2,000 records of sessions conducted by my colleagues, in Czechoslovakia and in the United States. The subjects in these experiments were "normal" volunteers, various groups of psychiatric patients, and individuals dying of cancer. The nonpatient population consisted of psychiatrists and psychologists, scientists from various other disciplines, artists, philosophers, theologians, students, and psychiatric nurses. The patients with emotional disorders belonged to a variety of diagnostic categories; among them were individuals with various forms of depression, psychoneurotics, alcoholics, narcotic drug addicts, sexual deviants, persons with psychosomatic disorders, borderline psychotics, and schizophrenics. The two major approaches used in this work—psycholytic and psychedelic therapy—have been described in detail elsewhere (Grof 1980).

During the years of my clinical work with psychedelics, it has become increasingly obvious that neither the nature of the LSD experience nor the numerous observations made in the course of psychedelic therapy can be adequately explained in terms of the Newtonian-Cartesian, mechanistic approach to the universe and, more specifically, in terms of the existing neurophysiological models of the brain. After years of conceptual struggle and confusion, I have concluded that the data from LSD research indicate an urgent need for a drastic revision of the existing paradigms for psychology, psychiatry, medicine, and possibly science in general. There is at present little doubt in my mind that our current understanding of the universe, of the nature of reality, and particularly of human beings, is superficial, incorrect, and incomplete.[7]

In what follows, I will briefly describe the most important observations from LSD psychotherapy that I consider to be serious challenges to contemporary psychiatric theory, to present medical beliefs, and to the mechanistic model of the universe based on the views of Isaac Newton and René Descartes. Some of these observations are related to certain formal characteristics of the psychedelic states, others to their content, and yet others to some extraordinary connections that seem to exist between them and the fabric of external reality. I emphasize again at this point that the following discussion applies not only to psychedelic states, but also to a variety of nonordinary states of consciousness that occur spontaneously or are induced by nondrug means. Thus, all the issues in question have general validity for the understanding of the human mind in health and disease.

Let me begin with a brief description of the *formal characteristics of nonordinary states of consciousness.* In psychedelic sessions and other types of unusual experiences, dramatic sequences of various kinds can be experienced with a sensory vividness, reality, and intensity that match or surpass the ordinary perception of the material world. Although the optical aspects of these sequences tend to be prominent for most people, quite realistic experiences can occur in all the other sensory areas. On occasion, powerful isolated sounds, human and animal voices, entire musical sequences, intense physical pain and other somatic sensations, as well as distinct tastes and smells can either dominate the experience or play an important part in it. Ideation can be influenced in the most profound way, and the intellect can create interpretations of reality quite different from the one that is characteristic of the individual in his or her ordinary state of consciousness. The description of the essential experiential elements of unusual states of consciousness would not be complete without mentioning an entire range of powerful emotions that are their standard components.

Many psychedelic experiences appear to have a general quality similar to those in everyday life, with the sequences occurring in three-dimensional space and unfolding along a linear time continuum. However, quite typically, additional dimensions and experiential alternatives are readily available. The psychedelic state has a multilevel and multidimensional quality, and the Newtonian-Cartesian sequences, if they occur, appear to be arbitrarily teased out of a complex continuum of infinite possibilities. At the same time, they have all the characteristics that we associate with the perception of the material world of "objective reality."

Although LSD subjects frequently talk about images, these do not have the quality of still photographs. They are in constant dynamic movement and usually convey action and drama. But again, the term "inner movie" that so frequently occurs in LSD reports does not really correctly describe their nature. In cinematography, the three-dimensionality of scenes is artificially simulated by the movement of the camera. The perception of space must be read into the two-dimensional display, and ultimately it depends on the viewer's interpretation. In contrast, psychedelic visions are truly three-dimensional and have all the qualities of everyday perception, or at least they can have them in certain types of LSD experiences. They seem to occupy a specific space and can be seen from different directions and angles with a true parallax. It is possible to zoom in and selectively focus on different levels and planes of the experiential continuum, perceive or reconstruct fine textures, and see through transparent media of envisioned objects, such as a cell, an embryonic body, parts of a plant, or a precious stone. This intentional shift of focus is only one mechanism of blurring or clearing the images. The pictures can also be clarified by overcoming the distortions caused by fear, defenses, and resistances, or by letting the content evolve along the continuum of linear time.

An important characteristic of the psychedelic experience is that it transcends space and time. It disregards the linear continuum between the microcosmic world and the macrocosm that appears to be absolutely mandatory in the everyday state of consciousness. The represented objects cover the entire range of dimensions from atoms, molecules, and single cells to gigantic celestial bodies, solar systems, and galaxies. Phenomena from the "zone of middle dimensions," perceivable directly by our senses, appear on the same experiential continuum with those that ordinarily require such complicated technology as microscopes and telescopes to be accessible to human senses. From the experiential point of view, the distinction between the microcosm and macrocosm is arbitrary; they can coexist within the same experience and are readily interchangeable. An LSD subject can experience himself or herself as a single cell, as a fetus, and as a galaxy; these three states can occur simultaneously, or in an alternating fashion by a simple shift of focus.

In a similar way, the linearity of temporal sequences is transcended in unusual states of consciousness. Scenes from different historical contexts can occur simultaneously and appear to be meaningfully connected by their experiential characteristics. Thus a traumatic experience from childhood, a painful sequence of biological birth, and what seems to be the memory of a tragic event from a previous incarnation can all appear simultaneously as parts of one complex experiential pattern. And again, the individual has the choice of focusing selectively on any one of these scenes, experiencing them all simultaneously, or perceiving them in an alternating fashion, while discovering meaningful connections between them. The linear temporal distance that dominates everyday experience is disregarded, and events from different historical contexts appear in clusters when they share the same strong emotion or an intense physical sensation of a similar kind.

Psychedelic states offer many experiential alternatives to the Newtonian linear time and three-dimensional space that characterize our everyday existence. Events from recent and remote past and future can be experienced in nonordinary states with the vividness and complexity that in everyday consciousness are reserved only for the present moment. There are modes of psychedelic experience in which time appears to slow down or accelerate enormously, to flow backwards, or to be entirely transcended and cease to exist. It can appear to be circular, or circular and linear at the same time, can proceed along a spiral trajectory, or show certain

specific patterns of deflection and distortion. Quite frequently time
as a dimension is transcended and acquires spatial characteristics;
past, present, and future are essentially juxtaposed and coexist in
the present moment. On occasion, LSD subjects experience various
forms of time travels—regressing in historical time, passing through
time loops, or stepping out of the time dimension altogether and
reentering at another point in history.

The perception of space can undergo similar changes: unusual
states of mind clearly demonstrate the narrowness and limitation
of space with only three coordinates. LSD subjects frequently report
that they experience space and the universe as being curved and
self-enclosed, or are able to perceive worlds that have four, five,
or more dimensions. Others have a sense of being a dimensionless
point in consciousness. It is possible to see space as an arbitrary
construct and a projection of the mind that has no objective
existence at all. Under certain circumstances, any number of interpenetrating universes of different orders can be seen in holographic coexistence. As in the case of time travel, one can experience linear transfer to another place by mental space travel, direct
and immediate transport through a space loop, or by stepping out
of the space dimension altogether and reentering at another place.

Another important characteristic of psychedelic states is transcendence of the sharp distinction between matter, energy, and
consciousness. Inner visions can be so realistic that they successfully
simulate the phenomena of the material world, and, conversely,
what in everyday life appears as solid and tangible "material stuff"
can disintegrate into patterns of energy, a cosmic dance of vibrations, or a play of consciousness. The world of separate individuals
and objects is replaced by an undifferentiated pool of energy patterns or consciousness in which various kinds and levels of boundaries are playful and arbitrary. Those who originally considered
matter to be the basis of existence and saw the mind as its derivative,
can at first discover that consciousness is an independent principle
in the sense of psychophysical dualism and ultimately accept it as
the only reality. In the most universal and all-encompassing states
of mind, the dichotomy between existence and nonexistence is itself
transcended; form and emptiness appear to be equivalent and
interchangeable.

A very interesting and important aspect of psychedelic states
is the occurrence of complex experiences with condensed or com-

posite content. In the course of LSD psychotherapy, some of the experiences can be deciphered as multiply determined symbolic formations, combining in a most creative fashion elements from many different areas that are emotionally and thematically related.[8] There is a clear parallel between these dynamic structures and the dream images as analyzed by Sigmund Freud (1953b). Other composite experiences appear to be much more homogeneous; instead of reflecting many different themes and levels of meaning, including those of a contradictory nature, such phenomena represent a plurality of content in a unified form, achieved by summation of various elements. The experiences of dual unity with another person (that is, sense of one's own identity and simultaneously unity and oneness with another person), consciousness of a group of individuals, of the entire population of a country (India, czarist Russia, Nazi Germany), or all of humanity would belong to this category. Also the archetypal experiences of the Great or Terrible Mother, Man or Woman, Father, Lover, Cosmic man, or the totality of Life as a cosmic phenomenon can be mentioned as important examples.

This tendency to create composite images is not only manifested within the inner content of the psychedelic experience. It is also responsible for another common and important phenomenon— illusive transformation of the persons present in psychedelic sessions, or of the physical environment, by the emerging unconscious material in an LSD subject who keeps his or her eyes open. The resulting experiences represent complex amalgams, combining the perception of the external world with the projected elements originating in the unconscious. Thus a therapist can be simultaneously perceived in his or her everyday identity and as a parent, executioner, archetypal entity, or a character from a previous incarnation. The treatment room can be illusively transformed into the childhood bedroom, delivering uterus, prison, death cell, bordello, aboriginal hut, and many other physical settings, while at the same time retaining on another level its original identity.

The last extraordinary characteristic of unusual states of consciousness that should be mentioned is the transcendence of the difference between the ego and the elements of the external world, or, in more general terms, between the part and the whole. In an LSD session it is possible to experience oneself as somebody or something else, both with and without the loss of one's original identity. The experience of oneself as an infinitely small, separate fraction of the universe does not seem to be incompatible with being at the same time any other part of it, or the totality of existence. LSD subjects can experience simultaneously, or alternately, many different forms of identity. One extreme is full identification with a separate, limited and alienated biological creature inhabiting a material body, or actually being this body. In this form, the individual is different from everybody and everything else and represents only an infinitesimal and ultimately negligible fraction of the whole. The other extreme is full experiential identification with the undifferentiated consciousness of the Universal Mind or the Void and, thus, with the entire cosmic network and with the totality of existence. The latter experience has the paradoxical quality of being contentless, yet all-containing; nothing exists in it in a concrete form, but at the same time all of existence seems to be represented or present in a potential or germinal mode.

The observations related to the *content of nonordinary experiences* represent an even more critical challenge for the Newtonian-Cartesian paradigm than do their formal characteristics, described above. Any open-minded LSD therapist who has conducted numerous psychedelic sessions has been confronted with an avalanche of data that cannot be accounted for within existing scientific frameworks. In many instances, the explanation is not only unavailable because of lack of information about the possible causal links, but also theoretically unimaginable if the existing postulates of mechanistic science are maintained.

During my LSD work, I long ago found it impossible to continue blinding myself to a steady influx of astonishing data on the sole basis of their incompatibility with the basic assumptions of contemporary science. I also had to stop reassuring myself that some reasonable explanations must exist for them despite my inability to imagine them in my wildest fantasy. I became open to the possibility that our present scientific world view might prove to be superficial, inaccurate, and inadequate, like many of its historical predecessors. At this point, I started registering carefully all the puzzling and controversial observations without judging them or trying to explain them. Once I was able to give up my dependence on the old models and simply become a participant observer in the process, I gradually recognized that there are important models in both ancient or Oriental philosophies and modern Western science that offer exciting and promising conceptual alternatives.

I have described in detail elsewhere the most important observations from LSD research that represent a critical challenge to the mechanistic world view. In this chapter, I will only briefly review the most relevant findings and refer the interested readers to the original source.[9] Analyzing the content of the LSD phenomena, I have found it useful to distinguish four major types of psychedelic experience. The most superficial of these—in the sense of easy availability for an average person—are the *abstract* or *aesthetic* experiences. They have no specific symbolic content related to the personality of the subject and can be explained in terms of the anatomy and physiology of the sensory organs, as presented in traditional medical texts. I have found nothing on this level of psychedelic states that would defy interpretation in strictly Newtonian-Cartesian language.

The next type or level of the psychedelic experience is the *psychodynamic, biographical,* or *recollective* one. It involves complex reliving of emotionally relevant memories from various periods of the individual's life and symbolic experiences that can be deciphered as variations on, or recombinations of, biographical elements in a way quite similar to dream images as described by psychoanalysis. The Freudian theoretical framework is extremely useful for dealing with the phenomena on this level; most of these experiences leave the Newtonian-Cartesian model unchallenged. This is not very surprising since Freud himself used the principles of Newtonian mechanics quite explicitly and consciously when he was formulating the conceptual framework of psychoanalysis.

It might come as somewhat of a surprise that, on occasion, memories from the first days or weeks of life can be relived with photographic accuracy of detail. Also, memories of serious physical traumas, such as episodes of near drowning, injuries, accidents, operations, and diseases, appear to be of greater importance than those of psychological traumas emphasized by contemporary psychology and psychiatry. Such memories of physical traumas seem to be of direct relevance for the development of various emotional and psychosomatic disorders. This is true even for memories of experiences associated with operations that were conducted under general anesthesia. However, as new and surprising as some of

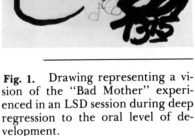

Fig. 1. Drawing representing a vision of the "Bad Mother" experienced in an LSD session during deep regression to the oral level of development.

Fig. 2. Deep regression to the early oral stage of libidinal development experienced in a psychedelic session. The large gaping mouth with the pharynx in the shape of a heart reflects the ambivalence characteristic for this stage; swallowing means destruction, as well as loving incorporation of the object.

these findings may be for medicine and psychiatry, they have little significance as indicators of the need for a major paradigm shift.

More serious conceptual problems are associated with the third type of psychedelic experience, which I term *perinatal*.[10] Clinical observations from LSD psychotherapy suggest that the human unconscious contains repositories or matrices, the activation of which leads to the reliving of biological birth and a profound confrontation with death. The resulting process of death and rebirth is typically associated with an opening of intrinsic spiritual areas in the human mind that are independent of the individual's racial, cultural, and educational background. This type of psychedelic experience presents important theoretical problems.

In this perinatal experience, LSD subjects can relive elements of their biological birth in all its complexity, and sometimes with astonishing objectively verifiable details. I have been able to confirm the accuracy of many such reports when the conditions were favorable; this frequently involved individuals who previously had had no knowledge of the circumstances of their birth. They have been able to recognize specificities and anomalies of their fetal position, detailed mechanics of labor, the nature of obstetric interventions, and the particulars of postnatal care. The experience of a breech position, placenta previa, the umbilical cord twisted around the neck, castor oil applied during the birth process, the use of forceps, various manual maneuvers, different kinds of anesthesia, and specific resuscitation procedures are just a few examples of the phenomena observed in the perinatal psychedelic experience.

The memories of these events appear to include the tissues and cells of the body. The process of reliving one's birth trauma can be associated with psychosomatic re-creation of all the appropriate physiological symptoms, such as acceleration of the pulse rate, choking with dramatic changes of skin color, hypersecretion of saliva or phlegm, excessive muscular tension with energy discharges, specific postures and movements, and the appearance of bruises and birthmarks. There are indications that the reliving of birth in LSD sessions may be associated with biochemical changes in the body that represent a replica of the situation at the time of the delivery, as exemplified by low oxygen saturation of the blood, biochemical indicators of stress, and specific characteristics of the carbohydrate metabolism. This complex reenactment of the birth situation, which extends to subcellular processes and chains of biochemical reactions, represents a difficult task for conventional scientific models.

However, other aspects of the death-rebirth process are even more difficult to account for. The symbolism that accompanies the experiences of dying and being born can be drawn from many different cultures, even if the corresponding mythological themes had not previously been known to the subject. On occasion, this involves not only the well-known symbolism for the death-rebirth process that exists in the Judaeo-Christian tradition—the humiliation and torture of Christ, death on the cross, and resurrection—but details of the Isis and Osiris legend, the myths of Dionysus, Adonis, Attis, Orpheus, Mithra, or the Nordic god Balder, and

Fig. 3. Picture of an LSD subject from a psychedelic session in which he relived his biological birth. The destructive uterine forces are represented as mythological bird-like monsters. The frail and frightened fetus is shown suspended on the umbilical cord.

their very little known counterparts from pre-Columbian cultures. The wealth of information involved in this process in some of the LSD subjects is truly remarkable.

The most critical and serious challenge for the Newtonian-Cartesian mechanistic model of the universe comes from the last category of psychedelic phenomena, an entire spectrum of experiences for which I have coined the term *transpersonal*. The common denominator of this rich and ramified group of unusual experiences is the individual's feeling that his or her consciousness has expanded beyond the ego boundaries and has transcended the limitations of time and space.

Many experiences belonging to this category can be interpreted as regression in historical time and exploration of one's biological,

Fig. 4.   An experience of death and rebirth from a perinatal LSD session. The subject's body rises from the realm of death and darkness with images of cemeteries, coffins and candles. Her arms are reaching up and her head is melting into the transcendental source of light.

Many LSD subjects have independently reported their insights that consciousness is not a product of the central nervous system and, as such, limited to humans and higher vertebrates. They saw it as a primary characteristic of existence that cannot be further reduced to, or derived from, anything else. Those individuals who have reported episodes of conscious identification with plants or parts of plants had sometimes remarkable insights into such botanical processes as germination of seeds, photosynthesis in the leaves, pollination, or exchange of water and minerals in the root system. Equally common is a sense of identification with consciousness of inorganic matter or processes, such as gold, granite, water, fire, lightning, tornado, volcanic activities, or even individual atoms and molecules. Like the preceding phenomena, these experiences can be associated with surprisingly accurate insights.

Another important group of transpersonal experiences involves telepathy, psychic diagnosis, clairvoyance, clairaudience, precognition, psychometry, out-of-the-body experiences, traveling clairvoyance, and other paranormal phenomena. Some of them are characterized by a transcendence of ordinary temporal limitations, others by transcendence of spatial barriers, or a combination of both. Since many other types of transpersonal phenomena also frequently involve access to new information through extrasensory channels, the clear boundary between psychology and parapsychology tends to disappear or become rather arbitrary when the existence of transpersonal experiences is recognized and acknowledged.

The existence of transpersonal experiences violates some of the most basic assumptions and principles of mechanistic science. They imply such seemingly absurd notions as the relativity and arbitrary nature of all physical boundaries, nonlocal connections in the universe, communication through unknown means and channels, memory without a material substrate, nonlinearity of time, or consciousness associated with all living forms (including unicellular organisms and plants) and even inorganic matter.

Many transpersonal experiences involve events from the microcosm and macrocosm—realms that cannot be directly reached by human senses—or from periods that historically precede the origin of the solar system, of planet Earth, of living organisms, of the nervous system, and of Homo sapiens. These experiences clearly suggest that, in a yet unexplained way, each of us contains the information about the entire universe or all of existence, has potential experiential access to all its parts, and in a sense *is* the whole cosmic network, as much as he or she is just an infinitesimal part of it, a separate and insignificant biological entity.

The content of the experiences discussed thus far involves elements of the phenomenal world. Although their content challenges the idea that the universe is composed of objectively existing material objects separated from each other, it does not go beyond what the Western world considers "objective reality" as perceived in ordinary states of consciousness. It is generally accepted that we have a complex pedigree of human and animal ancestors, that we are part of a specific racial and cultural heritage, and that we have undergone a complicated biological development from the fusion of two germinal cells to a highly differentiated Metazoan organism. Our everyday experiences indicate that we live in a world which involves an infinite number of elements other than ourselves—humans, animals, plants, and inanimate objects. We accept all this on the basis of direct sensory experience, consensual validation, empirical evidence, and scientific research. In transpersonal experiences that involve historical regression[11] or transcendence of spatial barriers, it is thus not the content that is surprising, but the possibility of having a direct experience of, and conscious identification with, various aspects of the phenomenal world outside of us. Under normal circumstances, we would consider those to be entirely separate from us and experientially inaccessible. With respect to lower animals, plants, and inorganic materials, we might also be surprised to find consciousness or awareness where we would not expect it. In the instances of classic extrasensory perception, again, it is not the content of the experiences that is unusual or surprising, but the way of acquiring certain information about other people, or perception of a situation that, according to common sense and the existing scientific paradigms, should be beyond our reach.

However, the theoretical challenge of these observations—formidable as it may be in itself—is further augmented by the fact that, in psychedelic sessions, transpersonal experiences correctly reflecting the material world appear on the same continuum and intimately interwoven with others whose content is not in agreement with the world view predominant in Western civilization. We can mention here the Jungian archetypes—the world of deities, demons, demigods, superheroes, and complex mythological, legendary, and fairy tale sequences. Even these experiences can be associated with accurate information about folklore, religious symbolism, and mythical structures of various cultures of the world that the subject has not been familiar with or interested in prior to the LSD session. The most generalized and universal experiences of this kind involve identification with cosmic consciousness, the Universal Mind, or the Void.

That transpersonal experiences can mediate access to accurate information about various aspects of the universe previously unknown to the subject requires in itself a fundamental revision of our concepts about the nature of reality and the relationship between consciousness and matter. Equally challenging is the discovery of archetypal and mythological realms or entities that seem to have existences of their own and cannot be explained away as derivatives of the material world. However, there are additional, quite striking observations that the new paradigm will have to account for or take into consideration.

In many instances, transpersonal experiences in psychedelic sessions seem to be inextricably interwoven with the fabric of events in the material world. Such *dynamic interconnections between inner experiences and the phenomenal world* suggest that somehow the network involved in the psychedelic process transcends the physical boundaries of the individual. A detailed discussion and analysis of this fascinating phenomenon must be reserved for a future publication, since it requires careful case histories. It is sufficient here to give a brief description of its general characteristics and a few specific examples.

When certain transpersonal themes emerge from the subject's unconscious during the psychedelic process, this is often associated with a highly improbable incidence of certain external events that appear to be related in a very specific and meaningful way to the inner theme. The life of such a person shows at this time a striking accumulation of most unusual coincidences; he or she might live temporarily in a world governed by synchronicity, in Carl Gustav Jung's terms (1960b), rather than simple linear causality. It has happened on a number of occasions that various dangerous events and circumstances started to accumulate in the lives of subjects who in their LSD sessions were approaching the experience of ego death. And, conversely, they cleared up in an almost magical way when this process was completed. It seemed as if these individuals had to face, for some reason, the experience of annihilation, but they had the choice of doing so in a symbolic way in the inner world or facing it in reality.

Similarly, when a Jungian archetype is emerging into the consciousness of an LSD subject during psychedelic therapy, its basic theme can become manifest and be enacted in the individual's life. Thus, at a time when the problems related to the Animus, Anima, or Terrible Mother are being confronted in the sessions, ideal representatives of these archetypal images tend to appear in the subject's everyday life. When elements of the collective, or racial, unconscious or mythological themes related to a specific culture dominate a person's LSD sessions, this can be accompanied in everyday life by a striking influx of elements related to this particular geographic or cultural area: appearance of the members of that particular ethnic group in the subject's life, unexpected letters from, or invitations to visit, the country involved, gifts of books or accumulation of the themes in question in movies or television programs shown at the time.

Another interesting observation of this kind was made in connection with past incarnation experiences in psychedelic sessions. Some LSD subjects occasionally experience vivid and complex sequences from other cultures and other historical periods that have all the qualities of memories and are usually interpreted by the individuals themselves as a reliving of episodes from previous lifetimes. As these experiences are unfolding, LSD subjects usually identify certain persons in their present lifetime as being important protagonists in these karmic situations. In that case present interpersonal tensions, problems, and conflicts with these persons are frequently recognized or interpreted as being direct derivatives of the destructive karmic patterns. The reliving and resolution of such karmic memories is typically associated with a sense of profound relief, liberation from oppressive "karmic bonds," and feelings of overwhelming bliss and accomplishment on the part of the LSD subject.

Careful examination of the dynamics of the interpersonal constellation that was allegedly a derivative of the resolved karmic pattern often brings astonishing results. The feelings, attitudes, and behavior of the individuals whom the LSD subject identified as protagonists in the past incarnation sequence tend to change in a specific direction in basic congruence with the events in the psychedelic session. It is important to emphasize that these changes happen quite independently and cannot be explained in terms of conventional linear understanding of causality. The persons involved might be hundreds or thousands of miles away at the time of the LSD subject's psychedelic experience. These changes can occur even if there is absolutely no physical communication between the persons involved. The feelings and attitudes of the alleged protagonists are influenced quite independently by factors that are in no way related to the subject's LSD experience, yet specific changes in all the persons involved seem to follow a common pattern and to happen at almost exactly the same time, within minutes of each other.

Similar instances of extraordinary synchronicities occur quite frequently in association with various other types of transpersonal phenomena. There seems to be a striking parallel between events of this kind and the basic assumptions of Bell's theorem in modern physics (1966), which will be discussed later. Such observations are in no way specific for psychedelic states and occur in the context of Jungian analysis or various forms of experiential psychotherapy, in the course of meditative practice, or during spontaneous upsurges of transpersonal elements into consciousness under the circumstances of everyday life.

Having described the most important observations from psychedelic research that challenge common sense and the existing scientific paradigms, it is of interest to explore *the changes in the world view* of the individuals who have had first-hand experiences of the perinatal and transpersonal realms. This should be particularly interesting in view of the focus in the following section of this book on the dramatic changes of the scientific world view in the course of this century.

As long as LSD subjects are confronting phenomena that are basically of a biographical nature, they do not encounter any major conceptual challenges. While systematically exploring their traumatic past, they tend to realize that certain aspects or sectors of their lives have been inauthentic, since they represent blind, automatonlike repetitions of maladjustive patterns established in early childhood. The reliving of specific traumatic memories underlying such patterns tends to have a liberating effect and makes it possible to perceive and differentiate more clearly, as well as respond more adequately, in the previously afflicted categories of relationships and situations. Typical examples of such situations would be the contamination of the attitude toward authority by one's traumatic experience with domineering parents, introduction of the elements of sibling rivalry into one's interactions with peers, or distortion of sexual relationships by patterns of interaction established in the relationship with the parent of the opposite sex.

As LSD subjects enter the perinatal realm and confront the twin experiences of birth and death, they typically realize that the distortion and inauthenticity of their lives does not limit itself to partial segments or areas. They suddenly see their entire picture of reality and general strategy of existence as false and inauthentic. Many previous attitudes and behaviors that used to appear natural and were accepted without questioning are now perceived as irrational and absurd. It becomes clear that they are derivatives of a fear of death and remnants of the unresolved trauma of birth. In this context, a driven and hectic life pattern, haunting ambitions, competitive drives, a need to prove oneself, and the inability to enjoy are seen as unnecessary nightmares from which one can awaken. Those who complete the death-rebirth process connect with intrinsic spiritual sources and realize that a mechanistic and materialistic world view is rooted in fear of birth and death.

Following the ego death, the ability to enjoy life typically increases considerably. The past and future appear to be relatively less important than the present moment, and excitement about the process of life replaces the compulsion to pursue the achievement of goals. The individual tends to see the world in terms of energy patterns instead of solid matter, and his or her boundaries against the rest of the world seem less absolute and more fluid. Although spirituality is now seen as an important force in the universe, the phenomenal world is still seen as objectively real. Time continues to be linear, space is Euclidean, and the principle of causality is unchallenged, although the roots of many problems are now seen in the birth process rather than in early childhood.

The most profound and basic changes in understanding the nature of reality occur in connection with various types of trans-individual experiences. As the LSD process extends into the transpersonal realms, the limits of linear causality are stretched ad infinitum. Not only biological birth, but various aspects and stages of embryonic development, and even circumstances of conception and implantation, appear to be plausible sources of important influences on the psychological life of the individual. The elements of ancestral, racial, and phylogenetic memories, conscious intelligence of the DNA molecule and metaphysics of the genetic code, dynamics of archetypal structures, and the fact of reincarnation with the law of karma must now be incorporated into the subject's thinking to account for the enormous expansion of his or her experiential world.

If one adheres to the old medical model in which a material substrate is necessary for memory, the nucleus of a single cell—the sperm or the ovum—would have to contain not only the information discussed in medical books concerning the anatomy, physiology, and biochemistry of the body, constitutional factors, hereditary dispositions to diseases, and parental characteristics, but also complex memories from the lives of our human and animal ancestors, and retrievable detailed data about all the cultures of the world. Since the LSD experiences also involve consciousness of plants and inorganic matter down to its molecular, atomic, and subatomic structures, as well as cosmogenetic events and geological history, one would ultimately have to postulate that the entire universe is in some way coded in the sperm and ovum. At this point, the mystical alternatives to the mechanistic world view appear to be much more appropriate and reasonable.

At the same time, various transpersonal experiences tend to undermine the belief in the mandatory nature of linear time and three-dimensional space by offering many experiential alternatives. Matter tends to disintegrate not only into playful energy patterns but into cosmic vacuum. Form and emptiness become relative and, ultimately, interchangeable concepts. After the individual has been confronted with a considerable sample of transpersonal experiences, the Newtonian-Cartesian world view becomes untenable as a serious philosophical concept and is seen as a pragmatically useful, but simplistic, superficial, and arbitrary system of organizing one's everyday experience.

Although for the practical purposes of daily life one still thinks in terms of solid matter, three-dimensional space, unidirectional time, and linear causality, the philosophical understanding of existence becomes much more complex and sophisticated; it approaches that found in the great mystical traditions of the world. The universe is seen as an infinite web of adventures in consciousness, and the dichotomies between the experiencer and the experienced, form and emptiness, time and timelessness, determinism and free will, or existence and nonexistence have been transcended.

New Understanding of Reality, Existence and Human Nature

The observations described in the preceding section, particularly those related to transpersonal experiences, are clearly incompatible with the most basic assumptions of mechanistic science. Yet, they are so consistent and come from so many independent sources that it is no longer possible to deny their existence. It is also hard to imagine that they could be assimilated into contemporary science at the expense of some minor or even major conceptual adjustments of the leading paradigm. The only solution seems to be a fundamental and drastic revision, a paradigm shift of enormous scope and far-reaching relevance.

In a sense, this development is quite logical and should not come as a surprise. Scientific thinking in contemporary medicine, psychiatry, psychology, and anthropology represents a direct extension of the seventeenth century Newtonian-Cartesian model of the universe. Since all the basic assumptions of this way of viewing reality have been transcended by twentieth-century physics, it seems only natural to expect profound changes sooner or later in all the disciplines that are its direct derivatives.

It can be demonstrated without much effort that most of the material from LSD psychotherapy, although quite puzzling and incomprehensible from the point of view of mechanistic science, presents far less difficulty when approached in the spirit of quantum-relativistic physics, information and systems theory, cybernetics, or recent discoveries in neurophysiology and biology. Modern consciousness research has produced much evidence supporting the world views of the great mystical traditions. At the same time, revolutionary developments in other scientific disciplines have seriously undermined and discredited the mechanistic world view, narrowing the gap between science and mysticism that in the past seemed absolute and unbridgeable.

It is interesting that many great scientists who have revolutionized modern physics, such as Albert Einstein, Niels Bohr, Erwin Schroedinger, Werner Heisenberg, Robert Oppenheimer, and David Bohm, have found their scientific thinking quite compatible with spirituality and the mystical world view. In recent years, the increasing convergence between science and mysticism has been discussed in a number of books and articles.[12]

To demonstrate the compatibility and complementarity between the world view emerging from quantum-relativistic physics and the observations from consciousness research discussed earlier, I will briefly review the conceptual revolution in twentieth century physics, following Fritjof Capra's comprehensive presentation in *The Tao of Physics* (1975). There is an interesting parallel here that is probably not just coincidental, but has a deeper meaning and significance. The Newtonian-Cartesian model was not only adequate but highly successful, as long as physicists were exploring the phenomena in the world of our everyday experience, or the "zone of middle dimensions." Once they started making excursions beyond the limits of ordinary perception into the microworld of subatomic processes and into the macroworld of astrophysics, the Newtonian-Cartesian model became untenable and had to be transcended. Similarly, deep conceptual and metaphysical changes occur automatically in LSD subjects, meditators, and other explorers of inner spaces as they enter experientially the transpersonal realms. Science that takes into account the testimony of nonordinary states of consciousness has no other choice but to free itself from the narrow confines of the Newtonian-Cartesian model.

The revolutionary changes in physics heralding the end of the Newtonian model started back in the nineteenth century with the famous experiments of Faraday and Maxwell's theoretical speculations concerning electromagnetic phenomena. The work of these two researchers led to the revolutionary concept of a force field, replacing the Newtonian concept of force. Unlike Newtonian forces, force fields could be studied with no reference to material bodies. This was the first major departure from Newtonian physics; it led to the discovery that light is a rapidly alternating electromagnetic field traveling through space in the form of waves. The comprehensive theory of electromagnetism based on this discovery was able to reduce the differences among radio waves, visible light, x-rays, and cosmic rays to differences in frequency, bringing them all under the common denominator of electromagnetic fields. However, for many years electrodynamics remained under the spell of Newtonian thinking. As a result, electromagnetic waves were conceived as vibrations of a very light, space-filling substance called "ether." The existence of ether was disproved by the Michelson-Morley experiment; it was Albert Einstein who stated clearly that electromagnetic fields were entities in their own right that could travel through empty space.

The first decades of this century brought unexpected discoveries in physics that shattered the very foundations of the Newtonian model of the universe. The milestones of this development were two papers published by Albert Einstein in 1905. In the first, he formulated the principles of his special theory of relativity; in the second, he suggested a new way of looking at light that was later elaborated by a team of physicists into the quantum theory of atomic processes. The theory of relativity and the new atomic theory undermined all the basic concepts of Newtonian physics: the existence of absolute time and space, the solid material nature of the universe, the definition of physical forces, the strictly deterministic system of explanation, and the ideal of objective description of phenomena without including the observer.

According to the relativity theory, space is not three-dimensional and time is not linear; neither of them is a separate entity. They are intimately interwoven and form a four-dimensional continuum called "space-time." The flow of time is not even and uniform, as in the Newtonian model; it depends on the position of the observers and their relative velocities in regard to the observed event. In addition, the general theory of relativity, formulated in 1915 and not yet conclusively confirmed by experiments, states that space-time is influenced by the presence of massive objects. The variations in the field of gravity in different parts of the universe have a curving effect on space that makes time flow at different rates.

Not only are all the measurements involving space and time relative, but the entire structure of space-time depends on the distribution of matter, and the distinction between matter and empty space loses its meaning. The Newtonian notion of solid material bodies moving in empty space with Euclidean characteristics is now considered to be valid only in the "zone of middle dimensions." In astrophysics and cosmological speculations, the concept of empty space has no meaning; conversely, the developments in atomic and subatomic physics have destroyed the image of solid matter.

The adventure of subatomic exploration began at the turn of the century with the discovery of x-rays and of the radiation emitted by radioactive substances. Rutherford's experiments with alpha particles demonstrated clearly that atoms were not hard and solid units of matter, but consisted of vast spaces in which small particles—the electrons—moved around the nucleus. The study of atomic processes presented scientists with a number of strange paradoxes that arose whenever they tried to explain the new observations in the framework of traditional physics. In the 1920s, an international group of physicists, including Niels Bohr, Louis de Broglie, Werner Heisenberg, Erwin Schroedinger, Wolfgang Pauli, and Paul Dirac, succeeded in finding mathematical formulations for the subatomic events.

The concepts of quantum theory and their philosophical implications were not easy to accept, although its mathematical formalism reflected adequately the processes involved. The "planetary model" showed atoms as consisting of empty space with only miniscule particles of matter; quantum physics demonstrated that even these were not solid objects. It turned out that the subatomic particles had very abstract characteristics and showed a paradoxical, dual nature. Depending on the arrangement of the experimental situation, they appeared sometimes as particles and sometimes as waves. Similar ambiguity was also observed in the research exploring the nature of light. In some experiments light showed the properties of an electromagnetic field, in others it seemed to have the form of distinct energy quanta, or photons, that were massless and always traveled with the speed of light.

The ability of the same phenomenon to manifest itself as particles as well as waves obviously involves a violation of Aristotelian logic. The image of a particle implies an entity confined to a small volume or a finite region of space, whereas that of a wave is diffuse and spread over vast regions of space. In quantum physics, these two descriptions are mutually exclusive, but equally necessary, for a comprehensive understanding of the phenomena involved. This was expressed in a new logical instrument that Niels Bohr (1934; 1958) called the *complementarity principle*. This new ordering principle in science codifies the paradox instead of resolving it. It accepts the logical discrepancy between two aspects of reality that are mutually exclusive yet equally necessary for an exhaustive description of a phenomenon. According to Bohr, this discrepancy results from an uncontrollable interaction between the object of observation and the agency of observation. In the domain of the quantum, there can be no question of causality or complete objectivity as these were once ordinarily understood.

The seeming contradiction between the particle and wave images was solved in quantum theory in a manner that shatters the very foundations of the mechanistic world view. At the subatomic level, matter does not exist with certainty at definite places, but rather shows "tendencies to exist," and atomic events do not occur with certainty at definite times and in definite ways, but rather "show tendencies to occur." These tendencies can be expressed as mathematical probabilities that have the characteristic properties of waves. The wave image of light or subatomic particles should not be understood in a concretistic way. The waves involved are not three-dimensional configurations, but mathematical abstractions or "probability waves" reflecting the chances of finding the particles at a certain time and at a certain place.

Quantum physics thus suggests a scientific model of the universe in sharp contrast with that of classical physics. At the subatomic level the world of solid material objects dissolves into a complex pattern of probability waves. In addition, careful analysis of the process of observation has shown that the subatomic particles have no meaning as isolated entities; they can only be understood as interconnections between the preparation of an experiment and the subsequent measurement. The probability waves, thus, do not ultimately represent probabilities of things, but probabilities of interconnections.

The exploration of the subatomic world did not end with the discovery of the atomic nuclei and the electrons. At first, the atomic model was extended to include three "elementary particles"—the proton, the neutron, and the electron. As physicists refined their experimental techniques and developed new devices, the number of subatomic particles kept increasing; at present, their number runs into the hundreds. During this experimentation, it became clear that a complete theory of subatomic phenomena must include not only quantum physics but also the theory of relativity, because the speed of the particles involved frequently approaches the speed of light. According to Einstein, mass has nothing to do with sub-stance, but is a form of energy; the equivalence of the two is expressed by his famous equation, $E=mc^2$.

The most spectacular consequence of the theory of relativity was the experimental demonstration that material particles can be created from pure energy and can be made to turn into pure energy in a reverse process. Relativity theory has not only drastically affected the conception of particles, but also the picture of the forces between them. The mutual repulsion and attraction of the particles are seen in relativistic description as an exchange of other particles. Thus, both force and matter are now considered to have their origin in dynamic patterns called particles. The presently known particles cannot be further subdivided. In high-energy phys-ics, using collision processes, matter can be divided repeatedly but never into smaller pieces; the resulting fragments are particles created out of the energy involved in the collision process. The subatomic particles are thus destructible and indestructible at the same time.

The field theories have transcended the classic distinction be-tween material particles and the void. According to both Einstein's theory of gravity and quantum field theory, particles cannot be separated from the space that surrounds them. They represent nothing but condensations of a continuous field that is present throughout space. The field theory suggests that particles can come into being spontaneously out of the void and disappear again into the void. The discovery of the dynamic quality of the "physical vacuum" is one of the most important findings of modern physics. It is in a state of emptiness and nothingness, yet it contains the potentiality for all forms of the particle world.[13]

This brief outline of the developments in modern physics would be incomplete without mentioning a radical school of thought that is particularly relevant for our further discussion—the so-called bootstrap approach formulated by Geoffrey Chew (1968). Although it has been specifically elaborated for only one type of subatomic particles—the hadron—it represents in its consequences a com-prehensive philosophical understanding of nature. According to "bootstrap philosophy," nature cannot be reduced to any such fundamental entities as elementary particles or fields; it must be understood entirely through its self-consistency. In the last analysis, the universe is an infinite web of mutually interrelated events. None of the properties of any part of this web is elementary and fundamental; they all reflect the properties of the other parts. It is therefore the overall consistency of their mutual interrelations that determines the structure of the entire network, rather than any specific constituents. The universe cannot be understood, as in the Newtonian model and its derivatives, to be an assemblage of entities that cannot be further analyzed and represent a priori givens. The bootstrap philosophy of nature not only rejects the existence of basic constituents of matter, it accepts no fundamental laws of nature or mandatory principles whatsoever. All the theories of natural phenomena, including natural laws, are considered in this view to be creations of the human mind. They are conceptual schemes that represent more or less adequate approximations and should not be confused with accurate descriptions of reality or with reality itself.

The history of twentieth century physics has not been an easy process; it has involved not only brilliant achievements, but also conceptual turmoil, confusion, and dramatic human conflicts. It took physicists a long time to abandon the basic assumptions of classical physics and the agreed-upon view of reality. The new physics necessitated not only changes in the concepts of matter, space, time, and linear causality, but also the recognition that paradoxes represent an essential aspect of the new model of the universe. Long after the mathematical formalism of the theories of relativity and of quantum theory have been completed, accepted, and assimilated into mainstream science, physicists are still far from unanimous with respect to the philosophical interpretation and metaphysical implications of these systems of thought. Thus, in relation to the quantum theory alone, there are several major interpretations of the mathematical formalism involved (Jammer 1974; Pagels 1982).

Theoretical physicists, however advanced and revolutionary in their views, have been brought up to experience every day reality as endowed with the properties ascribed to it by classical physics. Many of them, refusing to deal with the unsettling philosophical questions raised by the quantum theory, opt for a strictly *pragmatic approach*. They are satisfied with the fact that the mathematical formalism of quantum theory accurately predicts the results of the experiments and insist that this is all that really matters.

Another important approach to the problems of quantum theory is one based on *stochastic interpretations*. In dealing with the events in the phenomenal world, physicists use statistical approaches whenever they do not know all the mechanical details of the system they are studying. They refer to these unknown factors as "hidden variables." Those scientists who favor the stochastic interpretation of quantum theory are trying to demonstrate that it is basically a classic theory of probabilistic processes, and that a radical departure from the conceptual framework of classic physics was unnecessary and misleading. Many believe with Einstein that the quantum theory is a kind of statistical mechanics that gives only average values of the measured quantities. At a deeper level, each individual system is governed by deterministic laws that will be discovered in the future by more refined research. In classic physics, the hidden variables are local mechanisms. John Bell presented a proof that in quantum physics such hidden variables—if they exist—would have to be nonlocal connections to the universe operating instantly.

The *Copenhagen interpretation*, associated with Niels Bohr and Werner Heisenberg, was, until 1950, the leading view in quantum physics. It emphasizes the principle of local causality at the expense of undermining the objective existence of the microworld. According to this view, there is no reality until that reality is perceived. Depending on the experimental arrangement, various complementary aspects of reality will become apparent. It is the fact of observation that disrupts the unbroken wholeness of the universe and generates paradoxes. The instantaneous experience of reality does not appear paradoxical at all. It is only when the observer attempts to construct the history of his or her perception that paradoxes emerge. This is because there is no clear dividing line between ourselves and the reality we observe to exist outside ourselves. Reality is constructed by mental acts and depends on the choice of what and how we observe.

There have also been tendencies among theoretical physicists to solve the paradoxes of quantum physics by work on the basis of scientific theory. Certain developments in mathematics and philosophy have led to the idea that the reason for the impasse might be in the logic underlying the theory. A search along these lines has led to attempts to replace the Boolean logic of ordinary language by *quantum logic*, in which the usual logical meaning of such words as "and" and "either—or" is changed.

By far the most fantastic interpretation of quantum theory is the *many worlds hypothesis* associated with Hugh Everett III, John Archibald Wheeler, and Neill Graham. This approach eliminates the inconsistencies in conventional interpretations and the "collapse of the wave function" produced by the act of observation. However, this becomes possible at the expense of a drastic revision of our most fundamental assumptions about reality. This hypothesis postulates that the universe splits at every instant of time into an infinity of universes. Due to this multiple branching, all the possibilities suggested by the mathematical formalism of the quantum theory become actually realized, although in different universes. Reality is the infinity of all these universes existing in a "superspace" that includes them all. Because the individual universes do not communicate with each other, no contradictions are possible.

Most radical from the point of view of psychology, psychiatry, and parapsychology are those interpretations that assume a *critical role of the psyche in quantum reality*. The authors who think along these lines suggest that mind or consciousness actually influences, or even creates, matter. The work of Eugene Wigner, Edward Walker, Jack Sarfatti, and Charles Musès is relevant here.

The nature and scope of this volume do not allow me to explore in greater detail the fascinating and far-reaching changes in the image of the universe and the nature of reality suggested by quantum-relativity physics. The interested reader will find more relevant information in special books on the subject written by experts in the field. However, one more issue that is of critical importance should be briefly mentioned in this connection. Einstein, whose work had initiated the development of quantum physics, showed until the end of his life great resistance to the fundamental role of probability in nature. He expressed it in his famous statement: "God does not play dice." Even after numerous discussions and arguments with the foremost representatives of quantum physics, he remained convinced that a deterministic interpretation in terms of "hidden local variables" would be found some time in the future. In order to show that Bohr's interpretation of quantum theory was wrong, Einstein devised a thought experiment, which later became known as the Einstein-Podolsky-Rosen (EPR) experiment. Ironically, several decades later, this experiment served as the basis for John Bell's theorem that proves that the Cartesian concept of reality is incompatible with quantum theory (Bell 1966; Capra 1982).

The simplified version of the EPR experiment involves two electrons spinning in opposite directions, so that their total spin is zero. They are made to move apart until the distance between them becomes macroscopic; their respective spins can then be measured by two independent observers. Quantum theory predicts that, in a system of two particles with a total spin of zero, the spins about any axis will always be correlated, that is, opposite. Although before the actual measurement one can only talk about tendencies to spin, once the measurement is made, this potential is transformed into certainty. The observer is free to choose any axis of measurement, and this instantly determines the spin of the other particle that might be thousands of miles away. According to the theory of relativity, no signal can travel faster than light, and therefore this situation should be impossible in principle. The instantaneous, nonlocal connection between these particles cannot be thus mediated by signals in the Einsteinian sense; communication of this kind transcends the conventional concept of information transfer. Bell's theorem leaves the physicists with an uncomfortable dilemma; it suggests that either the world is not objectively real, or it is connected by supraluminal links. According to Henry Stapp (1971), Bell's theorem proves "the profound truth that the universe is either fundamentally lawless or fundamentally inseparable."

Although quantum-relativity physics provides the most convincing and radical critique of the mechanistic world view, important revisions have been inspired by various avenues of research in other disciplines. Drastic changes of a similar kind have been introduced into scientific thinking by developments in cybernetics, information theory, systems theory, and the theory of logical types. One of the major representatives of this critical trend in modern science has been Gregory Bateson.[14] According to him, thinking in terms of substance and discrete objects represents a serious epistemological mistake—error in logical typing. In everyday life, we never deal with objects but with their sensory transforms or messages about differences; in Korzybski's sense (1933), we have access to maps, not the territory. The information, difference, form, and pattern that constitute our knowledge of the world are dimensionless entities that cannot be located in space or time. The information flows in circuits that transcend the conventional boundaries of the individual and include the environment. This way of scientific thinking makes it absurd to treat the world in terms of separate objects and entities, to see the individual, family, or species as Darwinian units of survival, to draw distinctions between mind and body, or to identify with the ego-body unit (Alan Watt's "skin-encapsulated ego"). As in quantum-relativistic physics, the emphasis has shifted from substance and object to form, pattern, and process.[15]

Systems theory has made it possible to formulate a new definition of the mind and mental functioning. It showed that every aggregate of parts and components that has the appropriate complexity of closed causal circuits and the appropriate energy relations will show mental characteristics—respond to difference, process information, and be self-corrective. In this sense, it is possible to talk about mental characteristics of cells, tissues, and organs of the body, of a cultural group or nation, of an ecological system, or even of the entire planet, as Lovelock has done in his Gaia theory (1979). And when we consider a larger mind that integrates all the hierarchies of the lower ones, even a critical and skeptical scientist like Gregory Bateson has to admit that this concept comes close to that of an immanent god.

Another profound criticism of the basic concepts of mechanistic science has emerged from the work of the Nobel laureate Ilya Prigogine (1980, 1984) and his colleagues in Brussels, Belgium, and Austin, Texas. Traditional science portrays life as a specific, rare, and ultimately futile process—an insignificant and accidental anomaly involved in a quixotic struggle against the absolute dictate of the second law of thermodynamics. This gloomy picture of the universe, dominated by an all-powerful tendency toward increasing randomness and entropy and moving relentlessly toward a thermal death, belongs now to the history of science. It was dispelled by Prigogine's study of the so-called dissipative structures[16] in certain chemical reactions and his discovery of a new principle underlying them—"order through fluctuation." Further research revealed that this principle is not limited to chemical processes, but represents a basic mechanism for the unfolding of evolutionary processes in all domains—from atoms to galaxies, from individual cells to human beings, and further to societies and cultures.

As a result of these observations, it has become possible to formulate a unified view of evolution in which the unifying principle is not the steady state, but the dynamic conditions of the non-equilibrium systems. Open systems on all levels and in all domains are carriers of an overall evolution which ensures that life will continue moving into ever newer dynamic regimes of complexity. In this view, life itself appears in a new light far beyond the narrow notion of organic life. Whenever systems in any domain become stifled by past entropy production, they mutate toward new regimes. The same energy and the same principles thus carry evolution on all levels, whether it involves matter, vital forces, information, or mental processes. Microcosm and macrocosm are two aspects of the same unified and unifying evolution. Life is no longer seen as a phenomenon unfolding in an inanimate universe; the universe itself becomes increasingly alive.

Although the simplest level on which self-organization can be studied is the level of dissipative structures that form in self-renewing chemical reaction systems, applying these principles to biological, psychological, and sociocultural phenomena does not involve reductionistic thinking. Unlike the reductionism of mechanistic science, such interpretations are based on fundamental homology, on the relatedness of the self-organizing dynamics on many levels.

From this point of view, humans are not higher than other living organisms; they live simultaneously on more levels than do life forms that appeared earlier in evolution. Here science has rediscovered the truth of perennial philosophy, that the evolution of humanity forms an integral and meaningful part of universal evolution. Humans are important agents in this evolution; rather than being helpless subjects of evolution, they *are* evolution.

Like quantum-relativistic physics, this new science of becoming, replacing the old science of being, shifts the emphasis from substance to process. Here, structure is an incidental product of interacting processes, which, in Erich Jantsch's words, is no more solid than a standing wave pattern in the confluence of two rivers or the grin of a Cheshire cat.[17]

The latest serious challenge to mechanistic thinking is the theory of the British biologist and biochemist, Rupert Sheldrake, expounded in his revolutionary and highly controversial book, *A New Science of Life* (1981). Sheldrake has offered a brilliant critique of the limitations of the explanatory power of mechanistic science and its inability to face problems of basic significance in the areas of morphogenesis during individual development and evolution of species, genetics, or instinctual and more complex forms of behavior. Mechanistic science deals only with the quantitative aspect of phenomena, with what Sheldrake calls the "energetic causation." It has nothing to say about the qualitative aspect—the development of forms, or the "formative causation." According to Sheldrake, living organisms are not just complex biological machines, and life cannot be reduced to chemical reactions. The form, development, and behavior of organisms are shaped by "morphogenetic fields" of a type that at present cannot be detected or measured and is not recognized by physics. These fields are moulded by the form and behavior of past organisms of the same species through direct connections across both space and time, and they show cumulative properties. If a critical number of members of a species develop certain organismic properties or learn a specific form of behavior, these are automatically acquired by other members of the species, even if there are no conventional forms of contact between them.[18] The phenomenon of "morphic resonance," as Sheldrake calls it, is not limited to living organisms and can be demonstrated for such elementary phenomena as the growth of crystals.

However implausible and absurd this theory might appear to a mechanistically oriented mind, it is testable, unlike the basic metaphysical assumptions of the materialistic world view. Even at present, in its early stages, it is supported by experiments in rats and observations in monkeys. Sheldrake is well aware that his theory has far-reaching implications for psychology and has himself discussed its relationship to Jung's concept of the collective unconscious.

This survey of new exciting developments in science would not be complete without mentioning the work of Arthur Young (1976a; 1976b). His *theory of process* is a serious candidate for a scientific metaparadigm of the future. It organizes and interprets in a most comprehensive way the data from a variety of disciplines—geometry, quantum theory and theories of relativity, chemistry, biology, botany, zoology, psychology and history—and integrates them into an all-encompassing cosmological vision. Young's model of the universe has four levels, defined by degrees of freedom and of constraint, and seven consecutive stages: light, nuclear particles, atoms, molecules, plants, animals, and humans. Young was able to discover a basic pattern of the universal process that repeats itself again and again on different levels of evolution in nature. The explanatory power of this paradigm is complemented by its predictive power. Like Mendeléev's periodic table of elements, it is capable of predicting natural phenomena and their specific aspects.

By assigning a critical role in the universe to light and the purposeful influence of the quantum of action, Young made it possible to bridge the gap between science, mythology, and perennial philosophy. His metaparadigm is thus not only consistent with the best of science, but also capable of dealing with nonobjective and nondefinable aspects of reality far beyond the accepted limits of science. Since one cannot do justice to Young's theory without detailed excursions into a variety of disciplines, the interested reader is referred to his original writings.

At present, it is clearly impossible to integrate all the various revolutionary developments in modern science discussed in this chapter into a cohesive and comprehensive new paradigm. However, they all seem to have one thing in common: their proponents share a deep belief that the mechanistic image of the universe created by Newtonian-Cartesian science should no longer be considered an accurate and mandatory model of reality.

The concept of the cosmos as a gigantic supermachine, assembled from countless separate objects and existing independently from the observer, has become obsolete and has been relegated to the historical archives of science. The updated model shows the universe as a unified and indivisible web of events and relationships; its parts represent different aspects and patterns of one integral process of unimaginable complexity. As predicted by James Jeans (1930) over fifty years ago, the universe of modern physics looks far more like a system of thought processes than like a gigantic clockwork. As scientists have probed into the deepest structure of matter and studied the multifarious aspects of the processes in the world, the notion of solid substance has gradually disappeared from the picture, leaving them only with archetypal patterns, abstract mathematical formulas, or universal order. Consequently, it does not seem extravagant to entertain the possibility that the connecting principle in the cosmic web is consciousness as a primary and further irreducible attribute of existence.[19]

After this review of some exciting developments in modern science, we now return to the observations from modern consciousness research. Most are clearly incompatible with the Newtonian-Cartesian paradigm of mechanistic science; it is therefore of great interest to explore their relationship to various elements of the emerging new scientific world view. The revolutionary potential of the data generated by modern consciousness research seems to vary with the level of observation. Thus, experiences of a biographical nature present no serious challenge to established ways of thinking and could be handled by minor adjustments of the existing theories. The perinatal experiences would require far more dramatic changes, but it is conceivable that they could be assimilated without a radical paradigm shift. However, the existence of transpersonal experiences represents a mortal blow to mechanistic thinking and requires changes at the very basis of the scientific world view. The necessary drastic revisions will specifically affect those disciplines that remain under the spell of the Newtonian-Cartesian paradigm, considering the principles of this seventeenth century model to be synonymous with the principles of science.

Fritjof Capra (1975; 1982) and others have demonstrated that the world view emerging from modern physics seems to be converging with the mystical world view. The same can be said to a far greater extent about modern consciousness research, since it deals directly with states of consciousness, the true domain of the mystical schools. Consequently, there is also an increasing compatibility between the revolutionary concepts of consciousness research and modern physics. These statements require a few words of explanation and specification. Convergence between physics and mysticism does not mean identity, or even a prospect of future merging. Tendencies to so interpret the situation have been justly criticized. A particularly incisive criticism has been offered by Ken Wilber. In his paper, *Physics, Mysticism, and the New Holographic Paradigm* (1979), he points out that perennial philosophy describes being and consciousness as a hierarchy of levels, from the densest and most fragmentary realms to the highest, subtlest, and most unitary ones. Most of the systems agree on the following major levels: (1) *physical*, involving nonliving matter/energy; (2) *biological*, focusing on living, sentient matter/energy; (3) *psychological*, dealing with mind, ego, and logical thinking; (4) *subtle*, comprising psychic and archetypal phenomena; (5) *causal*, characterized by formless radiance and perfect transcendence, and (6) *absolute consciousness* and suchness of all the levels of the spectrum.

In the mystical world view, each level of the spectrum transcends and includes its predecessors, but not vice versa. Since the
lower is, in perennial philosophy, created by the higher by a process
called "involution," the higher cannot be explained from the lower.
Each level has a more limited and controlled range of consciousness
than the level above it. The elements of lower worlds are unable
to experience the higher worlds and are unaware of their existence,
although they are interpenetrated by them.

The mystics distinguish two forms of interpenetration—horizontal within each level, and vertical between the levels. Holoarchy
exists within each level—all its elements are roughly equivalent in
status and mutually interpenetrating. Nonequivalence and hierarchy
exist between the levels. The discoveries of physics have confirmed
only a small fragment of the mystical world view. Physicists have
blasted the dogma of the primacy of indestructible, solid matter
that served as the basis of the mechanistic world view: in subatomic
explorations, matter disintegrated into abstract patterns and forms
of consciousness. Physicists have also demonstrated horizontal unity
and interpenetration of the first, the physical, level of the hierarchy
of perennial philosophy.

Information theory and systems theory have shown a similar
situation on levels two and three. The new discoveries in physics,
chemistry, or biology can say nothing about the higher levels of
the mystical hierarchy. The significance of these developments in
science in this respect is only indirect. By undermining the mechanistic world view that ridiculed mysticism and spirituality, they
are creating a more open-minded climate for consciousness research.
However, only discoveries in scientific disciplines that study consciousness directly can provide access to the remaining levels of
the spectrum covered by perennial philosophy. With this in mind,
we can now explore the relationship between the observations from
modern consciousness research and recent developments in other
scientific disciplines.

Transpersonal experiences fall into two major categories. The
first includes phenomena the content of which is directly related
to various elements of the material world, such as other people,
animals, plants, and inanimate objects or processes. The second
category involves experiential domains that are clearly beyond the
confines of what is agreed upon in the West as objective reality.
Here belong, for example, various archetypal visions, mythological

sequences, experiences of divine and demonic influences, encounters with discarnate or suprahuman beings, and experiential identification with the Universal Mind or the Supracosmic Void.

The first category can be further subdivided into two subgroups; the principle of division here is the nature of the conventional barrier that appears to be transcended. In the experiences of the first subgroup it is primarily the spatial partitioning and the condition of separateness; in those of the second one the limitations of linear time. Experiences of this kind represent an insurmountable obstacle for Cartesian-Newtonian science, which sees matter as solid, boundaries and separateness as absolute properties of the universe, and time as linear and irreversible. This is not true for the modern scientific world view that pictures the universe as an infinite and unified web of interrelations and considers any boundaries to be ultimately arbitrary and negotiable. It has transcended the sharp distinction between object and empty space and offers conceptual possibilities of direct subatomic connections that bypass the channels accepted or acceptable by mechanistic science. Also the possibility of consciousness existing outside the brains of humans and higher vertebrates is seriously entertained in the context of modern physics. Some physicists believe that consciousness will have to be included in future theories of matter and in speculations about the physical universe as a primary factor and connecting principle in the cosmic web. In some sense, if the universe represents an integral and unified web and some of its constituents are obviously conscious, this must be true for the entire system. Of course, it is conceivable that different parts are conscious in different degrees and that they manifest various forms of awareness.

From this point of view, the divisions of the ultimately indivisible cosmic web are incomplete, arbitrary, and changeable. In view of this, there is no reason why it should not be true for the experiential boundaries between the units of consciousness. It is conceivable that, under certain special circumstances, an individual could reclaim his or her identity with the cosmic network and consciously experience any aspect of its existence. Similarly, certain ESP phenomena that are based on transcending the conventional spatial boundaries can be reconciled with this model. For telepathy, psychic diagnosis, remote viewing, or astral projection, the question is no longer whether such phenomena are possible, but how to describe the barrier that prevents them from happening all the time. In other words, the new problem is: What creates the semblance of solidity, separateness, and individuality in an essentially empty and immaterial universe the true nature of which is indivisible unity?

Transpersonal experiences transcending spatial barriers are also quite compatible with the world view based on information theory and systems theory. This approach also involves an image of the world in which boundaries are arbitrary, solid matter is nonexistent, and pattern is all-important. Although consciousness is not explicitly discussed, it is conceivable in this context to talk about mental processes in connection with cells, organs, lower organisms, plants, ecological systems, social groups, or the entire planet.

In regard to experiences that involve transcendence of temporal barriers, the only interpretive alternative mechanistic science has to offer for retrieving records from the past is the material substrate of the central nervous system, or the genetic code. Possibly this approach could be applied, although with greatest difficulty, to certain past experiences, such as embryonic, ancestral, racial, and phylogenetic experiences. It would be entirely absurd in this context to consider seriously those experiences that seem to reenact historical episodes from situations with which the individual is not connected through any biological line as, for example, elements of the Jungian collective unconscious from racially unrelated cultures or past incarnation experiences. The same is true for periods that precede the origin of the central nervous system, life, this planet, or the solar system. So too, any experience of future events is inconceivable, since the future has not yet happened.

Modern physics offers some fascinating possibilities based on its broader understanding of the nature of time. Einstein's theory of relativity, which replaced three-dimensional space and linear time with the concept of a four-dimensional continuum of space-time, offers an interesting theoretical framework for understanding certain transpersonal experiences that involve other historical periods. The special theory of relativity allows for a reversed flow of time under certain circumstances. Modern physicists have grown used to treating time as a two-directional entity that can move forward or backward. Thus, for example, in the interpretation of the space-time diagrams of high-energy physics (Feynman diagrams), the movements of particles forward in time are equivalent to the movements of corresponding antiparticles backward in time.

Speculations expressed in John Wheeler's *Geometrodynamics* (1962) postulated parallels in the physical world to what happens experientially in certain unusual states of mind. Wheeler's concept of hyperspace allows, theoretically, for instant connections among all the elements of the universe without the Einsteinian limitations of the speed of light. Also, the extraordinary changes of space-time, matter, and causality postulated by Einstein's relativity theory in connection with the contraction of stars and black holes have their experiential parallels in nonordinary states of consciousness. Although it is at present impossible to relate the concepts of modern physics to the observations from modern consciousness research in a direct and easily comprehensible way, the parallels are quite striking. If we consider what extraordinary concepts modern physicists need to account for their observations on the simplest of all levels of reality, it becomes obvious how absurd it is that mechanistic psychology tends to deny the existence of phenomena that are in conflict with pedestrian common sense or that cannot be traced back to such tangible events as circumcision or toilet training.

In contrast with the phenomena described above the category of transpersonal experiences, which has a content with no parallels in material reality, is clearly beyond reach of physics. However, even then there seems to be a fundamental difference between their status in the Newtonian-Cartesian paradigm and the modern scientific world view. In the mechanistic model, the universe consists of an immense number of material particles and objects. The existence of nonmaterial entities that cannot be observed or detected by ordinary means and in the usual state of consciousness would be denied in principle. The experiences of such entities would be relegated to the world of altered states of consciousness and hallucinations and interpreted philosophically as distortions of reality derived somehow from the sensory input about "objectively existing elements."

In the modern world view, even the material constituents of the world can be traced to abstract patterns and to the "dynamic vacuum." In the unified web of the universe, any structures, forms, and boundaries are ultimately arbitrary, and form and emptiness are relative terms. A universe with these kinds of qualities does not, in principle, exclude the possibility of existence of entities of any scope and characteristics, including mythological and archetypal forms. In the world of vibrations selective tuning into cohesive and comprehensive systems of information has been successfully achieved in the radio and television.

We have also already mentioned that transpersonal experiences are frequently meaningfully associated with patterns of events in the external world in a way that cannot be explained in terms of linear causality. Carl Gustav Jung (1960b) observed many striking coincidences of this kind in his clinical work; to explain them, he postulated the existence of an acausal connecting principle, which he called *synchronicity*. He defined it as "simultaneous occurrence of a certain psychic state with one or more external events which appear as meaningful parallels to the momentary subjective state." Synchronistically connected events are obviously thematically related to each other, although there is no link of linear causality between them. Many individuals labeled as psychotic experience striking instances of synchronicities; during the casual and biased examinations by Newtonian-Cartesian psychiatrists, all references to meaningful coincidences tend to be routinely interpreted as delusions of reference. However, there is no doubt that there are genuine synchronicities besides the pathological interpretations of obviously unrelated events. Situations of this kind are too striking and too common to be disregarded. It is therefore quite encouraging and refreshing to see that modern physicists were obliged to acknowledge the existence of comparable phenomena in the meticulously controlled context of their laboratory experiments. Bell's theorem and the experiments inspired by it deserve special notice in this regard.

The parallels between the world view of modern physics and the experiential world of mystics and psychedelic subjects are truly far-reaching, and there are good reasons to believe that these similarities will continue to increase. The basic difference between the conclusions based on a scientific analysis of the external world and those emerging from deep self-exploration is that, in modern physics, the world of the paradoxical and transrational can only be expressed in abstract mathematical equations, whereas, in unusual states of consciousness, it becomes a direct and immediate experience.

LSD subjects sophisticated in mathematics and physics have repeatedly reported that in their psychedelic sessions they gained illuminating insights into a variety of concepts and constructs that are not imaginable and visualizable in the ordinary state of consciousness. Reports of this kind involved, for example, Riemann's geometry of an *n*-dimensional space, Minkowski's space-time, non-Euclidean geometry, the collapse of natural laws in a black hole, and Einstein's special and general theories of relativity. The curvature of space and time, an infinite but self-enclosed universe, the interchangeability of mass and energy, various orders of infinities, zeroes of different magnitudes—all these difficult concepts of modern mathematics and physics were subjectively experienced and understood in a qualitatively new way by some of the subjects. It was even possible to find direct experiential correlates for Einstein's famous equations based on Lorentz's transformations. These observations were so striking that they would justify a future project in which prominent physicists would have the opportunity to experience psychedelic states for theoretical inspiration and creative problem solving.

The fact that so many observations from deep experiential work are compatible with the developments in modern physics, clearly demonstrating the limitations of the Newtonian-Cartesian model, is highly encouraging and promising and should help to legitimize the new approaches in the eyes of the scientific community. The potential significance of consciousness research using psychedelics or nondrug methods transcends the narrow boundaries of psychology and psychiatry. Because of the complexity of their respective fields, these two disciplines tried in the past to find solid anchoring in physics, chemistry, biology, and medicine to achieve the reputation of exact sciences. These efforts, although historically and politically necessary, neglected the fact that the intricate phenomena studied by psychiatry and psychology cannot be described and explained in their totality by the constructs of sciences exploring simpler and more basic aspects of reality.

The findings of psychological research certainly should not contradict fundamental laws of physics and chemistry. However, the science that studies consciousness phenomena having quite unique and specific characteristics should be able to make a contribution in its own right to the understanding of the world and to use approaches or descriptive systems that are best suited for its purposes. Since ultimately all scientific disciplines are based on sensory perception and are products of the human mind, it would seem obvious that consciousness research can offer valid contributions to any area of exploration of the physical world. It should be emphasized that the knowledge about many of the phenomena described in this book preceded by centuries, or even millenia, the developments in modern physics with which they are compatible. They were discarded by psychiatrists or received psychopathological labels simply because they could not be integrated into the Newtonian-Cartesian model and contradicted its basic postulates.

It is interesting to look from this point of view at the convergence between modern physics, mysticism, and consciousness research. Although the parallels are far reaching and quite striking, they are mostly of a formal nature. They can explain only those transpersonal experiences in which the individual consciously identifies with various aspects of the material universe in the past, present, or future. The mystical literature describes an entire spectrum of additional realms of reality that elude the conventional approaches of materialistic science. The new model of reality described by quantum-relativistic physics has transcended the concept of solid, indestructible matter and separate objects and shows the universe as a complex web of events and relations. In the last analysis, the traces of material substance of any kind disappear into the primordial emptiness of the dynamic void. However, the physicist has very little to say about the variety of the specific forms the cosmic dance takes on various other levels of reality. The experiential insights from unusual states of consciousness suggest the existence of intangible and unfathomable creative intelligence aware of itself that permeates all realms of reality. This approach indicates that it is pure consciousness without any specific content that represents the supreme principle of existence and the ultimate reality. From it everything in the cosmos can be derived; it creates countless phenomenal worlds with a playful sense for exploration, adventure, drama, art, and humor. This aspect of reality, although beyond the reach of the methods of the exact sciences, might yet be indispensable for a true understanding of the universe and for its comprehensive description.

It is hard to imagine that at present, or at any time in the future, physics could find within the confines of its own discipline access to this ultimate mystery. It would therefore mean repeating the old mistake to borrow from physics its new paradigm and make it a mandatory basis for consciousness research. It is essential that a paradigm emerges from the needs of our own discipline and attempts to build bridges to other disciplines rather than emulating them. The significance of new developments in physics for the study of consciousness lies, therefore, more in the destruction of the conceptual straitjackets of mechanistic Newtonian-Cartesian science than in the offer of a new mandatory paradigm.

At this point, it seems appropriate to consider the consequences of the data from quantum-relativistic physics, modern consciousness research, and other areas of twentieth century science for the understanding of the psyche and human nature. In the past, mechanistic science has accumulated a vast body of evidence indicating that human beings can be understood and treated with a considerable degree of success as separate material entities—essentially biological machines assembled from their constituent parts, such as organs, tissues, and cells. In this approach, consciousness was viewed as a product of physiological processes in the brain.[20]

In light of the new facts from consciousness research presented here, the exclusive image of the human being as nothing but a biological machine is no longer tenable. In serious logical conflict with this traditional model, the new data support quite unambiguously the view that has been held by the mystical traditions of all ages: under certain circumstances, human beings can also function as vast fields of consciousness, transcending the limitations of the physical body, of Newtonian time and space, and of linear causality. This situation is quite similar to the dilemma modern physicists encountered in their study of subatomic processes in the form of the wave-particle paradox regarding light and matter. According to Niels Bohr's principle of complementarity, which addresses this paradox, in order to describe light and subatomic particles in a comprehensive way, it is necessary to see the wave picture and the particle picture as two complementary and equally necessary aspects of the same reality. Each of them is only partially correct, and each has a limited range of applicability. It depends on the experimenter and the arrangement of the experiment which of these two aspects will become manifest.

Bohr's principle of complementarity is related specifically to phenomena in the subatomic world and cannot be automatically transferred to other problem areas. However, it sets an interesting precedent for other disciplines by codifying a paradox instead of

solving it. It seems that the sciences studying human beings—
medicine, psychiatry, psychology, parapsychology, anthropology,
thanatology, and others—have accumulated a body of controversial
data sufficient to justify fully the formulation of a comparable
principle of complementarity.

Although it appears absurd and impossible from the point of
view of classic logic, human nature shows a peculiar ambiguity.
Sometimes it lends itself to mechanistic interpretations equating
human beings with their bodies and organismic functions. At other
times it manifests a very different image, suggesting that humans
can also function as unlimited fields of consciousness, transcending
matter, space, time, and linear causality. In order to describe
humans in a comprehensive and exhaustive way, we must accept
the paradoxical fact that they are both material objects, or biological
machines, and extensive fields of consciousness. In physics, the
results in subatomic experiments depend on the experimenter's
concept and approach; in some sense, wave questions bring wave
answers and particle questions yield particle answers. It is conceivable that in human situations the researcher's concept of human
nature and arrangement of the experiment could facilitate one or
the other modality.

We might follow Niels Bohr's example and be satisfied with a
simple juxtaposition of these two contradictory but complementary
images, that are both partially true. However, certain developments
in mathematics, physics, and brain research have revealed the
existence of new mechanisms which offer a promising perspective.
In the future it may be possible to synthetize and integrate the
two seemingly irreconcilable images of human nature in an elegant
and comprehensive way. The relevant data come from the field of
holography, David Bohm's theory of holomovement, and the brain
research of Karl Pribram. The following discussion of holographic
principles should be seen not as an outline of a new physical model
for consciousness research, but as a conceptual aid opening new
possibilities for imagination and future speculation. It does not
intend to suggest that the world is a hologram, but that holography
reveals and illustrates the existence of certain new principles that
may operate in the creation of the fabric of reality.

The Holonomic Approach: New Principles and New Perspectives

During the last three decades, important developments in the fields of mathematics, laser technology, holography, quantum-relativistic physics, and brain research have led to the discovery of new principles that have far-reaching implications for modern consciousness research and for science in general. These principles have been called *holonomic, holographic,* or *hologrammic,* because they open fascinating alternatives to conventional understanding of the relationship between the whole and its parts. Their unique nature can best be demonstrated in the process of storing, retrieving, and combining information with the technique of optical holography.

It is important to emphasize that it is premature to talk about the "holonomic theory of the universe and of the brain," as has been done in the past. At present, we are dealing with a mosaic of important and fascinating data and theories in different areas that have not yet been integrated into a comprehensive, conceptual framework. However, the holonomic approach, which emphasizes interference of vibratory patterns rather than mechanical interactions and information rather than substance, is a very promising tool in view of the modern scientific understanding of the vibratory nature of the universe. The new insights are related to such fundamental problems as the ordering and organizing principles of reality and of the central nervous system, the distribution of information in the cosmos and in the brain, the nature of memory, the mechanisms of perception, and the relationship between the whole and its parts.

The modern holonomic approach to the universe has its historical predecessors in the ancient Indian and Chinese spiritual philosophies and in the monadology of the great German philosopher and mathematician Gottfried Wilhelm von Leibniz (1951). The transcendence of the conventional distinction between the whole and the parts, which represents the major contribution of the holonomic models, is an essential characteristic of various systems of perennial philosophy.

The poetic image of the necklace of the Vedic god Indra is a beautiful illustration of this principle. In the *Avatamsaka Sutra* it is written: "In the heaven of Indra, there is said to be a network of pearls, so arranged that if you look at one, you see all the others reflected in it. In the same way, each object in the world is not merely itself, but involves every other object and, in fact, *is* everything else." And Sir Charles Eliot (1969), quoting this passage, adds: "In every particle of dust, there are present Buddhas without number."

A corresponding image from the ancient Chinese tradition can be found in the Hwa Yen school of Buddhist thought,[21] a holistic view of the universe that embodies one of the most profound insights the human mind has ever attained. The Empress Wu, who was unable to penetrate the complexity of Hwa Yen literature, asked Fa Tsang, one of the founders of the school, to give her a practical and simple demonstration of the cosmic interrelatedness. Fa Tsang first suspended a glowing candle from the ceiling of a room the entire interior of which was covered with mirrors, to demonstrate the relationship of the One to the many. Then he placed in the center of the room a small crystal and, showing how everything around it was reflected in it, illustrated how in the Ultimate Reality the infinitely small contains the infinitely large and the infinitely large the infinitely small, without obstruction. Having done this, Fa Tsang complained about the fact that this static model was unable to reflect the perpetual, multidimensional motion in the universe and the unimpeded mutual interpentration of Time and Eternity, as well as past, present, and future (Franck 1976).

In the Jain tradition, the holonomic approach to the world is presented in the most sophisticated and elaborate way. According to Jain cosmology, the phenomenal world consists of an infinitely complex system of deluded units of consciousness, or *jivas*, trapped in matter in different stages of the cosmic cycle. This system associates consciousness and the concept of jiva not only with the human and animal forms, but also with plants and inorganic objects, or processes. The monads in Leibniz's philosophy (1951) have many characteristics of the Jainist jivas; all the knowledge about the entire universe can be deduced from the information related to a single monad. It is interesting that Leibniz was also the originator of the mathematical technique that was instrumental in the development of holography.

The technique of holography can be used as a powerful metaphor for the new approach and as a dramatic illustration of its principles. Therefore, it seems appropriate to begin with a description of its basic technological aspects. Holography is three-dimensional, lensless photography capable of recreating unusually realistic images of material objects. The mathematical principles of this revolutionary technique were elaborated by the British scientist Dennis Gabor, in the late 1940s; in 1971, Gabor was awarded a Nobel price for his achievement. The holograms and holography cannot be understood in terms of geometrical optics in which light is treated as consisting of discrete particles or photons. The holographic method depends on the superposition principle and on interference patterns of light; it requires that light be understood as a wave phenomenon. The principles of geometric optics represent an adequate approximation for a variety of optical instruments, including telescopes, microscopes, and cameras. These utilize only the light reflected from the objects and the intensities of light, not the phase. There is no provision for recording the interference patterns of light in mechanical optics. However, this is precisely the essence of holography, which is based on interference of pure monochromatic and coherent light (light of a single wavelength with all the waves in step). In the actual technique of holography (fig. 6), the beam of laser light is split and made to interact with

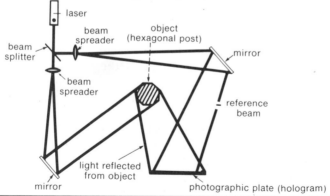

Fig. 6. *The Technique of Holography.* A laser beam is split by a half-silvered mirror. One part of it passes through, is directed to the photographed object, and having bounced off, it reaches the photographic plate (working beam). The other part is reflected directly to the plate (reference beam). When the two laser beams reconverge, the interference pattern is recorded in the film emulsion. Later illumination of this frozen interference pattern recreates a three dimensional image of the object.

the photographed object; the resulting interference pattern is then recorded on a photographic plate. Subsequent illumination of this plate by laser light makes it possible to recreate a three-dimensional image of the original object.

The holographic images have many characteristics that make them the best existing models of psychedelic phenomena and other experiences in unusual states of consciousness. They make it possible to demonstrate many of the formal properties of LSD visions, as well as various important aspects of their content. The reconstructed pictures are three-dimensional and have a vivid realism that approaches or even equals that of everyday perception of the material world. Unlike the pictures in contemporary cinematography, holographic images do not merely simulate three-dimensionality. They show genuine spatial characteristics, including an authentic parallax.[22] Holographic images offer the possibility of selective focusing on different planes and allow for perception of inner structures through transparent media. By a change of focus, it is possible to choose the depth of perception and to blur or clear various parts of the visual field. For example, new advanced techniques of holography using films with microscopic grain make it possible to produce a hologram of a leaf and to study its cellular structure under a microscope by changing the focus.

A property of holography that is particularly relevant for modeling the world of psychedelic and mystical phenomena is its incredible capacity for the storage of information; up to several hundred pictures can be recorded in the emulsion that, in conventional photography, would hold only a single image. Holography makes it possible to take a picture of two people or an entire group of persons by sequential exposures. Using just one film, this can be done either from the same angle or with slight change of angle for each exposure. In the former case, subsequent illumination of the developed film will yield a composite image of the couple or the group involved (for example, the entire staff of an institute or all the members of a football team). Occupying the same space, this image will thus represent no one of them and all of them at the same time. These genuinely composite images represent an exquisite model of a certain type of transpersonal experience, such as the archetypal images of the Cosmic Man, Woman, Mother, Father, Lover, Trickster, Fool, or Martyr, or generalized ethnic and professional visions, as exemplified by the Jew or the Scientist.

A similar mechanism seems to be involved in certain illusive transformations of persons or elements of the environment commonly observed in psychedelic sessions. Thus the sitter can be seen simultaneously in his or her real form and as father, mother, executioner, judge, devil, all men, or all women. The treatment room can oscillate between its everyday appearance and that of a harem, renaissance castle, medieval dungeon, death row, or a cottage on a Pacific island.

When holographic pictures are taken from different angles, all the individual images can be teased out sequentially and separately from the same emulsion by replicating the original conditions during exposure. This illustrates another aspect of visionary experiences, namely, that countless images tend to unfold in a rapid sequence from the same area of the experiential field, appearing and disappearing, as if by magic.

The individual holographic images can be perceived as separate but, at the same time, they are integral parts of a much broader undifferentiated matrix of interference patterns of light from which they originate. This fact can be used as an elegant model for some other types or aspects of transpersonal experience. The holographic pictures can be taken in such a way that the individual images occupy different spaces, as in simultaneous exposure of a couple or of a group of people. In that case the hologram shows them as two separate individuals or a group of persons. However, it is at the same time obvious to anybody familiar with the principles of holography that they can also be seen as an entirely undifferentiated field of light that, by specific patterns of interference, creates the illusion of separate objects. The relativity of separateness versus oneness, is of crucial importance for mystical and psychedelic experiences. It is difficult to imagine a more ideal conceptual aid and teaching device than holography to illustrate this otherwise incomprehensible and paradoxical aspect of nonordinary states of consciousness.

Probably the most interesting properties of holograms are those related to "memory" and information retrieval. An optical hologram has distributed memory; any small part of it large enough to contain the entire diffraction pattern contains the information about the whole gestalt. The decreasing size of the part of the hologram used for recreating the image will be associated with a certain loss of the power of resolution, or increase of information noise, but the overall characteristics of the whole will be retained. The holographic technique also makes it possible to synthetize new images of nonexisting objects by combining various individual inputs. This mechanism could account for the numerous combinations and symbolic variations of the unconscious material observed in psychedelic sessions or dreams.

They could account for the fact that each individual psychological gestalt, such as vision, fantasy, psychosomatic symptom, or thought form, contains an enormous amount of information about the subject's personality. Thus, free association and analytical work on each seemingly miniscule detail of the experience can bring a surprising amount of data about the individual involved.

However, the phenomenon of distributed memory is of the greatest potential relevance for understanding the fact that LSD subjects have, in certain special states of mind, access to information about almost any aspect of the universe. The holographic approach makes it possible to imagine how the information mediated by the brain is accessible in every cerebral cell, or how the genetic information about the entire organism is available in every single cell of the body.

In a model of the universe where the emphasis is on substance and quantity, as in the one created by mechanistic science, a part is different from the whole in an obvious and absolute way. In a model that depicts the universe as a vibratory system and emphasizes information rather than substance, this distinction no longer applies. This radical change that occurs when the emphasis shifts from substance to information can be illustrated by the human body. Although each somatic cell is a trivial part of the entire body, it has through the genetic code access to all the information about the body. It is conceivable that in a similar way all the information about the universe could be retrieved from any of its parts. The demonstration of how the seemingly irreconcilable difference between the part and the whole can be elegantly transcended is probably the single most important contribution of the holographic model to the theory of modern consciousness research.

Such parallels between holography and psychedelic experiences are remarkable, especially if one considers that this technology is in its initial stages; it is difficult to anticipate how far-reaching its developments might be in the near future. Although the problems related to three-dimensional holographic cinematography and television are considerable, their realization is certainly within the possibilities of modern technology. Another fascinating application of holography, which is at an early stage, is character, pattern, and symbol recognition and the capacity to translate from one symbolic language into another.

The hologram is a unique conceptual tool that can be extremely useful in understanding the notion of wholeness. However, it makes a static record of a movement of complex electromagnetic fields; this obscures certain important properties and possibilities of the holographic domain. In actuality, the movement of light waves (and other types of vibratory phenomena) is present everywhere and, in principle, enfolds the entire universe of space and time. These fields obey the laws of quantum mechanics implying the properties of discontinuity and nonlocality. Thus the totality of enfolding and unfolding goes far beyond what reveals itself to scientific observation.

Recent revolutionary discoveries of the Argentinian-Italian researcher Hugo Zucarelli extended the holographic model into the world of acoustic phenomena. Early in his life, Zucarelli became fascinated by the problems associated with the capacity of various organisms to localize sounds in auditory perception. By careful study and analysis of the mechanisms by which different species in the evolutionary pedigree arrive at precise identification of the sources of sound, he came to the conclusion that the existing models of hearing cannot account for important characteristics of human acoustic perception. The fact that humans can locate the source of sounds without movements of the head or positioning of the ear lobes clearly suggests that comparison of the intensity of acoustic input in the right and left ear is not the mechanism responsible for human abilities in this area. In additon, even individuals whose hearing has been destroyed on one side can still localize sounds. To explain all the characteristics of spatial hearing adequately, it is necessary to postulate that human acoustic perception uses holographic principles. This requires the assumption that the human ear is a transmitter, as well as a receiver.

By replicating this mechanism while recording sounds, Zucarelli developed the technology of holophonic sound. Holophonic recordings have an uncanny capacity to reproduce acoustic reality with all its spatial characteristics to such an extent that, without constant visual control, it is virtually impossible to distinguish the perception of recorded phenomena from actual events in the three-dimensional world. In addition, listening to holophonic recordings of events that stimulated other senses tends to induce synesthesia—the corresponding perceptions in other sensory areas.

Thus, the sound of scissors opening and closing near one's scalp will convey a realistic sense of one's hair being cut; the hum of an electric hairdryer can produce sensations of the stream of hot air blowing through the hair; listening to a person striking a match might be accompanied by a distinct smell of burning sulphur; and the voice of a woman whispering into one's ear will make one feel her breath.

Holophonic sound has clearly profound theoretical and practical implications for many fields and areas of human life—from revolutionizing the understanding of physiology and pathology of hearing to undreamed of applications in psychiatry, psychology and psychotherapy, mass media, entertainment, art, religion, philosophy, and many other realms.

These extraordinary effects of holophonic technology throw an entirely new light on the importance attributed to sound in various spiritual philosophies and mystical schools. The crucial role of the cosmic sound OM in the process of creation of the universe, discussed in ancient Indian systems of thought; the deep connection between various acoustic vibrations and the individual chakras in Tantra and Kundalini Yoga; the mystical and magical properties ascribed to the sounds of the Hebrew and Egyptian alphabet; and the use of sound as the technology of the sacred in shamanism and aboriginal healing ceremonies, as well as a powerful means of mediating experiences of other realities—these are just a few examples of the paramount role of sound in the history of religion. The discovery of holophonic sound is thus an important contribution to the emerging paradigm bridging modern science and ancient wisdom.

However exciting the possibilities of holography and holophony might be, one should not yet get carried away and apply them indiscriminately and too literally to consciousness research. After all, holograms and holophonic recordings can only replicate important aspects of events in the material world, whereas the spectrum of transpersonal experiences includes many phenomena that are undoubtedly active creations of the psyche, rather than just replicas of existing objects and events or their derivatives and recombinations. In addition, experiences in nonordinary states of consciousness include certain characteristics that cannot at present be directly modeled by holonomic technology, although some can occur in the form of synesthesia induced by holophonic sound. Among these are the experience of temperature changes, physical pain, tactile sensations, sexual feelings, olfactory and gustatory perceptions, and various emotional qualities.

In optical holography, the holographic images, the field of light that creates them, and the film that is their generating matrix all exist on the same level of reality, and they can all be simultaneously perceived or detected in the ordinary state of consciousness. Similarly, all the elements of a holophonic system are accessible to our senses and instruments in ordinary consciousness.

David Bohm,[23] a prominent theoretical physicist, former co-worker with Einstein, and author of basic texts on both relativity theory and quantum mechanics, has formulated a revolutionary model of the universe that extends the holonomic principles into realms that at present are not subject to direct observation and scientific investigation. In an effort to resolve the disturbing paradoxes of modern physics, Bohm resurrected the theory of hidden variables, long considered disproved by such emminent physicists as Heisenberg and von Neumann. The resulting vision of reality changes drastically the most fundamental philosophical assumptions of Western science. Bohm described the nature of reality in general, and consciousness in particular, as an unbroken and coherent whole that is involved in an unending process of change—the *holomovement.* The world is in a constant flux, and stable structures of any kind are nothing but abstractions; any describable object, entity, or event is considered to be a derivative of an undefinable and unknown totality.

The phenomena that we perceive directly through our senses and with the help of scientific instruments—the entire world studied by mechanistic science—represent only a fragment of reality, the *unfolded* or *explicate order.* It is a special form contained within, and emerging from, a more general totality of existence, the *enfolded* or *implicate order,* that is its source and generating matrix. In the implicate order, space and time are no longer the dominant factors determing relationships of dependence or independence of different elements. Various aspects of existence are meaningfully related to the whole, serving specific functions for a final purpose rather than being independent building blocks. The image of the universe thus resembles that of a living organism whose organs, tissues, and cells make sense only in relation to the whole.

Bohm's theory, although primarily conceived to deal with urgent problems of physics, has revolutionary implications for the understanding of not only physical reality but also of the phenomena of life, consciousness, and the function of science and knowledge in general. In Bohm's theory, life cannot be understood in terms of or derived from, inanimate matter. As a matter of fact, it is impossible to draw a sharp and absolute distinction between the two. Both life and inanimate matter have a common ground in the holomovement, which is their primary and universal source. Inanimate matter is to be considered a relatively autonomous sub-totality in which life is "implicit" but is not significantly manifested.

In contrast to both the idealists and materialists, Bohm suggests that matter and consciousness cannot be explained from, or reduced to, each other. They are both abstractions from the implicate order, which is their common ground, and thus represent an inseparable unity. In a very similar way, knowledge about reality in general and science in particular are abstractions from the one total flux. Rather than being reflections on reality and its independent descriptions, they are an integral part of the holomovement. Thought has two important aspects: when it functions on its own, it is mechanical and derives its—generally unsuitable and irrelevant—order from memory. However, it can also respond directly to intelligence, which is a free, independent, and unconditioned element, originating in the holomovement. Perception and knowledge, including scientific theories, are creative activities comparable to the artistic process, not objective reflections of independently existing reality. True reality is immeasurable, and true insight sees the immeasurable as the essence of existence.

The conceptual fragmentation of the world that is characteristic of mechanistic science tends to create a state of serious disharmony and has dangerous consequences. It tends not only to divide what is indivisible, but to unite what is not unitable and to create artificial structures—national, economic, political, and religious groups. To be confused about what is different and what is not means to be confused about everything. The inevitable result is emotional, economic, political and ecological crisis. Bohm pointed to the fact that the conceptual fragmentation is supported by the structure of our language which emphasizes divisions in terms of subject, verb, and object. He laid the foundations of a new language, the *rheomode*. It does not allow discussion of the observed facts in terms of separately existing things of an essentially static nature, but describes the world in a state of flux as a dynamic process.

According to Bohm, the present situation in Western science is intimately associated with the use of optical lenses. The invention of lenses made it possible to extend scientific explorations beyond the classical order into the domains of objects that are too small, too big, too far away, or moving too rapidly to be perceived by unaided vision. The use of lenses strengthened awareness of the various parts of the object and their interrelationships. This furthered the tendency to think in terms of analysis and synthesis.

One of the most important contributions of holography is its ability to help give a certain immediate perceptual insight into the undivided wholeness that is an essential feature of the modern world view emerging from quantum mechanics and the relativity theory. Modern natural laws should refer primarily to this undivided wholeness in which everything implicates everything else as suggested by holograms, rather than to analysis into the separate parts indicated by the use of lenses.

David Bohm probably went further than any other physicist by explicitly including consciousness in his theoretical speculations. Fritjof Capra considers Bohm's theory of holomovement (1980) and Chew's "bootstrap" philosophy of nature (1968) to be the most imaginative and philosophically profound approaches to reality. He points out the deep similarities between them and considers the possibility that they will merge in the future into a comprehensive theory of physical phenomena. They share the view of the universe as a dynamic web of relations, both emphasize the role of order, both employ matrices to portray change and transformation, and both use topology to describe categories of order.

It is hard to imagine how Bohm's ideas about consciousness, thinking, and perception could ever be reconciled with the traditional mechanistic approaches to neurophysiology and psychology. However, some recent revolutionary developments in brain research have changed the situation considerably. Neurosurgeon Karl Pribram (1971; 1976; 1977; 1981) developed an original and imaginative model of the brain which postulates that certain important aspects of cerebral functioning are based on holographic principles. Although Bohm's model of the universe and Pribram's model of the brain have not been integrated into a comprehensive paradigm, it is very exciting and encouraging that the two share the holographic emphasis.

Pribram, who has established his scientific reputation as a prominent brain researcher during several decades of experimental work in neurosurgery and electrophysiology, traces the beginnings of his holographic model to the investigations of his teacher, Karl Lashley. In his numerous experiments with rats, focusing on the problem of the localization of psychological and physiological func-

tions in various areas of the brain, Lashley discovered that memories
were stored in every part of the cortex and that their intensity
depended upon the total number of intact cortical cells. In his
book, *Brain Mechanisms and Intelligence* (1929), Lashley expressed
the opinion that the firing of billions of cerebral neurons results
in stable interference patterns that are diffused over the entire
cortex and represent the basis for all the information of the perceptual systems and memory. In his efforts to solve the conceptual
problems posed by experiments of this kind, Pribram became in-
trigued by certain fascinating properties of optical holograms. He
realized that a model based on holographic principles would account
for many of the seemingly mysterious properties of the brain—
vast storage capacity, distribution of memory storage, the imaging
capability of the sensory system, projection of the images away
from the storage area, certain important aspects of associative recall,
and so on.

Exploring this avenue of research, Pribram came to the conclusion that the holographic process must be seriously considered
as an explanatory device of extraordinary power for neurophysiology and psychology. In *Languages of the Brain* (Pribram 1971)
and in a series of articles, he formulated the basic principles of
what became known as the holographic model of the brain. According to his research, the holograms that showed the greatest
explanatory power and held the most promise were those that could
be expressed in the form of the so-called Fourier transforms. The
Fourier theorem holds that any pattern, no matter how complex,
can be decomposed into a set of completely regular sine waves.
Applying the identical transform then inverts the wave patterns
back into the image.

The holographic hypothesis does not contradict specific localization of function within various systems in the brain. Localization
of function depends in large part on connections between the brain
and peripheral structures; these determine *what* is encoded. The
holographic hypothesis addresses the problem of inner connectivity
within each system, which determines *how* events become encoded.
Another interesting approach to the problem of localization is based
on Dennis Gabor's suggestion that the Fourier domain may become
segmented into informational units, called *logons*, by the operation
of a "window" that limits band width. The window can be so
adjusted that processing sometimes occurs primarily in the holographic domain, at other times in the space/time domain. This

seems to throw interesting light on the puzzle that brain functions appear to be both localized and distributed.

Pribram's hypothesis represents a powerful alternative to the two models of brain function that were until recently seen as the only possibilities—the field theory and the feature correspondence theory. Both of these theories are *isomorphic*—they postulate that the representation in the central nervous system reflects the basic characteristics of the stimulus. According to the field theory, sensory stimulation generates fields of direct current that have the same shape as the stimulus. The feature correspondence theory suggests that a particular cell or assembly of cells responds uniquely to a certain feature of the sensory stimulus. In the holographic hypothesis, there is no linear correspondence or identity between the brain representation and the phenomenal experience, as there is no linear correspondence between the structure of the hologram and the image produced when the film is properly illuminated.

The holographic hypothesis does not aim to account for all brain physiology nor for all problems of psychology. However, even at this stage it is clear that it offers exciting new possibilities for future research. Convincing experimental data and precise mathematical descriptions have so far been given for the visual, auditory, and somatosensory systems.

Pribram (1977; 1981) was able to connect his holographic hypothesis with important aspects of brain anatomy and physiology. In addition to the standard transfer of neuronal impulses between the central nervous system and peripheral receptors or effectors, he also emphasizes slow-wave potentials occurring between synapses even in the absence of nerve impulses. These originate in cells with very rich dendritic ramifications and short axons or no axons at all. While the neuronal impulses operate in a binary "on-off" fashion, the slow potentials are graded and undulate continuously at the junctions between the neurons. Pribram believes that this "parallel processing" is of critical importance for the holographic functioning of the brain. The interaction of these two systems results in wave phenomena that follow holographic principles.[24]

Slow-wave potentials are very subtle and sensitive to a variety of influences. This provides an interesting basis for speculations about the interactions between consciousness and the brain mechanisms, as well as for theorizing about the psychological effects of psychoactive drugs and various nondrug mind-altering techniques. Particularly interesting from this point of view is the technique of holonomic integration, combining hyperventilation with music and focused body work; it is described in chapter 7. Approaches associated with slow-frequency waves, such as meditation and biofeedback, are also of special interest in this context.

As has already been mentioned, the theories of Bohm and Pribram are far from being unified and integrated into a comprehensive paradigm. Even if such a synthesis were accomplished in the future, the resulting conceptual framework could not provide satisfactory explanations for all the phenomena observed in modern consciousness research. Although both Pribram and Bohm address problems related to psychology, philosophy, and religion, they derive their scientific data primarily from the physical and biological domains, whereas many psychedelic and mystical states deal directly with nonmaterial realms of reality. However, there is no doubt that the holonomic perspective allows focusing of serious scientific interest on many genuine transpersonal phenomena for which the crude and heavy-handed mechanistic paradigms had no other alternative than conceited ridicule. As long as one attempts to relate the new data from consciousness research to the findings of other scientific disciplines, rather than ignore mainstream science altogether as some determined proponents of perennial philosophy do, the new conceptual frameworks offer exciting opportunities.

My own preference in the field of consciousness research is to create models that would draw primarily on observations from disciplines that study human experience—psychology, anthropology, parapsychology, thanatology, perennial philosophy, and others. The formulation of these models can draw inspiration from, and be influenced by, compatible, well-founded developments in other disciplines.

Since perfect integration has not been achieved even among different fields of physics that describe phenomena on the same level of reality, it would be absurd to expect a perfect conceptual synthesis between systems describing different hierarchical levels. However, it is conceivable that certain universal principles can be discovered that will be applicable in different domains, although they will take a different specific form in each domain. Prigogine's "order through fluctuation" (1980) and René Thom's catastrophe theory (1975) are important examples. With these reservations in mind, we can now discuss the relationship between various observations from consciousness research and the holonomic approach to the universe and the brain.

Bohm's concept of the unfolded and enfolded orders and the idea that certain important aspects of reality are not accessible to experience and study under ordinary circumstances are of direct relevance for the understanding of unusual states of consciousness. Individuals who have experienced various nonordinary states of consciousness, including well-educated and sophisticated scientists from various disciplines, frequently report that they entered hidden domains of reality that seemed to be authentic and in some sense implicit in, and supraordinated to, everyday reality. The content of this "implicate reality" would have to include, among others, elements of the collective unconscious, historical events, archetypal and mythological phenomena, and past incarnation dynamics.[25]

In the past, many traditional psychiatrists and psychologists have interpreted the manifestations of the Jungian archetypes as imaginary products of the human mind, abstracted or constructed from actual sensory perceptions of other people, animals, objects, and events in the material world. The conflict between Jungian psychology and mainstream mechanistic science regarding the archetypes is a modern replica of the disputes about the Platonic ideas that went on for centuries between the nominalists and the realists. The nominalists maintained that the Platonic ideas were nothing but "names" abstracted from phenomena in the material world, whereas for the realists, these had an independent existence of their own on another level of reality. In an extended version of the holonomic theory, the archetypes could be understood as phenomena *sui generis,* cosmic principles that are woven into the fabric of the implicate order.

The fact that certain kinds of archetypal visions can be so successfully modeled by holography suggests a possible deep link between archetypal dynamics and the operation of holonomic principles. This is particularly true for archetypal formations that represent generalized biological, psychological, and social roles, such as the images of the Great or Terrible Mother and Father, Child, Martyr, Cosmic Man, Trickster, Tyrant, Animus, Anima, or the Shadow. The experiential world of such culturally colored archetypes as various concrete deities and demons, demigods, heroes, and the mythological themes could be interpreted as phenomena of the implicate order that have a more specific connection with certain aspects of the explicate order. In any case, archetypal phenomena must be seen as ordering principles supraordinated to and preceding material reality, rather than its derivatives.

The transpersonal phenomena that can most easily be related to the holonomic theory are those that involve elements of "objective reality"—identification with other people, animals, plants, and inorganic reality in the past, present, and future. Here, some of the essential characteristics of the holonomic understanding of the world—relativity of boundaries, transcendence of the Aristotelian dichotomy between the part and the whole, and all the information enfolded in and distributed throughout the entire system—offer an explanatory model of extraordinary power. The fact that both space and time are enfolded in the holographic domain would then be compatible with the observation that transpersonal experiences of this kind are not bound by the usual spatial or temporal limitations.

Everyday experiences of the material world, fully compatible with the Newtonian-Cartesian model of the universe, would be seen in this context as reflecting selective and stabilized focus on the explicate or unfolded aspect of reality. Conversely, transcendental states of a highly undifferentiated, universal, and all-encompassing nature could be interpreted as direct experience of the implicate order or the holomovement in its totality. The concept of the implicate order would have to be much broader than Bohm's; it would have to be the creative matrix for all the levels described by perennial philosophy, not just those that seem immediately necessary for the description of phenomena on the physical or biological levels.

Other types of transpersonal experiences—such as sacralization of everyday life, manifestation of an archetype in everyday reality, seeing one's partner as a manifestation of the Animus, Anima, or of the divine—could then be seen as transitional forms, combining elements of the explicate and implicate order. All the above examples have one common denominator that is an absolutely necessary prerequisite for this kind of thinking: one must assume that consciousness has—at least in principle, if not always in actuality—access to all forms of the explicate and implicate order.

The holonomic approach also offers some exciting new possibilities in regard to certain extreme paranormal phenomena consistently reported in spiritual literature, but discounted as absurd by mechanistic science. Psychokinesis, materialization and dematerialization, levitation, and other supernormal feats, or *siddhis*, demonstrating the power of mind over matter might well deserve scientific reevaluation in this connection. If the basic assumptions of the holonomic theory about the explicate and implicate order reflect reality with a sufficient degree of accuracy, it is conceivable that certain unusual states of consciousness could mediate direct experience of, and intervention in, the implicate order. It would thus be possible to modify phenomena in the phenomenal world by influencing their generative matrix. This kind of intervention would be entirely inconceivable for mechanistic science because it would bypass the conventionally recognized chains of linear causality and not involve energy transfer within the explicate order of reality as we know it.

It seems obvious that we are approaching the time of a major paradigm shift. At present, there is a rich mosaic of new theoretical concepts that share certain general characteristics, as well as the fact of radical departure from the mechanistic models. The synthesis and integration of these exciting new developments in science will be a difficult and complex task and it is questionable whether it is at all possible. In any case, it seems that such a comprehensive paradigm of the future, capable of accommodating and synthesizing all the diversity of data from quantum-relativistic physics, systems theory, consciousness research, and neurophysiology, as well as from the ancient and Oriental spiritual philosophies, shamanism, aboriginal rituals, and healing practices would have to involve complementary dichotomies on three different levels: those of the cosmos, of the individual, and of the human brain.

The universe would have its phenomenal, explicate, or unfolded aspects and its transcendental, implicate, or enfolded aspects. The corresponding complementarity on the level of the human being would be the image of the Newtonian-Cartesian biological machine and that of an unlimited field of consciousness. A similar dichotomy would then be reflected in the dual aspects of the human brain, combining the digital computerlike functioning and parallel processing governed by holonomic principles. Although it is not possible at present to consolidate these images and create an internally consistent model, even in its preliminary forms the holonomic approach offers undreamed of possibilities in the controversial field of modern consciousness research.

CHAPTER TWO

Dimensions of the Human Psyche: Cartography of Inner Space

One of the most significant contributions of modern consciousness research to the emerging scientific world view has been an entirely new image of the human psyche. While the traditional model of psychiatry and psychoanalysis is strictly personalistic and biographical, modern consciousness research has added new levels, realms, and dimensions and shows the human psyche as being essentially commensurate with the whole universe and all of existence. A comprehensive presentation of this new model, beyond the scope of this book, can be found in a separate publication (Grof 1975). Here, I will briefly outline its essential features with special emphasis on its relationship to the emerging paradigm in science.

Although there are no clear boundaries and demarcations in the realm of consciousness, it seems useful for didactic purposes to distinguish four distinct levels or realms of the human psyche and the corresponding experiences: (1) the sensory barrier, (2) the individual unconscious, (3) the level of birth and death, and (4) the transpersonal domain. The experiences of all these categories are quite readily available for most people. They can be observed in sessions with psychedelic drugs and in various modern approaches of experiential psychotherapy using breathing, music, dance, and body work. Laboratory mind-altering techniques, such as biofeedback, sleep deprivation, sensory isolation or sensory overload, and various kinaesthetic devices can also induce many of these phenomena. A wide spectrum of ancient and Oriental spiritual practices are specifically designed to facilitate their occurrence. Many experiences of this kind can also occur during spontaneous episodes of nonordinary states of consciousness. The entire experiential spectrum related to the four realms has also been described by historians and anthropologists with respect to various shamanic procedures, aboriginal rites of passage and healing ceremonies, death-rebirth mysteries, and trance dancing in ecstatic religions.

The Sensory Barrier and the Individual Unconscious

Techniques that make it possible to enter experientially the realms of the unconscious mind tend initially to activate the sensory organs. Thus, for many individuals experimenting with such techniques, deep self-exploration starts with a variety of sensory experiences. These are of a more or less abstract nature and have no personal symbolic meaning; they can be aesthetically pleasing, but do not lead to increased self-understanding.

Changes of this kind can occur in any sensory area, although optical phenomena are by far the most frequent. The visual field behind closed eyelids becomes rich in color and animated, and the individual can see a variety of geometrical or architectural forms—dynamic kaleidoscopic patterns, mandalalike configurations, arabesques, naves of Gothic cathedrals, ceilings of Moslem mosques, and intricate designs resembling beautiful medieval illuminations or Oriental rugs. Visions of this kind can occur during any type of deep self-exploration; however, they are particularly dramatic after ingestion of psychedelics. The changes in the acoustic area

Fig. 7. Drawings of a Czech painter from one of the early LSD experiments conducted by Dr. J. Roubíček in Prague, representing dramatic unspecific distortions of the body image.

can take the form of ringing in the ears, chirping of crickets, buzzing, chimes, or continuous sounds of high frequency. This can be accompanied by a variety of unusual tactile sensations in various parts of the body. Also, smells and tastes can appear at this stage, but they are far less common.

Sensory experiences of this kind have little significance for the process of self-exploration and self-understanding. They seem to represent a barrier that one must pass through before the journey into one's unconscious psyche can begin. Some aspects of such sensory experiences can be explained from certain anatomical and physiological characteristics of the sense organs. Thus, for example, the geometrical visions seem to reflect the inner architecture of the retina and other parts of the optical system.

Fig. 8. Drawings of a Czech painter from one of the early LSD experiments conducted by Dr. J. Roubíček in Prague. *Picture a.* represents a combined vision of a hospital nurse with a vial of a revulsive medicine and an emetic basin and a waiter with a bottle of red wine. *Picture b.* shows an illusive transformation of a traffic policeman as the subject saw him when he was driven home after the experiment.

The next most easily available experiential realm is the domain of the individual unconscious. Although phenomena belonging to this category are of considerable theoretical and practical relevance, it is not necessary to spend much time on their description, because most of the traditional psychotherapeutic approaches are limited to this level of the psyche. There is abundant, though highly contradictory, literature on the nuances of psychodynamics in the biographical realm. Experiences belonging to this category are related to significant biographical events and circumstances of the life of the individual, from birth to the present moment, which have a strong emotional charge attached to them. On this level of self-exploration, anything from the life of the person involved that is an unresolved conflict, a repressed traumatic memory that has not been integrated, or an incomplete psychological gestalt of some kind, can emerge from the unconscious and become the content of the experience.

There is only one condition for its occurrence: the issue must be of sufficient emotional relevance. Herein lies a tremendous advantage of experiential psychotherapy in comparison with predominantly verbal approaches. Techniques that directly activate the unconscious seem to reinforce selectively the most relevant emotional material and facilitate its emergence into consciousness. They thus provide a kind of inner radar that scans the system and detects contents with the strongest emotional charge. This not only saves the therapist the effort of sorting the relevant from the irrelevant, but protects him or her from having to make such decisions, which would of necessity be biased by the therapist's own conceptual framework and many other factors.[1]

By and large, biographical material that emerges in experiential work is in agreement with the Freudian theory or one of its derivatives. However, there are several major differences. In deep experiential psychotherapy, biographical material is not remembered or reconstructed; it can be actually fully relived. This involves not only emotions but also physical sensations, pictorial elements of the material involved, as well as data from other senses. This happens typically in complete age regression to the stage of development when the event happened.

Another important distinction is that the relevant memories and other biographical elements do not emerge separately, but form distinct dynamic constellations, for which I have coined the term *COEX systems,* or *systems of condensed experience.* A COEX system is a dynamic constellation of memories (and associated fantasy material) from different periods of the individual's life, with the common denominator of a strong emotional charge of the same quality, intense physical sensation of the same kind, or the fact that they share some other important elements. I first became aware of COEX systems as principles governing the dynamics of the individual unconscious and realized that knowledge of them was essential for understanding the inner process on this level. However, later it became obvious that the systems of condensed experience represent a general principle operating on all the levels of the psyche, rather than being limited to the biographical domain.

Most biographical COEX systems are dynamically connected with specific facets of the birth process. Perinatal themes and their elements, then, have specific associations with related experiential material in the transpersonal domain. It is not uncommon for a dynamic constellation to comprise material from several biographical periods, from biological birth, and from certain areas of the transpersonal realm, such as memories of a past incarnation, animal identification, and mythological sequences. Here, the experiential similarity of these themes from different levels of the psyche is more important than the conventional criteria of the Newtonian-Cartesian world view, such as the fact that years or centuries separate the events involved, that ordinarily an abysmal difference appears to exist between the human and animal experience, or that elements of "objective reality" are combined with archetypal and mythological ones.

In traditional psychology, psychiatry, and psychotherapy, there is an exclusive focus on psychological traumas. Physical traumas are not thought to have a direct influence on the psychological development of the individual or to participate in the genesis of psychopathology. This contrasts sharply with observations from deep experiential work, where memories of physical traumas appear to be of paramount importance. In psychedelic work and other powerful experiential approaches, reliving life-threatening diseases, injuries, operations, or situations of near-drowning are extremely common and their significance clearly far exceeds that of the usual psychotraumas. The residual emotions and physical sensations from situations that threatened survival or the integrity of the organism appear to have a significant role in the development of various forms of psychopathology, as yet unrecognized by academic science.

Thus, when a child has a serious life-threatening disease, such as diptheria, and almost chokes to death, the experience of vital threat and extreme physical discomfort is not considered to be a trauma of lasting significance. Conventional psychology would focus on the fact that the child, having been separated from the mother at the time of hospitalization, experienced emotional deprivation. Experiential work makes it obvious that traumas involving vital threat leave permanent traces in the system and contribute significantly to the development of emotional and psychosomatic disorders, such as depressions, anxiety states and phobias, sadomasochistic tendencies, sexual problems, migraine headaches, or asthma.

The experiences of serious physical traumatization represent a natural transition between the biographical level and the following realm, which has as its main constituents the twin phenomena of birth and death. They involve events from the individual's life and are thus biographical in nature. Yet the fact that they brought the person close to death and involved extreme discomfort and pain connects them to the birth trauma. For obvious reasons, memories of diseases and traumas that involved interference with breathing, such as pneumonia, diptheria, whooping cough, or nearly drowning, are particularly significant.

Encounter with Birth and Death:
The Dynamics of Perinatal Matrices

As the process of experiential self-exploration deepens, the element of emotional and physical pain can reach such extraordinary intensity that it is usually interpreted as dying. It can become so extreme that the individual involved feels that he or she has transcended the boundaries of individual suffering and is experiencing the pain of entire groups of individuals, all of humanity, or even all of life. Experiential identification with wounded or dying soldiers, prisoners in concentration camps and dungeons, persecuted Jews or early Christians, mothers and children in childbirth, or animals being attacked and slaughtered by an enemy are typical.

Experiences on this level are usually accompanied by dramatic physiological manifestations, such as various degrees of suffocation, accelerated pulse rate and palpitations, nausea and vomiting, changes in the color of the complexion, oscillations of body temperature, spontaneous skin eruptions or bruises, twitches, tremors, and contortions or other striking motor phenomena.

Whereas on the biographical level only those individuals who have actually had a serious brush with death must deal during their self-exploration with vital threats, on this level of the unconscious the issue of death is universal and entirely dominates the picture. Those persons whose life history has not involved a serious threat to survival or bodily integrity can enter this experiential realm directly. For others, the reliving of serious traumas, operations or injuries tends to deepen and change into the experience of dying described above.

Experiential confrontation with death at this depth of self-exploration tends to be intimately interwoven with a variety of phenomena related to the birth process. Not only do individuals involved in experiences of this kind have the feeling of struggling to be born and/or of delivering, but many of the accompanying physiological changes that take place make sense as typical concomitants of birth. Subjects often experience themselves as fetuses and can relive various aspects of their biological birth with very specific and verifiable details. The element of death can be represented by simultaneous or alternating identification with aging, ailing, and dying individuals. Although the entire spectrum of experiences occurring on this level cannot be reduced to a reliving of biological birth, the birth trauma seems to represent an important core of the process. For this reason, I refer to this domain of the unconscious as *perinatal.*[2]

The connection between biological birth and the experiences of dying and being born as described above is quite deep and specific. This makes it possible to use the stages of biological delivery in constructing a conceptual model that helps to understand the dynamics of the unconscious on the perinatal level. The experiences of the death-rebirth process occur in typical thematic clusters; their basic characteristics can be logically derived from certain anatomical, physiological, and biochemical aspects of the corresponding stages of childbirth with which they are associated. As will be discussed later, thinking in terms of the birth model provides unique

new insights into the dynamic architecture of various forms of
psychopathology and offers revolutionary therapeutic possibilities.

In spite of its close connections with birth, the perinatal process
transcends biology and has important philosophical and spiritual
dimensions. It should not, therefore, be interpreted in a concretistic
and reductionistic fashion. To an individual who is totally immersed
in the dynamics of this level of the unconscious—experientially or
as a researcher—birth might appear as an all-explanatory principle.
In my own understanding, thinking in terms of the birth process
is a useful model with an applicability that is limited to phenomena
of a specific level of the unconscious. It has to be transcended and
replaced by a different approach when the process of self-exploration moves to transpersonal realms.

There are certain important characteristics of the death-rebirth
process that clearly indicate that perinatal experiences cannot be
reduced to a reliving of biological birth. Experiential sequences of
a perinatal nature have distinct emotional and psychosomatic aspects. However, they also produce a profound personality transformation. A deep experiential encounter with birth and death is
regularly associated with an existential crisis of extraordinary proportions, during which the individual seriously questions the meaning of existence, as well as his or her basic values and life strategies.
This crisis can be resolved only by connecting with deep, intrinsic
spiritual dimensions of the psyche and elements of the collective
unconscious. The resulting personality transformation seems to be
comparable to the changes that have been described as having
come about from participation in ancient temple mysteries, initiation
rites, or aboriginal rites of passage. The perinatal level of the
unconscious thus represents an important intersection between the
individual and the collective unconscious, or between traditional
psychology and mysticism or transpersonal psychology.

The experiences of death and rebirth reflecting the perinatal
level of the unconscious are very rich and complex. They appear
in four typical experiential patterns or constellations. There is a
deep correspondence between these thematic clusters and the clinical stages of the biological birth process. It proved very useful for
the theory and practice of deep experiential work to postulate the
existence of hypothetical dynamic matrices governing the processes
related to the perinatal level of the unconscious and to refer to
them as *Basic Perinatal Matrices (BPM)*.

Fig. 9. The experience of deep existential despair in a psychedelic session dominated by BPM II. The painting shows human life as "a trip from nowhere to nowhere in a rainy day."

In addition to having specific emotional and psychosomatic content of their own, these matrices also function as organizing principles for material from other levels of the unconscious. From the biographical level, elements of important COEX systems dealing with physical abuse and violation, threat, separation, pain, or suffocation are closely related to specific aspects of BPM. The perinatal unfolding is also frequently associated with various transpersonal elements, such as archetypal visions of the Great Mother or the Terrible Mother Goddess, Hell, Purgatory, Paradise or Heaven, mythological or historical scenes, identification with animals, and past incarnation experiences. As in the various layers of COEX systems, the connecting link is the same quality of emotions or physical sensations, and/or similarity of circumstances. The perinatal matrices also have specific relations to different aspects of the activities in the Freudian erogenous areas—the oral, anal, urethral, and phallic zones.

In the following text, I will briefly review the biological basis of the individual BPMs, their experiential characteristics, their function as organizing principles for other types of experience, and their connection with activities in various erogenous zones. A synopsis is presented in Table 1.

The significance of the perinatal level of the unconscious for a new understanding of psychopathology and specific relations between the individual BPMs and various emotional disorders is discussed in a later section.

First Perinatal Matrix (BPM I)

The biological basis of this matrix is the experience of the original symbiotic unity of the fetus with the maternal organism at the time of intrauterine existence. During episodes of undisturbed life in the womb, the conditions of the child can be close to ideal. However, a variety of factors of physical, chemical, biological, and psychological nature can seriously interfere with this state. Also, during late stages of pregnancy, the situation may become less favorable because of the size of the child, of increasing mechanical constraint, or of the relative insufficiency of the placenta.

Pleasant and unpleasant intrauterine memories can be experienced in their concrete biological form. In addition, subjects tuned in to the first matrix can experience an entire spectrum of images and themes associated with it, according to the laws of deep experiential logic. *The undisturbed intrauterine state* can be accompanied by other experiences that share with it a lack of boundaries and obstructions, such as consciousness of the ocean, an aquatic life form (whale, fish, jellyfish, anemone, or kelp), or interstellar space. Also images of nature at its best (Mother Nature), which is beautiful, safe and unconditionally nourishing, represent characteristic and quite logical concomitants of the blissful fetal state. Archetypal images from the collective unconscious that can be selectively reached in this state involve the heavens or paradises of different cultures of the world. The experience of the first matrix also involves elements of cosmic unity or mystical union.

The disturbances of intrauterine life are associated with images and experiences of underwater dangers, polluted streams, contaminated or inhospitable nature, and insidious demons. The mystical

Table 1 BASIC PERINATAL MATRICES

BPM I	BPM II	BPM III	BPM IV
	RELATED PSYCHOPATHOLOGICAL SYNDROMES		
Schizophrenic psychoses (paranoid symptomatology, feelings of mystical union, encounter with metaphysical evil forces); hypochondriasis (based on strange and bizarre physical sensations); hysterical hallucinosis and confusing daydreams with reality	Schizophrenic psychoses (elements of hellish tortures, experience of meaningless "cardboard" world); severe inhibited "endogenous" depressions; irrational inferiority and guilt feelings; hypochondriasis (based on painful physical sensations); alcoholism and drug addiction; psoriasis; peptic ulcer	Schizophrenic psychoses (sadomasochistic and scatological elements, automutilation, abnormal sexual behavior); agitated depression, sexual deviations (sadomasochism, male homosexuality, drinking of urine and eating of feces); obsessive-compulsive neurosis; psychogenic asthma, tics, and stammering; conversion and anxiety hysteria; frigidity and impotence; neurasthenia; traumatic neuroses; organ neuroses; migraine headache; enuresis and encopressis	Schizophrenic psychoses (death-rebirth experiences, messianic delusions, elements of destruction and recreation of the world, salvation and redemption, identification with Christ); manic symptomatology; female homosexuality; exhibitionism
	CORRESPONDING ACTIVITIES IN FREUDIAN EROGENOUS ZONES		
Libidinal satisfaction in all erogenous zones; libidinal feelings during rocking and bathing; partial approximation to this condition after oral, anal, urethral, or genital satisfaction and after delivery of a child	Oral frustration (thirst, hunger, painful stimuli); retention of feces and/or urine; sexual frustration; experiences of cold, pain and other unpleasant sensations	Chewing and swallowing of food; oral aggression and destruction of an object; process of defecation and urination; anal and urethral aggression; sexual orgasm; phallic aggression; delivering of a child, statoacoustic eroticism (jolting, gymnastics, fancy diving, parachuting)	Satiation of thirst and hunger; pleasure of sucking; libidinal feelings after defecation, urination, sexual orgasm, or delivery of a child

ASSOCIATED MEMORIES FROM POSTNATAL LIFE

Situations from later life in which important needs are satisfied, such as happy moments from infancy and childhood (good mothering, play with peers, harmonious periods in the family, etc.), fulfilling love, romances; trips or vacations in beautiful natural settings; exposure to artistic creations of high aesthetic value; swimming in the ocean and clear lakes, etc.	Situations endangering survival and body integrity (war experiences, accidents, injuries, operations, painful diseases, near drowning, episodes of suffocation, imprisonment, brainwashing, and illegal interrogation, physical abuse, etc.); severe psychological traumatizations (emotional deprivation, rejection, threatening situations, oppressive family atmosphere, ridicule and humiliation, etc.)	Struggles, fights, and adventurous activies (active attacks in battles and revolutions, experiences in military service, rough airplane flights, cruises on stormy ocean, hazardous car driving, boxing); highly sensual memories (carnivals, amusement parks and nightclubs, wild parties, sexual origies, etc.); childhood observations of adult sexual activities; experiences of seduction and rape; in females, delivering of their own children	Fortuitous escape from dangerous situations (end of war or revolution, survival of an accident or operation); overcoming of severe obstacles by active effort; episodes of strain and hard struggle resulting in a marked success; natural scenes (beginning of spring, end of an ocean storm, sunrise, etc.)

PHENOMENOLOGY IN LSD SESSIONS

Undisturbed intrauterine life: realistic recollections of "good womb" experiences; "oceanic" type of ecstasy, nature at its best ("Mother Nature"); experience of cosmic unity; visions of Heaven and Paradise; disturbances of intrauterine life: realistic recollections of "bad womb" experiences (fetal crises, diseases, and emotional upheavals of the mother, twin situation, attempted abortions), universal threat; paranoid idea-	Cosmic engulfment; immense physical and psychological suffering; unbearable and inescapable situation that will never end; various images of hell; feelings of entrapment and encagement (no exit); agonizing guilt and inferiority feelings; apocalyptic view of the world (horrors of wars and concentration camps, terror of the Inquisition; dangerous epidemics; diseases; decrepitude and death, etc.); meaninglessness	Intensification of suffering to cosmic dimensions; borderline between pain and pleasure; "volcanic" type of ecstasy; brilliant colors; explosions and fireworks; sadomasochistic orgies; murders and bloody sacrifice, active engagement in fierce battles; atmosphere of wild adventure and dangerous explorations; intense sexual orgiastic feelings and scenes of harems and carnivals; experiences of dying and being re-	Enormous decompression; expansion of space; "illuminative" type of ecstasy, visions of gigantic halls; radiant light and beautiful colors (heavenly blue, golden, rainbow, peacock feathers); feelings of rebirth and redemption; appreciation of simple way of life; sensory enhancement; brotherly feelings; humanitarian and charitable tendencies; occasionally manic activity and grandiose feelings, transition to elements

tion; unpleasant physical sensations ("hangover," chills and fine spasms, unpleasant tastes, disgust, feelings of being poisoned); encounter with demonic entities and other metaphysical evil forces

and absurdity of human existence; "cardboard world" or the atmosphere of artificiality and gadgets; ominous dark colors and unpleasant physical symptoms (feelings of oppression and compression, cardiac distress, hot flashes and chills, sweating, difficult breathing)

born; religions involving bloody sacrifice (Aztecs, Christ's suffering and death on the cross, Dionysus, etc.); intense physical manifestations (pressures and pains, suffocation, muscular tension and discharge in tremors and twitches, nausea and vomiting, hot flashes and chills, sweating, cardiac distress, problems of sphincter control, ringing in the ears)

of BPM I.); pleasant feelings can be interrupted by *umbilical crisis*: sharp pain in the navel, loss of breath, fear of death and castration, shifts in the body, but no external pressures

STAGES OF DELIVERY

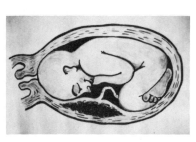

0

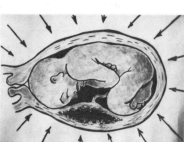

1

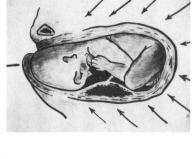

2

3

Fig. 10. A painting reflecting a sense of oneness and fusion with the therapist experienced in a psychedelic session which involved reliving of the symbiotic union with the maternal organism during intrauterine existence and nursing.

dissolution of boundaries is replaced by a psychotic distortion with paranoid undertones.

Positive aspects of BPM I are closely related to memories of symbiotic union on the breast, to positive COEX systems, and to recollections of situations associated with peace of mind, satisfaction, relaxation, and beautiful natural scenery. Similar selective connections exist also to various forms of positive transpersonal experiences. Conversely, negative aspects of BPM I tend to be associated with certain negative COEX systems and corresponding negative transpersonal elements.

In regard to Freudian erogenous zones, the positive aspects of BPM I coincide with the biological and psychological condition in which there are no tensions in these areas and all the partial drives

Fig. 11. The Oceanic Womb. A state of melted ecstasy experienced in an LSD session dominated by BPM I. Experiential identification with the intrauterine existence of the fetus coincides with a sense of becoming the ocean and fusing with various aquatic life forms.

Fig. 12. The Amniotic Universe. Experiential identification with the blissful existence of the fetus with a sense of unity with the entire cosmos. This painting was inspired by an LSD session governed by the first perinatal matrix.

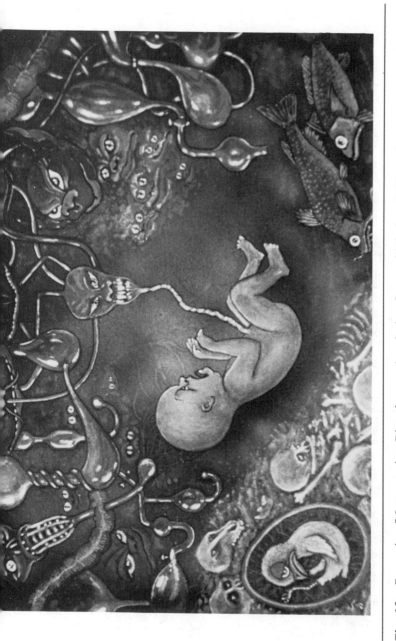

Fig. 13. Paranoia of Intrauterine Disturbance. A painting from a high-dose LSD session representing the toxic "bad womb". The subject identifies with a distressed fetus who is exposed to torture and horror in a diabolical laboratory run by insidious demons. Experiences of this kind are among important sources of paranoia. As the picture indicates, this state is related to the condition of a chicken embryo intoxicated by its own waste products and of fish in polluted waters.

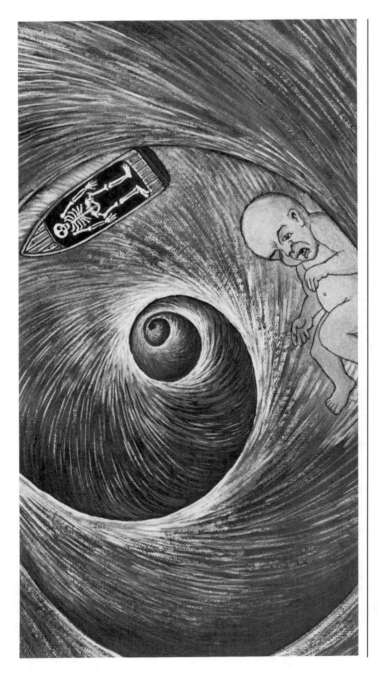

Fig. 14. The experience of the onset of biological delivery and of the beginning influence of BPM II. in a high-dose LSD session. In a full identification with a fetus, the subject feels drawn into a monstrous annihilating whirlpool; the overall atmosphere is reminiscent of Edgar Alan Poe's *A Descent into the Maelstrom.*

are satisfied. Negative aspects of BPM I seem to have specific links to nausea and intestinal dysfunction with dyspepsia.

SECOND PERINATAL MATRIX (BPM II)

This experiential pattern is related to the very onset of biological delivery and its first clinical stage. Here the original equilibrium of the intrauterine existence is disturbed, first by alarming chemical signals and then by muscular contractions. When this stage fully develops, the fetus is periodically constricted by uterine spasms; the cervix is closed and the way out is not yet available.

As in the previous matrix, this biological situation can be relived in a rather concrete and realistic fashion. The symbolic concomitant of the onset of delivery is the experience of *cosmic engulfment*. It involves overwhelming feelings of increasing anxiety and awareness of an imminent vital threat. The source of this danger cannot be

Fig. 15. Painting representing a vision from a psychedelic session governed by the initial phase of BPM II. The incipient uterine contractions are experienced as an attack by a monstrous octopus.

clearly identified, and the subject has a tendency to interpret the world in paranoid terms. Very characteristic for this stage is the experience of a three-dimensional spiral, funnel, or whirlpool, sucking the subject relentlessly toward its center. An equivalent of this annihilating maelstrom is the experience of being swallowed by a terrifying monster, such as a giant dragon, leviathan, python, crocodile, or whale. Equally frequent are experiences of attack by a monstrous octopus or tarantula. A less dramatic version of the same experience is the theme of descent into a dangerous underworld, a system of grottoes, or a mystifying labyrinth. The corresponding mythological theme seems to be the beginning of the hero's journey; related religious themes are the fall of the angels and paradise lost.

Some of these images may appear strange to the analytical mind; however, they show deep experiential logic. Thus, the whirlpool symbolizes serious danger for an organism floating freely in a watery environment and imposes on it a unidirectional motion. Similarly, the situation of being swallowed changes freedom into a life-threatening confinement comparable to that of the fetus being wedged into the pelvic opening. An octopus entangles, confines, and threatens organisms floating freely in an oceanic milieu, and a spider traps, constrains, and endangers insects previously enjoying freedom of flight in an unobstructed world.

The symbolic counterpart of a fully developed first clinical stage of delivery is the experience of *no exit* or *hell*. It involves a sense of being stuck, caged, or trapped in a claustrophobic, nightmarish world and experiencing incredible psychological and physical tortures. The situation is usually absolutely unbearable and appears to be endless and hopeless. The individual loses the sense of linear time and can see no possible end to this torment or any form of escape from it. This can produce experiential identification with prisoners in dungeons or concentration camps, inmates in insane asylums, sinners in hell, or archetypal figures symbolizing eternal damnation, such as the Wandering Jew Ahasuerus, the Flying Dutchman, Sisyphus, Tantalus, or Prometheus.

While under the influence of this matrix, the subject is also selectively blinded to anything positive in the world and in his or her own existence. Agonizing feelings of metaphysical loneliness,

Fig. 16. A demonic vision from a psychedelic session dominated by BPM II.

helplessness, hopelessness, inferiority, existential despair, and guilt are standard constituents of this matrix.

As far as the organizing function of BPM II is concerned, it attracts COEX systems with memories of situations in which the passive and helpless individual is subjected to, and victimized by, an overwhelming destructive force with no chance of escaping. It also shows affinity to transpersonal themes with similar qualities.

In regard to the Freudian erogenous zones, this matrix seems to be related to a condition of unpleasant tension or pain. On the oral level, it is hunger, thirst, nausea, and painful oral stimuli; on the anal level, rectal pain and retention of feces; and on the urethral level, bladder pain and retention of urine. The corresponding sensations on the genital level are sexual frustration and excessive tension, uterine and vaginal spasms, testicular pain and the painful

Fig. 17. Paintings by the Swiss painter Hansruedi Giger, a genius with uncanny ability to portray the nightmarish world of the negative perinatal matrices. *Picture a.* combines the anatomical frailty of the fetuses with aggressive machinery and constricting steel headbands suggestive of birth. *Picture b.* is a rich tapestry of distressed and sickened fetuses.

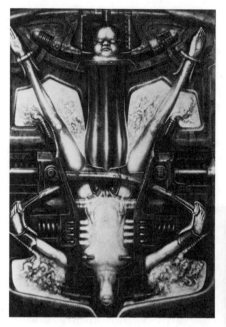

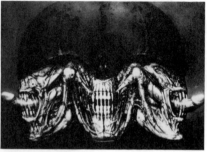

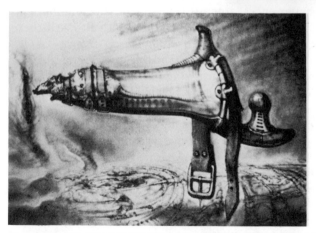

Picture c. shows the mother and child locked into a torturing stillbirth machine. *Picture d.* reflects the intimate fusion of sex and death characteristic of BPM III. *Picture e.* brings together elements of aggression, sexuality and scatology. (From Necronomicon).

contractions experienced by women in the first clinical stage of labor in childbirth.

THIRD PERINATAL MATRIX (BPM III)

Many important aspects of this complex experiential matrix can be understood from its association with the second clinical stage of biological delivery. In this stage, the uterine contractions continue, but unlike in the previous stage, the cervix is now dilated and allows a gradual propulsion of the fetus through the birth canal. This involves an enormous struggle for survival, crushing mechanical pressures, and often a high degree of anoxia and suffocation. In the terminal phases of the delivery, the fetus can experience intimate contact with such biological material as blood, mucus, fetal liquid, urine, and even feces.

From the experiential point of view, this pattern is somewhat ramified and complicated. Besides the actual, realistic reliving of various aspects of the struggle in the birth canal, it involves a wide variety of phenomena that occur in typical thematic sequences. The most important of these are the elements of titanic fight, sadomasochistic experiences, intense sexual arousal, demonic episodes, scatological involvement, and encounter with fire. All these occur in the context of a determined *death-rebirth struggle.*

The titanic aspect is quite understandable in view of the enormity of the forces involved in this stage of birth. The frail head of the child is wedged into the narrow pelvic opening by the power of uterine contractions that oscillate between 50 and 100 pounds. Facing this aspect of BPM III, the subject experiences powerful streams of energy building up to explosive discharges. Characteristic symbolic themes are raging elements of nature (volcanoes, electrical storms, earthquakes, tidal waves, or tornadoes), violent scenes of war or revolutions, and high-power technology (thermonuclear reactions, atomic bombs, and rockets). A mitigated form of this experiential pattern includes participation in dangerous adventures—hunting or fights with wild animals, exciting explorations, and the conquest of new frontiers. Related archetypal themes are images of the Last Judgment, the extraordinary feats of superheroes, and mythological battles of cosmic proportions involving demons and angels or gods and Titans.

Sadomasochistic aspects of this matrix reflect the mixture of aggression inflicted on the fetus by the female reproductive system and the biological fury of the child's response to suffocation, pain, and anxiety. Frequent themes are bloody sacrifice, self-sacrifice, torture, execution, murder, sadomasochistic practices, and rape.

The experiential logic of the sexual component of the death-rebirth process is somewhat less obvious. It can be explained by well-known observations indicating that suffocation and inhuman suffering in general generate a strange form of intense sexual arousal. The erotic themes on this level are characterized by an overwhelming intensity of the sexual drive, its mechanical and unselective quality, and pornographic or deviant nature. The experiences that belong to this category combine sex with death, danger, biological material, aggression, self-destructive impulses, physical pain, and spirituality (proximity of BPM IV).

The fact that, on the perinatal level, sexual excitement occurs in the context of vital threat, anxiety, aggression, and biological material is essential for the understanding of sexual deviations and other forms of sexual pathology. These connections are discussed later in greater detail.

The demonic element of this stage of the death-rebirth process can represent specific problems for both therapists and clients. The uncanny quality of the material involved can lead to reluctance to face it. The most common themes observed here are the elements of the Witches' Sabbath (Walpurgis Night), satanic orgies or Black Mass rituals, and of temptation. The common denominator of the birth experience at this stage and the Witches' Sabbath or Black Mass is the peculiar experiential amalgam of death, deviant sexuality, fear, aggression, scatology, and distorted spiritual impulse.

The scatological facet of the death-rebirth process has its natural biological basis in the fact that, in the final stages of birth, the child can come into close contact with excreta and other forms of biological material. However, these experiences typically exceed by far anything that the newborn might have actually experienced. They can involve the sense of wallowing in excrement, crawling in offal or sewage systems, eating feces, drinking blood or urine, or revolting images of putrefaction.

The element of fire is either experienced in its ordinary form—as identification with victims of immolation—or in an archetypal form of purifying fire (pyrocatharsis) that seems to destroy whatever

Fig. 18. *The Witches' Sabbath according to De Lancre.* The guests are shown arriving on brooms, Billy-goats, and various fantastic animals. In the upper right corner on thrones sit Master Leonard and two fallen angels. In the lower right corner are participants involved in the diabolic feast. At the bottom are three witches cooking the Sabbath brew. In the lower left corner are children playing with toads in a pool of holy water. In various other parts of the picture participants engage in music, dance, and orgies.

is corrupted and rotten in the individual, preparing him or her for spiritual rebirth. This is the least comprehensible element of the birth symbolism. Its biological concomitant could be the culminating overstimulation of the newborn with indiscriminate "firing" of peripheral neurons. It is interesting that its experiential counterpart can be found in the delivering mother, who often feels in this stage that her vagina is on fire. It is also worth mentioning here that, in the process of burning, solid forms are converted into energy; the experience of fire accompanies the ego death, after which the individual identifies philosophically with patterns of energy, rather than solid matter.

The religious and mythological symbolism of this matrix draws particularly on those systems that glorify sacrifice or self-sacrifice.

Fig. 19. The famous woodcut by Gustav Doré entitled *La Danse du Sabbat.* It shows the devil presiding at a wild ecstatic frenzy, characteristic activity at the Sabbath of the Witches.

Quite frequent are scenes from pre-Columbian sacrificial rituals, visions of crucifixion or identification with Christ, and worship of the Terrible Goddesses Kali, Coatlicue, or Rangda. The scenes of satanic worship and Walpurgis Night have already been mentioned. Another group of images is related to religious rituals and ceremonies combining sex and wild rhythmic dance, such as phallic worship, fertility rites, or various aboriginal tribal ceremonies. A classic symbol of the transition from BPM III to BPM IV is the legendary bird, the Phoenix, whose old form dies in fire and new form rises from the ashes and soars toward the sun.

Several important characteristics of this experiential pattern distinguish it from the previously described no-exit constellation. The situation here does not seem hopeless and the subject is not helpless. He or she is actively involved and has the feeling that the suffering has a definite direction and goal. In religious terms, this situation would be closer to the concept of purgatory than to that of hell. In addition, the subject does not play exclusively the

Fig. 20. An old German woodcut showing the Sabbath of the Witches on Blocksberg. One of the most famous European sites associated with the Sabbath, Blocksberg was also the scenery of the Valpurgi's Night in Goethe's *Faust*. The picture portrays the famous scene of ritual kissing of Master Leonard's anus and the beginning orgies.

role of a helpless victim. He is an observer and can at the same time identify with both sides to the point that it might be difficult to distinguish whether he is the aggressor or the victim. While the no-exit situation involves sheer suffering, the experience of the death-rebirth struggle represents the borderline between agony and ecstasy and the fusion of both. It seems appropriate to identify this type of experience as "volcanic ecstasy" in contrast to the "oceanic ecstasy" of the cosmic union.

Fig. 21. Two paintings by the Swiss painter Hansruedi Giger with blasphemic distortion of religious themes characteristic of BPM III. *Picture a.* combines elements of aggression, crucifixion, and death with a demonic atmosphere. *Picture b.* adds to these themes the motifs of sexuality and boa constrictor-type serpentine loops, further stressing the perinatal source of this imagery. (From Necronomicon).

Specific experiential characteristics link BPM III to COEX systems that are formed by memories of intense and precarious sensual and sexual experiences, fights and combats, exciting but hazardous adventures, rape and sexual orgies, or situations involving biological material. Similar connections exist also to transpersonal experiences of this kind.

In regard to the Freudian erogenous zones, this matrix is related to those physiological activities that bring sudden relief and

Fig. 22. Experiential identification with the legendary bird Phoenix at the moment of transition from BPM III to BPM IV that occurred in a high-dose LSD session. It is a very appropriate symbol of death-rebirth, since it involves death in fire, birth of the new and movement toward the light source.

relaxation after a prolonged period of tension. On the oral level, it is the act of chewing and swallowing food (or conversely of vomiting); on the anal and urethral level, the process of defecation and urination; on the genital level, the buildup to sexual orgasm and the feelings of the delivering woman in the second stage of labor.

FOURTH PERINATAL MATRIX (BPM IV)

This perinatal matrix is meaningfully related to the third clinical stage of the delivery, the actual birth of the child. In this final stage, the agonizing process of the birth struggle comes to an end; the propulsion through the birth canal culminates and the extreme build-up of pain, tension, and sexual arousal is followed by a sudden relief and relaxation. The child is born and, after a long period of darkness, faces for the first time the intense light of the day (or the operating room). After the umbilical cord is cut, the physical separation from the mother has been completed and the child begins its new existence as an anatomically independent individual.

As with the other matrices, some of the experiences belonging here seem to represent an accurate replay of the actual biological events involved in birth, as well as specific obstetric interventions. For obvious reasons, this aspect of BPM IV is much richer than the concrete elements experienced in the context of the other matrices. The specific details of the relived material are also easier to verify. They involve specifics of the birth mechanism, types of anesthesia used, nature of manual or instrumental intervention, and details of postnatal experience and care.

The symbolic counterpart of this final stage of delivery is the *death-rebirth experience;* it represents the termination and resolution of the death-rebirth struggle. Paradoxically, while only one step from a phenomenal liberation, the individual has a feeling of impending catastrophe of enormous proportions. This results frequently in a strong determination to stop the experience. If allowed to happen, the transition from BPM III to BPM IV involves a sense of annihilation on all imaginable levels—physical destruction, emotional debacle, intellectual defeat, ultimate moral failure, and absolute damnation of transcendental proportions. This experience of "ego death" seems to entail an instant merciless destruction of all previous reference points in the life of the individual. When experienced in its final and most complete form,[3] it means an irreversible end of one's philosophical identification with what Alan Watts used to call "skin-encapsulated ego."

This experience of total annihilation and of "hitting the cosmic bottom" is immediately followed by visions of blinding white or golden light of supernatural radiance and beauty. It can be associated with astonishing displays of divine archetypal entities, rainbow spectra, or intricate peacock designs. Also, visions of nature reawakened in spring or refreshed after a tempest and cloudburst can appear in this context. The subject experiences a deep sense of spiritual liberation, redemption, and salvation. He or she typically feels freed from anxiety, depression, and guilt, purged and unburdened. This is associated with a flood of positive emotions toward

Fig. 23. A sequence of experiences encountered during the transition from BPM III to BPM IV. The first picture shows a gigantic and threatening Golem-like figure blocking the access to the source of light. The second picture reflects a later stage of the process, during which the obstacle has been overcome and the subject faces and embraces the unobstructed rising sun. (From the collection of Dr. Milan Hausner, Prague, Czechoslovakia).

oneself, other people, and existence in general. The world appears to be a beautiful and safe place and the zest for life is distinctly increased.[4]

Fig. 24. The experience of a fundamental emotional and spiritual break-through represented in the first picture occurred in a perinatal LSD session at the time when the patient relived her biological birth. The lower part of the painting represents the "quagmire" of the patient's unconscious with various dangerous monsters—essentially the image of the psyche that she brought into therapy. The upper part—free cosmic space with celestial bodies—is the entirely new area that opened up in therapy. At the interface the monsters turn into friendly creatures. The patient herself appears as a little princess with a crown, as a divine child (she herself made the connection to "crowning").

The second picture shows how this newly achieved peace can be disturbed by negative influences from the external world. On a deeper level this reflects another wave of uterine contractions encroaching on the embryonal paradise of the fetus.

Fig. 25. In this picture of a transition from BPM III to BPM IV as it was experienced in an LSD session, the subject is shown climbing a steep mountain in her effort to reach the light. Ascent of a mountain is cross-culturally a symbol of rebirth and spiritual search. The predatory birds attacking her represent the dark forces that are trying to prevent this development.

The symbolism of the death-rebirth experience can be drawn from many areas of the collective unconscious, since every major culture has the appropriate mythological forms for this phenomenon. Ego death can be experienced in connection with various destructive deities—Moloch, Shiva, Huitzilopochtli, Kali, or Coatlicue—or in full identification with Christ, Osiris, Adonis, Dionysus, or other sacrificed mythical beings. The divine epiphany can involve an entirely abstract image of God as a radiant source of light, or more or less personified representations from different religions. Equally common are experiences of encounter or union with great mother goddesses, such as the Virgin Mary, Isis, Lakshmi, Parvati, Hera, or Cybele.

The related biographical elements involve memories of personal successes and the termination of dangerous situations, the end of wars or revolutions, the survival of accidents, or recoveries from serious diseases.

In relation to the Freudian erogenous zones, BPM IV is associated on all levels of libidinal development with the state of satisfaction immediately following activities that release unpleasant tension—satiation of hunger by swallowing food, relieving vomiting, defecation, urination, sexual orgasm, and delivery of a child.

Beyond the Brain: Realms of Transpersonal Experiences

Transpersonal experiences have many strange characteristics that shatter the most fundamental assumptions of materialistic science and the mechanistic world view. Although these experiences occur in the process of deep individual self-exploration, it is not possible to interpret them simply as intrapsychic phenomena in the conventional sense. On the one hand, they form an experiential continuum with biographical and perinatal experiences. On the other hand, they frequently appear to be tapping directly, without the mediation of the sensory organs, sources of information that are clearly outside of the conventionally defined range of the individual. They can involve conscious experience of other humans and members of other species, plant life, elements of inorganic nature, microscopic and astronomic realms not accessible to the unaided senses, history and prehistory, the future, remote locations, or other dimensions of existence.

The recollective-analytical level draws on the individual history and is clearly biographical in nature. Perinatal experiences seem to represent an intersection or frontier between the personal and transpersonal—a fact reflected in their connection with birth and death, the beginning and end of individual existence. Transpersonal phenomena reveal connections between the individual and the cosmos that seem at present to be beyond comprehension. All we can say in this respect is that, somewhere in the process of perinatal unfolding, a strange qualitative Möbiuslike leap seems to occur in which deep exploration of the individual unconscious turns into a process of experiential adventures in the universe-at-large, involving what can best be described as the superconscious mind.

Fig. 26. A shattering encounter with the Terrible Mother in the form of the Indian Goddess Kali experienced in a psychedelic session at the moment of the ego death. Archetypal surrender to the female principle, expressed in ritual kissing of the bleeding genitals of the goddess, coincides with reliving the memory of oral contact with the maternal vagina at the moment of birth.

The common denominator of this otherwise rich and ramified group of phenomena is the subject's feeling that his or her consciousness has expanded beyond the usual ego boundaries and has transcended the limitations of time and space. In the "normal" or usual state of consciousness, we experience ourselves as existing within the boundaries of the physical body (the body image) and our perception of the environment is restricted by the physically determined range of exteroceptors. Both our internal perception (interoception) and the perception of the external world (exteroception) are confined by the usual spatial and temporal boundaries. Under ordinary circumstances, we vividly experience only our present situation and our immediate environment; we *recall* past events and *anticipate* the future or fantasize about it.

In transpersonal experiences, one or several of the above limitations appear to be transcended. Many experiences belonging to this category are interpreted by the subjects as regression in historical time and exploration of their biological or spiritual past. It is rather common in various forms of deep experiential work to experience quite concrete and realistic episodes identified as fetal and embryonic memories. Many subjects report vivid sequences on the level of cellular consciousness that seem to reflect their existence in the form of a sperm or ovum at the moment of conception. Sometimes the regression appears to go even further and the individual has a convinced feeling of reliving memories from the lives of his or her ancestors, or even drawing on the racial and collective unconscious. On occasion, LSD subjects report experiences in which they identify with various animal ancestors in the evolutionary pedigree or have a distinct feeling of reliving episodes from their existence in a previous incarnation.

Some other transpersonal phenomena involve transcendence of spatial rather than temporal barriers. Here belong the experiences of merging with another person in a state of dual unity* or completely identifying with him or her, tuning into the consciousness of an entire group of persons, or expanding one's consciousness to the extent that it seems to encompass all of humanity. In a similar way, one can transcend the limits of the specifically human experience and tune in to what appears to be the consciousness of

* Dual unity – a sense of fusing with another organism into a unitive state without losing sense of identity

Fig. 27. Two pictures from a transpersonal LSD session in which the patient experienced elements of the collective unconscious. She became the member of an ancient culture that she could not identify by name, historical period, or geographical location; however, she was able to draw and paint in its artistic style.

animals, plants, or even inanimate objects and processes. In the extreme, it is possible to experience the consciousness of all creation, of our planet, on the entire material universe. Another phenomenon related to the transcendence of normal spatial limitations is consciousness of certain parts of the body—various organs, tissues, or individual cells. An important category of transpersonal experiences involving transcendence of time and/or space are the various ESP phenomena, such as out-of-body experiences, telepathy, precognition, clairvoyance, and clairaudience, and space and time travel.

In a large group of transpersonal experiences, the extension of consciousness seems to go beyond both the phenomenal world and the time-space continuum as we perceive it in our everyday life. Common examples are the experiences of encounters with spirits of deceased human beings or suprahuman spiritual entities. LSD subjects also report numerous visions of archetypal forms, individual deities and demons, and complex mythological sequences. Intuitive understanding of universal symbols, experience of the flow of *chi* energy as it is described in Chinese medicine and philosophy, or the arousal of Kundalini and activation of various chakras are additional examples of this category. In the extreme form, individual consciousness seems to encompass the totality of existence and identify with the Universal Mind or with the Absolute. The ultimate of all experiences appears to be that of the Supracosmic and Metacosmic Void, the mysterious primordial emptiness and nothingness that is conscious of itself and contains all existence in germinal form.

This expanded cartography of the unconscious is of critical importance for any serious approach to such phenomena as psychedelic states, shamanism, religion, mysticism, rites of passage, mythology, parapsychology, and schizophrenia. This is not simply a matter of academic interest; as will be discussed later, it has deep and revolutionary implications for the understanding of psychopathology and offers new therapeutic possibilities undreamed of by traditional psychiatry.

The Spectrum of Consciousness

The cartography of inner space which includes the biographical, perinatal and transpersonal levels throws interesting light on the present confusion in the world of depth psychotherapy and the conflicts among its various schools. While in its totality such a cartography resembles none of the existing approaches, its various levels can be described quite adequately in terms of various modern psychological systems or ancient spiritual philosophies. I observed fairly early in my psychedelic research that an average patient during psycholytic therapy with LSD tends to move from a Freudian stage to a Rankian-Reichian-existentialist stage, and then to the Jungian stage (Grof 1970). The names of these stages reflect the fact that the corresponding conceptual systems seemed to be the best available frameworks for describing the phenomena observed in these consecutive periods of therapy. It also became obvious that no Western psychotherapeutic system was adequate to describe certain phenomena occurring in advanced stages of therapy or levels of psychedelic experience. Here, one had to resort to the ancient and Oriental spiritual philosophies, such as Vedanta, different systems of yoga, Kashmir Shaivism Mahayana Buddhism, Vajrayana, Taoism, or Sufism. It became altogether clear that the entire spectrum of human experience cannot be described by a single psychological system and that each major level of the evolution of consciousness requires an entirely different explanatory framework.

The same idea was independently developed by Ken Wilber and presented in a most articulate and well-documented form in *Spectrum of Consciousness* (1977), *The Atman Project* (1980), and *Up From Eden* (1981). Wilber's concept of spectrum psychology involves a model of consciousness that integrates the insights of major Western schools of psychology with the basic principles of what can be called "perennial psychology"—an understanding of human consciousness that expresses the basic insights of "perennial philosophy" in a psychological language. According to Wilber, the great diversity of psychological and psychotherapeutic schools reflects not so much interpretation of, and opinion about, differences in the same set of problems or differences in methodology, as a real difference in the levels of the spectrum of consciousness to which they have adapted themselves. The major mistake of these discrepant schools is that each tends to generalize its approach and apply it to the entire spectrum, whereas it is appropriate only for a particular level. Each of the major approaches of Western psychotherapy is thus more or less "correct" when addressing its own level and grossly distorting when applied inappropriately to other bands. A truly encompassing and integrated psychology of the future will make use of the complementary insights offered by each school of psychology.

The key notion of Wilber's model of the spectrum of consciousness is the insight of perennial philosophy that human personality is a multilevel manifestation of a single consciousness, the Universal Mind. Each level of the spectrum of consciousness that constitutes the multidimensional nature of a human being is characterized by a specific and easily recognizable sense of individual identity. This covers a wide range from the supreme identity of cosmic consciousness through several gradations or bands, to the drastically reduced and narrowed identification with egoic consciousness.

Since the publication of *The Spectrum of Consciousness* (1977), Wilber has revised, refined and further developed his model and applied it successfully to the development of individual human consciousness and human history. In *The Atman Project* (1980), he outlined a transpersonal view of both ontology and cosmology, integrating in a creative way many schools of Western psychology and systems of perennial philosophy. This encompassing vision covers the evolution of consciousness from the material world and the individual to Atman-Brahman, as well as the opposite movement from the absolute to the manifest worlds. The process of the evolution of consciousness, then, involves the outward arc, or movement from subconsciousness to self-consciousness, and the inward arc, or the progression from self-consciousness to superconsciousness. Wilber's views on this subject and the concept of the Atman project are so important for the subject of this book that they deserve special notice.

Wilber's description of the outward arc of consciousness evolution starts with the *pleromatic stage,* the undifferentiated state of consciousness of the newborn, which is timeless, spaceless, and objectless and does not know the distinction between self and the material world. The following *uroboric stage,* closely related to the alimentary functions, involves the first primitive and incomplete distinction between the subject and the material world. It coincides with the early oral period of libidinal development. The *typhonic stage* is characterized by the first full differentiation, which creates the organic or body-ego self, dominated by the pleasure principle and instinctual urges and discharges. This period includes the anal and phallic phase of libidinal development. The acquisition of language, and of mental and conceptual functions, marks the *verbal-membership stage.* Here the self differentiates from the body and emerges as a mental and verbal being. This process then continues into the *mental-egoic stage* associated with the development of linear, abstract, and conceptual thinking and identification with a self-concept. The ordinary personal development culminates in the *centauric stage,* a high-order integration of ego, body, persona, and shadow.

The level of the centaur is the highest level of consciousness acknowledged and taken seriously by Western mechanistic science.

Western psychiatrists and psychologists either deny the existence of any higher states, or use pathological labels for them. In the past, those individuals interested in knowledge of higher states of consciousness had to turn to the great sages and mystical schools of the East and West. In the last decade, transpersonal psychology has undertaken the complex task of integrating the wisdom of perennial philosophy and psychology with the conceptual frameworks of Western science. Ken Wilber's work is a major accomplishment in this development.

Wilber's model of consciousness evolution does not end with the centaur. He sees the centaur as a transitional form leading toward transpersonal realms of being that are as far beyond the ego-mind as the ego-mind is from the typhon. The first of these realms of consciousness evolution is the *lower subtle level*, which includes the astral-psychic domain. On this level consciousness, differentiating itself further from the mind and body, is able to transcend the ordinary capacities of the gross body-mind. Here belong the out-of-the-body experiences, occult phenomena, auras, astral travel, precognition, telepathy, clairvoyance, psychokinesis, and related phenomena. The *higher subtle level* is the realm of genuine religious intuition, symbolic visions, perception of divine lights and sounds, higher presences, and archetypal forms.

Beyond the high subtle level lies the *causal realm.* Its lower level involves the supreme divine consciousness, the source of archetypal forms. In the higher causal realm, all forms are radically transcended and merge into the boundless radiance of Formless Consciousness. On the *level of the ultimate unity*, consciousness totally awakens to its original condition, which is also the suchness of all of existence—gross, subtle, and causal. At this point, the entire world process arises, moment to moment, as one's own being, outside of and prior to which nothing exists. Forms are identical with the Void, and the ordinary and extraordinary, or the mundane and supernatural, are the same. This is the ultimate state toward which all cosmic evolution drives.

In Wilber's model, cosmology involves a process that is the reverse of the above. It describes how phenomenal worlds are created from the original unity by progressive reduction and enfolding of higher structures into the lower. In this, Wilber follows exclusively the text of the *Tibetan Book of the Dead,* or Bardo Thödol, which describes the movements through the intermediate states, or bardos, at the time of death.

One of the most original contributions of Wilber's work is his detection of essentially identical, or at least similar, principles and mechanisms behind the confusing diversity of the many stages of consciousness evolution and involution. His concepts of deep and surface structures of various levels of consciousness, translation versus transformation, different types of the unconscious (ground, archaic, submergent, embedded, and emergent), evolution and involution of consciousness, outward and inward arc, and disidentification versus dissociation, as well as redefinition of the terms "eros" and "thanatos," will undoubtedly become standard elements of transpersonal psychology of the future.

However, most fundamental and revealing is Wilber's concept of the Atman project. He succeeded in demonstrating most convincingly that the motivating force on all the levels of evolution (except that of the original unity of Atman itself), is a determined search by the individual for the original cosmic unity. Because of inherent restraints, this happens in ways that allow for only unsatisfactory compromises, which explains the failures of the project that lead to abandoning the levels involved and to transformation to the next stage. Each new higher-order level is another substitute, although closer to the Real, until the soul grounds itself in the superconscious all which it has desired all along.

Wilber applied the described model not only to individual development, but also to human history. In his book *Up From Eden* (1981), he offered nothing less than a drastic reformulation of both history and anthropology. Space prevents my doing justice to his unique contributions to transpersonal psychology, and the interested reader should resort to Wilber's original books and papers. However, I shall outline briefly the areas in which my own work and the concepts I have described here differ from Wilber's model in spite of otherwise far-reaching agreement.

Wilber has done extraordinary work successfully synthesizing seemingly disparate data from a vast variety of areas and disciplines. His knowledge of the literature is truly encyclopedic, his analytical mind is systematic and incisive, and the clarity of his logic remarkable. It is therefore somewhat surprising that he has not taken into consideration a vast amount of data from both ancient and

modern sources—data suggesting the paramount psychological significance of prenatal experiences and the trauma of birth. In my
opinion, knowledge of the perinatal dynamics is essential for any
serious approach to such problems as religion, mysticism, rites of
passage, shamanism, or psychosis. Wilber's description of consciousness evolution begins with the undifferentiated pleromatic consciousness of the newborn and ends with the ultimate unity of the
Absolute. His description of consciousness involution, following
closely the *Tibetan Book of the Dead,* proceeds from the ultimate
consciousness, the immaculate and luminous Dharmakaya, through
the three bardo realms, to the moment of conception. The complexity of embryonic development and of the consecutive stages of
biological birth receives no attention in this sophisticated system,
which is elaborated in meticulous detail in all other areas.

Another major difference between my own observations and
Wilber's model involves the phenomenon of death. For Wilber,
the concept of thanatos is associated with the transformation of
consciousness from one level to the next. He equates dying with
abandoning the exclusive identification with a particular structure
of consciousness, which makes it possible to transcend that structure
and move to the next level. He makes no distinction between dying
to a developmental level and the experience associated with biological death. This approach is in sharp contrast with the observations from psychedelic therapy and other forms of deep experiential self-exploration, where memories of life-threatening events,
including biological birth, represent a category of special significance.

This material clearly suggests that it is essential to distinguish
the process of transition from one developmental stage to another
from the birth trauma and other events that endanger the survival
of the organism. The latter experiences are of a different logical
type and are in a meta-position in relation to the processes that
Wilber includes under the description of thanatos. They endanger
the existence of the organism as an individual entity without regard
to the level of its development. Thus, a critical survival threat can
occur during embryonic existence, in any stage of the birth process,
or at any age, without regard to the level of consciousness evolution.
A vital threat during prenatal existence or in the process of childbirth actually seems to be instrumental in creating a sense of

separateness and isolation, rather than destroying it, as Wilber suggests.[5]

In my opinion, without a genuine appreciation of the paramount significance of birth and death, the understanding of human nature is bound to be incomplete and unsatisfactory. The integration of these elements would give Wilber's model more logical consistency and greater pragmatic power. Without this, his model cannot account for important clinical data, and his description of the therapeutic implications of his model will remain the least convincing part of his work for clinicians used to dealing with the practical problems of psychopathology.

Finally, I should mention Wilber's emphasis on linearity and on the radical difference between prephenomena and transphenomena (prepersonal versus transpersonal, or preegoic versus postegoic). As much as I agree with him in principle, the absoluteness of his statements seems to me too extreme. The psyche has a multidimensional, holographic nature, and using a linear model to describe it will produce distortions and inaccuracies. This will be a serious problem for each description of the psyche that is limited to rational and verbal means.

My own observations suggest that, as consciousness evolution proceeds from the centauric to the subtle realms and beyond, it does not follow a linear trajectory, but in a sense enfolds into itself. In this process, the individual returns to earlier stages of development, but evaluates them from the point of view of a mature adult. At the same time, he or she becomes consciously aware of certain aspects and qualities of these stages that were implicit, but unrecognized when confronted in the context of linear evolution. Thus, the distinction between pre- and trans- has a paradoxical nature; they are neither identical, nor are they completely different from each other.

When this understanding is then applied to the problems of psychopathology, the distinction between evolutionary and pathological states may lie more in the context, the style of approaching them and the ability to integrate them into everyday life than in the intrinsic nature of the experiences involved. Detailed discussion of the above issues and some other questions that Wilber's exciting and inspiring work raises must await a special presentation.

CHAPTER THREE

The World of Psychotherapy: Towards an Integration of Approaches

The observations from psyche-delic research and other forms of experiential self-exploration have made it possible to bring an element of clarity and simplification into the hopeless labyrinth of conflicting and competing systems of psychotherapy.[1] Even a cursory look at Western psychology reveals fundamental disagreements and controversies of enormous proportions concerning the basic dynamics of the human mind, the nature of emotional disorders, and techniques of psychotherapy. This is true not only for schools that are products of a priori incompatible philosophical approaches, such as behaviorism and psychoanalysis, but also for those orientations with founders who originally started from the same or very similar premises. This can be best illustrated by comparing the theories of classical psycho-analysis formulated by Sigmund Freud and the conceptual systems of Alfred Adler, Wilhelm Reich, Otto Rank, and Carl Gustav Jung, all of whom were initially his admirers and devoted disciples.

This situation gets even more complicated when we take into consideration the psychological systems developed by the major spiritual traditions in both East and West, such as various forms of yoga, Zen Buddhism, Vipassana, Vajrayana, Taoism, Sufism, alchemy, or Kabbalah. There is an abysmal gap between most Western schools of psychotherapy and these refined and sophisticated theories of the mind based on centuries of a deep study of consciousness.

Observations of systematic changes in the content of psychedelic experiences related to variations in dosage and to the increasing number of serial sessions have helped to resolve some of the most striking contradictions in a rather unexpected way. In psycholytic therapy, a typical patient would confront in the initial LSD sessions a variety of biographical issues. During this recollective-analytical work, much of the experiential material could be interpreted in terms of classical psychoanalysis. Occasionally, the nature of the biographical experiences was such that they rendered themselves equally well, or better, to interpretations in Adlerian terms. Certain aspects of the transference dynamics during psychedelic sessions, and particularly in the periods following drug experiences, have important interpersonal components that can be understood and approached through Sullivan's principles.

However, once the subjects moved beyond this 'Freudian" stage, the sessions focused on a profound experiential confrontation with death and on reliving biological birth. At this point, the Freudian system became useless for the understanding of the processes involved. Certain aspects of the death-rebirth process, particularly the significance of death and the crisis of meaning, allowed for interpretation in terms of existential philosophy and psychotherapy. Orgiastic discharges of energy and the resulting dissolution of the muscular "character-armor"—which, in a less dramatic form, occurs also during the biographical stage—reach extreme dimensions during the perinatal process. With some modifications, the theoretical concepts and therapeutic maneuvers developed by Wilhelm Reich can prove extremely useful for dealing with this aspect of the psychedelic experience.

The central element in the complex dynamics of the death-rebirth process seems to be reliving the biological birth trauma. Its significance for psychology and psychotherapy was discovered and discussed by Otto Rank in his pioneering book, *The Trauma of Birth* (1929). Although Rank's understanding of the nature of this trauma does not exactly coincide with the observations from psychedelic work, many of his formulations and insights can be of great value when the process focuses on the perinatal level. Because of this, I sometimes refer to this stage of psychedelic therapy as "Rankian"; this does not accurately reflect clinical reality, since the death-rebirth process involves much more than just a reliving of biological birth.

Jungian psychology has been well aware of the importance of psychological death and rebirth and has studied carefully various cultural variations of this theme. It is extremely useful in approaching the specific content of many perinatal experiences, particularly the nature of mythological images and themes that frequently occur in this context. However, it seems to miss the relationship of this pattern to the biological birth of the individual and the important physiological dimensions of this phenomenon. The participation of archetypal elements in the death-rebirth process reflects the fact that deep experiential confrontation with the phenomena of death and birth typically results in a spiritual and mystical opening and mediates access to the transpersonal realms. This connection has its parallels in the spiritual and ritual life and practices of various cultures all through the ages, such as the shamanic initiations, rites of passage, meetings of ecstatic sects, or the ancient mysteries of death and rebirth. In some instances, one of the symbolic frameworks used by these systems can be more appropriate for the interpretation and understanding of a particular perinatal session than an eclectic combination of Rankian, Reichian, existentialist, and Jungian concepts.

Once the psychedelic sessions move into the transpersonal realms, beyond the gateway of birth and death, Jungian psychology and, to some extent, Assagioli's psychosynthesis are the only schools of Western psychology that have genuine understanding of the processes involved. At this point, the LSD experiences have a philosophical, spiritual, mystical, and mythological emphasis. Coming from Western psychological and psychiatric tradition, I tend to refer to this stage of the psychedelic therapy as "Jungian," although Jungian psychology does not cover many of the phenomena that occur in this context. Psychotherapy on this level is indistinguishable from the spiritual and philosophical quest for one's cosmic identity. Various forms of perennial philosophy and the associated spiritual and psychological systems provide excellent guidance at this advanced stage, both for the client and the therapist, if those terms are still appropriate for two individuals who have now become fellow seekers and travelers.

So far I have focused on the changes in the content of the sessions with the increasing number of exposures to the drug; however, a similar progression can be demonstrated in regard to increasing dosage. Thus, smaller dosages tend to reach the biographical level, perhaps in combination with some abstract sensory experiences. A higher dose usually leads to a confrontation with the perinatal level and gives the individual a better chance to connect with the transpersonal realms. Here we can speak of levels of a psychedelic experience, rather than stages of the transformative process. These relations can be observed only in the initial psychedelic sessions; an individual who has thoroughly worked through the biographical material and integrated the perinatal contents will in subsequent sessions respond to even smaller dosages with transpersonal experiences. In this case the dosage will be related to the intensity of the experience and not its type.

According to my experience, the above observations—although first made in the context of psychedelic therapy—are equally applicable to nondrug experiential approaches. Thus less powerful techniques will allow exploration of biographical realms, whereas more potent procedures can connect the individual to the perinatal process or mediate access to transpersonal realms. Similarly, systematic use of an effective experiential technique will typically result in a progression from biographical issues through the death-rebirth process to transpersonal self-exploration. It is not necessary to emphasize that this statement should be interpreted in statistical terms; in individual cases, this development is not necessarily linear, and it is also critically dependent on the specific characteristics of the techniques used, on the orientation of the therapist, the personality and attitude of the client, and the quality of the therapeutic relationship.

These observations indicate clearly that the confusing situation in Western psychology, with its almost inpenetrable jungle of rival schools, can be vastly simplified by the realization that they are not all talking about the same subject. As was brought out in connection with spectrum psychology, there are different realms in the psyche and different levels of consciousness, each of which has specific characteristics and laws. The phenomena of the psyche in its totality cannot therefore be reduced to simple common denominators of general validity and applicability, especially not to a few basic biological and physiological mechanisms. In addition, the world of consciousness has not only many levels, but many dimensions. For that reason, any theory that is limited to the Newtonian-Cartesian model of the world and to linear description is bound to be incomplete and fraught with inner inconsistencies. It is also likely to be in conflict with other theories that emphasize different fragmentary aspects of reality without explicitly knowing that they are doing so.

Thus, the major problem in Western psychotherapy seems to be that, for various reasons, individual researchers have focused their attention primarily on a certain level of consciousness and generalized their findings for the human psyche as a whole. For this reason, they are essentially incorrect, although they may give a useful and reasonably accurate description of the level they are describing, or one of its major aspects. Therefore, although many of the existing systems can be utilized during certain stages of the process of experiential self-exploration, none is sufficiently encompassing and complete to justify its use as an exclusive tool. Truly effective psychotherapy and self-exploration requires a broad theoretical framework based on recognition of the multilevel nature of consciousness that would transcend the sectarian chauvinism of the present approaches.

The following discussion will cover specific insights into the concepts of the major schools of psychotherapy, based on observations from deep experiential work both with and without psychedelic drugs. After a brief delineation of each of these systems, I will point out its major theoretical and practical problems, areas of disagreement with other schools, and the revisions or reformulations necessary for its integration into a comprehensive theory of psychotherapy.

Sigmund Freud and Classical Psychoanalysis

The discovery of the basic principles of depth psychology was the remarkable achievement of one man, the Austrian psychiatrist Sigmund Freud. He invented the method of free association, demonstrated the existence of an unconscious mind and described its dynamics, formulated the basic mechanisms involved in the etiology of psychoneurosis and many other emotional disorders, discovered infantile sexuality, outlined the techniques of dream interpretation, described the phenomenon of transference, and developed the basic principles of psychotherapeutic intervention. Since Freud explored singlehandedly the territories of the mind previously unknown to Western science, it is understandable that his concepts kept changing as he confronted new problems.

However, one element that remained constant during all these changes was Freud's deep need to establish psychology as a scientific discipline. He started his work with a firm belief that science will eventually introduce order and clear understanding into the apparent chaos of mental processes and explain them in terms of brain functions. Although he found the task of translating mental phenomena into physiological processes an insurmountable one and subsequently resorted to purely psychological techniques of exploration, he never lost the perspective of this ultimate goal. He was always open to the idea that psychoanalysis would have to adjust to new scientific discoveries, whether within psychology itself or in physics, biology, or physiology. It is, therefore, interesting to explore which of Freud's ideas withstood the test of new discoveries and which of them require fundamental revision. Some of these revisions reflect the limitations inherent in the Newtonian-Cartesian paradigm and the drastic change that has taken place in basic philosopical and metaphysical foundations of science since Freud's time. Others are due more specifically to his own personal limitations and cultural conditions.

It deserves special attention in this connection that Freud was deeply influenced by his teacher Ernst Bruecke, founder of the scientific movement known as the Helmholtz School of Medicine. According to his view, all biological organisms were complex systems of atoms governed by strict laws, particularly the principle of the conservation of energy. The only forces active in biological organisms were the physicochemical processes inherent in matter, which could ultimately be reduced to the force of attraction and repulsion. The explicit goal and ideal of the movement was to introduce the principles of Newton's scientific thinking into other disciplines. It was in the spirit of the Helmholtz school that Freud modeled his description of psychological processes after Newton's mechanics. The four basic principles of the psychoanalytic approach—dynamic, economic, topographical, and genetic—exactly parallel the basic concepts of Newtonian physics.

The Dynamic Principle. In Newton's mechanics, material particles and objects are moved around by forces that are different from matter: their collisions are governed by specific laws. Similarly, in psychoanalysis all mental processes are explained in terms of interaction and collisions of psychological forces. These can potentiate each other, inhibit each other, or be in conflict and create various compromise formations. They manifest definite directions, moving toward motor expression or away from it. The most important of the forces contributing to mental dynamics are instinctual drives. Newton's principle of action and reaction was also adopted by Freud, and it deeply influenced his thinking concerning opposites. His tendency to describe various aspects of mental functioning as a series of contrasting phenomena has been seen by some psychoanalysts as a serious conceptual limitation.

The Economic Principle. The quantitative aspect of Newtonian mechanics became a major factor in its pragmatic success and scientific prestige. Masses, forces, distances, and velocities could be expressed in the form of measurable quantities and their interrelations and interactions represented by mathematical equations. Although Freud could not even remotely approach these rigid criteria of physics, he often emphasized the importance of the energetic economy in psychological processes. He attributed to the mental representations of instinctual drives, and to the forces opposing them, charges of definite quantities of energy, or cathexis. The distribution of energy between input, consumption, and output was of crucial significance. The function of the mental apparatus was to prevent a damming of these energies and to keep the total amount of excitation as low as possible. The quantity of excitation was seen as the driving force behind the pleasure-pain principle that played an important role in Freud's thinking.

The Topographical or Structural Principle. Whereas in modern physics separate material entities of the phenomenal world appear as inseparably interconnected dynamic processes, Newtonian mechanics deals with individual material particles and objects that occupy Euclidean space and interact in it. Similarly, in Freud's topographical descriptions, dynamic processes that are intimately interwoven appear as specific individual structures of the psychic apparatus that interact with each other in psychological space with Euclidean properties. Freud on occasion warned that such concepts as id, ego, and superego are just abstractions that should not be taken literally and referred to every attempt to relate them to specific cerebral structures and functions as "brain mythology" (*Gehirnmythologie*). However, in his writings they have all the characteristics of Newtonian material objects—extension, mass, position, and movement. They cannot occupy the same space and thus cannot move without displacing each other. They impose on each other and get involved in collisions; they can be suppressed, overwhelmed, and demolished. The extreme of this approach is the concept that the amount of libido and even love is limited. In classical analysis, object love and self-love are in conflict and compete with each other.

The Genetic or Historical Principle.[2] One of the most characteristic features of Newtonian mechanics is its strict determinism; collisions between particles and objects occur in linear chains of cause and effect. The spatiotemporal description of events and their causal description are united and combined into a visualizable trajectory. The initial conditions of the system thus uniquely determine its state at all later times. In principle—if all variables were known— the complete knowledge of the present condition of the studied system should allow for its description at any point in the past and future.

The notion of strict determinism of mental processes was one of Freud's major contributions. Every psychological event was seen as the result of and, at the same time, the cause of other events. The psychogenetic approach of psychoanalysis tries to explain the experiences and behavior of the individual in terms of previous ontogenetic stages and modes of adaptation. A complete understanding of present behavior requires exploration of its antecedents, particularly the psychosexual history of early childhood. The individual's experiences in successive stages of libidinal development, solution of the childhood neurosis, and conflicts about infantile sexuality thus critically determine all subsequent life. Like Newtonian mechanics, classical psychoanalysis uses the concept of a visualizable trajectory in regard to instinctual drives involving source, impetus, aim, and object.

Another important characteristic that psychoanalysis shares with Newtonian-Cartesian science is the concept of the objective and independent observer. As in Newtonian physics, the observation of the patient can take place without any appreciable interference. Although this concept has been modified considerably in ego psychology, in classical psychonalysis the patient's life continues to be determined during therapy quite uniquely by the initial historical-psychogenetic conditions.

Following this account of the general principles on which psychoanalysis is built, we can outline its most important specific contributions. They can be divided into three thematic categories: the theory of instincts, the model of the psychic apparatus, and the principles and techniques of psychoanalytic therapy. By and large, Freud believed that the psychological history of the individual begins after birth; he referred to the newborn as a *tabula rasa* (a "blank" or "erased tablet"). He occasionally mentioned the possibility of vague constitutional predispositions or even archaic memories of a phylogenetic nature. According to him, the little boy's fantasy of castration might be a remnant from times when cutting off the penis was actually used as punishment, or certain totemistic elements in the psyche might reflect the historical reality of brutal patricide by a fraternal coalition. Similarly, certain aspects of dream symbolism cannot be explained from the individual's life experience and seem to reflect an archaic language of the psyche. However, for all practical purposes, the mental dynamics can be understood in terms of biographical factors, beginning with the events from early childhood.

Freud ascribed a critical role in mental dynamics to instinctual drives that he saw as forces bridging between the psychic and somatic spheres. In the early years of psychoanalysis, Freud postulated a basic dualism involving the sexual drive, or libido, and the nonsexual ego instincts related to self-preservation. He believed that mental conflicts resulting from the clash between these instincts were responsible for psychoneuroses and a variety of other psychological phenomena. Of the two instincts, the libido attracted much more of Freud's attention and received preferential treatment.

Freud (1953a) discovered that the origins of sexuality lie in early childhood and formulated a developmental theory of sex. According to him, the psychosexual activities start during nursing when the mouth of the infant functions as an erogenous zone (oral phase). During the period of toilet training the emphasis shifts, first, to sensations associated with defecation (anal phase) and, later, with urination (urethral phase). Finally, around the age of four, these pregenital partial drives become integrated under the domination of genital interest involving the penis or clitoris (phallic phase). This also coincides with the development of the Oedipus or Electra complex, a predominantly positive attitude toward the parent of the opposite sex and an aggressive stance toward that of the same sex. At this time, Freud attributes a crucial role to the overvaluation of the penis and the castration complex. The boy gives up his Oedipal tendencies because of castration fears. The girl moves from her primary attachment to her mother toward the father because she is disappointed by the "castrated" mother and hopes to achieve a penis or child from her father.

Overindulgence in erotic activities or, conversely, frustrations, conflicts, and traumas interfering with them, can cause fixation on different stages of libidinal development. Such fixation and a failure to resolve the Oedipal situation may result in psychoneuroses, sexual perversions, or other forms of psychopathology. Freud and his followers developed a detailed dynamic taxonomy linking different emotional and psychosomatic disorders to specific vicissitudes of libidinal development and of the maturation of the ego. Freud also traced difficulties in interpersonal relationships to factors interfering with the evolution from the stage of primary narcissism of the infant, characterized by self-love, toward differentiated object relations, where the libido is invested in other people.

During the early stages of his psychoanalytical explorations and speculations, Freud put great emphasis on the pleasure principle, or an inborn tendency to seek pleasure and avoid pain, as

the main regulatory principle governing the psyche. He related
pain and distress to an excess of neuronal stimuli and pleasure to
the discharge of tension and reduction of excitation. The counterpart of the pleasure principle, then, was the reality principle, a
learned function reflecting the demands of the external world and
necessitating delay or postponement of immediate pleasure. In his
later investigations, Freud found it increasingly difficult to reconcile
clinical facts with the exclusive role of the pleasure principle in
psychological processes.

Originally, he considered aggression largely in terms of sadism,
believing that it manifests itself at every level of psychosexual
development in the context of partial instincts. Since aggression
had some clearly nonsexual aspects, he classified it for some time
as an ego instinct. Later he distinguished nonsexual aggression and
the hate that belonged to the ego instincts from the libidinal aspects
of sadism that were clearly related to the sexual instinct. Sadism
itself was then seen as a fusion of sex and aggression due primarily
to frustration of desires.

However, Freud had to face an even more serious problem.
He became aware of the fact that in many instances aggressive
impulses were not serving the purpose of self-preservation and,
therefore, should not be attributed to the ego instincts. This was
quite obvious in the case of the self-destructive tendencies of depressed patients, including suicide, automutilations occurring in
certain mental disorders, self-inflicted injuries among masochistic
individuals, the inexplicable need to suffer manifested by the human
psyche, the repetition compulsion involving self-damaging behavior
or painful consequences, and wanton destructiveness normally occurring in small children.

Consequently, Freud decided to treat aggression as a separate
instinct the source of which was in the skeletal muscles, and the
aim, destruction. This gave the final touch to an essentially negative
image of human nature depicted by psychoanalysis. According to
this view, the psyche is not only driven by base instincts, but it
contains destructiveness as its intrinsic and essential component. In
Freud's earlier writings, aggression was seen as a reaction to frustration and to thwarting of libidinal impulses.

In his late speculations, Freud postulated the existence of two
categories of instincts—those that serve the goal of preserving life
and those that counteract it and tend to return it to an inorganic

condition. He saw a deep relationship between these two groups of instinctual forces and the two opposing trends in the physiological processes of the human organism—anabolism, and catabolism. Anabolic processes are those that contribute to growth, development, and storage of nutriments; catabolic processes are related to the burning of metabolic reserves and to expenditure of energy.

Freud also linked the activity of these drives to the destiny of two groups of cells in the human organism—germinal cells, which are potentially eternal, and regular somatic cells that are mortal. The death instinct operates in the organism from the very beginning, gradually converting it into an inorganic system. This destructive drive can and must be partially diverted from its primary self-destructive aim and be directed against other organisms. It seems to be irrelevant whether the death instinct is oriented toward objects in the external world or against the organism itself, as long as it can achieve its goal, which is to destroy.

Freud's final formulations concerning the role of the death instinct appeared in his last major work, *An Outline of Psychoanalysis* (1964). There the basic dichotomy between two powerful forces, the love instinct (eros) and the death instinct (thanatos), became the cornerstone of his understanding of mental processes—a concept that dominated Freud's thinking in the last years of his life. This major revision of psychonalytic theory generated little enthusiasm among Freud's followers and has never been fully incorporated into mainstream psychoanalysis. Rudolf Brun (1953), who has conducted an extensive statistical review of papers concerned with Freud's theory of the death instinct, found that most of them were clearly unfavorable to Freud's concept. Many of the authors have considered Freud's interest in death and the incorporation of thanatos into the theory of instincts as an alien enclave in the development of his psychological framework. There have also been inferences that intellectual decline in old age and personal factors were the basis for this unexpected dimension in Freud's thinking. His later ideas have been interpreted by some as a result of his own pathological preoccupation with death, his reaction to the cancer that was afflicting him, and the demise of close family members. Brun, in the aforementioned critical study, suggested that Freud's theory of the death instinct was also deeply influenced by his reaction to mass killing during the First World War.

Freud's early topographical theory of the mind, outlined at
the beginning of this century in his *Interpretation of Dreams* (1953b),
was derived from analysis of dreams, of the dynamics of psycho-
neurotic symptoms, and of the psychopathology of everyday life.
It distinguishes three regions of the psyche that are characterized
by their relationship to consciousness—the unconscious, the preconscious, and the conscious. The unconscious contains elements
that are essentially inaccessible to consciousness and can become
conscious only through the preconscious which controls them by
means of psychological censorship. It contains mental representations of instinctual drives that had once been conscious, but were
unacceptable and therefore banned from consciousness and repressed. All the activity of the unconscious is to pursue the pleasure
principle—to seek discharge and wish fulfillment. For this purpose
it uses the primary-process thinking that disregards logical connections, has no conception of time, knows no negatives, and readily
permits contradictions to coexist. It attempts to reach its goals by
means of such mechanisms as condensation, displacement, and
symbolization.

The preconscious contains those elements that, under certain
circumstances, are capable of surfacing into consciousness. It is not
present at birth, but develops in childhood in connection with the
evolution of the ego. It is aimed at avoiding unpleasantness and
delaying instinctual discharge; for this purpose, it uses the second-
ary-process thinking governed by logical analysis and reflecting the
reality principle. One of its important functions is to execute
consorship and to repress instinctual desires. The system—conscious
then, is related to the organs of perception, to controlled motor
activity, and to the regulation of a qualitative distribution of psychic
energy.

This topographical theory encountered serious problems. It
became obvious that the defense mechanisms warding off pain or
unpleasantness were themselves initially not accessible to consciousness; hence the agency of repression could not be identical with
the preconscious. Similarly, the existence of unconscious needs for
punishment contradicted the concept that the moral agency responsible for repression was allied with preconscious forces. In
addition, the unconscious clearly contained some archaic elements
that had never been conscious, such as primordial fantasies of a

phylogenetic nature and certain symbols that could not possibly have been generated by personal experience.

Eventually, Freud replaced the concept of system-conscious and system-unconscious by his famous model of the mental apparatus, which postulated dynamic interplay of three separate structural components of the psyche—id, ego, and superego. Here the id represents a primordial reservoir of instinctual energies that are ego-alien and governed by the primary process. The ego retains its original close connection to consciousness and external reality, yet it performs a variety of unconscious functions, warding off id impulses by specific mechanisms of defense.[3] In addition, it also controls the apparatus of perception and motility. The superego is the youngest of the structural components of the mind; it comes fully into being with the resolution of the Oedipus complex. One of its aspects represents the ego ideal, reflecting the attempt to recover a hypothetical state of narcissistic perfection that existed in early childhood and positive elements of identification with the parents. The other aspect reflects the introjected prohibitions of the parents backed by the castration complex; this is conscience or the "demon." Characteristically, the striving toward masculinity in the boy and femininity in the girl leads to a stronger identification with the superego of the parent of the same sex.

The operations of the superego are mainly unconscious; in addition, Freud noticed that a certain aspect of the superego is savage and cruel, betraying its unmistakable origins in the id. He made it responsible for extreme self-punishment tendencies and self-destructive tendencies observed in certain psychiatric patients. More recent contributions to Freudian theory have emphasized the role in the development of the superego of the drives and object attachments formed in the pre-oedipal period. These pregenital precursors of the superego reflect projections of the child's own sadistic drives and a primitive concept of justice based on retaliation.

Freud's revised model of the mind was associated with a new theory of anxiety, the symptom that represents the fundamental problem of dynamic psychiatry. His first theory of anxiety emphasized its biological basis in the sexual instinct. In the so-called actual neuroses—neurasthenia, hypochondriasis and anxiety neurosis—anxiety was attributed to inadequate discharge of libidinal energies as a result of abnormal sexual practices (abstinence or coitus interruptus) and the consequent lack of appropriate psychic elaboration of sexual tensions.

In psychoneuroses, the interference with normal sexual functioning was due to psychological factors. In this context, anxiety was seen as a product of repressed libido. This theory did not take into consideration the objective anxiety that arises in response to realistic danger. It also involved a disquieting vicious circle in logical reasoning. Anxiety was explained in terms of repression of libidinal impulses; in turn, repression itself was caused by unbearable emotions, which certainly included anxiety.

Freud's new theory of anxiety distinguished real from neurotic anxiety, both of them occurring as a response to danger to the organism. In real anxiety, the danger has a concrete, external source; in neurotic anxiety, the source is not known. In infancy and childhood, anxiety occurs as a result of excessive instinctual stimulation; later it arises in anticipation of danger, rather than as a reaction to it. This signal anxiety mobilizes protective measures—avoidance mechanisms to escape real or imagined danger from without, or psychological defenses to cope with the excess of instinctual excitation. Neuroses then result from partial failure of the defense system; a more complete breakdown of the defenses leads to disorders of psychotic proportions that involve greater distortions of the ego and of the perception of reality.

The psychoanalytical concept of the treatment situation, and of the actual therapeutic technique, shows equally strong influences of the Newtonian-Cartesian mechanistic science as Freudian theory. The basic therapeutic arrangement, with the patient lying on the couch and the invisible, detached therapist sitting behind his or her head, embodies the ideal of the "objective observer." It reflects the deep-seated belief of mechanistic science that one can make scientific observations without interfering with the studied object or process.

The Cartesian dichotomy between mind and body finds its expression in psychoanalytic practice in its exclusive focus on mental processes. The physical manifestations are discussed during the psychoanalytic process as reflections of psychological events or, conversely, as triggers of psychological reactions. However, the technique itself involves no direct physical interventions. There is actually a strong taboo against any physical contact with the patient. Some psychoanalysts have even advised strongly against shaking hands with patients as a potential hazard from the point of view of the transference-countertransference process.

The mind-body split of Freudian psychoanalysis is complemented by a rigorous isolation of the problem from its broader interpersonal, social, and cosmic context. Psychoanalysts typically refuse to interact with, or otherwise include, spouses and other family members and disregard most of the social factors of their cases; further, they are closed to any genuine acknowledgment of transpersonal and spiritual factors in the dynamics of emotional disorders. The dynamic foundations of the observable external phenomena are the instinctual impulses striving for discharge and the various counterforces that inhibit them. The therapeutic efforts of the analyst are focused on eliminating the obstacles that prevent a more direct expression of these forces. In this analysis of resistance, he or she has to rely entirely on verbal tools.

The therapist has the task of reconstructing—from certain given manifestations—the constellation of forces that produced symptoms, allowing these forces to be reenacted in the therapeutic relationship and, by transference analysis, freeing the originally repressed infantile sexual strivings, turning them into adult sexuality and enabling them to participate in the development of the personality.

In a psychoanalytic session, the patient is in a passive, submissive, and highly disadvantageous situation. He or she lies on the couch, does not see the analyst, and is expected to free-associate and not to ask questions. The analyst has total control of the situation, seldom answers questions, chooses to be silent or interpret, and tends to refer to any disagreement as resistance on the part of the patient.[4] The analyst's interpretations, based on Freudian theory, explicitly or implicitly guide the process, keep it within the narrow limits of its conceptual framework, and leave no space for excursions into new territories. The therapist is expected to be uninvolved, objective, impersonal, and unresponsive and to control any indications of "counter-transference."

The patient contributes free associations, but it is the therapist and his or her interpretations that are considered to be instrumental in therapeutic change. The therapist is seen as a mature and healthy individual possessing the necessary knowledge and therapeutic technique. The influence of the medical model in the psychoanalytic situation is thus very strong and clearly discernible in spite of the fact that psychoanalysis represents a psychological, not a medical approach to emotional disorders.

The primary focus of analysis is on the reconstruction of the traumatic past and its repetition in the present transference dynamics; it is thus based on a strictly deterministic, historical model. Freud's understanding of improvement is quite mechanistic—it emphasizes freeing of pent-up energies and their use for constructive purposes (sublimation). The goal of therapy as explicitly described by Freud is indeed modest, particularly in view of the extraordinary investment of time, money, and energy: to "change the extreme suffering of the neurotic into the normal misery of everyday life."

This outline of the basic concepts of classical psychoanalysis and its theoretical and practical vicissitudes provides a basis for considering Freud's contributions in the light of the observations from deep experiential psychotherapy, particularly LSD research. In general, it is possible to say that psychoanalysis appears to be an almost ideal conceptual framework, so long as the sessions focus on the biographical level of the unconscious. If recollective-analytical experiences were the only type of phenomena observed in this context, LSD psychotherapy could be considered to be almost a laboratory proof of the basic psychoanalytic premises.

The psychosexual dynamics and the fundamental conflicts of the human psyche as described by Freud are manifested with unusual clarity and vividness even in sessions of naive subjects who have never been analyzed, have not read psychoanalytic books, and have not been exposed to any other forms of explicit or implicit indoctrination. Under the influence of LSD, such subjects experience regression to childhood and even early infancy, relive various psychosexual traumas and complex sensations related to infantile sexuality, and are confronted with conflicts involving activities in various libidinal zones. They have to face and work through the basic psychological problems described by psychoanalysis, such as the Oedipus or Electra complex, the trauma of weaning, castration anxiety, penis envy, and conflicts around toilet training. The LSD work also confirms the Freudian dynamic cartography of psychoneuroses and psychosomatic disorders and their specific connections with various libidinal zones and stages of ego development.

However, two major revisions must be introduced into the Freudian conceptual framework to account for certain important and common experiences from the biographical level of the unconscious. The first of these is the concept of dynamic governing systems, organizing emotionally relevant memories, for which I have coined the term *COEX systems*. (They have been briefly described in chapter 2; a more detailed discussion can be found in my book *Realms of the Human Unconscious* [1975].) The second revision involves the paramount significance of physical traumas, such as operations, diseases, or injuries, which Freudian psychology has not recognized. Such memories play an important role in the genesis of various emotional and psychosomatic symptoms in their own right, as well as by providing an experiential bridge to corresponding elements of the perinatal level.

However, these are minor problems that could be easily corrected. The fundamental fallacy of psychoanalysis is its exclusive emphasis on biographical events and on the individual unconscious. It tries to generalize its findings, which are highly relevant for one superficial and narrow band of consciousness, to other levels and to the totality of the human psyche. Thus, its major shortcoming is that it has no genuine recognition of the perinatal and transpersonal levels of the unconscious. According to Freud, the etiology and dynamics of emotional disorders is almost entirely explainable from the sequences of postnatal events.

Experiential therapies bring overwhelming evidence that childhood traumas do not represent the primary pathogenic causes, but create conditions for the manifestation of energies and contents from deeper levels of the psyche. The typical symptoms of emotional disorders have a complex multilevel and multidimensional dynamic structure. The biographical layers represent only one component of this complex network; important roots of the problems involved can almost always be found on the perinatal and transpersonal levels.

The incorporation of the perinatal level into the cartography of the unconscious has far-reaching consequences for psychoanalytic theory; it clarifies many of its problems and puts them in a very different perspective without invalidating the Freudian approach as a whole. The shift of emphasis from biographically determined sexual dynamics to the dynamics of the basic perinatal matrices (BPM) without rejecting most of the important findings of psychoanalysis is possible because of the deep experiential similarity between the pattern of biological birth, sexual orgasm, and the physiological activities in the individual erogenous zones (oral, anal, urethral, and phallic). The dynamic connections between these biological functions are graphically represented in table 1, page 103.

The awareness of perinatal dynamics and its incorporation into the cartography of the unconscious provide a simple, elegant, and powerful explanatory model for many phenomena that have represented a crux for the theoretical speculations of Freud and his followers. In the realm of psychopathology, psychoanalysis has failed to provide satisfactory explanations for the phenomena of sado-masochism, automutilation, sadistic murder, and suicide. It did not adequately tackle the puzzle of the savage part of the superego, which seems to be a derivative of the id. The concept of feminine sexuality, or femininity in general, as outlined by Freud represents without doubt the weakest aspect of psychoanalysis and borders on the bizarre and the ridiculous. It lacks any genuine understanding of the female psyche or the feminine principle and treats women essentially as castrated males. Further, psychoanalysis offers only superficial and unconvincing interpretations for an entire spectrum of phenomena occurring in psychiatric patients, a subject that will be taken up at length later.

In terms of a broader application of Freudian thinking to cultural phenomena, we can add its failure to provide a convincing explanation for a number of anthropological and historical observations, such as shamanism, rites of passage, visionary experiences, mystery religions, mystical traditions, wars, genocide, and bloody revolutions. None of these can be adequately understood without the concept of the perinatal (and transpersonal) level of the psyche. The general lack of efficacy of psychoanalysis as a therapeutic tool should also be mentioned as one of the serious shortcomings of this otherwise fascinating system of thought.

On a number of occasions, Freud's genius came quite close to an awareness of the perinatal level of the unconscious. He discussed repeatedly some of its essential elements and many of his formulations dealt, although not explicitly, with problems intimately related to the death-rebirth process. He was the first one to express the idea that the vital anxiety associated with the trauma of birth might represent the deepest source and prototype for all future anxieties. However, he did not pursue this exciting idea any further, nor did he make an attempt to incorporate it into psychoanalysis.

Later, he opposed the speculations of his disciple, Otto Rank (1929), who published a drastic revision of psychoanalysis based on the paramount significance of this fundamental event of human life. In the writings of Freud and his followers, a surprisingly clear line is drawn between the interpretation and evaluation of prenatal, or perinatal, and postnatal events. The material in free associations or dreams that is related to birth or intrauterine existence is consistently called "fantasy" in contrast to material from postnatal time, which is usually seen as possibly reflecting memories of actual events. The exceptions to this rule are Otto Rank (1929), Nandor Fodor (1949), and Lietaert Peerbolte (1975), who have a genuine appreciation and understanding of perinatal and prenatal dynamics.

According to the literature of classic and mainstream psychoanalysis, death has no representation in the unconscious. Fear of death is interpreted alternately as fear of castration, fear of loss of control, fear of a powerful sexual orgasm, or death wishes toward another person, redirected by the relentless superego toward the subject (Fenichel 1945). Freud was never quite satisfied with his thesis that the unconscious or id does not know death, and he found it increasingly difficult to deny the relevance of death for psychology and psychopathology.

In his late formulations, he introduced the death instinct, or thanatos, into his theory as a counterpart at least equipotent to eros or libido. Freud's approach to death does not accurately portray its role in the perinatal dynamics; he was rather far from the insight that, in the context of the death-rebirth process, birth, sex, and death form an inextricable triad and are intimately related to ego death. However, Freud's recognition of the psychological significance of death was quite remarkable; here, as in many other areas, he was clearly far ahead of his followers.

The advantages of the model that includes perinatal dynamics are far-reaching. They not only offer a more adequate and comprehensive interpretation of many psychopathological phenomena and their dynamic interrelations, but they also bind these logically and naturally to anatomical, physiological, and biochemical aspects of the birth process. As I will discuss in detail later, the phenomenon of sadomasochism can be explained fairly easily from the phenomenology of BPM III, with its intimate connections among sex, pain, and aggression. The mixture of sexuality, aggression, anxiety, and scatology, which is another important characteristic of the third perinatal matrix, provides a natural context for the understanding of other sexual deviations and disturbances. On this level, sexuality and anxiety are two facets of the same process and neither can be explained from the other. This throws new light on Freud's frustrating attempts to explain anxiety from repression of libidinal feelings and, in turn, repression from anxiety and other negative emotions.

BPM III is also characterized by an excessive generation of various instinctual impulses with a simultaneous blockage of external motor expression of any kind in the context of an extremely brutal, life-threatening, and painful situation. This appears to be the natural basis for the deepest roots of the Freudian superego, which is cruel, savage, and primitive. Its connection to pain, masochism, self-mutilation, violence, and suicide (ego death) is easily comprehensible and constitutes no puzzle or mystery if seen as an introjection of the merciless impact of the birth canal.

In the context of perinatal dynamics, the concept of *dentate vagina*—female genitals that can kill or castrate—considered by Freud a product of primitive infantile fantasy, represents a realistic assessment based on a specific memory. In the course of delivery, innumerable children have been killed, almost killed, or severely damaged by this potentially murderous organ. The connection of the dentate vagina to castration fears becomes obvious when these can be traced back to their actual source—the memory of the cutting of the umbilical cord. This clarifies the paradox of the occurrence of castration fears in both sexes, as well as the fact that, in their free associations, subjects in psychoanalysis equate castration with death, separation, annihilation, and loss of breath. The image of the dentate vagina thus involves a generalization from an accurate perception. It is this generalization, not the perception itself, that is inappropriate.

The recognition of the perinatal level of the unconscious eliminates a serious logical gap in psychoanalytical thinking that is hard to explain in view of the intellectual acuity of its representatives. According to Freud, his followers, and many theoreticians inspired by him, very early events that occurred during the oral period of the infant's life can have profound influence on later psychological development. This is generally accepted even for influences that are of a relatively subtle nature. Thus, Harry Stack Sullivan (1955) expected the nursing infant to distinguish experiential nuances in the oral erogenous zone, such as a "good," "evil," and "wrong nipple."[5] How, then, could the same organism that is a connoisseur of female nipples possibly have missed experiencing, a few days or weeks earlier, the extreme conditions of delivery—life-threatening anoxia, extreme mechanical pressures, agonizing pain, and a whole spectrum of other alarming signals of vital danger? According to the observations from psychedelic therapy, various biological and psychological subtleties of nursing are of great importance. However, as one could expect from the above, the relevance of the birth trauma is of a far higher order. A certainty about the supply of life-giving oxygen is necessary before one can feel hunger or cold, notice whether the mother is present or absent, or distinguish the nuances of the nursing experience.

Birth and death are events of fundamental relevance that occupy a metaposition in relation to all the other experiences of life. They are the alpha and omega of human existence; a psychological system that does not incorporate them is bound to remain superficial, incomplete, and of limited relevance. The lack of applicability of psychoanalysis to many aspects of psychotic experiences, to a number of anthropological observations, to parapsychological phenomena, and to serious social psychopathology (such as wars and revolutions, totalitarianism, and genocide) reflects the fact that these aspects are characterized by substantial participation of perinatal and transpersonal dynamics and thus are clearly beyond the reach of classical Freudian analysis.

This description of psychoanalysis may not satisfy its contemporary practitioners, since, being limited to classical Freudian concepts, it does not take into consideration important recent developments in the field. In view of this, it is appropriate to touch on the theory and practice of ego psychology. The origins of ego psychology can be found in the writings of Sigmund Freud and Anna Freud. Over the last four decades, its present form was developed by Heinz Hartmann, Ernst Kris, Rudolph Loewenstein, René Spitz, Margaret Mahler, Edith Jacobson, Otto Kernberg, Heinz Kohut, and others (Blanck and Blanck 1965). The basic theoretical modifications of classical psychoanalysis include a sophisticated development of the concept of object relations, an appreciation of their central role in the development of the personality, and a focus on the problems of human adaptation, inborn ego apparatus, conflict-free zones in the psyche, average expectable environment, narcissism, and many others. Ego psychology considerably expands the spectrum of psychoanalytic interests, including, on the one hand, normal human development and, on the other, severe psychopathologies. These theoretical changes have also found their reflection in the therapeutic techniques. Such technical innovations as ego building, drive attenuation, and correction of distortion and structure, made it possible to extend psychotherapeutic work to patients with precarious ego strength and borderline psychotic symptomatology.

As significant as these developments are for psychoanalysis, they share with classical Freudian thought the serious limitation of its narrow biographical orientation. Since they do not recognize the perinatal and transpersonal levels of the psyche, they cannot reach a true comprehension of psychopathology; instead, they spin out refinements of concepts related to a layer of the psyche that is not sufficient for its understanding. Many borderline and psychotic states have significant roots in the negative aspects of perinatal matrices, or in the transpersonal domain.

By the same token, ego psychology cannot conceive of and utilize powerful mechanisms of healing and personality transformation that are available through experiential access to transindividual realms of the psyche. In light of the therapeutic strategies presented in this book, the main problem is not to protect and build up the ego through sophisticated verbal maneuvers, but to create a supportive framework within which it can be experientially transcended. The experience of ego death and the ensuing unitive experiences, both of a symbiotic-biological and transcendental nature, then become the sources of new strength and personal identity. Understanding of concepts and mechanisms of this kind is as far beyond the reach of ego psychology as it was for classical Freudian analysis.

The Famous Renegades: Alfred Adler,
Wilhelm Reich, and Otto Rank

Freud's epoch-making discoveries in the field of depth psychology attracted a small group of brilliant researchers and thinkers who became members of his Viennese inner circle. Because of the complexity and novelty of the subject, as well as the intellectual independence of some of Freud's best disciples, the psychoanalytic movement was from the very beginning fraught with controversy and dissent. Over the years, several of Freud's prominent followers chose to leave the movement, or were forced to leave it, and founded their own schools. It is interesting that many elements of the conceptual framework presented here were contained in the revisions of these famous renegades. However, they were presented as mutually exclusive alternatives and have not been integrated into mainstream psychoanalysis or academic psychology. Instead of following the actual historical sequence of events, I will discuss these theoretical and practical departures from classical psychoanalysis with respect to the level of consciousness that was their main focus.

Alfred Adler's individual psychology (1932) remained limited to the biographical level, as Freudian psychoanalysis, but its focus differed. In contrast with Freud's deterministic emphasis, Adler's approach was clearly teleological and finalistic. Freud explored historical and causal aspects of the pathogenesis of neurosis and other mental phenomena, whereas Adler was interested in their purpose and final goal. According to him, the guiding principle of every neurosis is the imaginary aim to be a "complete man." The sexual drives and the tendencies toward sexual perversions of various kinds, emphasized by Freud, are only secondary expressions of this guiding principle. The preponderance of sexual material in the fantasy life of the neurotic is simply jargon, a *modus dicendi*, expressing strivings toward the masculine goal. This drive for superiority, totality, and perfection reflects a deep need to compensate for all-pervasive feelings of inferiority and inadequacy.

Adler's individual psychology puts great stress, in the dynamics of neurosis, on the "constitutional inferiority" of some organs or systems of organs, which can be morphological or functional. The striving for superiority and success follows a strictly subjective pattern. It is based on one's self-perception and self-esteem and the methods it uses for its achievement reflect the circumstances of one's life, particularly one's biological endowment and early childhood environment. Adler's concept of inferiority is broader than it appears at first sight; it includes, among other elements, insecurity and anxiety. Similarly, the striving for superiority is in the last analysis striving for perfection and completion and implies also a search for meaning in life. A deeper, hidden dimension behind the inferiority complex is the memory of the infantile helplessness, and at its bottom is impotence in view of the dictate of death. The inferiority complex can lead through the mechanism of overcompensation to superior performance and in the extremes create a genius. Adler's favorite example was a stammering boy with a tick, Demosthenes, who became the most powerful orator of all time. In less fortunate cases, this mechanism can create a neurosis.

In contrast to Freud's image of the human being as fragmented and driven by his past, Adler's concept depicts an organic, purposeful system with the goal of self-realization and social survival. The individual and his survival must be understood in terms of dynamically interwoven, somatic, psychological and social processes. The individual's need for integration into the social milieu, and for differentiation from it, results in a pattern of active adaptation. The growing child selects from its complex history a consistent and coherent life style. According to Adler, conscious and unconscious processes are not in conflict; they represent two aspects of a unified system serving the same purpose. Events that do not fit into it are considered unimportant and are forgotten. We are unaware of thoughts and feelings that painfully contradict our self-concept. The problem is not that human beings are pawns of historically codetermined forces of their unconscious, but that they are unaware of the goals and values that they themselves have created or accepted.

Adler puts great emphasis on social feelings as an important criterion for mental health; a healthy lifestyle is oriented toward achieving competence and social success by working toward the goal of social usefulness. The concept of normal development includes a unique, self-consistent, active, and creative life style, striving for a subjectively conceived goal, innate social interests, and a capacity for social living.

A neurotic disposition is created by a childhood history of overprotection or neglect, or both. This is conducive to a negative self-concept, a sense of helplessness, and an image of the social environment as basically unfriendly, hostile, punishing, depriving, demanding, or frustrating. As a result, the insecure individual develops a manipulative, self-centered and uncooperative private life style, rather than one that reflects common sense and is integrated with societal interests. Adler has discussed extensively the different forms and manifestations of "private logic"—that of neurotics, psychotics, addicts, and criminals. In general, he was always more interested in the observation and description of the unique individual than in diagnostic categories and clinical classifications. According to him, a neurotic cannot cope with problems and enjoy social life, because he has developed as a result of childhood experiences a complex private map that has a primarily protective function. It has an inner cohesion and is resistant to change, because it represents the only adaptive pattern the person has been able to construct. The individual is afraid of facing new corrective experiences and continues to view a variety of highly idiosyncratic and faulty assumptions about people and the world as accurate and generally valid. While a neurotic suffers a sense of real or imaginary failure, the psychotic does not accept social reality as the ultimate criterion, but instead resorts to a private world of fantasies that compensate for his sense of hopelessness and despair for not having achieved significance in the real world.

In his therapeutic practice, Adler greatly emphasized the active role of the therapist. He interpreted the society to the patient, analyzed his life style and goals, suggested specific modifications, gave encouragement, instilled hope, restored the patient's faith in himself, and helped him to realize his strength and ability. He considered the therapist's understanding of the patient to be essential for successful reconstruction of the patient: the patient's insight into his motivations, intentions, and goals was not a prerequisite for therapeutic change. Adler saw the Freudian concept of transference as erroneous and misleading, as an unnecessary obstacle to therapeutic progress. He emphasized that the therapist should be warm, trustworthy, reliable, and interested in the patient's well-being in the here and now.

The observations from LSD work and other experiential approaches bring an interesting new perspective and insight into the theoretical conflict between Adler and Freud. In general, this controversy is based on the erroneous belief that the complexity of the psyche can be reduced to some simple fundamental principles. This cornerstone of mechanistic science is now being abandoned even in physics, in relation to material reality, as exemplified by Geoffrey Chew's "bootstrap" philosophy of nature (1968). The human mind is so complex that many different theories can be constructed, all of which appear to be logical, coherent, and reflective of certain major observations, yet at the same time are mutually incompatible or actually contradict each other. More specifically, the disagreements between psychoanalysis and individual psychology reflect a lack of awareness of the spectrum of consciousness with its different levels. In this sense, both systems are incomplete and superficial, since they operate exclusively on the biographical level and do not acknowledge the perinatal and transpersonal realms. Projections of various elements from these neglected areas of the psyche, then, appear in both systems in a distorted and diluted form.

The conflict between the emphasis on the sexual drive and on the will to power and masculine protest appears to be important and irreconcilable only as long as one's knowledge of the psyche is limited to the biographical level, excluding the dynamics of the perinatal matrices. As has already been described, intense sexual arousal (including oral, anal, urethral, and genital components) and feelings of helplessness alternating with attempts at aggressive self-assertion represent integral and inseparable aspects of the dynamics of BPM III. Although in respect to the death-rebirth process, there may, temporarily, be more emphasis on the sexual aspect or the power aspect of the perinatal unfolding, the two are inextricably interwoven. The study of the sexual profile of men in power (Janus, Bess, and Saltus 1977), discussed elsewhere (pp. 218–19) can be mentioned here as an important example.

The deep roots of sexual pathology can be found in the third perinatal matrix, where strong libidinal arousal is associated with vital anxiety, pain, aggression, and the encounter with biological material. Feelings of inadequacy, inferiority, and low self-esteem can be traced beyond the biographical conditioning in early childhood to the helplessness of the child in the life-threatening and overpowering situation of birth. Thus, both Freud and Adler, because of an insufficient depth of their approach, focused selectively on two categories of psychological forces that on a deeper level represent two facets of the same process.

The awareness of death, the crucial theme of the perinatal process, had a powerful impact on both researchers. Freud postulated in his final theoretical formulations the existence of the death instinct as a decisive force in the psyche. His biological emphasis prevented him from seeing the possibility of psychological transcendence of death, and he created a gloomy and pessimistic image of human existence. The theme of death played also an important role in his personal life, since he suffered from a severe thanatophobia. Adler's life and work were also very strongly influenced by the problem of death. He saw the inability to prevent and control death as the deepest core of the feelings of inadequacy. It is interesting in this connection that Adler was aware that his decision to become a physician—a member of the profession trying to control and conquer death—was deeply influenced by his near-death experience at the age of five. It is likely that the same factor also functioned as a prism that shaped the form of his theoretical speculations.

From the viewpoint of observations from deep experiential therapy, determined striving for external goals and the pursuit of success in the world are of little value in overcoming the feelings of inadequacy and low self-esteem, no matter what the actual outcome of these endeavors turns out to be. The feelings of inferiority cannot be resolved by mobilizing one's forces to over-compensate for them, but by confronting them experientially and surrendering to them. They are then consumed in the process of ego death and rebirth, and a new self-image emerges from the awareness of one's cosmic identity. True courage lies in the willingness to undergo this awesome process of self-confrontation, not in a heroic pursuit of external goals. Unless the individual succeeds in finding his or her true identity within, any attempts to give meaning to life by manipulating the outside world and external achievement will be a futile and ultimately self-defeating, quixotic crusade.

Another important psychoanalytic renegade was the Austrian psychiatrist and political activist, Wilhelm Reich. Maintaining Freud's main thesis concerning the paramount importance of sexual factors in the etiology of neuroses, he modified his concepts substantially by emphasizing "sex economy"—the balance between energy charge and discharge, or sexual excitement and release. According to Reich, the suppression of sexual feelings together with the characterological attitude that accompanies it constitutes the true neurosis; the clinical symptoms are only its overt manifestations. The original traumas and sexual feelings are held in repression by complex patterns of chronic muscular tensions—the "character armor." The term "armoring" refers to the function of protecting the individual against painful and threatening experiences from without and within. For Reich, the critical factor that contributed to incomplete sexual orgasm and congestion of bioenergy was the repressive influence of society. A neurotic individual maintains balance by binding his excess energy in muscular tensions, in this way limiting sexual excitement. A healthy individual does not have such a limitation; his or her energy is not bound in muscular armoring and can flow freely.

Reich's contribution to therapy (1949) is of great significance and lasting value. His dissatisfaction with the methods of psychoanalysis led him to the development of a system called "character analysis" and, later, "character analytic vegetotherapy." It was a radical departure from classical Freudian techniques, since it concentrated on the treatment of neuroses from a biophysical point of view and involved physiological elements. Reich used hyperventilation, a variety of body manipulations, and direct physical contact to mobilize the jammed energies and remove the blocks. According to him, the goal of therapy was the patient's capacity to surrender fully to the spontaneous and involuntary movements of the body that are normally associated with the respiratory process. If this was accomplished, the respiratory waves produced an undulating movement of the body that Reich called the "orgasm reflex." He believed that those patients who achieve it in therapy are then capable of surrendering fully in the sexual situation, reaching a state of total satisfaction. The full orgasm discharges all the excess energy of the organism, and the patient remains free of symptoms.

As he was developing his theories and trying to implement his ideas, Reich became increasingly controversial. Seeing the repressive role of society as one of the main factors in emotional disorders, he combined his innovative work in psychotherapy with radical political activity as a member of the Communist Party. This resulted eventually in his break with both the psychoanalytic circles and the Communist movement. After Reich's conflict with Freud, his name was dropped from the roster of the International Psychoanalytic Association. The publication of his fierce criticism of the mass psychology of fascism led to his excommunication from the Communist Party. In later years, Reich became increasingly convinced about the existence of a primordial cosmic energy that is the source of three large realms of existence, which arise from it through a complicated process of differentiation—mechanical energy, inorganic mass, and living matter (1973). This energy that Reich called *orgone* can be demonstrated visually, thermically, electroscopically, and by means of Geiger-Mueller counters. It is different from electromagnetic energy, and one of its main properties is pulsation. According to Reich, the dynamics of orgone and the relationship between "mass-free orgone energy" and "orgone energy that has become matter" is essential for any true functional understanding of the universe, nature, and the human psyche. The streaming of orgone and its dynamic superimpositions can explain as diverse phenomena as the creation of subatomic particles, the origin of life forms, growth, locomotion, sexual activity and the reproductive processes, psychological phenomena, tornadoes, the aurora borealis, and the formation of galaxies.

Reich designed special orgone accumulators, boxes that he claimed collected and concentrated orgone for use for therapeutic purposes. Orgone therapy is based on the assumption that the soma and psyche are both rooted bioenergetically in the pulsating pleasure system (blood and vegetative apparatus); it addresses itself to this common source of psychological and somatic functions. Orgone therapy is, therefore, neither a psychological nor a physiological-chemical therapy, but rather a biological therapy dealing with disturbances of pulsation in the autonomic system. Wilhelm Reich's work, which began originally as highly innovative therapeutic experimentation, moved gradually into increasingly remote areas— physics, biology, cellular biopathy, abiogenesis, meteorology, astronomy, and philosophical speculations. The end of his stormy scientific career was tragic. Because he used, and advocated the use of, orgone generators, which were denounced by the Food and Drug Administration, he got into serious conflicts with the U.S. Government. After a series of harrassments, he was twice imprisoned, and finally died in jail from a heart attack.

From the point of view of the concepts presented in this book, Reich's major contribution seems to be in the areas of bioenergetic processes and the psychosomatic correlations in the genesis of emotional disorders, and in their therapy. He was fully aware of the enormous energies underlying neurotic symptoms and of the futility of purely verbal approaches to them. Also, his understanding of armoring and the role of musculature in neuroses is a contribution of lasting value. The observations from LSD work confirm

the basic Reichian concepts of energetic stasis and involvement of
the muscular and the vegetative systems in neurosis. A patient's
experiential confrontation of his or her psychological problems is
typically accompanied by violent tremors, shaking, jerks, contortions, prolonged maintaining of extreme postures, grimacing, ut-
tering sounds, and even occasional vomiting. It is quite clear that
psychological aspects of the process, such as perceptual, emotional,
and ideational elements, and dramatic physiological manifestations
are intimately interconnected, representing two sides of the same
process. The basic difference between my own point of view and
the Reichian theory lies in the interpretation of this process.

Wilhelm Reich put great emphasis on the gradual accumulation
and congestion of sexual energy in the organism due to interference
of societal influences with full sexual orgasm (1961). As a result
of repeated incomplete discharge, the libido jams in the organism
and finally finds deviant expressions in a variety of psychopathological phenomena, from psychoneuroses to sadomasochism. Effective therapy, then, requires release of pent-up libidinal energies,
dissolution of the "body armor," and achievement of total orgasm.
LSD observations indicate clearly that this energetic reservoir is
not a result of chronic sexual stasis resulting from incomplete
orgasms. Much of this energy seems, rather, to represent powerful
forces from the perinatal level of the unconscious. The energies
released during therapy can best be understood in terms of a
belated discharge of the excessive neuronal excitation generated
by the stress, pain, fear, and suffocation in the course of the
biological birth process. The deepest basis of much of the character
armor seems to be in the introjected dynamic conflict between the
flood of neuronal overstimulation associated with the birth process
and the unrelenting straitjacket of the birth canal, preventing
adequate response and peripheral discharge. The dissolution of the
armor coincides to a great extent with the completion of the death-
rebirth process; however, some of its elements have even deeper
roots in the transpersonal realms.

Perinatal energy can be mistaken for jammed libido because
BPM III has a substantial sexual component and because of the
similarity between the pattern of birth and sexual orgasm. Activated
perinatal energy seeks peripheral discharge, and the genitals represent one of the most logical and important channels. This seems
to form the basis for a vicious circle: aggression, fear, and guilt

associated with the third perinatal matrix interfere with full orgastic ability; conversely, the absence or incompleteness of sexual orgasm blocks an important safety valve for the birth energies. The situation thus seems to be the opposite of what Reich postulated. It is not that societal and psychological factors interfering with full orgasm lead to accumulation and stasis of sexual energy, but that deep-seated perinatal energies interfere with adequate orgasm and create psychological and interpersonal problems. To rectify this situation, these powerful energies must be discharged in a nonsexual, therapeutic context and reduced to a level that the patient and the partner can comfortably handle in a sexual context. Many phenomena discussed by Reich, from sadomasochism to the mass psychology of fascism, can be explained more adequately from perinatal dynamics than from incomplete orgasm and the jamming of sexual energy.

Reich's speculations, although unconventional and at times undisciplined, are in their essence frequently compatible with modern developments in science. In his understanding of nature, he came close to the world view suggested by quantum-relativistic physics, emphasizing the underlying unity, focusing on process and movement rather than substance and solid structure, and acknowledging the active role of the observer (1972). Reich's ideas about the joint origin of inorganic matter, life, consciousness, and knowledge are occasionally reminiscent of the philosophical speculations of David Bohm (1980). His arguments against the universal validity of the principle of entropy and the second law of thermodynamics essentially resemble the conclusions of the careful and systematic work of Prigogine (1980) and his colleagues.

In the field of psychology, Reich came close, both theoretically and practically, to the discovery of the perinatal realm of the unconscious. His work on muscular armoring, his discussion of the dangers of sudden removal of the armor, and his concept of total orgasm clearly involve important elements of perinatal dynamics. However, he showed determined resistance to its most critical elements—the psychological significance of the experiences of birth and death. This is evident from his passionate defense of the primary role of genitality and his rejection of Rank's concept of the birth trauma, Freud's speculations about death, and Abraham's assumptions of a psychological need for punishment.

In many ways, Reich teetered on the edge of transpersonal understanding. He was obviously close to cosmic awareness, which found its expression in his speculations about the orgone. True religion for him was unarmored oceanic merging with the dynamics of the universal orgone energy. In sharp contrast with perennial philosophy, Reich's understanding of this cosmic energy was quite concrete; orgone was measurable and had specific physical characteristics. Reich never reached a true understanding and appreciation of the great spiritual philosophies of the world. In his passionate critical excursions against spirituality, he tended to confuse mysticism with certain superficial and distorted versions of mainstream religious doctrines. In his polemics (1972), he thus argued against literal belief in devils with tails and pitchforks, winged angels, formless blue-gray ghosts, dangerous monsters, heavens, and hells. He then discounted these as projections of unnatural, distorted organ sensations and, in the last analysis, as misperceptions of the universal flow of the orgone energy. Similarly, Reich was also strongly opposed to Jung's interest in mysticism and his tendency to spiritualize psychology.

For Reich, mystical inclinations reflected armoring and serious distortion of orgone economy. Mystical search, then, could be reduced to misunderstood biological urges. Thus: "Fear of death and dying is identical with unconscious orgasm, anxiety and the alleged death instinct. The longing for dissolution, for nothingness, is unconscious longing for orgastic release" (Reich 1961). "God is the representation of the natural life forces, of the bioenergy in man, and is nowhere so clearly expressed as in the sexual orgasm. Devil then is the representation for the armoring that leads to perversion and distortion of these life forces" (Reich 1972). In direct contrast with psychedelic observations, Reich claimed that the mystical experiences disappear if therapy succeeds in dissolving the armor. In his opinion, "Orgastic potency is not found among mystics any more than mysticism is found among the orgastically potent" (Reich 1961).

The system of psychology and psychotherapy developed by Otto Rank represents a considerable departure from mainstream Freudian psychoanalysis. In general, Rank's concepts are humanistic and voluntaristic, while Freud's approach is reductionistic, mechanistic, and deterministic. More specifically, the major areas of disagreement were Rank's emphasis on the paramount significance of the birth trauma as compared to sexual dynamics, negation of the crucial role of the Oedipus complex, and a concept of ego as an autonomous representative of the will rather than a slave of the id. Rank also offered modifications of the psychoanalytic technique that were as radical and drastic as his theoretical contributions. He suggested that a verbal approach to psychotherapy is of limited value and the emphasis should be experiential. According to him, it was essential that the patient relive in therapy the trauma of birth; without it, treatment should not be considered complete.[6]

As far as the role of the birth trauma in psychology is concerned, Freud was actually the first to draw attention to the possibility that it might be the prototype and source of all future anxieties. He discussed this issue in several of his writings, but refused to accept Rank's extreme formulations. There was also a major difference in the concepts of the birth trauma as seen by Freud and Rank. While Freud emphasized the extreme physiological difficulties involved in the birth process as being the source of anxiety, Rank related anxiety to the separation from the maternal womb as a paradisean situation of unconditional and effortless gratification.

Rank saw the trauma of birth as the ultimate cause responsible for the fact that separation is the most painful and frightening human experience. According to him, all later frustrations of partial drives can be seen as derivatives of this primal trauma. Most of the events experienced by the individual as traumatic derive their pathogenic power from their similarity to biological birth. The entire period of childhood can be seen as a series of attempts at abreacting and mastering psychologically this fundamental trauma. Infantile sexuality can be reinterpreted as the child's desire to return to the womb, the anxiety associated with it, and curiosity about where he or she came from.

But Rank did not stop here; he believed that all human mental life has its origin in the primal anxiety and primal repression precipitated by the birth trauma. The central human conflict consists of the desire to return to the womb and in the fear of this wish. As a result of it, any change from a pleasurable situation to an unpleasant one will give rise to feelings of anxiety. Rank also offered an alternative to the Freudian interpretation of dreams. Sleep is a condition that resembles the intrauterine life, and dreams can be understood as attempts to relive the birth trauma and return to the prenatal state. Even more than the act of sleep itself, they represent a psychological return to the womb. The analysis of dreams provides the strongest support for the psychological significance of the birth trauma. Similarly, the cornerstone of Freudian theory, the Oedipus complex, is reinterpreted with the emphasis on the trauma of birth and the desire to return to the womb. At the core of the Oedipus myth is the mystery of the origin of man that Oedipus tries to solve by returning to the mother's womb. This happens not only literally, in the act of marriage and sexual union with his mother, but symbolically through his blindness and disappearance into the cleft rock leading into the Underworld.

In Rankian psychology, the birth trauma also plays a crucial role in sexuality; its importance is based on the deep desire to return to the intrauterine existence that governs the human psyche. Much of the difference between the sexes can be explained by women's ability to replay through their bodies the reproductive process and find their immortality in procreation, whereas for men sex represents mortality and their strength lies in nonsexual creativity.

Analyzing human culture, Rank found the birth trauma to be a powerful psychological force behind religion, art, and history. Every form of religion tends ultimately toward the reinstitution of the original succoring and protecting primal situation of the symbiotic union in the womb. The deepest root of art is the "autoplastic imitation" of one's own growing and origin from the maternal vessel. Art, being a representation of reality and at the same time a denial of it, is a particularly powerful means of coping with the primal trauma. The history of human dwellings, from the search for primitive shelters to elaborate architectural structures, reflects instinctive memories of the warm, protective womb. The use of implements and weapons is, in the last analysis, based on an "insatiable tendency to force one's way completely into the mother."

LSD psychotherapy and other forms of deep experiential work have brought strong support for Rank's general thesis about the paramount psychological significance of the birth trauma. However, substantial modifications of the Rankian approach are necessary to increase its compatibility with actual clinical observations. Rank's theory focuses on the element of separation from the mother and loss of the womb as the essential traumatic aspects of birth. For him the trauma consists in the fact that the postnatal situation is far less favorable than the prenatal one. Outside the womb, the child has to face irregularity of food supply, absence of the mother, oscillations of temperature, and loud noises. He or she has to breathe, swallow food, and dispose of the waste products.

In the LSD work the situation appears much more complicated. Birth is not traumatic just because the child is transferred from the paradisean situation of the womb into the adverse conditions of the external world; the passage through the birth canal itself entails enormous emotional and physical stress and pain. This fact was emphasized in Freud's original speculations about birth, but almost entirely neglected by Rank. In a sense, Rank's concept of the birth trauma applied to the situation of a person born by elective Cesarean section rather than physiological childbirth.

However, most of the psychopathological conditions are rooted in the dynamics of BPM II and BPM III, which reflect experiences undergone during the hours inserted between the undisturbed intrauterine state and the postnatal existence in the external world. In the process of reliving and integrating the birth trauma, the individual can be craving a return to the womb or, conversely, completion of birth and emergence from the birth canal, depending on the stage of perinatal unfolding. The tendency to externalize and discharge the pent-up feelings and energies generated during the birth struggle represents a deep motivational force for a broad spectrum of human behaviors. This is especially true for aggression and sadomasochism, two conditions for which the Rankian interpretation was particularly unconvincing. In addition—as with Freud, Adler, and Reich—Rank misses a genuine understanding of the transpersonal realms. In spite of all these shortcomings, Rank's discovery of the psychological relevance of the birth trauma and its many ramifications was a truly remarkable achievement that preceded the LSD findings by several decades.

It is interesting to note that several other psychoanalytic researchers recognized the significance of various aspects of the birth trauma. Nandor Fodor, in his pioneering book *The Search For The Beloved* (1949), described in considerable detail the relations between various facets of the birth process and many important psychopathological symptoms in a way that has far-reaching congruence with the LSD observations. Lietaert Peerbolte produced a comprehensive book, *Prenatal Dynamics* (1975), in which he discussed in great detail his unique insights into the psychological relevance of prenatal existence and the birth experience. This topic also received a great deal of attention in a series of original and imaginative, although more speculative and less clinically grounded, books by Francis Mott (1948; 1959).

The list of famous psychoanalytic renegades would be incomplete without Carl Gustav Jung, who was one of Freud's favorite disciples and the designated "crown prince" of psychoanalysis. Jung's revisions were by far the most radical, and his contributions were truly revolutionary. It is not an exaggeration to say that his work moved psychiatry as far beyond Freud as Freud's discoveries were ahead of his own time.

Jung's analytical psychology is not just a variety or modification of psychoanalysis; it represents an entirely new concept of depth psychology and psychotherapy. Jung was well aware that his findings could not be reconciled with Cartesian-Newtonian thinking, and that they required a drastic revision of the most fundamental philosophical assumptions of Western science. He was deeply interested in the revolutionary developments of quantum-relativistic physics and had fruitful exchanges with some of its founders.

Unlike the rest of the theoreticians of psychoanalysis, Jung also had a genuine understanding of the mystical traditions and great respect for the spiritual dimensions of the psyche and of human existence. His ideas are much closer to the conceptual system I am presenting here than those of any other school of Western psychotherapy. Jung was the first transpersonal psychologist, without calling himself one, and his contributions will be taken up in the section on the transpersonal approaches to psychotherapy.

It seems logical to conclude this exposition of the world of psychotherapy by mentioning another prominent pioneer and member of the inner circle of Freud's Viennese group, Sandor Ferenczi. Although he is not usually listed among the renegades of psychoanalysis, his speculations took him far beyond traditional analysis. Also, his support of Otto Rank clearly indicated that he was far from a conforming and docile follower of Freud. In his theoretical framework, he considered seriously not only perinatal and prenatal events, but also elements of phylogenetic development. Being one of the few disciples of Freud who immediately accepted his concept of thanatos, Ferenczi also integrated into his conceptual system a metaphysical analysis of death.

In his remarkable essay, "Thalassa" (1938), Ferenczi described the entire sexual evolution as an attempt to return to the maternal womb. According to him, in sexual intercourse the interacting organisms share in the gratification of the germ cells. Men have the privilege of penetrating the maternal organism directly and in a real sense, while women entertain fantasy substitutes or identify with their children when they are pregnant. This is the essence of the "Thalassa regressive trend," the striving to return to the original aquatic mode of existence that had been abandoned in primeval times. In the last analysis, the amniotic fluid represents the water of the ocean introjected into the maternal womb. According to this view, terrestrial mammals have a deep organismic craving to reverse the decision they once made when they left their oceanic existence and opted for a new form of existence. This would be the solution actually carried out millions of years ago by the ancestors of today's whales and dolphins.

However, the ultimate goal of all life might be to arrive at a state characterized by the absence of irritability and, finally, to the inertness of the inorganic world. It is possible that death and dying are not absolute and that germs of life and regressive tendencies lie hidden even within inorganic matter. One could then conceive of the entire organic and inorganic world as a system of perpetual oscillations between the will to live and the will to die, in which an absolute hegemony on the part of either life or death is never attained. Ferenczi thus clearly came close to the concepts of perennial philosophy and mysticism, although his formulations were expressed in the language of the natural sciences.

A historical review of the conceptual disagreements in the early psychoanalytic movement is of great interest from the point of view of the ideas presented in this volume. It demonstrates clearly that many of the concepts that may at first sight appear surprisingly new and without precedent in Western psychology were in one form or another seriously considered and passionately discussed by the early pioneers of psychoanalysis. The major contribution of this book is thus a re-evaluation of the various approaches in light of the findings of modern consciousness research and their integration and synthesis in the spirit of spectrum psychology, rather than an entirely original system of thought.

Existential and Humanistic Psychotherapies

By the middle of the twentieth century, American psychiatry and psychology were dominated by two influential theories, psychoanalysis and behaviorism. However, an increasing number of prominent clinicians, researchers, and thinkers felt deeply dissatisfied with the mechanistic orientation of these two schools. The external expression of this trend was the introduction of existential psychotherapy by Rollo May (1958) and the development of humanistic psychology. Since both existential and humanistic psychology emphasize the freedom and importance of individual human beings, there has been a considerable overlapping between the two orientations. These two movements are of great interest from the point of view of our discussion, since they represent a bridge between mainstream academic psychotherapy and the views presented in this book.

Existential psychotherapy has its historical roots in the philosophy of Søren Kierkegaard and the phenomenology of Edmund Husserl. It emphasizes that each individual person is unique and inexplicable in terms of any scientific or philosophical system. The individual has freedom of choice, which makes his or her future unpredictable and a source of anxiety. A central theme in existential philosophy is the inevitability of death. This fact found the most articulate expression in Martin Heidegger's *Sein und Zeit* (1927). According to his description, human beings are cast into an unfriendly world, desperately trying to achieve goals, the relevance of which will be mercilessly annihilated by death. They might try to avoid the thought of this final destiny by living in a superficial and conventional way; however, this gives life an inauthentic quality. The only way to be true to oneself is to be constantly aware of one's eventual death.

It is impossible to review here the vast, complex, and often contradictory writings of existential philosophers and psychotherapists. However, there is no doubt that this orientation is closely associated with perinatal dynamics. Individuals who are under the psychological influence of BPM II typically experience a deep confrontation with death, mortality, and impermanence of material existence. This is accompanied by a deep existential crisis—a sense of the meaninglessness and absurdity of life and a desperate search for meaning. From this vantage point, all the subject's life in the past appears to have been unauthentic—a "treadmill" or "rat-race" type of existence—and characterized by futile attempts to deny the ultimate inescapability of death. Existential philosophy thus offers a powerful and accurate description of one aspect of the perinatal level of consciousness.[7] The major mistake of the existential approach is that it generalizes its observations and presents them as universally valid insights about the human condition. From the point of view of deep experiential work, the existential approach is limited to the perinatal level of consciousness and loses its relevance with the experience of ego death and transcendence.

Viktor Frankl's existential analysis, or logotherapy (1956) is an approach that puts great emphasis on the sense of meaning in life. Although Frankl does not specifically recognize perinatal dynamics and the twin problems of birth and death that it entails, it is significant that the development of his system of therapy was deeply influenced by his drastic experiences in a concentration camp (1962). The extreme suffering of the inmates of concentration camps is a characteristic perinatal theme, and so is the search for meaning. However, the resolution of this search that occurs in the context of the death-rebirth process is quite different from the one suggested by Frankl. Rather than an intellectual fabrication of a meaningful goal in life, it involves an experiential embrace of a philosophical and spiritual way of being in the world that appreciates the life process as it is.

Ultimately, one cannot justify life and find meaning in it by intellectual analysis and the use of logic. One must reach a state in which he or she experiences emotionally and biologically that it is worthwhile to be alive and feels active excitement about the fact of existence. Agonizing philosophical preoccupation with the problem of the meaning of life, instead of being a legitimate philosophical issue, should be seen as a symptom indicating that the dynamic flow of the life process has been obstructed and blocked. The only effective solution of this problem is to be found not in the invention of contrived life goals, but in a profound inner transformation and shift in consciousness that reinstates the flow of vital energy. A person who is actively engaged in the life process and experiences zest and joy will never question whether life has any meaning. In this state, existence appears to be precious and miraculous, and its value is self-evident.

The dissatisfaction with the mechanistic and reductionistic orientation of American psychology and psychotherapy found its most powerful expression in the development of humanistic and, later, transpersonal psychology. The most outstanding representative and articulate spokesman of this opposition was Abraham Maslow (1962; 1964; 1969). His penetrating critique of psychoanalysis and behaviorism became a powerful impetus for the movement and provided a focus for the crystalization of new ideas. Maslow rejected Freud's grim and pessimistic view of humanity as hopelessly dominated by base instincts. According to Freud, such phenomena as love, appreciation of beauty, or sense of justice are interpreted either as sublimation of low instincts or as a reaction formation against them. All higher forms of behavior are seen as acquired or imposed on the individual and not as natural to the human condition. Maslow also disagreed with Freud's exclusive concentration on the study of neurotic and psychotic populations. He pointed out that focusing on the worst in humanity instead of the best results in a distorted image of human nature. This approach leaves out man's aspirations, his realizable hopes, his godlike qualities.

Maslow's criticism of behaviorism was equally incisive and determined. In his opinion, it was erroneous to see humans simply as complex animals responding blindly to environmental stimuli. The behaviorist's heavy reliance on animal experimentation is highly problematic and of limited value. Such studies can provide information about those characteristics that humans share with other animal species, but are useless as an approach to specifically human qualities. The exclusive focus on animals guarantees neglect of those aspects and elements that are uniquely human—conscience, guilt, idealism, spirituality, patriotism, art, or science. The mechanistic approach exemplified by behaviorism can at best be seen as a strategy for certain kinds of research, but it is too narrow and limited to qualify as a general or comprehensive philosophy.

While behaviorism focused almost exclusively on external influences, and psychoanalysis on introspective data, Maslow advocated that psychology should combine objective observations with introspection. He emphasized the use of human data as a source for human psychology, and his special contribution was the focus on psychologically healthy and self-actualizing individuals, the "growing tip" of the population. In a comprehensive study of subjects who have had spontaneous mystical states ("peak experiences"), Maslow (1962) demonstrated that such experiences should be considered supernormal rather than pathological phenomena, and that they are associated with a tendency toward self-realization. Another important contribution was Maslow's concept of "metavalues" and "metamotivations." In sharp contrast with Freud, Maslow (1969) believed that human beings have an innate hierarchy of higher values and needs, as well as corresponding tendencies to pursue them.

Maslow's ideas were among the most important influences shaping the development of humanistic psychology, or the Third Force as he called it. The new movement emphasized the central significance of human beings as subjects for study and of human objectives as criteria for determining the value of research findings. It put a high value on personal freedom and the ability of the individual to predict and control his or her own life. This was in direct contrast with behaviorism in which the objective is to predict and control the behavior of other people. The humanistic approach is holistic; it studies individuals as unified organisms, rather than as merely a sum total of separate parts.

Humanistic psychotherapies are based on the assumption that humanity has become too intellectual, technologized, and detached from sensations and emotions. The therapeutic approaches of humanistic psychology are designed as corrective experiential procedures to remedy the resulting alienation and dehumanization. They emphasize experiential, nonverbal, and physical means of personality change and aim for individual growth or self-actualization, rather than adjustment. Humanistic psychology provided a broad umbrella for the development of new therapies and the rediscovery of some old techniques that overcome to various degrees the limitations and shortcomings of traditional psychotherapy.

The humanistic approaches represent an important step toward a holistic understanding of human nature, as compared to the one-sided emphasis on either body or psyche characterizing mainstream psychology and psychiatry. Another significant aspect of humanistic psychotherapy is a shift from intrapsychic or intraorganismic orientation to the recognition of interpersonal relations, family interaction, social networks, and sociocultural influences and the introduction of economic, ecological, and political considerations. The spectrum of humanistic therapies is broad and so rich that it is impossible here to do much more than name and briefly define the most important techniques.

The physical emphasis of the human potential movement was deeply influenced by Wilhelm Reich, who first used body work in the analysis of character neuroses. The most important of the neo-Reichian approaches is *bioenergetics* (Lowen 1976), a therapeutic system developed by Alexander Lowen and John Pierrakos. It utilizes the energetic processes in the body and body language to influence mental functioning. The bioenergetic approach combines psychotherapy with a wide range of exercises involving breathing, postures, movements, and direct manual intervention.

Lowen's therapeutic goals are broader than those of Wilhelm Reich, whose single aim was the sexual fulfillment of his patients. The emphasis is on integration of the ego with the body and its striving for pleasure. This involves not only sexuality but also other basic functions, such as breathing, moving, feelings, and self-expression. Through bioenergetics one can connect with one's "first nature," a condition of being free from structured physical and psychological attitudes, as compared to the "second nature," psychological stances and muscular armouring imposed on the individual that prevent one's living and loving.

Another neo-Reichian approach is the *Radix Intensive*, developed by Reich's disciple Charles Kelley and his wife Erika. It is a therapeutic form that combines the intimacy of individual work with the energy and dynamism of the group. The Kelleys employ a spectrum of techniques that involve some of Reich's original approaches, bioenergetics, sensory awareness, and other body-oriented methods. The emphasis is on freeing the muscular armor which releases feelings of fear, rage, shame, pain, or grief that have been held since childhood. As the client accepts and works through these negative feelings, he or she discovers a new capacity for pleasure, trust, and love.

While the neo-Reichian approaches have an explicit psychotherapeutic component, the focus of some other important human potential techniques is primarily physical. This is certainly true for Ida Rolf's structural integration, Feldenkrais exercises, and Milton Trager's psychophysical integration and mentastics. The method of *structural integration,* or *Rolfing* (Rolf 1977), as it is popularly known, was developed by Ida Rolf as a method for improving the physical structure of the body, particularly in regard to its adjustment to the gravitational field. According to Rolf, humans as bipeds should keep their weight distributed about a central vertical axis. However, most people do not maintain such ideal distribution, which guarantees optimal functioning of the skeletomuscular system and the entire organism. The consequences are tightness and shortening of the fascia with a resulting restriction of motility, constriction of circulation, chronic muscular tension, pains, and certain psychological disturbances of somatic origin. The purpose of Rolfing is to relieve this condition, restore the proper fascial structure, realign the body's weight segments, and restore normal body movements. In a standardized series of sessions, the Rolfer uses powerful physical interventions to achieve this goal.

Moshe Feldenkrais (1972) created a program of systematic correction and re-education of the nervous system using movement sequences that engage most unusual combinations of muscles. These exercises, known as *Feldenkrais,* are designed to expand the possibilities of the neuromuscular system and stretch its habitual boundaries. They relieve tension, increase the flexibility and range of movements, improve posture and the alignment of the spine, develop paths of ideal action, facilitate coordination of the flexor and extensor muscles, deepen breathing, and introduce awareness into these physical activities. The subtlety of the Feldenkrais exercises is in sharp contrast with Rolfing, which utilizes deep pressure and massage and can be very painful when the area involved is blocked.

Milton Trager's *psychophysical integration* (1982) is another elegant and effective body technique of the human potential movement. Through a systematic sequence of passive rolling, shaking, and vibratory movements, the clients achieve a state of deep physical and mental relaxation. The spectrum of the human potential techniques focusing on the body would not be complete without mentioning the various forms of *massage* that have become increasingly popular, from its sensual forms to techniques that represent a deep intervention in the body energies, such as polarity massage.

Two of the new experiential therapies deserve special attention because of their intimate relation to my own subject. The first of these is *gestalt therapy,* developed by Fritz Perls (1976a; 1976b), which has rapidly become one of the most popular approaches in the field. In his development, Perls was influenced by Freud, Reich, existentialism, and particularly by gestalt psychology. The basic assumption of the German gestalt school is that human beings do not perceive things as unrelated and isolated, but organize them during the perceptual process into meaningful wholes. Gestalt therapy has a holistic emphasis; it is a technique of personal integration, based on the idea that all of nature is a unified and coherent gestalt. Within this whole, the organic and inorganic elements constitute continuous and everchanging patterns of coordinated activity.

The emphasis in gestalt therapy is not on interpreting problems, but on re-experiencing conflicts and traumas in the here and now, introducing awareness into all the physical and emotional processes, and completing the unfinished gestalts from the past. The client is encouraged to take full responsibility for the process and free himself or herself from dependence on parents, teachers, spouses, and the therapist. Gestalt therapy frequently uses individual work in a group context. The emphasis is on breathing and full awareness of one's physical and emotional processes as the fundamental prerequisites. The therapist pays great attention to the client's uses of different ways to interrupt his or her experiences. He identifies these tendencies and facilitates full and free experience and expression of the unfolding psychological and physiological processes.

Another experiential technique that is of great interest from the point of view of our discussion is *primal therapy*, developed by Arthur Janov (1970; 1972a; 1972b). The origins of primal therapy were strictly empirical; they were inspired by several accidental observations of dramatic relief and change of basic attitudes in patients who allowed themselves to emit an inarticulate, primordial scream. According to the theory that Janov built around his observations of deliberately induced "primals," as he calls them, neurosis is a symbolic behavior that represents a defense against excessive psychobiological pain associated with childhood traumas. Primal pains are related to early occurrences in life that have not been acted upon. Instead, the emotions and sensations have been stored up as tensions, or in the form of defenses. In addition to several layers of primal pain from various periods of childhood, Janov also recognizes the role of pain rooted in the memory of traumatic birth. Primal pains are disconnected from consciousness because to become conscious of them would mean unbearable suffering. They interfere with the authenticity of one's life experience and prevent one from "being a real person," according to Janov.

The therapeutic focus is on overcoming the defenses and working through the primal pains by experiencing them fully and reliving the memories of the events that created them. The major therapeutic outlet encouraged in this approach is the "primal scream," an involuntary, deep, and rattling sound that expresses in a condensed way the patient's reaction to past traumas. Janov believes that repeated primals can gradually eliminate the layers of pain, reversing the process of successive appositions by which they have been created. According to Janov, primal therapy dispels the "unreal" system that drives one to drink, smoke, take drugs, or otherwise act in a compulsive or irrational way in response to an inner buildup of unbearable feelings. Postprimal patients who have become "real"—free from anxiety, guilt, depression, phobias, and neurotic habits—are capable of acting without the compulsion to satisfy neurotic needs of their own or of others.

Janov initially made extreme statements about the efficacy of primal therapy that have not withstood the test of time. He claimed originally a 100 percent success with his patients, as illustrated by the title of his first book, *The Primal Scream: Primal Therapy—The Cure For Neurosis* (1970). The sensational improvements of emotional problems were allegedly accompanied by equally stunning physical changes. These included development of breasts in flat-chested women, the appearance of hair in previously hairless men, improved circulation and a rise of peripheral temperature, increased sexual appetite and orgastic potency, and improved performance in tennis. Although primal therapy continues to be a popular form of treatment, the results lag far behind the original claims. Many patients have been in primal therapy for several years without making substantial progress, and occasionally there is a worsening of the clinical condition instead of improvement. Many primal therapists have disassociated themselves from Janov and his Los Angeles-based organization and formed their own independent primal centers because of serious disagreements about both theory and practice.

The human potential movement also includes many techniques utilizing group dynamics. The advent of humanistic psychology represented a real renaissance of group therapy, which ranged from a renewed interest in psychodrama to the development of such new group techniques as transactional analysis, T-groups, and encounter, marathon, and nude marathon sessions.

It is interesting to look at the different therapeutic avenues of the human potential movement from the point of view of the observations from LSD research. Such an approach brings a strong support for Maslow's criticism of academic psychology. Only in the early stages of therapy, when subjects deal with biographical issues and certain aspects of perinatal dynamics, do the observations endorse the Freudian image of human nature as dominated by instinctual drives, such as sexuality and aggression. Once the individual moves beyond the death-rebirth process and gains experiential access to the realms of the transpersonal, he or she connects with a system of higher values that roughly correspond with Maslow's metavalues (1969). Thus, continued penetration into the unconscious does not reveal increasingly bestial and hellish regions, as indicated by psychoanalysis, but rather extends into the cosmic realms of the superconscious.

Similarly, the richness of the various experiential areas underlying the everyday experience of both the healthy and neurotic or psychotic individual makes the behaviorist's point of view look simplistic and absurd. Instead of reducing the uniqueness of the human psyche to the simple neurological reflexes of the rat or pigeon, observations of this kind reveal dimensions of cosmic consciousness behind the existence of these animals. Anybody who has seriously studied the material from psychedelic sessions is left with no doubt that subjective data are essential for the study of the human psyche.

The observations from LSD research also clearly support the basic thesis of humanistic psychology about the unity of mind and body. Powerful experiences in psychedelic sessions always have important correlates in psychosomatic processes. Resolution of psychological issues have characteristically physical concomitants, and, vice versa, clearing of somatic blocks is always accompanied by corresponding changes in the psyche. This connection is quite obvious in the body-oriented human potential techniques. As originally developed by Ida Rolf, structural integration was strictly a physical procedure (Rolf 1977). However, many of her followers have noticed that their clients occasionally experience dramatic emotional release and have powerful experiences of a biographical, perinatal, or even transpersonal nature. As a result, some of them decided to combine Rolfing with systematic psychotherapeutic work (Schutz and Turner 1982). A similar development seems to have taken place with the Feldenkrais exercises, Trager mentastics, polarity massage, and even acupuncture.

Of all the therapeutic techniques of humanistic psychology, Fritz Perls's gestalt practice is probably closest to the system described in this book. His main emphasis is on a full, here-and-now experience with all its physical, perceptual, emotional, and ideational characteristics, rather than remembering and intellectual analysis. Although gestalt therapy was originally designed to deal with problems of a biographical nature, individuals involved in systematic gestalt work can occasionally experience various perinatal sequences and even such transpersonal phenomena as embryonal, ancestral, and racial memories, animal identification, or encounters with archetypal entities. This can happen in spite of the sitting position of the client, the use of verbal ploys, and the biographical orientation that characterize the work of most gestalt therapists. It is important to emphasize that there is no reason why the basic principles of the gestalt approach could not be applied to the work on perinatal and transpersonal issues, if the conceptual framework of the therapist includes them. Some gestalt practitioners, such as Richard and Christine Price, have already moved in that direction by allowing the reclining position, restricting verbal exchange in certain situations, and giving the experiencer unlimited freedom to enter any experiential realms.

The implosion-explosion paradigm that characterizes so much of gestalt practice should also be mentioned; although it is usually experienced in a biographical context, it seems to reflect the deeper underlying dynamics of the perinatal level. Another observation that is highly relevant for our discussion is the fact that, during the reliving of complex scenes in psychedelic sessions, individuals frequently spontaneously experience simultaneous or successive identification with all the protagonists involved. This is exactly what the gestalt practice tries to accomplish by specific guidance and a structured sequence of interactions, particularly in the work with dreams and fantasies. In general, the basic principles of the gestalt approach are thus quite similar to the ideas advocated here. The basic differences are in the biographical emphasis of gestalt therapy and its lack of recognition of the perinatal and transpersoanl levels of the unconscious.

Another technique that deserves special attention is Arthur Janov's primal therapy. His description of layered primal pain shows remarkable parallels with my concept of the COEX systems, first outlined in a preprint for the International Congress of LSD Psychotherapy in Amsterdam (1966), and elaborated in my book, *Realms of the Human Unconscious* (1975). Janov also acknowledges the significance of the birth trauma, although his understanding of it is purely biological and far narrower than the concept of perinatal matrices. However, he lacks any recognition of the trans-personal dimensions of the psyche. Thus, the major dilemma he faces seems to be that the technique he employs is sufficiently powerful not only to take clients into perinatal realms, but also to induce transpersonal phenomena, such as memories of a past in-carnation, archetypal sequences, states of possession, and mystical experiences. However, his theoretical system, which is superficial, mechanistic, and antispiritual, does not account for, let alone ap-preciate, the whole range of experiences that his technique is capable of triggering. Increasing numbers of Janov's followers find themselves, after months of intensive therapy, in an unsolvable dilemma and painful confusion, being propelled by the use of the primal technique into transpersonal realms for which the straitjacket of Janov's theory does not allow. The external manifestation of this development has been a deep schism in the primal movement and creation of renegade factions seeking a more open-minded framework.

Perinatal and also transpersonal experiences have occasionally been observed in encounter groups, marathon sessions, and, par-ticularly, in Paul Bindrim's nude marathons and aquaenergetic sessions (n.d.). They occur quite frequently in the rebirthing sessions of Leonard Orr (1977) and Elisabeth Feher (1980).

In many ways, the experiential techniques of humanistic psy-chology show many similarities with the approach I am advocating. The major difference is that most of them have only a superficial and incomplete understanding of the perinatal level of the uncon-scious and a total lack of awareness of the transpersonal realms. This shortcoming was overcome by the development of transper-sonal psychology, a movement that has fully recognized and ac-knowledged the importance of the spiritual dimension in human life.

Psychotherapies with Transpersonal Orientation

During the rapid development of humanistic psychology in the 1960s, it became increasingly obvious that a new force had begun to emerge within its inner circles for which the humanistic position emphasizing growth and self-actualization was too narrow and limited. The new emphasis was on recognition of spirituality and transcendental needs as intrinsic aspects of human nature and on the right of every individual to choose or change his or her "path." Many leading humanistic psychologists exhibited a growing interest in a variety of previously neglected areas and topics of psychology, such as mystical experiences, transcendence, ecstasy, cosmic consciousness, theory and practice of meditation, or interindividual and interspecies synergy (Sutich 1976).

The crystalization and consolidation of the originally isolated tendencies into a new movement, or Fourth Force, in psychology was primarily the work of two men—Anthony Sutich and Abraham Maslow—both of whom had earlier played an important role in the history of humanistic psychology. Although transpersonal psychology was not established as a distinct discipline until the late 1960s, transpersonal trends in psychology had preceded it by several decades. The most important representatives of this orientation have been Carl Gustav Jung, Roberto Assagioli, and Abraham Maslow. Also the most interesting and controversial systems of dianetics and scientology developed by Ron Hubbard (1950) outside of the professional circles should be mentioned in this context. A powerful impetus for the new movement was clinical research with psychedelics, particularly LSD psychotherapy, and the new insights into the human psyche that it made possible.

Carl Gustav Jung can be considered the first modern psychologist; the differences between Freudian psychoanalysis and Jung's theories are representative of the differences between classical and modern psychotherapy. Although Freud and some of his followers suggested rather radical revisions of Western psychology, only Jung challenged its very core and its philosophical foundations—the Cartesian-Newtonian world view. As June Singer so clearly pointed out, he stressed "the importance of the unconscious rather than consciousness, the mysterious rather than the known, the mystical rather than the scientific, the creative rather than the productive, and the religious rather than the profane" (1972).

Jung put great emphasis on the unconscious and its dynamics, but his concept of it was radically different from Freud's. He saw the psyche as a complementary interplay between its conscious and unconscious elements, with a constant energy exchange and flow between the two. The unconscious for him was not a psychobiological junkyard of rejected instinctual tendencies, repressed memories, and subconsciously assimilated prohibitions. He saw it as a creative and intelligent principle binding the individual to all humanity, nature, and the entire cosmos. According to him, it is not governed by historical determinism alone, but has also a projective, teleological function.

Studying the specific dynamics of the unconscious, Jung (1973a) discovered functional units for which he coined the term *complexes*. Complexes are constellations of psychic elements—ideas, opinions, attitudes, and convictions—that are clustered around a nuclear theme and associated with distinct feelings. Jung was able to trace complexes from biographically determined areas of the individual unconscious to myth-creating primordial patterns that he called *archetypes*. He discovered that, in the nuclei of the complexes, archetypal elements are intimately interwoven with various aspects of the physical environment. At first he saw it as an indication that an emerging archetype creates a disposition for a certain type of frame. Later on, studying instances of extraordinary coincidences or *synchronicities* accompanying this process, he concluded that the archetypes must in some way influence the very fabric of the phenomenal world. Because they seemed to represent a link between matter and psyche or consciousness, he referred to them as *psychoids* (1960a).

Jung's image of the human being is not that of a biological machine. He recognized that in the individuation process humans can transcend the narrow boundaries of the ego and of the personal unconscious and connect with the Self that is commensurate with all humanity and the entire cosmos. Jung, thus, can be considered the first representative of the transpersonal orientation in psychology.

By careful analysis of his own dream life, the dreams of his patients, and the fantasies and delusions of the psychotic, Jung discovered that dreams commonly contain images and motifs that can be found not only in widely separated places all over the earth, but also in different periods throughout the history of mankind. He came to the conclusion that there is—in addition to the individual unconscious—a collective or racial unconscious, which is shared by all humanity and is a manifestation of the creative cosmic force. Comparative religion and world mythology can be seen as unique sources of information about the collective aspects of the unconscious. According to Freud, myths can be interpreted in terms of the characteristic problems and conflicts of childhood, and their universality reflects the commonality of human experience. Jung found this explanation unacceptable; he observed repeatedly that the universal mythological motifs—or mythologems—occurred among individuals for whom all knowledge of this kind was absolutely out of the question. This suggested to him that there were myth-forming structural elements in the unconscious psyche that gave rise both to the fantasy lives and dreams of individuals and to the mythology of peoples. Dreams can thus be seen as individual myths, and myths as collective dreams.

Freud showed all through his life a very deep interest in religion and spirituality. He believed that it was in general possible to get a rational grasp of the irrational processes and tended to interpret religion in terms of unresolved conflicts from the infantile stage of psychosexual development. In contrast to Freud, Jung was willing to accept the irrational, paradoxical, and even mysterious. He had many religious experiences during his lifetime that convinced him of the reality of the spiritual dimension in the universal scheme of things. Jung's basic assumption was that the spiritual element is an organic and integral part of the psyche. Genuine spirituality is an aspect of the collective unconscious and is independent of childhood programming and the individual's cultural or educational background. Thus, if self-exploration and analysis reach sufficient depth, spiritual elements emerge spontaneously into consciousness.

Jung (1956) differed from Freud also in the understanding of the central concept of psychoanalysis, that of the libido. He did not see it as a strictly biological force aiming at mechanical discharge, but as a creative force of nature—a cosmic principle comparable to *élan vital*. Jung's genuine appreciation of spirituality and his understanding of libido as a cosmic force found their expression also in a unique concept of the function of symbols. For Freud, symbol was an analagous expression of, or allusion to, something already known. In psychoanalysis, one image is used instead of another one, usually of a forbidden sexual nature. Jung disagreed with this use of the term symbol and would refer to Freudian symbols as signs. For him, a true symbol points beyond itself into a higher level of consciousness. It is the best possible formulation of something that is unknown, an archetype that cannot be represented more clearly or specifically.

What makes Jung truly the first modern psychologist is his scientific method. Freud's approach was strictly historical and deterministic; he was interested in finding rational explanations for all psychic phenomena and in tracing them back to biological roots, following the chains of linear causality. Jung was aware that linear causality is not the only mandatory connecting principle in nature. He originated the concept of *synchronicity* (1960b), an acausal connecting principle that refers to meaningful coincidences of events separated in time and/or space. He was keenly interested in the developments of modern physics and maintained contact with its prominent representatives.[8] Jung's willingness to enter the realm of the paradoxical, mysterious, and ineffable included also an open-minded attitude toward the great Eastern spiritual philosophies, psychic phenomena, the I Ching, and astrology.

The observations from LSD psychotherapy have repeatedly confirmed most of Jung's brilliant insights. Although even analytical psychology does not cover adequately the entire spectrum of psychedelic phenomena, it requires the least revisions or modifications of all the systems of depth psychotherapy. On the biographical level, Jung's description of psychological complexes (1973a) is quite similar to that of COEX systems, although the two concepts are not identical. He and his followers were aware of the significance of the death-rebirth process, and they discussed and analyzed cross-cultural examples of this phenomenon, ranging from ancient Greek mysteries to the rites of passage of many aboriginal cultures. However, Jung's most fundamental contribution to psychotherapy is his recognition of the spiritual dimensions of the psyche and his discoveries in the transpersonal realms.

The material from psychedelic research and deep experiential work brings strong support for the existence of the collective unconscious and for the dynamics of archetypal structures, Jung's understanding of the nature of libido, his distinction between the ego and the Self, recognition of the creative and prospective function of the unconscious, and the concept of the individuation process. All these elements can be independently confirmed even in psychedelic work with unsophisticated subjects who are unfamiliar with Jung's theories. Material of this kind also emerges frequently in LSD sessions guided by therapists who are not Jungians and have no Jungian training. In a more specific way, the literature of analytical psychology is very useful in understanding various archetypal images and themes that surface spontaneously in experiential sessions, reflecting the transpersonal level of the unconscious. Deep experiential work has also independently confirmed Jung's observations on the significance of synchronicity.

The differences between the concepts presented in this book and Jung's theories are relatively minor as compared to the far-reaching correspondences. It has already been mentioned that the concept of the COEX system is similar to, but not identical with, Jung's description of a psychological complex. Jungian psychology has a good general understanding of the death-rebirth process as an archetypal theme, but seems not to recognize and acknowledge its special position and certain significant specific characteristics that distinguish it from all others. The perinatal phenomena with their emphasis on birth and death represent a critical interface between the individual and the transpersonal realms. Experiences of death and rebirth are instrumental in the individual's philosophical dissociation from an exclusive identification with the ego-body unit and with the biological organisation. Deep experiential confrontation of this level of the psyche is typically associated with a sense of serious threat for survival and with a life-death struggle. Death-rebirth experiences have an important biological dimension; they are usually accompanied by a broad spectrum of dramatic physiological manifestations, such as powerful motor discharges, feelings of suffocation, cardiovascular distress and disturbances, loss of control of the bladder, nausea and vomiting, hypersalivation, and profuse sweating.

In Jungian analysis, which uses more subtle techniques than psychedelic therapy or some of the new powerful experiential approaches, the emphasis is on the psychological, philosophical, and spiritual dimensions of the death-rebirth process, while the psychosomatic components are seldom, if ever, effectively dealt with. Similarly, Jungian analysis seems to pay little attention to the actual biographical aspects of perinatal phenomena. In experiential psychotherapy, one always encounters an amalgam of actual detailed birth memories and concomitant archetypal themes. In the theory and practice of analytical psychology, memories of concrete events during delivery seem to play a negligible role.

In the transpersonal realm, Jungian psychology seems to have explored certain categories of experiences in considerable detail, while entirely neglecting others. The areas that have been discovered and thoroughly studied by Jung and his followers include the dynamics of the archetypes and of the collective unconscious, mythopoic properties of the psyche, certain types of psychic phenomena, and synchronistic links between psychological processes and phenomenal reality. There seems to be no genuine recognition of transpersonal experiences that mediate connection with various aspects of the material world. Here belong, for example, authentic identification with other people, animals, plants, or inorganic processes, and experiences of historical, phylogenetic, geophysical, or astronomical events that can mediate access to new information about various aspects of "objective reality." In view of Jung's deep interest and scholarship in the Eastern spiritual philosophies, it is astonishing that he has almost entirely overlooked and neglected the realm of past incarnation phenomena, which are of critical importance in any deep experiential psychotherapy.

The last major distinction between Jungian analysis and the approaches discussed in this book, psychedelic therapy and holonomic integration, is the emphasis on deep, direct experience that has both psychological and actual physical dimensions. Although the biological component appears in the most dramatic form in connection with the perinatal phenomena, various experiences of a biographical and transpersonal nature can have significant somatic manifestations. Authentic infantile grimacing, voice, and behavior, or presence of the sucking reflex during age regression; specific postures, movements, and sounds accompanying animal identification; and frantic movements, "mask of evil," or even projectile vomiting related to an emerging demonic archetype are important examples. Despite all the above differences, Jungians seem to be, in general, best conceptually equipped to deal with the material described in this book, provided they can get used to the dramatic form of the phenomena occurring in psychedelic therapy, during the sessions of holonomic integration, or in the course of other deep experiential approaches.

Another interesting and important transpersonal system of psychotherapy is *psychosynthesis,* developed by the late Italian psychiatrist, *Roberto Assagioli* (1976), who originally belonged to the Freudian school and was one of the pioneers of psychoanalysis in Italy. However, in his doctoral thesis, written in 1910, he presented his serious objections to Freud's approach and discussed the shortcomings and limitations of psychoanalysis. In the following years, Assagioli outlined an expanded model of the psyche and developed psychosynthesis as a new technique of therapy and self-exploration. His conceptual system is based on the assumption that an individual is in a constant process of growth, actualizing his or her hidden potential. It focuses on the positive, creative, and joyous elements of human nature and emphasizes the importance of the function of will.

Assagioli's cartography of the human personality bears some similarity to the Jungian model, since it includes the spiritual realms and collective elements of the psyche. The system is complex and consists of seven dynamic constituents. The lower unconscious directs the basic psychological activities, such as primitive instinctual urges and emotional complexes. The middle unconscious, where experiences are assimilated before reaching consciousness, seems to correspond roughly to the Freudian preconscious. The superconscious realm is the seat of higher feelings and capacities, such as intuitions and inspirations. The field of consciousness comprises analyzable feelings, thoughts, and impulses. The point of pure awareness is referred to as the conscious self, while the higher self is that aspect of the individual that exists apart from the consciousness of mind and body. All these components are then enclosed in the collective unconscious. An important concept of Assagioli's psychosynthesis is that of subpersonalities, dynamic substructures of the human personality that have a relatively separate existence. The most common of these are related to the roles we play in life, such as that of the son, father, lover, doctor, teacher, and officer.

The therapeutic process of psychosynthesis involves four consecutive stages. At first the client learns about various elements of his or her personality. The next step is disidentification from those elements and subsequent ability to control them. After the client has gradually discovered his or her unifying psychological center, it is possible to achieve psychosynthesis, characterized by a culmination of the self-realization process and integration of the selves around the new center.

The approach described in this book shares with psychosynthesis the spiritual and transpersonal emphasis, the concepts of the superconscious and of the collective unconscious, and the notion that certain states labeled currently as psychotic can be more appropriately seen as spiritual crises that have a potential for personality growth and transformation (Assagioli 1977). Another major similarity is the concept of gaining control over various aspects of the psyche by full experience of, and identification with, them.

The major difference between the two approaches lies in dealing with the dark and painful aspects of the personality. While I share Assagioli's emphasis on the creative, superconscious, and radiant potential of the psyche, it has been my experience that direct confrontation of its dark side whenever it manifests itself in the process of self-exploration is beneficial and conducive to healing, spiritual opening, and consciousness evolution. Conversely, a one-sided emphasis on the light, problem-free, and joyful side of life is not without dangers. It can be used in the service of repression and denial of the shadow, which can then become manifest in less obvious forms and color or distort the spiritual process. The end result can be various spiritual aberrations ranging from an unconvincing, exaggerated caricature of a spiritual person to tyranny and control of others in the name of transpersonal values. It seems preferable to approach inner exploration in the spirit of "transcendental realism," willing to confront all aspects of one's psyche and of the universe in their dialectic and complementary interplay of opposites.

Like Jungian analysis, psychosynthesis seems to focus on the emotional, perceptual, and cognitive aspects of the process and lacks adequate recognition of its biological components. In its focus on the symbolic language of the psyche, it also seems to neglect those transpersonal experiences that represent a direct reflection of specific elements of the phenomenal world. Some of the sub-personalities that, in a fantasy exercise, might appear as more or less abstract intrapsychic structures would, in the process of self-exploration using psychedelics or controlled breathing and music, be deciphered as reflections of genuine ancestral, phylogenetic, racial, and past incarnation matrices, or as authentic experiences of consciousness of other people, animals, or other aspects of the phenomenal world. Thus, beside playful use of human, animal, and natural symbolic forms, the individual psyche also seems to be able to draw on holographically stored information about the entire phenomenal world—present, past, and future.

The major practical difference between Assagioli's psychosynthesis and the strategies presented in this book would be the degree of formal structure and guidance by the therapist. While psychosynthesis offers a comprehensive system of highly structured exercises, the approach advocated here emphasizes unspecific activation of the unconscious and reliance on spontaneous emergence of the material reflecting the autonomous dynamics of the client's psyche.

The credit for the first explicit formulation of the principles of transpersonal psychology belongs to *Abraham Maslow*, whose role in the development of the movements of humanistic and transpersonal psychology has already been described. At this point it is appropriate to discuss those aspects of his work that have direct relevance for transpersonal theory, comparing them with the observations from psychedelic therapy and deep nondrug experiential work.

One of Maslow's lasting contributions is his study of individuals who had spontaneous mystical or "peak" experiences, as he called them (1964). In traditional psychiatry, mystical experiences of any kind are usually treated in the context of serious psychopathology; they are seen as indications of a psychotic process. In his comprehensive and careful study, Maslow was able to demonstrate that persons who had spontaneous "peak" experiences frequently benefited from them and showed a distinct trend toward "self-realization" or "self-actualization." He suggested that such experiences might be supernormal, rather than subnormal or abnormal, and laid the foundations of a new psychology reflecting this fact.

Another important aspect of Maslow's work was his analysis of human needs and his revision of the instinct theory. He suggested that higher needs represent an important and authentic aspect of the human personality structure and cannot be reduced to, or seen as, derivatives of the base instincts. According to him, higher needs have an important role in mental health and disease. Higher values (metavalues) and the impulses to pursue them (metamotivations) are intrinsic to human nature; the recognition of this fact is ab-

solutely necessary for any meaningful theory of human personality
(Maslow 1969).

Observations from deep experiential therapy provide powerful
support for Maslow's theories. Ecstatic unitive experiences occurring
in this context—if properly integrated—have beneficial consequences that match in minute detail the descriptions from Maslow's
study of spontaneous "peak" experiences. Their healing potential
is incomparably greater than that of anything the armementarium
of modern psychiatry has to offer, and there is absolutely no reason
to treat them as pathological phenomena.

Furthermore, Maslow's basic model of human personality gets
strong support from experiential therapy. Only the early stages of
the process, when subjects deal with biographical and perinatal
traumas, seem to endorse Freud's gloomy picture of human beings
driven by powerful instinctual forces operating from the inferno
of the individual unconscious. As the process moves beyond the
experience of ego death and into transpersonal realms, intrinsic
sources of spirituality and cosmic feelings are discovered beyond
this screen of negativity. Individuals gain access to a new system
of values and motivations that are independent of base instincts
and meet the criteria of Maslow's metavalues and metamotivations
(1969).

There are far-reaching parallels between the concepts presented in this book and L. Ron Hubbard's controversial *dianetics*
and *scientology* (1950). The comparison of the two systems—since
there are many differences as well as similarities—would require
a special study. Unfortunately, Hubbard's remarkable insights have
been discredited by their practical application within a dubious
organizational structure lacking professional credibility and com-
promising itself by its pursuit of power. However, that fact should
not diminish their value for an open-minded researcher who will
find scientology to be a gold mine of brilliant ideas. A comparison
of Hubbard's findings with the observations from psychedelic research is presented in a special essay by Klaus Gormsen and Jørgen
Lumbye (1979). It is sufficient here to summarize some of their
most important points.

Scientology is the only other system that emphasizes the psychological significance of physical traumas, as revealed by LSD
work and holotropic therapy. Hubbard distinguishes between "engrams"—mental records of times of physical pain and unconscious-

ness—and "secondaries"—mental images containing such emotions as grief or anger. The secondaries derive their power from the engrams, which are more fundamental, representing the deepest source of psychological problems. Some additional parallels include recognition of the paramount significance of the birth trauma and prenatal influences (including the experience of conception), ancestral and evolutionary memories (or "experiences on the genetic line," as Hubbard calls them), and the emphasis on past incarnation phenomena.

During the last decade, transpersonal psychology has shown consistent growth and expansion. Its prominent representatives, include Angeles Arrien, Arthur Deikman, James Fadiman, Daniel Goleman, Elmer and Alyce Green, Michael Harner, Arthur Hastings, Jean Houston, Dora Kalff, Jack Kornfield, Stanley Krippner, Lawrence Leshan, Ralph Metzner, Claudio Naranjo, Thomas Roberts, June Singer, Charles Tart, Frances Vaughan, Roger Walsh, and Ken Wilber. They have made significant theoretical contributions to the field and established it firmly as a respectable scientific endeavor. While in the early years the transpersonal movement was quite isolated, it has now established meaningful connections with revolutionary developments in other disciplines that have already been described. These connections found expression in the International Transpersonal Association (ITA), which has an explicitly interdisciplinary and international emphasis.

In conclusion, it seems appropriate to define the relationship between the practice of transpersonal psychology and more traditional psychotherapeutic approaches. As Frances Vaughan (1980) has so clearly pointed out, what characterizes a transpersonal therapist is not content, but context; the content is determined by the client. A transpersonal therapist deals with all the issues that emerge during the therapeutic process, including mundane affairs, biographical data, and existential problems. What truly defines the transpersonal orientation is a model of the human psyche that recognizes the importance of the spiritual or cosmic dimensions and the potential for consciousness evolution. No matter what level of consciousness the therapeutic process is focusing on, a transpersonal therapist maintains the awareness of the entire spectrum and is willing at all times to follow the client into new experiential realms when the opportunity occurs.

CHAPTER FOUR

The Architecture of Emotional Disorders

The observations from LSD psychotherapy and from the experiential nondrug techniques have shed new light on the conceptual controversies among the competing schools of depth psychology by providing unique insights into the complex and multilevel structure of various psychopathological syndromes. The rapid and elemental, spontaneous unfolding of the therapeutic process that characterizes most of these innovations of psychotherapy minimizes the distortions and restrictions imposed on the patient during verbal forms of therapy. The material that emerges through these new approaches seems to reflect more genuinely the actual dynamic constellations underlying clinical symptoms and frequently comes as a total surprise to the therapist, instead of bearing out his or her conceptual bias.

In general, the architecture of psychopathology manifested under these new techniques is infinitely more intricate and ramified than it appears in the models presented by any of the individual schools of depth psychology. Although each of the conceptual frameworks of these schools is right in a certain limited sense, none depicts correctly the true state of affairs. In order to reflect adequately the network of unconscious processes that underlie the psychopathological conditions encountered in clinical psychiatry, one must think in terms of the extended cartography of the psyche described earlier; it encompasses not only the analytical-recollective biographical level, but also the perinatal matrices and the entire spectrum of the transpersonal domain.

Observations from experiential psychotherapies clearly suggest that very few emotional and psychosomatic syndromes can be explained solely from the dynamics of the individual unconscious. Because psychotherapeutic schools do not acknowledge transbiographical sources of psychopathology, they have very superficial and incomplete models of the human mind. Moreover, therapists of these schools are not fully effective in their work with patients because they do not utilize the powerful therapeutic mechanisms available on the perinatal and transpersonal level. There is a wide range of clinical problems that have their deep roots in the dynamics of the death-rebirth process. They are meaningfully related to the trauma of birth and to fear of death and can be therapeutically influenced by experiential confrontation with the perinatal level of the unconscious. Thus, systems of psychotherapy that incorporate the perinatal dimension have, *ceteris paribus*, a much greater therapeutic potential than those limited to biographical exploration and manipulation.

However, many emotional, psychosomatic, and interpersonal problems are dynamically anchored in the transpersonal realms of the human psyche. Only those therapists who acknowledge the healing power of transpersonal experiences and respect the spiritual dimensions of the human psyche can expect success with patients whose problems fall into this category. In many instances, psychopathological symptoms and syndromes show a complex, multilevel dynamic structure and are meaningfully connected with all the major areas of the unconscious—the biographical, perinatal, and transpersonal. To work effectively with problems of this kind, a therapist must be prepared to acknowledge and confront successively the material from all these levels; this requires great flexibility as well as freedom from conceptual orthodoxy.

In presenting the new insights into the "architecture of psychopathology," I will first focus on the problems of sexuality and aggression, because these two aspects of human life have played a crucial role in the theoretical speculations of Freud and many of his followers. Succeeding sections will systematically describe specific emotional disorders, including depressions, psychoneuroses, psychosomatic diseases, and psychoses.

Varieties of Sexual Experience: Dysfunctions,
Deviations, and Transpersonal Forms of Eros

The sexual drive, or libido, in its manifold manifestations and transformations, occupies an extremely significant role in psychoanalytic speculations. Freud, in his classic study, *Three Essays on the Theory of Sexuality* (1953a), traced the problems of human sexuality back to their origins in the early stages of infantile psychosexual development. He postulated that the child passes successively through several distinct stages of libidinal organization, each of which has an association with one of the erogenous zones. In the course of psychosexual evolution, the child thus derives primary instinctual satisfaction, first, from oral activities and, later, from anal and urethral functions during toilet training. At the time of the oedipal crisis, the libidinal attention shifts to the phallic area and the penis, or the clitoris, becomes the dominant focus. If this development is normal, the individual's partial drives—oral, anal, and urethral—are at this stage integrated under the hegemony of the genital drive.

Traumatic influences and psychological interferences in various stages of this development can result in fixations and conflicts conducive to later disturbances of sexual life and specific psychoneuroses. Freud and his followers have elaborated an intricate dynamic taxonomy linking specific emotional and psychosomatic disorders to fixations in various stages of libidinal development and to the history of the ego. In everyday psychoanalytic practice, the relevance of these fixed connections has been repeatedly confirmed by the patients' free associations. Any theory that would challenge the explanatory system of psychoanalysis must deal with the problem of why sexuality and biographical data of a specific kind seem to show a uniquely causal connection in regard to various psychopathological syndromes, and it must offer a convincing alternative interpretation of this fact.

A close look at the history of psychoanalysis shows that several of Freud's followers felt the need to modify the ideas he put forward in his *Three Essays on the Theory of Sexuality*. It became obvious that Freud's descriptions of the individual stages of libidinal development and their implications for psychopathology represented ideal abstractions that did not exactly match the observations from daily psychoanalytic practice. In the actual clinical pictures presented by psychiatric patients, the problems related to various erogenous zones do not come in a pure form, but are intimately interwoven. For example, many patients tend to block sexual orgasm for fear of losing control over the urinary bladder; for anatomical reasons, this fear is far more common in women. In other instances, the fear of letting go in a sexual orgasm is associated with concerns about inadvertant passing of intestinal gas or even about loss of bowel control. In some patients, analysis of the factors underlying the inability to achieve erection or orgasm reveals a deep-seated and primitive unconscious fear that the loss of control involved would result in the act of devouring the partner, or in being devoured.

Sandor Ferenczi attempted to explain these and similar clinical problems in his extraordinary essay, "Thalassa" (1938). He postulated that the originally separate activities in the individual erogenous zones can show secondary fusion and functional overlapping, which he called *amphimixis*. In basic agreement with the theories of Otto Rank (1929), Ferenczi also believed that a full psychological understanding of sexuality must include an unconscious tendency to undo the trauma of birth and return to the maternal womb. However, he was even more radical than Rank in recognizing behind this intrauterine regressive tendency a deeper phylogenetic drive to return to the conditions that had existed in the primeval ocean.

Wilhelm Reich (1961) generally accepted Freud's emphasis on the sexual drive, but saw it as an almost hydraulic force that had to be freed by direct energetic manipulation if therapeutic effects were to be achieved. Two more important revisions of Freud's sexual theory by his disciples should be mentioned. Alfred Adler's psychology (1932) put primary emphasis on the inferiority complex and will to power; for him sexuality was subservient to the power complex. The most far-reaching criticism of Freud's sexual theory came from Carl Gustav Jung (1956), for whom libido was not a biological force but a manifestation of a cosmic principle comparable to *élan vital.*

The observations from psychedelic therapy and some of the experiential nondrug techniques present sexuality and sexual problems in an entirely new light; they strongly suggest that these problems are far more complex than any of the previous theories suspected. As long as the process of self-exploration remains focused on the biographical level, the experiential material emerging from these therapeutic sessions seems to support the Freudian theory. However, only seldom can one see significant therapeutic results in patients with sexual disorders and deviations, as long as the sessions focus primarily on biographical issues. Patients working on sexual problems will sooner or later discover the deeper roots of their difficulties, on the level of perinatal dynamics or even in various transpersonal realms.

Conditions that involve considerable reduction or total absence of libidinal drive and sexual appetite are typically associated with deep depressions.[1] As we will discuss later, this usually indicates a deep dynamic connection with BPM II. An individual under the influence of the second perinatal matrix experiences total emotional isolation from the environment and complete blockage of energy flow; both of these conditions effectively prevent the development of sexual interest and the experience of sexual excitement. Under these circumstances, one can frequently hear that sexual activity is the last thing in the world the individual would possibly consider. However, sexual material from the past or present life often emerges in this condition and is reviewed by the individual in the negative context of agonizing guilt and disgust. Occasionally, depressive states with lack of sexual interest can also have transpersonal roots.

Most of the serious disturbances and deviations of sexuality are psychogenetically connected with BPM III; the understanding of this liaison requires a discussion of the deep relationship between the pattern of sexual orgasm and the dynamics of this matrix. Extreme amounts of libidinal tension, and driving energy in general, represent one of the most important characteristics of the final stages of the death-rebirth process and constitute an intrinsic and integral aspect of BPM III. This tension can take the form of undifferentiated energy that permeates the entire organism or find, in addition, a more focused manifestation in the individual erogenous zones—oral, anal, urethral, or genital.

As described earlier, the phenomenology of the third perinatal matrix combines the elements of titanic fight, destructive and self-destructive tendencies, a sadomasochistic mixture of aggressive and erotic impulses, a variety of deviant sexual drives, demonic themes, and scatological preoccupation. In addition, this unusually rich combination of emotions and sensations occurs in the context of a deep confrontation with death and reliving of birth, which entails extreme physical pain and vital anxiety. The above connections represent a natural basis for the development of all clinical conditions in which sexuality is intimately linked with, and contaminated by, anxiety, aggression, suffering, guilt, or preoccupation with such biological material as urine, feces, blood, or genital excretions. A simultaneous activation of all erogenous zones in the context of perinatal unfolding can also explain why many clinical disorders are characterized by a functional overlapping of the activities in the oral, anal, urethral, and genital areas.

The deep functional interconnectedness of all the major erogenous zones in the context of biological delivery—for both the mother and the child—is clearly manifested in situations where the preparation of the mother does not involve enema and catheterization. Under these circumstances, the mother can not only experience a powerful sexual orgastic release, but also pass gas, defecate, and urinate. In a similar way, the child can show reflex urination and pass fetal feces, or meconium. If we include intensive activation of the oral zone and engagement of the chewing muscles that occur in both mother and child during the final stages of the birth process, and the buildup and release of sexual energy in the child generated by suffocation and extreme pain, we have the image of a total functional and experiential amalgam of all major activities that Freud refers to as erogenous.[2]

The clinical observations that Sandor Ferenczi tried to relate to the secondary fusion of partial drives, or amphimixis, simply reflect the fact that the Freudian successive development of activities in the erogenous zones is superimposed on the dynamics of the perinatal matrices, where all the functions involved are engaged simultaneously. The main key to a deeper understanding of the psychology and psychopathology of sex is the fact that, on the perinatal level of the unconscious, sexuality is intimately and inextricably connected with the sensations and emotions associated with both birth and death. Any theoretical or practical approach to sexual problems that fails to recognize this fundamental liaison and treats sexuality in isolation from these other two fundamental aspects of life is necessarily incomplete, superficial, and of limited efficacy.

The association of sex with birth and death and the deep involvement of sexual energy in the psychological death-rebirth process are not easy to explain. However, the existence of this link is unquestionable and can be illustrated by numerous examples from anthropology, history, mythology, and clinical psychiatry. The emphasis on the triad of birth, sex, and death seems to be the common denominator in all the rites of passage of various preindustrial cultures, temple mysteries, rituals of ecstatic religions, and initiation into secret societies. In mythology, male deities symbolizing death and rebirth, such as Osiris and Shiva, are frequently represented with an erect phallus; similarly, there are important female goddesses whose functions reflect these same connections. The Indian goddess Kali, Middle-Eastern Astarte, and pre-Columbian Tlacolteutl are important examples. Observations of delivering women show that the experience of childbirth has a very important sexual component, as well as a strong element of the fear of death. This connection does not seem particularly mysterious, since the genital area is instrumental in the process of delivery, and passage of the child obviously entails a strong stimulation of the uterus and vagina, with a powerful buildup and subsequent release of tension. Also, the element of death is clearly logical, since childbirth is a serious biological event that occasionally endangers the life of the mother.

However, it is far from clear why the reliving of one's own biological birth should involve a strong sexual component. It seems that this connection reflects a deep physiological mechanism built into the human organism; its existence can be illustrated by examples from many different areas. Thus, extreme physical agony, especially if it is associated with severe suffocation, tends to elicit intense sexual arousal and even religious ecstasy. Many psychiatric patients who have tried to commit suicide by hanging themselves and were rescued in the last moment, have related retrospectively that a high degree of suffocation resulted in excessive sexual excitation. It is also well known that male criminals dying on the gallows tend to have erections and even ejaculations during the terminal agony. Patients suffering from the so-called bondage syndrome feel a deep need to experience sexual release in connection with physical confinement and choking. Others use various contraptions, such as scarves and nooses attached to nails, doorknobs, or branches that enable them to masturbate while they experience strangulation.

It seems that all human beings, when subjected to extreme physical and emotional tortures, have the capacity to transcend suffering and reach a state of strange ecstasy (Sargant 1957). This fact can be documented by observations from the Nazi concentration camps, where human subjects were used for bestial experiments, by material from Amnesty International, as well as reports of American soldiers who were tortured by the Japanese in the Second World War, or as prisoners of war during the Korean and Vietnamese conflicts. Similarly, members of the religious sects of flagellants have all through the ages severely tortured themselves and their peers to evoke strong libidinal feelings, states of ecstatic rapture, and eventually the experience of union with God. Experiential transcendence of inhuman suffering in the religiously motivated torture and death of martyrs also falls into this category. Many other examples of spiritual pathology could be mentioned in which self-mutilation, torture, sacrifice, sexuality, fear-provoking procedures, and scatological maneuvers are combined into a strange experiential amalgam and woven into the fabric of religious or quasi-religious ceremonies.

Additional observations of a similar kind are related to the psychology of wars, revolutions, and totalitarian systems. Thus, the atmosphere of vital danger in bloody battles tends to induce sexual excitement in many soldiers. At the same time, the unleashing of the aggressive and sexual impulse in war situations seems to be associated with perinatal elements. The speeches of military leaders and politicians declaring wars and igniting masses for bloody revolutions abound in metaphors pertaining to biological birth. The atmosphere of concentration camps combines sexual, sadistic, and scatological elements in a most unusual way. The sociopolitical implications of these facts are discussed in detail in chapter 8.

A possible neurophysiological basis of such phenomena might be the anatomical arrangement and functional characteristics of the limbic system of the brain. This archaic part of the central

nervous system contains in close association areas that are instrumental in the self-preservation of the organism, and thus related
to aggression, and those that play an important role in the preservation of the species, and are thus connected with sexuality. It
is conceivable that these centers could be stimulated simultaneously,
or that the excitation of one could spill over to the other.

The rich spectrum of phenomena related to human sexuality
cannot be adequately described and explained, if theoretical speculations remain limited to elements of biological nature and to
biographically determined psychological factors. The observations
from psychedelic psychotherapy demonstrate beyond any doubt
that, subjectively, sexuality can be experienced on many different
levels of consciousness and in many different ways, although its
biological, physiological, and behavioral manifestations might appear quite similar to an external observer. Comprehensive understanding of sexuality is impossible without an intimate knowledge
of the dynamics of the perinatal and transpersonal levels of the
unconscious.

In what follows, I will focus on various sexual experiences and
behaviors and discuss them in the light of observations from modern
consciousness research conducted both with and without the use
of psychedelic drugs. The problems involved fall into the following
thematic categories: (1) "normal" sexuality; (2) disorders and dysfunctions of sexual life; (3) sexual variations, deviations, and perversions; and (4) transpersonal forms of sexuality.

1. "Normal" sexuality. Although it is generally recognized that
a full sexual experience should involve more than merely adequate
biological functioning, present medical criteria for sexual normalcy
are somewhat mechanical and limited. They do not involve such
elements as deep respect for the partner, a sense of synergy and
emotional reciprocity, or feelings of love and unity in the everyday
interaction between partners, or during sexual intercourse. It is
generally considered sufficient for adequate sexual functioning, if
a male is capable of developing an erection and maintaining it for
a reasonable amount of time before ejaculation. Similarly, women
are expected to respond to a sexual situation by an adequate
lubrication of the genitals and the ability to reach a vaginal orgasm.
The concept of normalcy for both sexes also entails heterosexual

preference and a sufficient degree of sexual appetite to perform the sexual act with statistically established average frequency.

LSD subjects and individuals undergoing experiential psychotherapy frequently experience profound sexual changes during the course of treatment. Sooner or later, their understanding of sexuality expands considerably and they find these criteria superficial, insufficient, and problematic. They discover that the sexual orgasm, male or female, is not an all-or-none phenomenon: there are many degrees of both the intensity of the experience and the completeness of release. In many instances, individuals who, before therapy, thought they had adequate sexual orgasms experience a surprising increase of orgastic potency. This is usually directly related to a new capacity of surrendering to the process and the letting go that occurs as a result of the experiences of death-rebirth and of cosmic unity.

Another important insight involves the fact that our present definition of normal sex does not exclude even severe contamination of the sexual situation by preoccupation with dominance versus submission, use of sex for a variety of nonsexual goals, and maneuvers that have more relevance for self-esteem than for sexual gratification. In our culture individuals of both sexes commonly use military concepts and terminology in referring to sexual activities. They interpret the sexual situation in terms of victory or defeat; conquering or penetrating the partner, and, conversely, being defeated and violated; and proving oneself or failure. Concerns about who seduced whom and who won, in this situation, can all but overshadow the question of sexual gratification.

Similarly, material gains, or pursuit of a career, status, fame, or power can completely override more genuine erotic motives. When sex is subordinated to self-esteem, sexual interest in the partner may entirely disappear once the "conquest" has been accomplished or the number of partners seduced becomes more important than the quality of interaction. Moreover, the fact that the partner is not approachable or is deeply committed to another person can become a decisive element of sexual attraction.

According to the insights from psychedelic therapy, competition, maneuvers involving self-esteem, lack of respect for the partner, selfish exploitation, or mechanical emphasis on discharge of tension during sexual interaction—all represent serious distortions and reflect a tragic misunderstanding of the nature of the sexual union. Such a contamination of sexuality usually has important biographical determinants, that is, specific traumatic memories from childhood; however, the roots of such problems always reach deep into the perinatal level of the unconscious. When the perinatal energies are discharged and the content of the perinatal matrices is worked through and integrated, individuals automatically move to a synergistic and complementary understanding of sex.

To persons so integrated, it becomes absolutely clear that there cannot be selective victories or losses in a genuine sexual interaction. Since it is by definition a complementary situation that involves mutual satisfaction of various categories of needs, both partners are either winners or losers, depending on circumstances. Sexuality can be experienced in many different contexts and it can satisfy an entire spectrum of hierarchically arranged needs that range from the biological to the transcendental. Sexual interaction that focuses only on primitive needs is less a problem of moral inferiority than one of ignorance and missed opportunity. High forms of sexual communication that satisfy the entire range of human needs necessarily have a spiritual emphasis and involve the archetypal dimensions, as it occurs in the oceanic and tantric sex described later in this section.

2. Disorders and dysfunctions of sexual life. In the course of LSD psychotherapy and other forms of deep experiential treatment, the sexual life of clients undergoes dramatic changes. These involve both sexual experiences and behavior during the therapeutic sessions and dynamic shifts that can be observed in the intervals between treatments. In certain stages of therapy, various sexual disorders can be alleviated, completely disappear, or be strikingly transformed and modified. Conversely, confrontation of certain areas of the unconscious can be associated with the appearance of new symptoms and difficulties in sexual life that the client had not had before. Careful observation and study of these dynamic changes and oscillations offer unique insights into the dynamic structure of sexual functioning and malfunctioning.

It has already been mentioned that the dynamic influence of BPM II is associated with a deep inhibition of sexual life. When the client is experiencing elements of the second perinatal matrix toward the end of a therapeutic session and does not reach resolution, he or she can show in the postsession interval symptoms of an inhibited depression, characterized by a total lack of libido and disinterest in sex. In addition, under these circumstances, anything related to sexuality may be perceived as illicit, dirty, sinful, disgusting, and fraught with guilt. Although one might find more superficial biographical determinants that seemingly explain the presence of this problem in a patient, the therapeutic context in which it occurs clearly suggests that it is rooted in BPM II.

Most functional disturbances of sex seem to be related to the dynamics of the third perinatal matrix and can be logically understood from its basic characteristics, described in chapter 2. When, during the termination period of a therapeutic session, a person is under the influence of the sexual facet of BPM III and does not reach resolution in the transition to BPM IV, this can result in an enormous increase of sexual appetite, which is clinically termed "satyriasis" or "nymphomania." In this condition, the insatiable drive for repeated sexual intercourse is typically associated with a sense of incomplete release and lack of satisfaction following sexual orgasm. It thus represents a strange combination of hypersexuality with orgastic impotence. On closer inspection, it becomes obvious that this situation appears sexual only on the surface; in reality, it is pseudosexual and has very little to do with sex in a narrower sense. The core of the problem is that the individual is flooded with perinatal energies that are seeking discharge through any possible means. Because of the similarity between the pattern of sexual orgasm and the orgasm of birth, the genitals, under these circumstances, become an ideal channel for peripheral discharge of these energies. Since the reservoirs of perinatal energies are enormous, repeated sexual intercourse and even orgasms bring no relief or satisfaction.

It is not uncommon under these circumstances for a male to have sexual intercourse as many as fifteen times in a single night and have a complete but unsatisfactory orgasm each time. Within a matter of minutes after coitus, the perinatal energies, present in enormous quantities, tend to recreate a state of tension sufficient to induce an erection and initiate another intercourse. Hypersexuality of this kind in both men and women is frequently associated with promiscuity. This seems to be related to the fact that because of the lack of orgastic release the sexual act is unsatisfactory. It is common under these circumstances to blame the partner instead of recognizing that the real problem is the perinatal outpouring of energy. Frequent change of partners also seems to reflect a tendency to compensate for an abysmally low self-esteem that is typically associated with the perinatal unfolding, as well as a strong drive toward erratic behavior due to chaotic energies seeking discharge.

If the intensity of the perinatal energies is excessive, the possibility of discharge can be perceived as extremely dangerous, although the nature of this danger might not be clearly defined. Under these circumstances the individual might sense deep fear of losing control of these elemental forces and unconsciously block the sexual experience. Since the discharge pattern of perinatal energies is inextricably connected with the pattern of sexual orgasm, this situation will result, for men, in an inability to achieve or maintain an erection and, for women, in an absence of sexual orgasm—conditions that old psychiatry and colloquial jargon refer to as "impotence" and "frigidity." Traditionally, impotence was seen as a symptom of energetic deficiency or lack of masculine power, and frigidity was interpreted as a lack of erotic sensitivity and of sexual responsiveness. However, these concepts are completely erroneous and, as a matter of fact, could not be further from the truth.

Impotence and frigidity of psychogenic origin are due to the exact opposite—a tremendous excess of driving sexual energy. The problem is not only the enormous amount of these feelings and sensations, but also that they express not pure sexual energy but sexually colored perinatal energy. Consequently, this driving energy is associated with sadomasochistic impulses, vital anxiety, profound guilt, fear of loss of control, and a gamut of psychosomatic symptoms characteristic of BPM III. These involve fear of suffocation, cardiovascular distress, painful muscular and intestinal spasms, uterine cramps, and concerns about loss of control over the bladder or anal sphincter. In the last analysis, this energy represents the unfinished gestalt of birth and an organismic state of vital threat.

A person suffering from impotence or frigidity, then, does not lack sexual energy, but is literally sitting on a volcano of instinctual forces. Since, under these circumstances, the sexual orgasm cannot be experienced in isolation from these forces, letting go in orgasm would unleash an experiential inferno. The unconscious fear of orgasm and loss of control thus becomes equivalent with the fear of death and destruction.

This new interpretation of frigidity and impotence is supported by the dynamics of therapeutic changes observed in the course of successful treatment. When the excess of perinatal energies is discharged in a structured nonsexual situation, one can observe the development of transient hypersexuality—satyriasis or nymphomania—before the client reaches a state in which the remaining sexual energies can be comfortably handled in a sexual context. Finally, when in the course of the death-rebirth process the individual experiences elements of BPM IV and BPM I, he or she becomes fully sexually competent and, in addition, the orgastic ability tends to reach unusual heights.

In psychoanalytic literature, the problem of impotence is closely related to the castration complex and to the concept of *vagina dentata,* or the vagina seen as a dangerous organ that is capable of killing or castrating. These issues deserve special attention from the point of view of the extended cartography of the unconscious that includes the perinatal level. There are certain aspects of the castration complex that classical psychoanalysis with its biographical orientation failed to explain in a satisfactory way. The castration complex can be found in both sexes; Freud presumed that males experienced actual fear of losing the penis, while females unconsciously believed that they once had it and lost it because of bad behavior. He tried to relate this to the masochistic tendencies and greater proneness to guilt found in women. Another mysterious aspect of the castration complex is that, unconsciously, castration seems to be equated with death. Even if one accepts that the penis is, psychologically, grossly overestimated, its equivalence with life makes little sense. Moreover, in free associations of psychoanalytic patients, suffocation, separation, and loss of control seem to be images that occur in close connection with castration (Fenichel 1945).

Observations from LSD psychotherapy bring an unexpected solution to these inconsistencies; here, the castration fears represent only a biographical overlay and secondary elaboration of a far more fundamental problem. A deepening of the therapeutic process made possible by the catalyzing effect of psychedelics or some powerful nondrug techniques will inevitably reveal that the castration fears have their roots in the cutting of the umbilical cord. They are thus derivatives of a fundamental biological and psychological trauma of human existence that has life and death relevance. It is a common occurrence that typical castration themes, such as the memory of circumcision or the operation for preputial adhesions, develop into reliving of the umbilical crisis. This regularly involves sharp pains in the navel, radiating into the pelvis and projecting into the penis, testicles, and urinary bladder.[3] These are frequently associated with fear of death, suffocation, and strange shifts in the body anatomy. In women, the umbilical crisis typically underlies memories of urinary infections, abortions, and uterine curettage. The reason why there can be experiential overlapping and confusion between perinatal umbilical sensations and genital or urinary pain seems to be an inability to localize pelvic pain clearly; this is true in general and in early developmental stages in particular.

Cutting the umbilical cord represents the final separation from the maternal organism and, thus, a biological transition of fundamental significance. Following it, the child must achieve a total anatomical and physiological reconstruction; it has to create its own system of oxygen supply, removal of waste products, and digestion of food. Once we realize that the castration fears are related to an actual memory of a biological event that has relevance for life and death, rather than to an imaginary loss of genitals, it is easy to understand some of their otherwise mysterious characteristics, mentioned earlier. It becomes immediately clear why these fears occur in both sexes, are closely associated with separation anxiety, are interchangeable with fear of death and annihilation, and why they suggest loss of breath and suffocation.

Also, the famous Freudian concept of the dentate vagina appears suddenly in an entirely new light when the cartography is extended beyond the biographical realms to include the perinatal matrices. In psychoanalytic literature the unconscious representation of the vagina as a dangerous organ that can damage, castrate, or kill is discussed as if it were an absurd and irrational fantasy of the naive child. Once the possibility is accepted that the memory of birth is recorded in the unconscious, this simply becomes a realistic evaluation. The delivery is a serious and potentially dangerous event, and during birth female genitals have killed or almost killed a number of children.

For a male in whom the memory of the birth trauma is too close to the surface, the image of the vagina as a murderous organ is so compelling that this organ cannot be seen and approached as a source of pleasure. The traumatic memory has to be relived and worked through before the way to women as sexual objects is free. A female psychologically close to the memory of her birth will have difficulty in accepting her own femininity, sexuality, and reproductive functions, because she associates being a woman and having a vagina with torture and murder. Working through the memory of the birth trauma is essential if she is to become comfortable with her sexuality and female role.

3. *Sexual variations, deviations, and perversions.* The inclusion of perinatal dynamics into the cartography of unconscious processes offers some unexpected solutions to problems that have plagued psychoanalysis almost from its beginning. The key to this new understanding is the phenomenology of BPM III, a matrix that involves an intimate association of sexual arousal with anxiety, physical pain, aggression, and scatology. It was above all the existence of *sadomasochism* that challenged Freud's belief about the hegemony of the pleasure principle in the human psyche. If the pursuit of pleasure were the only leading principle and motivating force of mental life, it would certainly be hard to explain the determined and consistent search for physical and emotional suffering that characterizes masochistic patients. This issue became a real crux for Freud's theoretical speculations; it forced him finally to change the entire structure of psychoanalysis and include the controversial concept of the death instinct, or thanatos, in his thinking.

The speculations about the death instinct in connection with sadomasochism reflected Freud's intuitive insight that this clinical phenomenon involves matters of life and death relevance. Consequently, it cannot be explained from some relatively trivial biographical situations in which active aggression and pain are intimately connected. Explanations offered by some psychoanalysts focus on traumas that do not provide a convincing model for the depth of sadomasochistic impulses. Kučera's (1959) theory linking sadomasochism to the experience of teething, when active efforts of the child to bite become painful, is a case in point. However, it was not only the combination of active and passive destructiveness in sadomasochism that psychoanalysis found puzzling, but also the peculiar fusion of aggression and sexuality. The model of perinatal matrices can provide a very logical explanation for the most relevant aspects of this disorder.

In the process of perinatal unfolding, sadistic as well as masochistic manifestations and experiences appear with great constancy and can be related quite naturally to certain characteristics of the birth process. Physical pain, anxiety, and aggression are combined, in BPM III, with intense sexual arousal, the nature and origin of which has already been discussed. In the memory of the birth process, the introjected assault of the uterine forces coincides and alternates with active aggression oriented outward, representing a reaction against this vital threat. This explains not only the fusion of sexuality and aggression, but also the fact that sadism and masochism are two sides of the same coin and constitute one clinical unit, sadomasochism.

The need to create a sadomasochistic situation and exteriorize the above unconscious experiential complex can be seen not only as symptomatic behavior, but also as an attempt to expurgate and integrate the original traumatic imprint. The reason why this effort is unsuccessful and results in no self-healing is the absence of introspection, insight, and awareness of the nature of the process. The experiential complex is acted out and attached to the external situation instead of being faced internally and recognized as a historical replay.

Individuals experiencing elements of BPM III show all the typical elements of sadomasochism, such as alternation between the role of the suffering victim and that of the cruel aggressor, a need for physical confinement and pain, and rapture of peculiar volcanic ecstasy that represents a mixture of agony and intense sexual pleasure. It was mentioned earlier that the potential for transcending extreme suffering and reaching ecstasy seems to be inherent in the human personality structure, although it is most clearly expressed in sadomasochistic patients.

Some extreme cases of criminal sexual pathology, such as *rapes, sadistic murders,* and *necrophilia,* clearly betray definite perinatal roots. Individuals experiencing the sexual aspects of BPM III frequently talk about the fact that this stage of the birth process has many features in common with *rape.* This comparison makes a lot of sense if one considers some of the essential experiential features of rape. For the victim, it involves the element of serious danger, vital anxiety, extreme pain, physical restraint, a struggle to free oneself, choking, and imposed sexual arousal. The experience of the rapist, then, involves the active counterparts of these elements—endangering, threatening, hurting, restricting, choking, and enforcing sexual arousal. While the experience of the victim has many elements in common with that of the child in the birth canal, the rapist exteriorizes and acts out the introjected forces of the birth canal, while simultaneously taking revenge on a mother surrogate. Because of this similarity between the experience of rape and the birth experience, the rape victim suffers a psychological trauma that reflects not only the impact of the immediate situation, but also the breakdown of the defenses protecting her against the memory of biological birth. The frequent long-term emotional problems following rapes are very probably caused by the emergence into consciousness of perinatal emotions and psychosomatic manifestations.

The involvement of the third perinatal matrix is even more obvious in the case of *sadistic murders,* which are closely related to rapes. In addition to a combined discharge of the sexual and aggressive impulses, these acts involve the elements of death, mutilation, dismemberment, and scatological indulgence in blood and intestines; this is an association characteristic of the reliving of the final stages of birth. As will be discussed later, the dynamics of bloody suicide is closely related to that of sadistic murder; the only difference is that in the former the individual overtly assumes the role of the victim, whereas in the latter, that of the aggressor. In the last analysis, both roles represent separate aspects of the same personality, that of the aggressor reflecting the introjection of the oppressive and destructive forces of the birth canal; that of the victim, the memory of the emotions and sensations of the child during delivery.

A similar combination of elements, but in somewhat different proportions, seems to underlie the clinical picture of *necrophilia.* This aberration covers a wide range of phenomena from sexual arousal at the sight of corpses to actual sexual activities involving dead bodies and taking place in morgues, funeral homes, and cemeteries. Analysis of necrophilia reveals that same strange amalgam of sexuality, death, aggression, and scatology so characteristic of the third perinatal matrix.

Although one can always find in the history of the individual specific biographical events that seem instrumental in the development of necrophilia, these are not its causes, but only necessary conditions or precipitating factors. Genuine understanding of the problems involved is impossible without acknowledging the paramount role of perinatal dynamics.

Necrophilia occurs in many different forms and degrees, from fairly innocuous to manifestly criminal. Its most superficial varieties involve sexual excitement produced by the sight of a corpse or attraction to cemeteries, graves, or objects connected with them. More serious forms of necrophilia are characterized by a strong craving to touch corpses, smell or taste them, and indulge in putrefaction and decay. The next step is actual manipulation of corpses with a sexual emphasis, culminating in actual intercourse with the dead. Extreme cases of this sexual perversion combine sexual abuse of corpses with acts of mutilation, dismemberment of the bodies, and cannibalism.

The observations from clinical work with LSD also provided new insights into the peculiar sexual deviations of *coprophilia, coprophagia,* and *urolagnia.* Individuals showing these aberrations indulge in biological materials that are usually considered repulsive, become sexually aroused by them, and tend to incorporate the excretory functions into their sexual life. In the extremes, such activities as being urinated or defecated on, smeared with feces, eating excrements, and drinking urine can be a necessary condition for reaching sexual satisfaction. A combination of sexual excitement and scatological indulgence is a rather common occurrence, both in psychiatric patients and normal subjects, during the final stages of the death-rebirth process. This experience seems to reflect the fact that, in the old-fashioned deliveries where no catheterization or enemas were used, many children experienced intimate contact with feces and urine; blood, mucus, and fetal liquid are, of course, biological materials commonly encountered in the course of childbirth.

My clinical experiences with patients from this category clearly indicate that a deep root of this problem is fixation on the memory of the moment of birth. The natural basis of this seemingly extreme and bizarre deviation is the patient's having experienced as a newborn child oral contact with feces, urine, blood, or mucus at the moment when, after many hours of agony and vital threat, the head was released from the firm grip of the birth canal. Intimate contact with such material thus became the symbol of this fundamental orgastic experience.

According to psychoanalytical literature, the infant is originally attracted to various forms of biological material and only secondarily develops aversion as a result of parental and societal influences. Observations from psychedelic research suggest that this is not necessarily so. The deepest attitude toward biological material seems to be established during the birth experience. Depending on the specific circumstances, this attitude can be extremely positive or negative.

It certainly makes a difference whether, on the one hand, the child simply encounters mucus or feces as symbols and concomitants of physical and emotional liberation, or, on the other, it emerges from the birth canal choking on this material and has to be freed from it by artificial resuscitation. In several instances of unsupervised home deliveries, patients were left in the biological material for a long time before help arrived; the accuracy of these memories relived in psychedelic sessions was later verified in interviews with the patients' mothers. Thus the birth situation has a potential for both positive and negative encounters with biological material, and the individual's specific experience will then become the basis for further biographical elaboration.

The same factors that underlie the above aberrations also operate, in a more subtle form, under the circumstances of everyday life. Thus the memory of the encounter with biological material during the birth experience can determine a man's attitude toward oral-genital sex. It is well known that the reactions to *cunnilingus* cover a wide range, from intense disgust and aversion to preference and irresistible attraction. There is no doubt that on the deepest level these attitudes are determined by the nature of the experience of the oral contact with the maternal vagina at the time of birth. Similarly, the reaction of both sexes to the contact with the mucous membrane of the mouth and tongue during deep kissing is colored not only by the memories of nursing, but also those of the contact with the vaginal mucous membrane during delivery. A woman's intolerance of the physical weight of her partner during intercourse, or revulsion from close embrace, is based on reluctance to face a combination of sensations characteristic of BPM III. Similarly, one of the important reasons for a deep aversion to *fellatio* seems to be the memory of the combination of sexual arousal and choking during birth.

A rich source of illustrations and examples for many of these issues is *A Sexual Profile of Men in Power*, by Janus, Bess, and Saltus (1977). The study is based on more than 700 hours of interviews with high-class call girls from the East Coast of the United States. Unlike many other researchers, the authors were less interested in the personalities of the prostitutes than in the preferences and habits of their customers. Among these were many prominent representatives of American politics, business, law, and justice.

The interviews revealed that only an absolute minority of the clients sought straight sexual activities. Most were interested in various devious erotic practices and "kinky sex." A common request was for bondage, whipping, and other forms of torture. Some clients were willing to pay high prices for the enactment of complex sadomasochistic scenes, such as that of an American pilot captured in Nazi Germany and subjected to ingenious tortures by bestial Gestapo women. Among the frequently requested and highly priced practices were the "golden shower" and "brown shower," being urinated and defecated on in a sexual context.[4] After sexual orgasm, many of these extremely ambitious and influential men regressed to an infantile state, wanting to be held and to suck on the prostitutes' nipples—behavior in sharp contrast to the public image they had been trying to project.

The authors offer interpretations that are strictly biographical and Freudian, linking tortures to parental punishments, the "golden shower" and the "brown shower" to problems related to toilet training, nursing needs to a mother fixation, and the like. However, closer inspection reveals that the clients typically enacted classical perinatal themes rather than postnatal childhood events. The combination of physical restraint, pain and torture, sexual arousal, scatological involvement, and subsequent regressive oral behavior are unmistakable indications of the activation of BPM III.

The conclusions of Janus, Bess, and Saltus deserve special notice. They appeal to the American public not to expect their politicians and other prominent figures to be models of sexual behavior. In light of their study, excessive sexual drives and an inclination to deviant sexuality are inextricably linked to the extreme degree of ambition that it takes in today's society to become a successful public figure.

The authors thus suggest a solution to the old conflict between Freud and Adler (concerning the primacy of sex or will to power as dominant forces in the psyche) by proposing that these are really two sides of the same coin. This is in perfect agreement with the perinatal model. In the context of BPM III, excessive sexual drive and self-assertive impulse, compensating for a sense of helplessness and inadequacy, are two aspects of one and the same experience.

Homosexuality has many different types and subtypes and undoubtedly many different determinants; it is therefore impossible to make any generalizations about it. In addition, my clinical experience with homosexuality was rather biased, since it was limited almost entirely to individuals who volunteered for treatment because they considered homosexuality a problem and had a serious conflict about it. There is a large category of persons who clearly have homosexual preference and enjoy their way of life; their major problem seems to be a conflict with intolerant society rather than an intrapsychic struggle. My patients who were homosexual usually had other clinical problems, such as depression, suicidal tendencies, neurotic symptoms, or psychosomatic manifestations. These considerations are important in approaching the following observations.

Most of the male homosexual patients I have worked with were able to form good social relations with women, but were incapable of relating to them sexually. During treatment, this problem could be traced back to what psychoanalysis would call "castration fears"; I have already pointed out that the castration complex and the Freudian image of the dentate vagina can be deciphered during psychedelic therapy as fear of female genitals, based on the memory of the birth trauma. In addition to this problem, which might be interpreted as an unconscious fear of repeating in relation to female genitals the role of the child during delivery, there seems to be another element underlying male homosexuality, apparently based on identification with the delivering mother. This involves a specific combination of sensations characteristic of BPM III—the feeling of a biological object inside one's body, a mixture of pleasure and pain, and a combination of sexual arousal with anal pressure. The fact that anal intercourse tends to have a strong sadomasochistic component can be used as an additional illustration of the deep connection between male homosexuality and the dynamics of the third perinatal matrix.

On a more superficial level, my male patients frequently showed a deep craving for affection from a male figure; although the real nature of this desire was the need of a child for paternal attention, in adulthood the only way to satisfy it would be in a homosexual relationship. I have also encountered homosexual subjects with minimal conflicts about their sexual life who were able to trace their sexual preference to roots in the transpersonal realms, such as an unfinished gestalt of a previous incarnation as a female, or as a male from ancient Greece with homosexual preference.

My comments concerning lesbian tendencies must be presented with reservations similar to those on male homosexuality, since my sample was equally limited and biased. In general, *female homosexuality* seems to have more superficial psychological roots than its male counterpart. One important factor is certainly an unsatisfied need for intimate contact with the female body, which reflects a period of serious emotional deprivation in infancy. It is interesting that female subjects frequently experience homosexual fears when, during deep regression into infancy, they approach periods of emotional starvation and start craving contact with a woman. This fear usually disappears when they realize that for an infant girl the need for the physical affection of a woman is quite normal and natural.

Another important component in lesbianism seems to be a tendency to return psychologically to the memory of release at the time of birth, which occurred in close contact with female genitals. This factor would be essentially the same as that discussed earlier in connection with male heterosexual preference for oral-genital practices. Another element related to the memory of birth might be the fear of being dominated, overpowered, and violated in the sexual act. Very frequently negative experiences with a father figure in childhood represent additional motives for seeking women and avoiding men. In general, female homosexuality seems to be less connected with perinatal dynamics and issues of life and death relevance than it was in the male homosexuals I worked with. Lesbian tendencies reflect a positive perinatal component of attraction toward the maternal organism, while male homosexuality is associated with the memory of the life-threatening dentate vagina. Society's greater tolerance of lesbianism than of male homosexual manifestations seems to support this view.

Even if the emphasis in the interpretation of the sexual variations and deviations described above was on perinatal dynamics, this does not mean that biographical events are irrelevant for the development of these phenomena. As a matter of fact, the psychogenic factors discussed in psychoanalytic literature have been consistently confirmed both by psychedelic work and in experiential nondrug therapy. The only difference between the Freudian point of view and the explanations presented here is that the biographical events are seen here not as causes of these problems, but as conditions for their development. Biographical factors are of such relevance because they selectively reinforce certain aspects or facets of perinatal dynamics, or seriously weaken the defense system that usually prevents the perinatal energies and contents from emerging into consciousness. It is also important to emphasize that in many instances some of the conditions described above have significant transpersonal components. These cannot be described systematically and must be discovered in each individual case by unbiased and open-minded experiential work.

4. Transpersonal forms of sexuality. In sexual experiences that have transpersonal dimensions, the individual has the sense of having transcended his or her identity and ego boundaries as they are defined in the ordinary state of consciousness. This can involve experiencing oneself in a different historical, ethnic, or geographical context, or in full identification with other persons, animals, or archetypal entities. Experiences of this kind can occur as entirely intrapsychic phenomena when the subject is not involved in actual sexual activities but, rather, in a process of deep self-exploration, or they can occur as part of an actual sexual interaction with a partner. In the latter case, the altered state of consciousness can precede the act of love making—as in partners who have sex while under the influence of marijuana or LSD—or can actually be triggered by it.

In all these instances, one can either experience only one's own feelings in the sexual situations involved or have simultaneous access to the emotional states and physical sensations of a partner. Thus, on a number of occasions, LSD subjects have experienced what seemed to be the sexual feelings of their mothers at the time of the symbiotic union of pregnancy, delivery, or nursing. Sometimes, the intrauterine experiences were associated with a sense of witnessing parental intercourse from the point of view of the fetus; this was associated with a distinct sexual experience of its own kind. Less common were instances when a person in a nonordinary state of consciousness had a convinced sense of reliving the sexual experiences of one of his or her ancestors. Sometimes, this involved more immediate ancestors, such as parents or grandparents; at other times, these episodes seemed to have come from very remote historical periods and had the quality of a racial memory. Occasionally, LSD subjects experienced themselves as participants in complex sexual rituals and ceremonies of different cultures, such as fertility festivals, rites of passage, ancient temple prostitution, or scenes of phallic worship. Experiences of this kind frequently convey very specific and detailed, historically or anthropologically correct information that was not previously available to the subject. When such phenomena lack the feeling of an actual biological link with the persons involved, they can best be described in terms of Jung's collective unconscious. Occasionally, they can be associated with the sense of identity and a deep spiritual link with the protagonists and have an experiential quality of a memory. These are the characteristics of one of the most important groups of transpersonal experiences—karmic, or past incarnation, memories.

A fascinating category of transpersonal sexual experiences involves full identification with various animal forms. Whether these are other mammals, lower vertebrates, or such invertebrates as insects, mollusks, and coelenterates, these episodes entail the corresponding body image, emotional and other experiential responses, and characteristic behavior sequences. All the sensations involved appear to have a very authentic quality; they are always quite specific and unique for the species in question and typically far beyond what the fantasy of an uninformed person could contrive. Like the experiences of the collective and racial unconscious they frequently mediate a great amount of accurate information that far transcends the educational background and training of the individual involved.

Accurate new insights obtained during such episodes can be related not only to animal psychology, the dynamics of instincts, and specific courting behavior, but also to the details of sexual anatomy, physiology, and sometimes even chemistry. Usually this involves identification with just one specific life form at a time, but occasionally many of them can be combined into a complex experience. The resulting constellation then seems to represent the archetype of love making in nature, or to express and illustrate the overwhelming power and beauty of sexual union. Experiences of this kind can occur as part of oceanic sex and during the divine unitive experience of the Shiva-Shakti type (which will both be described later), or in the context of the opening of the second chakra when sexual energy appears to be the most dominant force in the universe. On several occasions, LSD subjects have also reported sexual feelings in connection with plant identification, such as, for example, conscious experiences associated with the process of pollination.

Another important and common transpersonal form of sexual experience is that of *divine intercourse*. There are two distinct varieties of this most interesting phenomenon. In the first, the individual has the sense of sexual communion with the divine, but maintains his or her original identity. The ecstatic raptures of Saint Theresa of Avila could be mentioned here as nondrug examples of this experience. Spiritual states of this kind also occur in the practice of the devotees of bhakti yoga. The second variety involves a sexual experience in full identification with the divine being. It can occur in a more or less abstract form, as the cosmic union of the male and the female principles, like the divine interplay of yin and yang in the Taoist tradition. Its more elaborate archetypal manifestations are the mystical marriage or hierogamy, the alchemical mysterium coniunctionis, or identification with a specific god or goddess, experiencing sexual union with the appropriate consort (e.g., Shiva-Shakti, Apollo-Aphrodite or the Tibetan tantric deities with their shaktis).

Three transpersonal forms of sexuality are so distinct that they deserve special treatment; they are the satanic, oceanic, and tantric. The first of these, *satanic sexuality,* is psychologically related to the birth process, and more specifically to BPM III. Images and experiences of satanic orgies appear quite frequently in the final stages of the perinatal unfolding. They are characterized by a peculiar mixture of death, sex, aggression, scatology, and religious feelings. In one important variety of this theme, individuals have visions of or even a sense of participating in complex *Black Mass rituals.* The element of death is represented by the favorite setting of these ceremonies—graveyards with open tombs and coffins. The rituals themselves involve the defloration of virgins, the sacrifice of animals or little children, and couples fornicating in open tombs and caskets, or in warm entrails of sacrificed and disemboweled animals. A diabolic feast with a menu that includes excrement, menstrual blood, and cut-up fetuses is another frequent motif. Yet, the atmosphere is not that of a perverted orgy, but of a peculiar religious ritual of uncanny power—service to the Dark God. Many LSD subjects have reported independently that the phenomenology of this experience involves elements identical to the final stages of birth and seems to be meaningfully related to it. The common denominators of the satanic orgies and the culmination of biological birth are sadomasochism, a strong sexual arousal of a deviant nature, the involvement of repulsive biological material, an atmosphere of death and macabre horror, and yet a sense of the proximity of the divine.

Another variation of the same theme is the imagery of the *Witches' Sabbath*, or *Walpurgis Night*, and the experiences associated with it. This archetype, available in unusual states of consciousness, was actually manifested historically in medieval Europe, where certain covens of witches knew the secret of psychoactive potions and ointments. The plants used in such preparations were the deadly nightshade (Atropa belladonna), henbane (Hyoscyamus niger), thorn-apple or Jimson weed (Datura stramonium), and mandrake (Mandragora officinarum); sometimes animal ingredients were added, such as toad or salamander skin.[5] Following the ingestion of the potion, or application of the ointment on the skin or in the vagina, the witches had relatively stereotyped experiences of participating in the Witches' Sabbath.

Although this phenomenon is well documented historically, it comes as somewhat of a surprise when similar experiences occur spontaneously in certain stages of the psychedelic process or in the course of nondrug experiential psychotherapy. The general atmosphere of the Witches' Sabbath is that of wild excitement and an arousal of otherwise illicit instinctual drives. The sexual element is represented in a sadomasochistic, incestuous, and scatological form. The president of the Witches' Sabbath is the devil in the form of a large black male goat, by the name of Master Leonard. He conducts painful ritual defloration of virgins with his gigantic scaly penis, copulates indiscriminately with all the women present,

Fig. 28. Scenes from the Sabbath of the Witches showing the traditional vehicles of the magic flight—Billy-goats, hogs and brooms (painting combining elements from medieval carvings and etchings).

receives adulatory kisses on his anus, and encourages participants to engage in wild orgies of an incestuous nature. Mothers and sons, fathers and daughters, brothers and sisters get involved in the course of this peculiar ritual in unbridled sexual interaction.

The scatological element is represented in the form of a strange diabolical feast involving such biological materials as menstrual blood, semen, excrement, and cut-up fetuses served with condiments. A characteristic aspect of the Witches' Sabbath is blasphemy, mockery, and the inversion of Christian symbolism. Little children play with ugly toads in puddles of holy water; the toads are dressed in little pieces of purple cloth, suggesting a cardinal's robe, and fed the Eucharist. The mock Eucharist used in the Witches' Sabbath is produced from dough that has been kneaded on the buttocks of a nude girl.

Fig. 29. A scene from the Sabbath of the Witches showing adoration of Master Leonard, the devil in the form of a large black Billy-goat who is the president of the meeting; the ritual involves kissing of his anus that emits indescribable stench.

An important part of the ceremony is the vow of the neophytes to renounce Christ and all Christian symbolism. This element seems to be of particular interest, since, in the perinatal unfolding, identification with Christ and his suffering represents the next archetypal step of the death-rebirth process, which frees the experient from the nightmarish atmosphere of the satanic orgies, or the Walpurgis Night and mediates experiential transition to pure spiritual opening. The renunciation of Christian elements thus commits the participants of the Sabbath ritual to perpetuation of its macabre activities, arrests the archetypal unfolding, and prevents them from reaching spiritual liberation.

Musical instruments made of bones, skins, and wolves' tails add to the bizarre atmosphere of this extraordinary ritual. As in the satanic orgies previously described, the strange mixture of wild

Fig. 30. A painting illustrating the blasphemic element of the Sabbath of the Witches. It shows children playing with ugly toads in puddles of holy water, feeding them eucharist and dressing them in cardinal's robes.

excitement, deviant sex, aggression, scatology, and the spiritual element in the form of a blasphemous inversion of traditional religious symbolism betrays the deep connection between this experiential pattern and the third perinatal matrix. In contrast with the hellish elements of BPM II, the experient is not a tortured victim of evil forces; he or she is tempted to unleash all the forbidden impulses from within in an ecstatic orgy. The danger here is that of becoming evil rather than being a helpless victim of evil.

It is interesting that many of the procedures used by the Inquisition against the actual satanists and witches, as well as thousands of innocent victims, bore a strange similarity to these rituals of the Witches' Sabbath. Diabolically ingenious tortures and other sadistic procedures, mass autos-da-fé, endless questioning about sexual aspects of the Sabbath and satanic orgies or about the devil's sexual anatomy and physiology, examination of the genitals of alleged witches for signs of intercourse with the dark god *(signa diaboli)*—all this was conducted with a sense of religious fervor, rather than a perversion of immense proportions. According to the insights from the psychedelic process, there was little difference between the state of mind of the Inquisitors and the satanists or witches; their behavior was motivated by the same deep unconscious forces related to BPM III. The advantage for the Holy Office of the Inquisition was that its practices were backed by legal codes and actual worldly power.

The elements of these archetypal patterns can be found in a more mitigated form in a variety of deviations and distortions of sexual life and, to some extent, even in sexual activities that, according to present criteria, would pass for "normal." All the sexual phenomena we have so far discussed have a common basis in the sexuality that was experienced during the life-death struggle with the maternal organism. Those individuals who connect experientially with the elements of BPM IV and BPM I tend to develop very different approaches to sexuality. These are based on the memory of the intrauterine and postnatal state, in which libidinal feelings were experienced in a synergistic and complementary interaction with another organism. Such forms of sexuality have a very definite numinous or spiritual quality; the most important examples in this category are oceanic sex and the tantric approach to sexuality.

Oceanic sex is a concept of sexuality, approach to it, and experience of it that is diametrically different from those derived from the dynamics of the third perinatal matrix. I coined this term myself after having failed to find in the literature an appropriate name for this form of sexuality or even a description of it. Its development is associated with the experience of cosmic unity and, on a more superficial level, with the ecstatic symbiotic union between the child and the maternal organism during pregnancy and periods of nursing (good womb and good breast experiences). It is a new understanding and a new strategy of sexuality that tends to emerge spontaneously after full experiential confrontation with BPM IV and BPM I. Once experienced, it tends to persist indefinitely in everyday life as a philosophical concept and ideal, if not as experiential reality.

In oceanic sex, the basic model for sexual interaction with another organism is not that of a liberating discharge and release after a period of strenuous effort and struggle, but that of a playful and mutually nourishing flow and exchange of energies resembling a dance. The aim is to experience the loss of one's own boundaries, a sense of fusion and melting with the partner into a state of blissful unity. The genital union and orgasmic discharge, although powerfully experienced, are here considered secondary to the ultimate goal, which is reaching a transcendental state of union of the male and female principles. Although the ascending curve of the sexual orgasm itself can reach numinous or archetypal dimensions in this form of sexuality, it is not considered the only or final goal. Some of the subjects who have reached this form of sexuality, when asked what function the genital orgasm has in it, would respond that it serves the purpose of "removing biological noise from a spiritual system." If two sexually charged partners attempt to fuse, they will experience, after a certain period of interaction, localized genital tension. This tension has to be discharged in a genital orgasm before a more total and diffuse unifying experience is possible.

A characteristic aspect of this approach to sex is a tendency of the partners to remain in close physical contact and loving nongenital interaction for long periods following the sexual orgasm. Intense forms of oceanic experiences always have a powerful spiritual component; the sexual union is perceived as a sacrament and has a definitely numinous quality. The partner can assume an archetypal form and be experienced as the representative of all the members of his or her sex. The situation has a paradoxical quality, being simultaneously the sexual interaction of two human beings and a manifestation of the male-female union on a cosmic scale in the sense of the Chinese yin and yang polarity. At the same time, the partners can be connecting with mythological dimensions, experiencing themselves and each other as divine personages, or tapping various phylogenetic matrices. In the latter case, the sexual union is experienced as a very complex, multilevel and multidimensional event that portrays sexuality as an overwhelming natural force of cosmic proportions. The partners, while making love, can also be recognizing that parts of their bodies move in patterns and rhythms that represent the courtship dances and mating behavior of other species and life forms all through the evolutionary pedigree.

The last distinct transpersonal form of sexuality is *tantric sex;* the goal of this approach is the experience of transcendence and enlightenment, and the genitals and sexual energy are used simply as convenient vehicles. It is questionable to refer to this form of interaction as sexual, since it is a spiritual technique of yoga and not an activity striving for satisfaction of biological needs. In this sexual strategy, the genital union is used to activate libidinal forces, but does not result in orgasmic discharge and ejaculation; as a matter of fact, biological satisfaction through a sexual orgasm would be considered a failure.

The followers of Vāma mārga, or the "left-hand path" of tantra, participate in elaborate rituals called "Pancha-makāra." This name refers to five important components of these rites that all begin with the letter M: madya (wine), māmsa (meat), matsya (fish), mudrā (parched cereal), and maithuna (sexual union). The ritual sexual union is performed collectively in a special location and at a time carefully chosen by the guru. The ceremony has great aesthetic emphasis, using purification, ritual bathing, fresh flowers, beautiful costumes, fragrant incense and perfumes, music, chants, and specially prepared food and wine. Ayurvedic herbal preparations combining powerful aphrodisiacs and psychedelic mixtures are important parts of the ritual (Mookerjee 1982).

While the "right-hand path," or Dakshina mārga, remains in its practice on a symbolic and metaphorical level, the "left-hand path" is concrete and literal in conducting the ritual. Its fundamental principle is that spiritual liberation will not be achieved by avoiding desires and passions, but by transforming those very elements that ordinarily make us fall. During the culmination of the ritual, the partners assume special sexual yogic postures, or tantra-āsanas. They breathe and meditate together in full genital union in a concentrated effort to prolong and experientially explore the very last moment before the orgastic release.

This activity awakens and arouses the dormant spiritual energy in the sacral part of the spinal cord, described in the tantric literature as Kundalini, or the Serpent Power. In its active form, or Shakti, this energy then flows up the spine through conduits in the subtle body called the "Ida" and "Pingala" and causes opening and activation of the seven centers of psychic energy, or chakras. Under these circumstances, the tantric partners experience a sense of cosmic union of the male and female principles and a connection with the transcendental divine source.

Unlike oceanic sex, in which the localized sexual tension is discharged prior to the male-female fusion, here the genital union and tension is used as a vehicle and the sexual energy is transformed into a spiritual experience. In many instances, LSD subjects discovered the tantric approach to sex quite spontaneously in their psychedelic sessions and continued to practice it in their everyday life, usually alternately with oceanic sex, or even more conventional forms of sexuality. Transpersonal sexual experiences and deep changes of sexual life can also occur in the context of various nondrug experiential approaches.

Roots of Violence: Biographical, Perinatal, and Transpersonal Sources of Aggression

In the light of everyday clinical observations during psychedelic therapy and other forms of experiential self-exploration, I became increasingly aware that the explanations presented by mainstream, analytically oriented psychiatry for the majority of emotional disorders were superficial, incomplete, and unconvincing. This was particularly striking in those cases that involved extreme violence or self-destructive activity. It became quite obvious that psychodynamic material of a biographical nature, no matter how traumatic, cannot provide an adequate explanation for such serious and drastic psychopathological phenomena as the automutilations, bloody suicide, sadomasochism, bestial murders, or indiscriminate impulsive killing seen in individuals running amok. A history of emotional deprivation in childhood, painful teething, or even physical abuse by parents and their surrogates certainly do not impress one as adequate psychological motives for blood-curdling acts of criminal psychopathology.

Since these are acts the consequences of which have life and death relevance, the forces that underlie them must be of comparable scope. Explanations based entirely on the analysis of biographical material appear even more absurd and inadequate when applied to extremes of social psychopathology, as exemplified by the insanity of mass extermination and genocide, the apocalyptic horrors of concentration camps, the collective support given by

entire nations to grandiose and megalomaniacal schemes of autocratic tyrants, the sacrifice of millions in the name of naive utopian
visions, or the holocaust of absurd wars and bloody revolutions. It
certainly is hard to take seriously psychological theories that would
try to relate mass pathology of such depth to a history of childhood
spanking, or some comparable emotional and physical trauma. The
instinctivistic speculations of such researchers as Robert Ardrey
(1961; 1966), Desmond Morris (1967), and Konrad Lorenz (1963),
suggesting that this destructive behavior is phylogenetically programmed, are of little help because the nature and scope of human
aggression has no parallels in the animal kingdom.

Let us now consider some of the most important observations
from in-depth experiential work, with and without psychedelic
drugs, that seem emminently relevant for the problem of human
aggression. In general agreement with Erich Fromm (1973), this
clinical material clearly indicates the need to distinguish *defensive*
or *benign aggression,* which is in the service of the survival of the
individual and of the species, from *malignant destructiveness* and
sadistic cruelty. The latter seems to be specific for humans and tends
to increase rather than decrease with the advance of civilization.
It is this malignant form of aggression—without any serious biological or economic reason, nonadaptive, and not programmed
phylogenetically—that constitutes the real problem for humanity.
In view of the powerful modern technology at its disposal, this
malignant aggression has become in the last few decades a serious
threat not only to the existence of the human species, but to the
survival of life on this planet. According to Fromm, it is therefore
important to differentiate between the aggressiveness of an instinctual nature and those forms of destructiveness that are rooted in
the personality structure; the latter can be described as "nonin-
stinctual, character-rooted passion."

The observations from clinical psychotherapy with LSD and
other experiential techniques have added some important new
dimensions to this insight. They strongly indicate that the patterns
of malignant aggression are understandable in terms of the dynamics
of the unconscious, if the model of the human mind is extended
to include the perinatal and transpersonal levels. This finding has
some far-reaching theoretical and practical consequences. It shows
malignant aggression not as a phenomenon that is fatally rooted
in the hardware of the central nervous system and its rigid instinc-

Fig. 31. Unleashing of powerful instinctual forces of an aggressive nature is quite characteristic for experiences related to the death-rebirth process. These four drawings represent various manifestations of murderous aggression in an LSD session dominated by BPM III.

Fig. 32.   Aggression oriented both outward and inward is one of the most typical manifestations of BPM III. This is reflected in the above symbolic self-portrait of a psychiatric patient, drawn after a powerful perinatal LSD session. A stylized bird of prey is crushing with his right claw a helpless mouse. The left claw is transformed into a cannon turned against the predator's own head. The antique car on top reflects a play on words (self-portrait=auto-portrait), but also the relationship of this type of aggression to reckless driving and accident-proneness.

tual programs, but as a manifestation of the flexible and changeable functional matrices, or software, of the brain.

Furthermore, this finding puts malignant aggression in the context of the death-rebirth process and thus connects it with the striving for transcendence and with the mystical quest. If faced internally and worked through in a safe, structured, and socially sanctioned framework, experiences of malignant aggression and self-destructiveness can become an important instrument in the process of spiritual transformation. From this point of view, much of the senseless violence, oriented toward both self and others, and both individual and collective, appears to be the result of misunderstood and warped spiritual drives. In many instances, in a therapeutic framework and with the use of appropriate techniques, these energies can be redirected to their spiritual goals. It is useful at this point to focus more specifically on the sources of malignant aggression and its clinical and social manifestations.

In general agreement with psychoanalytic concepts, much aggression appears to be related to traumatic material from childhood and other biographical factors. It is usually connected with the reliving of memories that involved interference with the satisfaction of the basic needs or security of the child and the ensuing sense of frustration. Conflicts around the achievement of pleasure in various libidinal zones, emotional deprivation and rejection by parents or their surrogates, and gross physical abuse are the most typical examples of such situations. The involvement of the oral and anal zones seems to be particularly relevant from this point of view. If the psychotherapeutic process uses techniques with rather limited power to penetrate the unconscious, such as face-to-face discussions or Freudian free associations, all the aggression may appear to be connected with biographical material, and the client, as well as the therapist, never reaches a deeper level of understanding of the processes involved. However, with the use of psychedelics or some powerful experiential techniques, an entirely different image begins to emerge quite early in therapy.

Initially, the individual may experience aggression in connection with various biographical events from childhood, but the intensity of the destructive impulses attached to these events seems excessive and out of proportion to the nature and relevance of the situations involved. In some instances, various seemingly psychological traumas may be found to derive their emotional power from physical traumas in the person's life to which they are thematically related. However, even this mechanism cannot itself provide a full and satisfactory explanation. As the process of experiential self-exploration deepens, it becomes obvious that the secret of the enormity of the emotions and sensations involved lies in the underlying perinatal level and in meaningful thematic connections between the biographical material involved and specific facets of the birth trauma, which is the true source of these aggressive impulses.

Thus an extreme oral aggression with murderous feelings and vicious tendencies to bite experienced in relation to some unsatisfactory aspect of nursing is suddenly identified as being also the rage of a baby who is desperately fighting for life and breath in the clutch of the birth canal. Emotions and sensations that were originally attributed to the trauma of circumcision and related castration fears are recognized as belonging to the frightening separation from the mother when the umbilical cord was cut at birth. A combination of violent aggressive impulses, anal spasms, and fears of biological material that seemed related to severe toilet training is reinterpreted as reaction to the life-and-death struggle during the final stage of the birth process. And similarly, rage associated with suffocation that, on the biographical level seemed to be a metaphorically somatized reaction to the coercive, restricting, and "choking" influence of a domineering mother is experientially linked to the literally confining and strangling maternal organism during the time of biological delivery.

Once it becomes clear that only a small portion of the murderous aggressive impulses belongs to the traumatic situations from childhood and that their deeper source is the trauma of birth, the magnitude, intensity, and malignant nature of the violent impulses begins to make sense. The vital threat to the organism involved in the birth process, extreme physical and emotional stress, excruciating pain, and fear of suffocation make this situation a plausible source of malignant aggression. It is understandable that the reactivation of the unconscious record of an event in which survival was seriously threatened by another biological organism could result in aggressive impulses that would endanger the life of the individual or others.

Phenomena that are obscure and puzzling so long as we try to see them as being only biographically determined, such as automutilation, bloody suicide, sadistic murder or genocide, certainly make more sense when we realize that their experiential source is a process of comparable scope and relevance. The fact that all the Freudian erogenous zones are deeply engaged in the birth process provides a natural bridge to later traumas during the various stages of libidinal development. Difficult and painful experiences involving the oral, anal, urethral, and phallic areas and functions are thus not only traumatic in their own right, but also through their close thematic association with specific perinatal elements. As a result of this connection, they provide experiential channels through which different aspects of perinatal dynamics can, under certain circumstances, influence conscious processes. Childhood experiences, therefore, are not the actual primary sources of malignant aggression. They only contribute to the existing abysmal repository of perinatal aggression, weaken the defenses that normally prevent it from emerging into consciousness, and color specifically its manifestations in the individual's life.

The connection between malignant aggression and perinatal dynamics finds important support in certain rather common observations from psychedelic therapy. If the pharmacological effect of LSD wears off at a time when the subject is under the dynamic influence of BPM III and the experience does not reach the point of resolution by shifting to BPM IV, a highly characteristic clinical picture tends to develop. It involves extreme physical and emotional tension of a generalized nature, accompanied by sensations of great pressure in various parts of the body, as well as localized discomfort in some of the erogenous zones. The specific pattern of this condition in terms of the relative involvement of different anatomical regions and physiological functions varies greatly from one situation to another.

This condition is associated with an overwhelming upsurge of aggressive impulses into consciousness; it frequently requires an extreme effort to maintain control and prevent violent acting out. The individuals involved describe themselves as "time-bombs" ready to explode any minute. This destructive energy is oriented both inward and outward; elemental self-destructive impulses and aggression oriented toward persons and objects in the environment can coexist, or alternate in rather rapid sequences. If these volcanic forces were allowed to manifest themselves or override the individual's defenses, suicide and homicide would be equally plausible outcomes. Although both destructive and self-destructive tendencies are always present, in some instances one or the other direction can be clearly dominant.

These observations indicate a clear psychogenic link between violence, murder, self-destructive behavior, and bloody suicide, on the one hand, and the dynamics of the third perinatal matrix, on the other. They are also highly relevant for the understanding of various situations in which the individual kills indiscriminately and then directly or indirectly commits suicide. The phenomenon of

running amok—a culture-bound syndrome occurring in Malaysia—
is an extreme example. Even a cursory analysis of the lives of mass
murderers, such as the Boston Strangler, the Texas gunman White,
or Charles Manson, reveals that their dreams and fantasies, as well
as their everyday lives, abound in themes directly related to BPM
III.

A sociocultural example of behavior reflecting psychologically
the dynamics of BPM III is the kamikaze warrior; he causes massive
destruction and killing and in the process he dies himself. At the
same time, this act is viewed in a broader spiritual framework as
a sacrifice for a higher cause and for the Emperor, who is the
personification of the divine. A mitigated form of activation of the
third perinatal matrix will result in a state of irritability, anger,
and a strong tendency to provoke conflicts, attract the aggression
of others, and invite self-punishing situations.

Similar observations also shed new light on various self-destructive behaviors that result in *physical automutilation;* as in the
above examples, the key is again the dynamics of BPM III. When
individuals experience in their sessions intense painful sensations
that form an intrinsic part of the death-rebirth struggle, they
frequently feel a strong need for externally induced suffering that
would involve sensations congruent with their experience. Thus, a
person who has an excruciating pain in the neck or the small of
the back might demand painful massage in those places. Similarly,
feelings of suffocation can result in a craving for, or attempts at,
strangulation. In the extreme, individuals who experience excruciating pains in various parts of their bodies may believe that they
need to be cut by a knife or stabbed by a sharp object to achieve
relief from their unbearable suffering. During some psychedelic
sessions of this kind, the sitters actually have to prevent subjects
from hurting themselves by assuming dangerous positions that could
damage their necks, hitting their heads against the wall, scratching
their faces, or poking their eyes.

Deeper analysis reveals that these phenomena, which on the
surface suggest gross psychopathology, are motivated by an attempt
at self-healing. When an individual experiences intense pain or strong
negative emotion without an adequate external stimulus, this is an
indication that traumatic material is emerging from the unconscious.
In the context of this underlying gestalt, the same unpleasant
emotion or physical sensation is represented with an intensity which

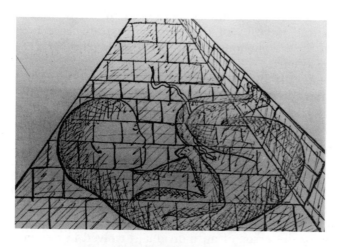

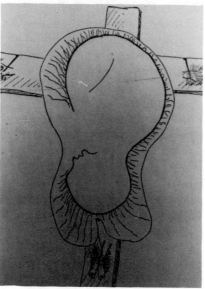

Fig. 33. Drawings reflecting deep regression to prenatal existence and to biological birth. First picture depicts the tranquillity of intrauterine existence by equating it with the atmosphere in the interior of a pyramid. The second picture reveals a profound insight into the connection between the suffering of the child during birth and Christ's agony on the cross by portraying a crucified fetus.

surpasses that consciously experienced by the subject. When the nature and intensity of the conscious experience exactly matches that of the unconscious gestalt, the problem has been resolved and healing occurs.

Thus, the insight that it is important to experience more of the same discomfort to reach resolution is essentially accurate. However, for this to happen, the experiential pattern must be completed internally, not acted out. It is essential that the subject relive the original situation in a complex way and with full conscious insight; experiencing a modified replica of it, without experiential access to the level of the unconscious to which it belongs, perpetuates the problem rather than solving it. The major mistake of those individuals who tend to mutilate themselves is confusion of the inner process with the elements of external reality. It is quite similar to the error of an individual involved in reliving a painful birth process who seeks an open window, seeing it as an escape route from the clutch of the birth canal. The above examples clearly indicate the absolute indispensability of an experienced sitter who can create a safe environment and prevent possible serious accidents based on inadequate reality testing by the client.

When a session dominated by BPM III is poorly resolved, various degrees of self-mutilating tendencies can persist in everday life for indefinite periods of time. A condition of this kind can be indistinguishable from a tendency to automutilation that one sees in naturally occurring psychopathological conditions. When this occurs, it is essential to continue the uncovering work with the use of various experiential techniques to reach the resolution. If that is insufficient, another psychedelic session should be planned as soon as possible. In some instances, various degrees of self-mutilation do not reflect the existence of a specific feeling in the unconscious, but are motivated by lack of feeling. In this case the individual may attempt to pinch, stab, cut, or burn himself or herself in order to overcome a sense of physical and emotional anesthesia and to experience some feelings. In the last analysis, even this problem typically reflects the existence of powerful forces operating in the unconscious. Lack of feeling frequently means not a lack of sensitivity, but a clash of conflicting forces that cancel each other out. Dynamic conflict of this kind quite commonly has perinatal roots.

We have already discussed in the preceding section certain psychopathological phenomena that involve aggression in combination with sexuality and scatology as characteristic manifestations of BPM III. For sadomasochism, rapes, sexual murders, and necrophilia, the participation of the sexual and scatological elements is so essential that it seemed preferrable to treat them in the context of sexuality rather than aggression.

The relevance of the new insights from deep experiential psychotherapy for the understanding of malignant aggression becomes even more obvious when we move from individual psychopathology into the realm of mass psychology and social pathology. The new insights into the psychology of wars, bloody revolutions, totalitarian systems, concentration camps, and genocide are of such fundamental theoretical and practical relevance that they will be examined separately in chapter 8, which deals with human culture.

Although for all practical purposes the most important repositories of aggressive impulses are the negative perinatal matrices, many transpersonal experiences can function as additional sources of destructive energy. Thus, large amounts of hostility are typically associated with reliving the memories of various embryonic crises, particularly attempted abortions. In some instances, a strong charge of negative emotions can be attached to a traumatic or frustrating ancestral, racial, or collective memory. A large variety of rather specific forms of aggression accompanies authentic identification with different animal forms; these can involve the roles of fighting enemies and rivals of the same species, or of animal, avian, reptilian, and other predators, hunting smaller victims for food.

Another important source of aggressive feelings is the reliving of traumatic memories from previous incarnations. It is important to relive the events involved, including the emotions and physical sensations, in order to free oneself from the bondage of anger and other negative affects and reach the ability to forgive and be forgiven. Mythology abounds in themes involving aggression and violence; many of the archetypal sequences stage horrific demons and wrathful deities, the fierce combats of gods, heroes, and legendary creatures, as well as scenes of destruction of incredible dimensions. Much destructive energy is also tied to transpersonal scenes of inorganic processes, such as volcanic eruptions, earthquakes, ocean storms, the destruction of celestial bodies, and black holes.

The transpersonal realms thus represent a rich repository of negative energies of various kinds and degrees. Like the biographical and perinatal sources, they are of great significance for the understanding of psychopathology and for psychotherapy. In actual clinical work, the transpersonal roots of aggression sometimes represent the deepest layer of a multilevel arrangement that also involves biographical and perinatal components; at other times the specific transpersonal forms immediately underlie the emotional or psychosomatic symptoms. In either case, the clinical problems with this dynamic structure cannot be solved unless and until the individual allows himself or herself to experience the transpersonal gestalts involved.

Dynamics of Depressions, Neuroses, and Psychosomatic Disorders

The extended cartography of the human psyche provides the basis for a deeper understanding of many psychopathological conditions encountered in everyday psychiatric practice. Where biographically oriented theories offer dynamic explanations for various clinical phenomena, the new model provides an interpretation that is more accurate and encompassing and, in many instances, simpler. It describes far more adequately the complicated mutual interrelations and interactions between the individual symptoms and syndromes and reflects more precisely everyday clinical observations. However, it also integrates in a comprehensive way certain syndromes or their aspects that the old theories could not account for, or, were able to explain only through elaborate, contrived, and ultimately unconvincing speculations. This is particularly true in the case of malignant aggression, sadomasochism, serious sexual perversions, various forms of suicide, most psychotic manifestations, and instances of spiritual pathology.

At the same time, the conceptual framework presented here is described and used with the explicit knowledge that it is a model and not an accurate description of reality. As such, it is at best a useful organization of the presently available observations and data and will have to be revised, extended, or replaced when new data emerge or new explanatory principles are discovered. The most important criteria of its validity are the power to reflect correctly

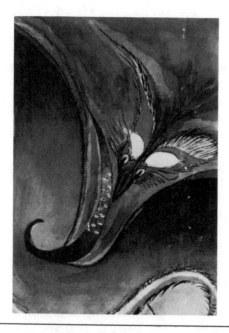

Fig. 34. *Vision from a perinatal session dominated by BPM III.* The bird-like monster represents vital threat and aggression; concomitant feelings of revulsion are attached to the mangy rat-tail at the bottom of the picture.

and to synthetize observations from many different fields, the use of new therapeutic mechanisms and approaches that far surpass those existing at present, and the capacity to provide exciting ideas for future research and exploration of new areas. Although the descriptions of the biographical level of the unconscious found in mainstream psychoanalysis require only minor adjustments for incorporation into the presented model, the role of perinatal and transpersonal dynamics in the understanding of psychopathology must be discussed in considerable detail, because of its novelty, as well as its critical importance.

The dynamics of the perinatal matrices is of particular theoretical and practical relevance. The perinatal phenomena are easily available; they are manifested regularly in dreams and even under the circumstances of everyday life. For many people, it is generally more difficult to keep these forces under control than to gain conscious access to them. When new understanding, reassurance, and a supportive framework are provided, intensive breathing and music are usually sufficient to facilitate experiential access to the perinatal material. The inclusion of the concept of perinatal matrices and of the birth trauma in psychiatric theory opens up new and exciting perspectives. It makes possible natural and logical explanations for most major psychopathological disorders, based on the connections between this level of the psyche and the anatomy, physiology, and biochemistry of the biological birth process.

Transcending the narrow biographical orientation of contemporary psychiatry also has far-reaching implications for therapy. In the new context, based on the understanding of perinatal dynamics, most of the standard psychopathological categories suddenly appear as relatively stabilized, difficult stages of a transformational and evolutionary process. When the therapeutic strategy involves activation and acceptance, rather than suppression, mechanisms of healing and personality transformation become available that surpass anything known to traditional psychotherapy and psychiatry.

Manifestations related to the dynamics of perinatal matrices are usually seen by psychiatrists as indications of serious mental disease that should be supressed by all possible means. The routine application of this therapeutic strategy, which is a direct outgrowth of the medical model, makes much of psychiatry an essentially antitherapeutic force, because it specializes in interfering with a process that has intrinsic healing potential. In many instances, providing a new understanding of the process, and encouraging and facilitating it by psychological or pharmacological means should be considered a method of choice, or at least acknowledged as an important alternative.

It is appropriate at this point to focus more specifically on the new understanding of psychopathology based on the concept of perinatal matrices. It is generally accepted that thinking in terms of clearly defined disease entities of agreed-upon etiology and pathogenesis is not applicable to psychiatry. The few exceptions, such as mental dysfunctions associated with general paresis, circulatory and degenerative diseases of the central nervous system, meningitis and encephalitis, or different forms of brain tumors, are actually problems that are diagnosed and treated by techniques developed by neurology. Patients with these disorders will be referred to psychatric facilities if they present serious management problems.

For the majority of disorders in the psychiatrist's daily practice, it is more appropriate to think in terms of symptoms and syndromes. *Symptoms* are emotional and psychosomatic manifestations that represent basic units, constituents, or building blocks of psychopathology. *Syndromes* are typical clusters or constellations of symptoms encountered in clinical practice.

A careful analysis of observations from deep experiential psychotherapy reveals that a conceptual model that includes perinatal dynamics can derive logically most psychiatric symptoms from the specific characteristics of the biological birth process. It can also explain quite naturally why individual psychiatric symptoms, such as anxiety, aggression, depression, guilt, inferiority feelings, or obsessions and compulsions tend to cluster into typical syndromes.

Anxiety, generally considered to be the single most important psychiatric symptom, is a logical and natural concomitant of the birth process in view of the fact that delivery is a situation of vital emergency involving extreme physical and emotional stress. The possibility that all anxiety could have its origin in the trauma that the child experienced in the birth canal was first mentioned by Sigmund Freud. However, Freud himself did not pursue this idea, and the theory of the birth trauma as the source of all future anxieties was later elaborated by his renegade disciple, Otto Rank. These theoretical speculations of the pioneers of psychoanalysis preceded by three decades their confirmation by psychedelic research.

Aggression of extreme proportions is equally comprehensible in relation to the birth process as a reaction to excessive physical and emotional pain, suffocation, and threat to survival. A comparable abuse imposed on an unconstrained animal would result in outbursts of rage and a motor storm. However, the child trapped in the narrow confines of the birth canal has no outlet for the flood of emotional and motor impulses, since he or she cannot move, fight back, leave the situation, or scream. It is therefore conceivable that an enormous amount of aggressive impulses and general tension would be, under these circumstances, fed back into the organism and stored for belated discharge. This enormous reservoir of pent-up energies can later become the basis not only for aggression and violent impulses, but also for various motor phenomena that typically accompany many psychiatric disorders, such as *generalized muscular tension, tremors, twitches, tics,* and *seizurelike activity.*

The fact that the closed system of the birth canal prevents any external expression of the biological fury involved seems to provide a natural model for Freud's concept of depression as aggression turned inward, using the individual as a target. This connection is clearly illustrated by the fact that the extreme outcome of both depression and aggression is murder. Homicide and suicide differ only in the direction the destructive impulse takes. Thus also, the symptom of *depression* has its perinatal prototype; for inhibited depression, it is the no-exit situation of the second perinatal matrix that effectively prevents any energetic discharge or flow, and, for agitated depression, it is the third perinatal matrix that allows some limited expression of aggression.

The psychological, emotional, and physical manifestations of depressed patients represent a combination of elements, some of which reflect the role of the suffering victim and others powerful

Fig. 35. An experience of deep depression and despair in a psychedelic session dominated by BPM II.

restrictive, repressive and self-punishing forces. In regressive experiential work, the victim aspects of depression can be traced back to the experience of the child during delivery, while the hostile, coercive, and self-destructive elements are identified as introjection of the uterine contractions and the pressures of the constricting birth canal. The perinatal roots of the major types of depression can explain many emotional, physiological, and even biochemical characteristics of these disorders. These connections are described in greater detail below.

It is somewhat more difficult to account for the fact that *guilt,* another basic psychiatric symptom, can typically be traced back to birth. Working with patients who suffer from overwhelming irrational feelings of guilt, one usually detects relevant biographical factors that seemingly explain them, such as constant reproaches from parents, explicit guilt-producing comments, and even the common use of references to labor pains ("If you knew how much I suffered giving birth to you, you would not behave this way"). However, such biographical factors represent only an overlay; their deeper source is a pool of primordial guilt of metaphysical dimensions that is closely associated with the perinatal matrices. This connection can be also illustrated by mythological and archetypal examples. Thus, the "primal sin" of the Bible links guilt to the expulsion from the paradisean situation of the Garden of Eden. More specifically, God's punishment of Eve involves an explicit reference to female reproductive functions: "In pain and sorrow shalt thou bring forth children."

On occasion, subjects in LSD therapy and other forms of deep experiential work offer interpretations of the connection between guilt and birth as they saw it in their sessions. Some attribute guilt to the reversal of the causal nexus between the loss of the intrauterine state and the intense negative emotions during delivery. According to this view, the aggressive and other instinctual forces unleashed during biological birth are interpreted as indicative of inherent evil, and the loss of the womb and the agony in the birth canal are seen as punishment for it. Others feel that guilt reflects a sense of reponsibility for suffering of the mother during delivery. However, the most common and most plausible explanation relates guilt to the recognition or awareness of how much suffering is recorded in the human organism or how much pain has been inflicted on it. Since a great portion of the emotional and physical pain that the individual has experienced during his or her lifetime was associated with the birth trauma, it seems quite logical that the sense of guilt reaches enormous proportions when the process of self-exploration or awareness reaches the perinatal level.

The individual who gets in touch experientially with the amount of suffering associated with the memory of birth has two possible interpretations. The first is to accept the fact that we live in an entirely capricious universe, where the most horrible things can happen to us without any good reason, quite unpredictably, and without our having the slightest degree of control. The alternative interpretation involving the sense of guilt emerges when the individual is unable or reluctant to accept this image of the universe and has a deep need to see the cosmos as a system governed by fundamental moral law and order. It is interesting in this connection that persons who discover that they have cancer or some other incurable and painful disease tend to respond to it with feelings of guilt: "Where did I go wrong? What did I do to deserve this? Why are 'they' doing this to me?" The logic behind this response can be explicated as: "Something this horrible would not have been done to me (or would not be happening to me), unless I had done something comparably bad to deserve it."

The degree of unconscious guilt thus seems to be commensurate with, and directly proportionate to, the amount of unconscious pain. Although the individuals involved frequently tend to project guilt onto specific situations that they consciously remember, such as forbidden sexual activities or various other forms of unacceptable behavior, its deepest nature is very vague, abstract, and unconscious. It consists in the conviction of having committed some horrible deed and not having the slightest idea what it was. It therefore makes good sense to see guilt as the result of a desperate effort to rationalize the absurdity of suffering that was imposed on the individual without any intelligible reason.[6]

The above explanation, however plausible on this level of consciousness, is not final and absolute. When the process of self-exploration reaches the transpersonal level, new possibilities occur that the individual could not have conceived of while totally immersed in biographical issues or in the perinatal process. The traumatic aspects of birth can suddenly be identified as the workings of condensed bad karma. The suffering involved is then seen not as absurd and capricious, but as reflecting the individual's karmic responsibility for actions in previous incarnations. The deepest transpersonal roots of guilt seem to reflect the recognition of one's identity with the creative principle responsible for all the suffering built into the divine play of existence. This would represent an error in logical typing, since the ethical standards that are part of creation backfire and are applied against the creator.

We have already described in detail how the excessive sexual arousal that is an intrinsic part of the third perinatal matrix forms a natural basis for a variety of *sexual dysfunctions and deviations.* We have also discussed at lenth how *unusual attitudes toward biological material and excretory functions* can be explained quite logically from the events accompanying biological birth. The fact that spiritual opening and intrinsic mystical feelings form integral aspects of perinatal dynamics provides fascinating new insights into the *psychopathology of religion,* as well as various clinical conditions that have a strong spiritual component, such as obsessive compulsive neurosis and certain types of psychosis. These issues are dealt with later in connection with specific psychopathological disorders, the new understanding of psychoses, and the role of spirituality in human life (obsessive-compulsive neuroses, psychoses and spiritual energencies are discussed later this chapter; spirituality in human life is discussed in Chapter 5 and 6).

Emotional disorders are almost invariably accompanied by specific *psychosomatic manifestations.* This is true for various forms of depressions, psychoneuroses, alcoholism and drug addiction, borderline psychotic states, psychoses, and particularly for psychosomatic diseases. The nature and certain specific features of the typical physical concomitants of emotional disorders can also be understood quite logically from their connection with the birth experience. In the past, there have been endless arguments between the organic and psychological schools of psychiatry as to whether biological or psychological factors play a primary role in emotional disorders. Introducing the perinatal level of the unconscious into psychiatric theory bridges to a great extent the gap between these two extreme orientations and offers a surprising alternative: since the birth experience is simultaneously an emotional, physiological, and biochemical process, the question as to what is primary and what is derived is irrelevant on this level of the psyche. The emotional and biological phenomena represent two sides of the same coin, and both can be reduced to the same common denominator—the birth process.

The typical physical concomitants of various emotional disorders make much sense if considered in this light. They involve belt headaches or migraine headaches; palpitation and other cardiac complaints; a subjective sense of a lack of oxygen and breathing difficulties under emotional stress; muscular pains, tensions, tremors, cramps, and seizurelike activities; nausea and vomiting; painful uterine contractions; activation of the gastrointestinal tract, resulting in spastic constipation or diarrhea; profuse sweating; hot flashes alternating with chills; and changes of skin circulation and various dermatological manifestations. The same is true for some extreme psychiatric complaints that have both emotional and physical aspects, such as the sense of being overwhelmed by powerful erratic energies and losing control, fear of death and the experience of dying, and fear of an impending loss of sanity. Similarly, the frequent catastrophic expectations of psychiatric patients are not difficult to understand in the context of the emerging memory of the birth trauma.

The perinatal level of the unconscious thus represents a multifaceted and rich repository of emotional qualities, physical sensations, and powerful energies. It seems to function as a universal and relatively undifferentiated potential matrix for the development of most forms of psychopathology. To the extent to which the perinatal matrices reflect the actual trauma of birth, one would expect substantial variations in the overall extent of negative elements from individual to individual. It certainly should make a difference whether an individual was born within one hour, in an elevator or a taxi on the way to the hospital, or whether the delivery lasted fifty hours and involved forceps and other extreme measures.

However, with respect to the model presented here, the actual nature and duration of childbirth is not the only factor in the development of psychopathology. It is obvious that among individuals whose birth was comparable, some may be relatively normal, while others could show various types and degrees of psychopathology. The question is how to reconcile this variation with the obvious significance of the perinatal level of the unconscious. The pool of difficult emotions and physical sensations derived from the birth trauma represents only a potential source of mental disorders;

whether psychopathology develops, what specific form it takes, and how serious it will be are critically codetermined by the individual's postnatal history and, thus, by the nature and dynamics of the COEX systems.

Sensitive handling of the newborn, reinstitution of the symbiotic interaction with the mother, and sufficient time allowed for bonding seem to be factors of critical importance that can counteract much of the deleterious impact of the birth trauma. In view of the observations from modern consciousness research, a basic revision of present medical approaches, which emphasize impeccable body mechanics but violate fundamental biological and emotional bonds beween mother and child, is of critical importance for the mental health of humanity. The significance of alternative techniques of childbirth that attempt to rectify the present frightening situation, such as Frederick Leboyer's birth without violence (1975) and other new approaches respecting the needs of mother, father, and child, cannot be overestimated.

Individuals who relive their birth in psychedelic sessions or some nondrug experiential work repeatedly report that they have discovered a deep connection between the pattern and circumstances of their delivery and the overall quality of their life. It seems as if the experience of birth determines one's basic feelings about existence, image of the world, attitudes toward other people, the ratio of optimism to pessimism, the entire strategy of life, and even such specific elements as self-confidence and the capacity to handle problems and projects.

From the point of view of the medical model and pedestrian common sense, the delivery appears to be an essentially passive act for the child; the work is all done by the mother and her uterine contractions, while the child is delivered more or less as an inanimate object. The dominant medical belief is that the child is not conscious of the environment and does not experience pain. Neurophysiology even denies the possibility of birth memory, because the cerebral cortex of the newborn is not mature and lacks the myelin sheaths on neurons. In light of all the clinical evidence from modern consciousness research, this position is the result of psychological repression and wishful thinking and should not be considered a scientific fact. Even on a rather superficial level, this approach significantly contradicts other experiments and observations that have demonstrated a remarkable sensitivity of the fetus during prenatal existence and others that suggest the presence of primitive forms of memory in unicellular organisms.

In any case, the reliving of birth in experiential clinical work clearly indicates that from the introspective point of view this process is perceived and interpreted as an ordeal that requires extreme active struggle and effort, a true hero's journey. Thus, the moment of birth is experienced under normal circumstances as a personal triumph. This can be illustrated by its characteristic association with images of victory in revolutions, wars, or the killing of wild and dangerous animals. It is not infrequent in the context of the birth memory that the individual experiences a condensed review of all his or her later successes in life. The experience of birth thus functions psychologically as the prototype of all future situations that represent a serious challenge for the individual.

When exposure to the birth situation has been reasonable and not excessive or debilitating and the postnatal situation sensitively handled, the individual is left with an almost cellular feeling of self-confidence in confronting difficulties and overcoming them. Individuals born under the influence of heavy general anesthesia repeatedly connect this with their later difficulties in completing projects. They indicate that they are capable of mobilizing enough energy and enthusiasm in the early stages of any major endeavor, but later lose the sense of focus and feel that their energies become diffused and diluted. As a result, they never experience the feeling of clean completion of a project and the satisfaction derived from it. When manual help or forceps were used to terminate the delivery, the ensuing pattern is somewhat similar. The individual involved is capable of working with adequate energy and enthusiasm in the initial phases of a project, but loses confidence just before its termination and has to rely on external help for the "final push." Persons whose birth was induced report that they dislike being pushed into projects before they feel ready, or may sense that they are being pushed into projects even if objectively this is not so.

From the point of view of the presented model, it is of course of utmost theoretical and practical importance to study individuals who were born by Caesarean section. For this purpose it is essential to differentiate between elective or nonlabor Caesarean section and emergency Caesarean section. The former is planned ahead of time for various reasons: the pelvis may be too narrow, the baby too large, the uterus scarred by a previous Caesarean section, or the vogue allows the mother to choose a Caesarean operation for cosmetic purposes. The child born in this way entirely bypasses the situation characteristic of BPM II and III. It must still face the crisis of separation from the mother, the cutting of the umbilical cord, and possibly the effects of anesthesia. The emergency Caesarean is usually performed after many hours of traumatic delivery, when it becomes obvious that to continue would be dangerous for the mother or child. In this case, the overall trauma is regularly far greater than that associated with normal delivery.

Since I have worked with only a few elective Caesareans, the following observations represent first clinical impressions that require further validation. Unless programmed negatively by the circumstances of their life, they seem to be quite open to the spiritual dimension and have easy experiential access to the transpersonal realm. They accept quite naturally many phenomena that give an average person great conceptual difficulty; such as the possibility of extrasensory perception, reincarnation, or the archetypal world. In psychedelic sessions they can reach the traspersonal level in a short-cut fashion and characteristically they need not confront elements of BPM II and III. Instead, their reliving of biological birth includes experiences characteristic of Caesarean birth, such as surgical cuts, manual extraction from the womb, emerging into light through a bloody opening, and the effects of anesthesia.

When they reach the level of birth experientially, elective Caesareans report a sense of fundamental wrongness, as if they were comparing the way they came into this world with some phylogenetic or archetypal matrix indicating what birth should be like. Surprisingly, they miss the experience of normal birth—the challenge and stimulation it provides, the confrontation with obstacles, and the triumphant emerging from confinement. They sometimes ask the sitters to simulate the constricting situation of birth to allow them to struggle for their liberation. It seems that, as a result of the short-cut solution, they are not prepared for the future vicissitudes of life and lack the stamina for struggle or even the ability to see life in terms of projects and to get excited about them.

In addition, the exposure to the constraints of the birth canal seems to lay the foundations for one's sense of boundaries in the world. The elective Caesareans may lack the sense of what their place is in the world and how much they can reasonably expect from others. It is as if they feel that the entire world should be the nourishing womb, providing unconditionaly all they need. They tend to reach out and, if they get what they want, they ask for more. Since the world is substantially different from the womb, it strikes back sooner or later and the hurt individual withdraws into psychological isolation. The life pattern of a Caesarean may in extreme cases oscillate between indiscriminate and excessive demands and painful withdrawal.[7]

It is important to realize what a great difference there is between a normal birth and a Caesarean birth. During normal birth the intrauterine condition deteriorates and becomes unbearable, so that the moment of birth is experienced as a liberation and a fundamental improvement over the preceding one. In elective Caesarean birth the child moves from the symbiotic relationship in the womb directly into the external world, where it must face separation, hunger, cold, the need to breathe, and other difficulties. This situation is clearly worse than the intrauterine state that preceded it, although the womb in late pregnancy does not satisfy the needs of the child to the same degree that it does in early embryonic development.

If, following birth, the infant is handled with love and sensitivity, much of the immediate traumatic impact of this life-threatening situation can be compensated for or counterbalanced. This is particularly true if the pregnancy was satisfactory and the newborn has good psychological foundations. Such a child would spend nine months of life in a good womb and then be catapulted in the birth process. It is my belief that the event of birth will always be traumatic to some degree, even if its duration is short and the mother is psychologically stable, loving and well prepared. However, immediately after birth, this child would be put back on the mother's belly or breast, reestablishing a symbiotic relationship with her. The comforting impact of physical contact has been demonstrated experimentally, and it is well known that the heart beat can have a profound nourishing impact on the newborn.

The symbiotic situation on the good breast is quite close to the one experienced in the good womb. Under these circumstances, bonding can occur that, according to some recent studies (Klaus 1976; Quinn 1982), seems to have a decisive influence on the entire future relationship between mother and child. If the child is then put into lukewarm water, simulating the intrauterine conditions, as is done in the Leboyer approach, this is another powerful soothing and healing element.[8] It is as if the child is being told in a language that he or she understands: "Nothing horrible and irreversible happened; things were difficult for awhile, but now, by and large, you are where you were before. And this is the way life is; it can get rough, but if one persists it will be good again." This approach seems to imprint in the child, almost on a cellular level, a general optimism or realism toward life, a healthy self-confidence, and an ability to face future challenge. It answers positively for all of the individual's life the question that Einstein considered the crucial problem of existence: "Is the universe friendly?"

Conversely, if the child immediately after birth faces the contemporary "perfect medical treatment," the psychological situation is entirely different. The umbilical cord is usually cut almost instantly, the respiratory pathways are cleaned, and the child might be slapped on the buttocks to stimulate respiration. Then a drop of silver nitrate is administered to the baby's eyes to prevent possible infection by gonorrhea from the mother, and the child is hastily washed and examined. This is just about all the human interaction that the child receives to counteract the most serious trauma of human life—the depth of which is matched only by other life-threatening situations and, eventually, by biological death. After being shown to the mother, the child is taken to the nursery, being returned to her in the following days according to a scientifically prescribed schedule designed by obstetricians. A child treated in this way emerges with a deeply ingrained message that the intra-uterine paradise was lost once and forever, and things will never be good again. A sense of psychological defeat and a lack of confidence in confronting difficulties are engraved on the very core of his or her being.

It is difficult to believe that science, known for its meticulous exploration of all possible variables, could have developed such a one-sided and distorted approach to this fundamental event in human life. However, this situation is not isolated; similar conditions exist for the dying: a mechanical concern to prolong life has all but replaced the human dimensions of the experience of death. Intellectual knowledge and training of any depth and scope gives

no protection against emotional bias and, in regard to such shattering events as birth and death, this bias is paramount. For this
reason, with respect to being born and dying, scientific opinions
and theories frequently do not reflect objective facts, but are
sophisticated rationalizations of irrational emotions and attitudes.

Both the drastic and the tender aspects of the birth situation
represent powerful emotional stimuli, particularly for those who
have not confronted these areas in themselves in deep experiential
work. Even the reliving of birth in a group situation is an overwhelming emotional event that can trigger on the part of assisting
and observing persons a deep psychological process. Much of the
detached and overly technological approach to birth practiced by
contemporary medicine may not arise from factors of time and
money alone, but may also reflect the rigid training in detachment
from, and armoring against, emotions that are seen as professionally
disqualifying.

The pathogenic impact of birth is, therefore, not just a simple
function of the extent and the nature of the birth trauma itself;
it is also a function of the way the child was treated immediately
following the moment of birth. But even that is not the whole
story; emotionally important events from later life, both nourishing
and traumatic, are also significant factors determining the extent
to which the dynamics of perinatal matrices will be translated into
manifest psychopathology. In this sense, the psychoanalytic doctrine
about the relevance of childhood traumas remains valid in the new
model in spite of the fact that the latter emphasizes the birth
trauma and the transpersonal realms. However, the specific biographical events described by Freud and his followers are seen not
as the primary causes of emotional disorders, but as conditions for
the manifestation of deeper levels of the unconscious.

The new conceptual framework suggests that good mothering,
satisfaction, security, and a general predominance of positive experiences in childhood would create a dynamic buffering zone
protecting the individual from the direct and disturbing impact of
perinatal emotions, sensations, and energies. Conversely, continuing
traumatization in childhood would not only fail to create this
protective screen, it would further contribute to the pool of negative
emotions and sensations stored on the perinatal level. As a result
of this defect in the defense system, the perinatal elements could
at a later date emerge into consciousness in the form of psycho-

pathological symptoms and syndromes. The specific content of the traumatic experiences in childhood and their timing would then selectively emphasize certain aspects or facets of the birth experience or of the perinatal dynamics, thereby determining the final form of symptomatology that will become manifest in the individual's life.

Thus, traumatic situations in which the subject plays the role of a helpless victim selectively reinforce the dynamic relevance of BPM II. They can cover a wide range, from painful and threatening events that occurred in the life of a helpless infant to such adult situations as being trapped under the debris of a collapsed house during an air raid, near suffocation under an avalanche, or being imprisoned and tortured by the Nazis or Communists. In a more subtle way, the second perinatal matrix can be cultivated by daily situations in a family that victimizes the child and leaves no possible outlet.

Similarly, situations that include violence but allow some degree of active involvement on the part of the subject would reinforce BPM III. An experience of being raped would characteristically selectively reinforce the sexual aspect of the third perinatal matrix, since it involves a combination of fear, aggression, struggle, and sexuality. A childhood experience in which a child was confronted with feces or some other biological material in a painful, punishing manner would selectively emphasize the scatological facet of BPM III. There are many other similar examples, however, these should suffice to convey the general principles of the mechanisms involved.

Having established the relationship between perinatal matrices, the birth trauma, and psychopathology, I will now apply the concept of dynamic interplay between perinatal matrices and the COEX systems to the most important categories of emotional disorders and their specific forms. Emotional, psychosomatic, and interpersonal problems frequently have a multilevel dynamic structure that includes not only the biographical and perinatal elements, but also important roots in the transpersonal realm. I will therefore make occasional references to such deeper connections. The following discussion should not be seen as a speculative application of the new model to various forms of psychopathology. It is basically a collection of insights gathered from people who have explored and deciphered in deep experiential work the dynamic structure of the various problems that plagued their lives.

Severe inhibited depressions of endogenous and reactive nature have typically important roots in the second perinatal matrix. The phenomenology of the sessions governed by BPM II, as well as the postsession intervals dominated by this matrix, show all the essential features of deep depression. Under the influence of BPM II an individual experiences agonizing mental pain, despair, overwhelming feelings of guilt and inadequacy, deep anxiety, lack of initiative, loss of interest in anything, and an inability to enjoy existence. In this state, life appears to be utterly meaningless, emotionally empty, and absurd. In spite of the extreme suffering involved, this condition is not associated with crying or any other dramatic external manifestations; it is characterized by a general motor inhibition. The world and one's own life are seen as if through a negative stencil, with selective awareness of the painful, bad, and tragic aspects of life and blindness for anything positive. This situation appears to be, and indeed feels, utterly unbearable, inescapable, and hopeless. Sometimes this is accompanied by loss of the ability to see colors; when that happens, the entire world is perceived as a black-and-white film. Existential philosophy and the theater of the absurd seem to be the most accurate descriptions of this experience of life.

Inhibited depressions are characterized not only by a total obstruction of emotional flow, but also a total energetic blockage and severe inhibition of the major physiological functions of the body, such as digestion, elimination of waste products, sexual activity, the menstrual cycle, and the sleep rhythm. This is quite consistent with an understanding of this type of depression as a manifestation of BPM II. Its typical physical concomitants involve feelings of oppression, constriction, and confinement, a sense of suffocation, tension and pressure, headaches, retention of water and urine, constipation, cardiac distress, loss of interest in food and sex, and a tendency to hypochondriacal interpretation of various physical symptoms. The paradoxical biochemical findings, suggesting that people suffering from inhibited depression can show a high level of stress as indicated by the level of catecholamines and steroid hormones fit well the image of BPM II, which reflects a highly stressful situation with no external action or manifestation.

The theory of psychoanalysis links depression to early oral problems and emotional deprivation. Although this connection is obviously correct, it does not account for important aspects of depression—a sense of being stuck, of hopelessness with no exit, of energy blockage, and most of the physical symptoms, including biochemical findings. The present model shows the Freudian explanation as correct, but partial. While the deepest nature of inhibited depression can only be understood from the dynamics of BPM II, the COEX systems associated with it and instrumental in its development include biographical elements emphasized by psychoanalysis.

The connection of this biographical material with BPM II reflects deep experiential logic. This stage of biological delivery involves interruption of the symbiotic connection with the maternal organism through uterine contractions, isolation from any meaningful contact, termination of the supply of nourishment and warmth, and exposure to danger without protection.[9] It stands to reason, then, that the typical constituents of COEX systems dynamically related to depression involve rejection, separation from and absence of the mother, and feelings of loneliness, cold, hunger, and thirst, during infancy and early childhood. Other important biographical determinants include family situations that are oppressive and punishing for the child and permit no rebellion or escape. They thus reinforce and perpetuate the role of the victim in a no-exit situation, a characteristic of BPM II.

An important category of COEX systems instrumental in the dynamics of depression involves memories of events that constituted a threat to survival or body integrity, in which the individual played the role of a helpless victim. This is an entirely new observation, since psychoanalysis and psychotherapeutically oriented academic psychiatry emphasize the role of psychological factors in the pathogenesis of depression. The psychotraumatic effects of serious diseases, injuries, operations, and episodes of near drowning have been overlooked and grossly underestimated. These new observations suggesting the paramount significance of physical traumas in the individual's life for the development of depression would be difficult to integrate into psychoanalytic theory, which stresses the oral origins of depression. However, they are perfectly logical in the context of the presented model, where the emphasis is on the combined emotional-physical trauma of birth.

In contrast, the phenomenology of *agitated depression* is dynamically associated with BPM III; its basic elements can be seen in experiential sessions and postsession intervals governed by this matrix. Characteristic features of this type of depression are a high level of tension and anxiety, an excessive amount of psychomotor excitement and agitation, and aggressive impulses oriented both inward and outward. Patients with agitated depression cry and scream, roll on the floor, flail around, beat their heads against the wall, scratch their faces, and tear their hair and clothes. The typical physical symptoms associated with this condition are muscular tensions, tremors, and painful cramps, belt (or migraine) headaches, uterine and intestinal spasms, nausea, and breathing problems.

The COEX systems associated with this matrix deal with aggression and violence, cruelties of various kinds, sexual abuse and assaults, painful medical interventions, and diseases involving choking and a struggle for breath. Unlike the COEX systems related to BPM II, the subject involved in these situations is not a passive victim; he or she is actively engaged in attempts to fight back, defend oneself, remove the obstacles, or escape. Memories of violent encounters with parental figures or siblings, fist fights with peers, scenes of sexual abuse and rape, and episodes from military battles are typical examples of this kind.

There has been a strong feeling among psychoanalysts that the psychodynamic interpretation of *mania* is generally far less satisfactory and convincing than that of depression. However, most authors seem to agree that mania represents a means of avoiding an awareness of depression, and that it includes a denial of painful inner reality and a flight into the external world. It reflects the victory of ego over superego, a drastic decrease of inhibitions, an increase of self-esteem, and an abundance of sensual and aggressive impulses. In spite of all this, mania does not give the impression of genuine freedom. Psychological theories of manic-depressive disorders emphasize the intensive ambivalence of manic patients and the fact that simultaneous feelings of love and hate interfere with their ability to relate to others. The typical manic hunger for objects is usually seen as a manifestation of strong oral emphasis, and the periodicity of mania and depression as an indication of its relation to the cycle of satiety and hunger.

Many of the otherwise puzzling features of manic episodes become easily comprehensible when seen in their relation to the dynamics of the perinatal matrices. Mania is psychogenetically linked to the experiential transition from BPM III to BPM IV; it can be seen as a clear indication that the individual is partially under the influence of the fourth perinatal matrix, but nevertheless still in touch with the third. Here, the oral impulses reflect the state the manic patient is aiming for and has not yet achieved, rather than a "fixation" on the oral level. Relaxation and oral satisfaction are characteristic of a state following biological birth. To be peaceful, to sleep and to eat—the typical wishes found in mania—are the natural goals of an organism flooded by the impulses associated with the final stage of birth.

In experiential psychotherapy one can occasionally observe transient manic episodes *in statu nascendi* as phenomena suggesting incomplete rebirth. This usually happens when the subjects involved have already moved beyond the difficult experience of the death-rebirth struggle and gotten a taste and sense of release and escape from the birth agony. However, at the same time, they are unwilling and unable to face the remaining unresolved material related to the third matrix. As a result of anxious clinging to this uncertain and tenuous victory, the new positive feelings become accentuated to the point of a caricature. The image of whistling in the dark seems to fit this condition particularly well. The exaggerated and forceful nature of manic emotions and behavior clearly betrays that they are not expressions of genuine joy and freedom, but reaction formations to fear and aggression.

LSD subjects whose sessions terminate in a state of incomplete rebirth show all the typical signs of mania. They are hyperactive, move around at a hectic pace, try to socialize and fraternize with everybody in their environment, and talk incessantly about their sense of triumph and well-being, wonderful feelings, and the great experience they have just had. They extol the wonders of LSD treatment and spin messianic and grandiose plans to transform the world by making it possible for every human being to have the same experience. Extreme hunger for stimuli and social contact is associated with inflated zest, self-love, and self-esteem, as well as indulgence in various aspects of life. The breakdown of superego restraints results in seductiveness, promiscuous tendencies, and obscene talk.

The fact emphasized by Otto Fenichel (1945) that these aspects of mania link it to the psychology of carnivals—socially sanctioned unleashing of otherwise forbidden impulses—further confirms its deep connection with the dynamic shift from BPM III to BPM IV. In this connection, the hunger for stimuli and the search for drama and action serve the dual purpose of consuming the released impulses and engaging in an external situation with a turbulence that matches the intensity and quality of the inner turmoil.

When subjects experiencing this state can be convinced to turn inward, face the difficult emotions that remain unresolved, and complete the (re)birth process, the manic quality disappears from their mood and behavior. The experiences of BPM IV in their pure form are characterized by radiant joy, increased zest, deep relaxation, tranquility and serenity, peace, and total inner satisfaction; they lack the driven quality, grotesque exaggeration, and ostentatiousness characteristic of manic states.

The COEX systems superimposed on the perinatal mechanism for mania seem to involve episodes in which satisfaction has occurred under circumstances of insecurity and uncertainty about the genuineness and continuation of the gratification. Also an expectation or demand of overtly happy behavior in situations that do not quite justify it seems to feed into the manic pattern. In addition, one frequently finds in the history of manic patients contrary influences on their self-esteem, hypercritical and undermining attitudes of parental figures alternating with overestimation, psychological inflation, and a building up of unrealistic expectations. Also, the alternating experience of constraint and freedom that characterizes the custom of swaddling infants seems to be psychogenetically related to mania.

All the observations from experiential work seem to suggest that the memory of the final stage of birth, with its sudden shift from agony to a sense of dramatic relief, represents the natural basis for the alternating patterns of manic-depressive disorders. This, of course, does not exclude the participation of biochemical factors as important triggers for the shifts of these psychological matrices. However, even findings of consistent and relevant biochemical changes do not in themselves explain the specific nature and psychological features of this disorder. Even in a situation as clearly chemically defined as an LSD session, the administration of the drug does not explain the psychological content, and the occurrence of a depressive or manic state requires further clarification. In addition, there is always the question whether biological factors play a causal role in the disorder or are its symptomatic concomitants. It is conceivable that the physiological and biochemical changes in manic-depressive disorders represent an organismic replay of the conditions in the organism of a child who is being born.

The concept of basic perinatal matrices offers fascinating new insights into the *phenomenon of suicide,* which in the past has represented a serious theoretical challenge to psychoanalytically oriented theories. Two important questions related to suicide must be answered by any theory that tries to explain this phenomenon. The first is why a particular individual wants to commit suicide, an act that obviously violates the otherwise mandatory dictate of the self-preservation drive. The second, equally puzzling question is the specificity in the choice of the means of suicide. There seems to be a close connection between the state of mind the depressed person is in and the type of suicide he or she contemplates or attempts. The drive thus is not simply to terminate one's life but to do it in a particular way. It might seem natural that a person who takes an overdose of tranquilizers or barbiturates would not jump off the cliff or under a train. However, the selectivity of choice also works the other way around: a person who chooses bloody suicide would not use drugs, even if they were easily available.[10]

The material from psychedelic research and other forms of deep experiential work throws new light on both the deep motives for suicide and the intriguing question of the choice of methods. Suicidal ideation and tendencies can be occasionally observed in any stage of LSD psychotherapy; however, they are particularly frequent and urgent at the time when subjects are confronting the unconscious material related to the negative perinatal matrices. Observations from psychedelic sessions reveal that suicidal tendencies fall into two distinct categories that have very specific relations to the perinatal process. If we agree that the experience of inhibited depression is a manifestation of BPM II and that agitated depression is a derivative of BPM III, then various forms of suicidal fantasies, tendencies, and actions can be understood as unconsciously motivated attempts to escape these unbearable psychological states, using two routes reflecting the individual's biological history.

Suicide of the first type, or *nonviolent suicide,* is based on the unconscious memory that the no-exit situation of BPM II was preceded by the experience of intrauterine existence. An individual trying to escape the elements of the second perinatal matrix would thus choose a way that is most easily available in this state—that of regression into the original undifferentiated unity of the prenatal condition (BPM I). Since the level of the unconscious on which this decision is made is not usually experientially accessible, the subject is attracted to situations and means in everyday life that seem to involve similar elements. The basic underlying purpose is to reduce the intensity of painful stimuli and eventually eliminate them. The final goal is to lose the painful awareness of one's separateness and individuality and to reach the undifferentiated state of "oceanic consciousness" that characterizes embryonic existence. Mild forms of suicidal ideas of this type are manifested as a wish not to exist, or to fall into a deep sleep, forget everything and not to awaken ever again. Actual suicidal plans and attempts in this group involve the use of large doses of hypnotics or tranquilizers, inhalation of carbon monoxide or domestic gas, drowning, bloodletting in warm water, and freezing in snow.[11]

Suicide of the second type, or *violent suicide*, follows unconsciously the pattern once experienced during biological birth. It is closely associated with the agitated form of depression and thus related to BPM III. For a person under the influence of the third matrix, regression into the oceanic state of the womb is unavailable because it would lead through the hellish no-exit stage of BPM II, which is psychologically worse than BPM III. However, what is available as a psychological escape route is the memory that once a similar state was terminated by the explosive release and liberation at the moment of biological birth. As with nonviolent suicide, the individuals involved have no experiential access to the perinatal level and to the insight that the psychological solution would be to relive one's birth, complete the death-rebirth process internally, and connect experientially with the postnatal situation. Instead, they exteriorize the process and tend to enact a situation in the external world that involves the same elements and has similar experiential components.

The basic pattern here is to intensify the tension and suffering, bring them to a culmination point, and then reach liberation in the context of an explosive discharge of destructive impulses and amidst various forms of biological material. This applies equally to biological birth and violent suicide; both involve an abrupt termination of excessive emotional and physical tension, instant discharge of enormous energies, extensive tissue damage, and the presence of organic material, such as blood, feces, and entrails.

The juxtaposition of photographs showing biological birth and those depicting victims of violent suicide clearly demonstrate the deep formal parallels of the two situations. The similarity between them has been repeatedly reported by psychedelic subjects who experienced identification with individuals who have committed suicide; experiences of this kind occur frequently in perinatal sessions.

The suicidal fantasies and acts that belong to this category involve death under the wheels of a train, in the turbine of a hydroelectric plant, or in suicidal car accidents; cutting one's throat, blowing one's brains out, and stabbing oneself with a knife; throwing oneself from a window, tower, or cliff; and some exotic forms of suicide such as harakiri, kamikaze, and running amok. Suicide by hanging seems to belong to an earlier phase of BPM III, characterized by feelings of strangulation, suffocation, and strong sexual arousal.

The LSD work has also provided fascinating insights into the intriguing problem of the choice of a particular type and specific form of suicide that has been poorly understood in the past. Nonviolent suicide reflects a general tendency to reduce the intensity of painful emotional and physical stimuli. The specific choice of means seems to be determined by biographical elements of a relatively superficial nature. However, violent suicide involves a mechanism of an entirely different kind. Here I have repeatedly observed that the individuals who were contemplating a particular form of suicide were already experiencing the physical sensations and emotions that would be involved in its actual enactment.

Thus, those persons who are attracted to trains or hydroelectric turbines already suffer from intense feelings of being crushed and torn to pieces; it is easy to trace these feelings back to perinatal experiences. Those who have a tendency to cut or stab themselves complain about unbearable pains in the parts of their bodies that they intend to injure. Similarly, the tendencies to hang oneself are based on strong and deep preexisting feelings of strangulation and choking. Again, both the pains and choking sensations are easily recognizable as elements of the third perinatal matrix. The specific choice of violent suicide thus seems to be a special example of fundamental intolerance for cognitive-emotional dissonance; this important mechanism underlying much of psychopathology is discussed further on (p. 424–5). When an individual is overwhelmed by irrational emotions and incomprehensible physical sensations of

enormous intensity, then even acts that involve severe self-mutilation or self-destruction seem acceptable as ways to achieve congruence between the inner experience and external reality.

There are important exceptions to these general rules. The
mechanism of violent suicide requires a relatively clear memory of
the sudden transition from the struggle in the birth canal to the
external world and of the explosive liberation. If this transition
was blurred by heavy anaesthesia, the individual would be programmed for the future almost on a cellular level to escape from
severe stress into a drugged state. Under these circumstances, a
state characteristic of BPM III could result in a nonviolent suicide.
A physiological exposure to birth without or with minimum anesthesia would thus prepare the individual for future serious challenges and create a deep sense of confidence in one's ability to
cope with them. Under pathological circumstances, a birth not
seriously complicated pharmacologically would set a pattern for
violent suicide. Heavy anesthesia would then program the individual
to seek relief from severe stress in a drugged state and, under
extreme circumstances, in a drug death. However, in the study of
individual cases of suicide, detailed examination of the birth process
must be complemented by biographical analysis, since postnatal
events can significantly codetermine and color the pattern of suicide.

When suicidal individuals undergo psychedelic therapy and
complete the death-rebirth process, they see suicide retrospectively
as a tragic mistake based on lack of self-understanding. A person
who does not know that one can experience liberation from unbearable emotional and physical tension through a symbolic death
and rebirth and/or through reconnecting to the state of prenatal
existence without suffering any physical damage, might be driven
by the catastrophic dimensions of his or her agony to enact an
irreversible situation in the material world that involves similar
elements. Since the experiences of the first and fourth perinatal
matrices not only represent symbiotic biological states but also have
very distinct spiritual dimensions, suicidal tendencies of both types
appear, in light of the above observations, to be distorted and
unrecognized craving for transcendence. The best remedy for self-
destructive tendencies and the suicidal urge is, then, the experience
of ego death and rebirth and of cosmic unity. Not only are the
destructive energies and impulses consumed in the process, but the
individual connects with the transpersonal context in which suicide

no longer seems to be a solution. This sense of the futility of suicide is connected with the insight that the transformations of consciousness and the cycles of death and rebirth will continue after one's biological demise or, more specifically, with the recognition of the impossibility of escaping one's karmic patterns.

In general agreement with the psychoanalytical theory, *alcoholism* and *narcotic drug addiction* appear to be closely related to depressions and suicide. The most basic characteristic of alcoholics and addicts, and their deepest motive for taking intoxicant drugs, seems to be an overwhelming craving for experiences of blissful undifferentiated unity. Feelings of this kind are associated with periods of undisturbed intrauterine life and good nursing; it was emphasized above that both of these states have intrinsic numinous dimensions. Alcoholics and addicts experience a great amount of emotional pain derived from COEX systems and in the last analysis from negative perinatal matrices; these involve depression, general tension, anxiety, guilt, low self-esteem, and others. The excessive consumption of alcohol or narcotic drugs seems to be a mitigated analogue of suicidal tendencies. Alcoholism and addiction have frequently been described as prolonged and slow forms of suicide.

The mechanism characteristic of these groups is the same as for nonviolent suicide; it reflects an unconscious need to undo the birth process and return to the womb. Alcohol and narcotics tend to inhibit various painful emotions and sensations and produce a state of diffused consciousness and indifference toward one's past and future problems. Patients addicted to alcohol and drugs who had experienced in their psychedelic sessions states of cosmic unity, reported insights very similar to those of suicidal patients. They realized that they had been craving for transcendence, not for drug intoxication; this mistake was based on a certain superficial similarity between the effects of alcohol or narcotics and the experience of cosmic unity. However, resemblance is not identity and there are some fundamental differences between transcendental states and these intoxications. Whereas alcohol and narcotics dull the senses, obnubilate consciousness, interfere with intellectual functions, and produce emotional anesthesia, transcendental states are characterized by a great enhancement of sensory perception, serenity, clarity of thinking, abundance of philosophical and spiritual insights, and unusual richness of emotions.

Thus, instead of producing the state of cosmic consciousness in its entirety and with all its essential characteristics, these drugs create its pitiful caricature. However, for a hurting individual who is desperately looking for help and is incapable of accurate discrimination, the resemblance seems close enough to seduce him or her into systematic abuse. Repeated administration then leads to physiological addiction and damages the user physically, psychologically, and socially.

As mentioned in connection with suicide, there seems to be another mechanism underlying alcoholism and addiction, which reflects not the natural dynamics of the birth process, but artificial intervention. There are patients who clearly show signs of the psychological influence of BPM III and yet turn to alcohol and narcotics. It is common to find that at the time of their birth their mothers were under severe general anesthesia. As a result, their memory of birth is not that of an explosive liberation but of a slow awakening from drug intoxication. They thus tend to escape from the painful grip of BPM III, and intense stress in general, into chemically induced anesthesia, following the route shown to them by the obstetrician attending their birth.

The experience of cosmic unity characteristically results in negative attitudes toward the states of consciousness produced by intoxication with alcohol and narcotics. In our work with alcoholics and serious narcotic drug addicts, a dramatic reduction of the use of alcohol and narcotics was frequently observed even after a single high-dose psychedelic session. After the experiences of ego death and cosmic unity, abuse of alcohol and narcotics are seen as tragic mistakes produced by an unrecognized and misunderstood craving for transcendence; the parallel with the insights of depressed patients concerning suicide is quite obvious and striking.

A consuming need for transcendence seems to be the core problem of alcoholism and narcotic drug addiction, as improbable as this might appear to those familiar with the personality, behavior patterns, and life style of patients who belong to these categories. This can be clearly illustrated by statistics from psychedelic therapy programs conducted in the Maryland Psychiatric Research Center, in Baltimore. These two categories of patients had in their psychedelic sessions the highest incidence of mystical experiences among all the studied groups, including neurotics, mental health professionals, and individuals dying of cancer (Grof 1980).

It is important to emphasize that the perinatal dynamics, although crucial, does not in itself explain the personality structure of the alcoholic and the addict or the phenomenon of drug abuse. Additional factors of psychological relevance can be found in the biographies of the patients; these are basically congruent with the psychodynamic literature. Thus, the COEX systems associated with alcoholism and addiction involve early oral frustration, emotional deprivation, and craving for anaclitic satisfaction. In some instances, significant roots of alcoholism and drug addiction can reach into the transpersonal domain.

Although my clinical experiences with the treatment of the relatively rare *impulse neuroses*, such as running away from home and wandering (poriomania), gambling, quaternary drinking (dipsomania), stealing (kleptomania), and setting fires (pyromania) have been rather limited, it seems safe to hypothesize that they are psychogenetically related to manic-depressive disorders and thus to the transition from BPM III to BPM IV. In cases of *impulsive running away*, the hectic traveling activity represents an exteriorization of the driving energies characteristic of the third perinatal matrix. Here, running means running away from danger, restrictions, and punishment and toward security, freedom, and gratification. The typical fantasized goal of this erratic search is the image of an ideal home with a good mother who will satisfy all the individual's needs. It is easy to recognize this craving as the psychological search for the elements of BPM IV and, ultimately, BPM I. In *impulsive gambling*, the feverish atmosphere of the casino, the anxiety-laden excitement, and the extreme alternatives of a total annihilation or a magical transformation of one's life are characteristic features of the dynamics of the third perinatal matrix and of the approaching ego death and rebirth. The fantasized cornucopia associated with the positive outcome belongs to characteristic images associated with BPM IV. A strong emphasis on the sexual aspect of BPM III can give a distinct erotic coloring to gambling, connecting it to masturbatory activities. *Dipsomania*, the excessive use of alcohol that comes in periodic bouts, is closely related to poriomania; it represents a combination of impulse neurosis and alcoholism. The fundamental mechanism is an inability to tolerate extreme organismic tension and a need for instant discharge; one would expect the element of alcohol consumption or use of other drugs to be based on the administration of anesthetics or sedatives during the final stage of the individual's birth. The deep root of *kleptomania* seems to be a need to achieve satisfaction in the context of danger, tension, excitement and anxiety.

Pyromania is clearly psychogenetically related to the pyrocathartic aspect of BPM III. Archetypally, the final stages of the death-rebirth process are associated with the element of fire; LSD subjects would at this point experience visions of gigantic conflagrations, volcanic or atomic explosions, and thermonuclear reactions. This experience of fire is associated with intense sexual arousal and seems to have purifying properties. It is perceived as a cathartic destruction of the old structures, the elimination of biological impurities, and a preparation for spiritual rebirth. Obstetricians and midwives frequently observe the experiential counterpart of this phenomenon in delivering women who complain in the final stages of childbirth about burning sensations in their genitals, as if their vaginas were on fire.

A pyromaniac has the correct insight that he must go through the experience of fire to free himself from unpleasant tension and achieve satisfaction. However, he fails to recognize that this can be effective only if it is experienced internally as a symbolic transformative process. Instead of experiencing pyrocatharsis and spiritual rebirth, he projects the process outward, exteriorizes it and becomes an arsonist. Although watching the fire generates a state of excitement and sexual arousal, it fails to bring the anticipated satisfaction, since the expectations reflect the outcome of a process of inner transformation and cannot be met by witnessing an external event. Because the subject has an unconsciously true, and therefore convincing, insight that the experience of fire is essential for reaching liberation and full satisfaction, he or she keeps repeating the act in spite of all the failures.

The fundamental mistake behind all impulse activities is the exteriorization of the inner process, acting it out in a concrete way. The only solution is to approach these problems as internal processes and complete them on a symbolic level. The striving for the discharge of intolerable tension, the craving for sexual release, and the need for inner security—so characteristic for impulse neuroses—find simultaneous gratification in the context of ecstatic feelings associated with BPM IV and BPM I.

The complex and intricate dynamic structure of BPM III also contributes an important component to *obsessive-compulsive neuroses;*

Fig. 36. Painting depicting a sequence of death and rebirth experienced in an LSD session. It involved identification with the fetus passing through purifying fire into the celestial realm of the Great Mother Goddess.

Fig. 37. Immolation Sacrifice by a Wrathful Deity. Painting of a vision from a perinatal LSD session representing "Moloch"—a gigantic destructive deity appearing in fire and demanding sacrifice of the newborn. Such sacrifices to Moloch were allegedly practiced in Carthage and ancient Israel; during these awesome rituals mothers were throwing neonates into the fire burning inside metal statues of the deity. The combination of the newborn status, fire, sacrificial death, and epiphany of the divine is characteristic for the transition from BPM III to BPM IV.

however, the emphasis is on different aspects or facets of this matrix. Patients suffering from this disorder are tormented by ego-alien thoughts or feel compelled to perform repeatedly certain irrational and incomprehensible rituals. If they refuse to comply with these strange urges, they are overwhelmed by free-floating anxiety. There is a general agreement in psychoanalytical literature that conflicts related to homosexuality, aggression, and biological material form the psychodynamic basis of this disorder, together with an inhibition of genitality and a strong emphasis on pregenital drives.

It has already been pointed out that the unconscious fear of female genitals and the homosexual tendencies associated with it are related to birth anxiety. The inhibition of genitality is, in the last analysis, the result of the similarity between the pattern of sexual orgasm and the orgastic aspects of birth. In the context of BPM III, sexual arousal is intimately combined with anxiety and

Fig. 38. A scatological experience in the context of BPM III—wallowing in feces and drowning in a gigantic cesspool. Drawing by a subject who confronted this stage of the death-rebirth process in a psychedelic session with LSD.

aggression in an inextricable experiential complex. If the elements of this matrix are close to the surface, sexual excitement will tend to activate this particular aspect of the birth memory. Any attempts to control and suppress the anxiety and aggression involved will then automatically result in the inhibition of genital sexuality. The typical ambivalence about such biological material as feces, urine, mucus, and blood, has its natural roots in the final stages of biological birth, where the contact with this material can occur in either a negative or a positive context, as already discussed. Further, the attitude of obsessive-compulsive patients toward biological substances as potentially extremely dangerous and capable of killing makes sense in light of this association with the memory of an event that was life-threatening.

Another characteristic feature of obsessive-compulsive neurosis betrays its psychogenetic relation to BPM III, namely, the strong ambivalence of patients suffering from this disorder in regard to spirituality and religion. Many of them live in a constant conflict about God and religious faith, alternating between rebellion or blasphemy and desperate tendencies to repent, expiate, and undo their transgressions and sins. This kind of problem is altogether characteristic of the final stages of the death-rebirth process, in which determined resistance and revolt against an overwhelming higher force alternates with a wish to surrender and comply. This is usually associated with the awareness of the cosmic relevance of this situation and its spiritual significance.

LSD subjects who experience this higher force in a more figurative, archetypal form describe it as a strict, punishing, and cruel deity comparable with Jehovah of the Old Testament, or even the pre-Columbian gods demanding blood sacrifice. The biological correlate of this punishing deity is the restricting influence of the birth canal that prevents any external expression of the activated instinctual energies of sexual and aggressive nature and in turn inflicts extreme, life-threatening suffering on the individual. Postnatally, this coercion takes far more subtle forms, being executed by parental authorities, penal institutions, and religious precepts and commandments.

The restricting force of the birth canal thus represents a natural basis for the deep instinctual part of the superego that Freud saw as a derivative of the id; he considered it to be the savage and cruel element of the psyche that can drive an individual to self-

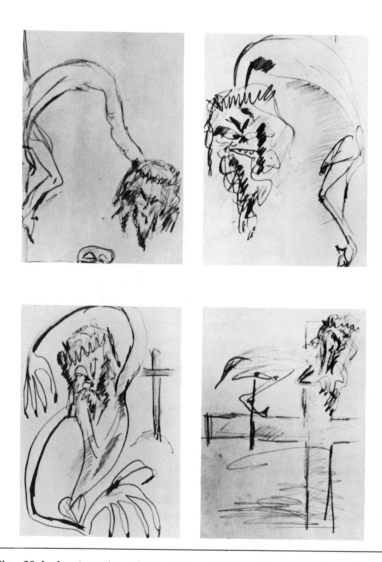

Fig. 39abcd. A series of drawings reflecting monstrous, blasphemous distortion of the most sacred religious themes and their contamination by "obscene biology"; this combination is quite characteristic for BPM III and the final stages of the death-rebirth process. The patient was flooded by similar images in an LSD session in which she was working through specific traumatic childhood experiences and elements of the birth trauma. Experiences of this kind are closely related to the theme of the Sabbath of the Witches and other satanic rituals.

Fig. 39e. The last picture of the series shows the resolution of the problems illustrated by the preceding drawings; this resolution occurred at the time when the patient connected experientially with the moment of biological birth. The image of "Purified Christ" is rising above the realm of "obscene biology" (stomach, intestines, bladder, and human embryo) and separating from it. The patient's hands are reaching for the "Black Sun", symbolizing the Divine Within-inner reality without any form that is even beyond Christ.

mutilation and suicide. In this context, obsessive-compulsive patients face a painful, paradoxical situation that involves a strange double bind. In view of the patterns of archetypal unfolding, one must experience elemental aggression and distorted sexual feelings of various kinds that are intrinsic to BPM III in order to connect experientially with the pure spiritual energy associated with BPM IV. However, the experience of these intense instinctual tendencies is seen as incompatible with the divine and is therefore suppressed.

The COEX systems that are psychogenetically associated with obsessive-compulsive neurosis involve traumatic experiences related to the anal zone and to biological material, such as a history of strict toilet training, painful enemas, and gastrointestinal diseases. Another important category of related biographical material includes memories of various situations representing a threat to genital organization. These observations are in basic agreement with the psychoanalytic understanding of the psychogenetic factors instrumental in the development of obsessive-compulsive neurosis.

According to psychoanalytic literature, the *pregenital conversions,* such as psychogenic asthma, various tics, and stammering, represent a combination of obsessive-compulsive disorders and conversion hysteria. The basic underlying personality structure of these patients clearly has obsessive-compulsive features, yet the principal mechanism of symptom formation is conversion. Deep experiential work reveals that pregenital conversions are derivatives of the third perinatal matrix. In *psychogenic asthma,* the breathing difficulties can be traced directly to the element of agony and suffocation experienced during biological birth and can be therapeutically influenced by confronting the death-rebirth process. Careful analysis of the physiological process involved in asthma suggests that many of its important aspects can be traced back to the biological dynamics of childbirth. Similarly, as in obsessive-compulsive neuroses, the anal emphasis reflects the general energy blockage and involvement of the anal zone at birth. The specific accentuation of the elements of suffocation and anal retention is due to biographical factors. In addition to the traumas described by psychoanalysis, one frequently finds a history of diseases, incidents, or accidents that involve interference with breathing.

We have discussed earlier how the agony, anguish, and suffocation that the child experiences in the birth canal seem to generate an enormous amount of neuronal stimulation that remains stored in the system and seeks belated discharge through different channels. *Psychogenic tics* represent, in the last analysis, such an attempt to release in a biographically codetermined fashion some of these pent-up energies accumulated during the hydraulic situation of birth. *Psychogenic stammering* has its deep dynamic roots in the conflicts around oral as well as anal aggression. The oral component reflects the distress the child experiences when his or her head is stuck in the birth canal with jaws forcefully locked. The anal element can be traced back to the increased intra-abdominal pressure and constriction of the sphincter accompanying the delivery. As in other emotional disorders, the specific selection of certain facets of the complex dynamics of BPM III in psychogenic stammering is determined by later biographical events. An important factor in this disorder seems to be repression of verbal aggression of a distinctly obscene quality.

The deep dynamic basis of *conversion hysteria* is quite similar to that of agitated depression; this is also reflected in a phenomenological resemblance of these two conditions. The relation between them can be used as an illustration of the intricate geometry of psychopathological syndromes. In general, agitated depression is a deep disorder and it manifests, in a far purer form the content and dynamics of BPM III. Observation of the facial expression and behavior of a patient with agitated depression leaves no doubt that it is a very serious condition. The high incidence of suicide and even suicide combined with murder found in these patients supports this impression.

A major hysterical seizure shows a superficial resemblance to agitated depression. However, the overall picture is far less serious; it lacks the depth of despair, appears stylized and contrived, and has definite theatrical features with sexual overtones. In general, a hysterical seizure has many basic characteristics of BPM III— excessive tension, psychomotor excitement and agitation, a mixture of depression and aggression, loud screaming, disturbances of breathing, and dramatic arching (arc de cercle). However, the experiential template appears here in a considerably more mitigated form than in agitated depression and is substantially modified and colored by later traumatic events. The nature and timing of these biographical components are in basic agreement with the Freudian theory. They are typically sexual traumas from the time when the patient reached the phallic stage of development and was solving the Oedipus or Electra complex. The movements of the hysterical seizure can be deciphered as symbolic allusions to certain specific aspects of the underlying childhood trauma.

The deep connection between agitated depression and conversion hysteria is clearly manifested in the course of LSD therapy. At first, the hysterical symptoms become amplified and the client has to relive and work through the specific sexual traumas from childhood. When this biographical work is completed, subsequent psychedelic sessions produce elements resembling agitated depression that the patient finally deciphers as derivatives of the birth struggle of BPM III. The resolution comes when an experiential connection is made to the elements of BPM IV.

Hysterical paralysis of the hands and arms, inability to stand (abasia), loss of speech (aphonia) and other conversion symptoms seem to be based on conflicting innervations reflecting the excessive and chaotic generation of neuronal impulses in the demanding situation of birth. The paralysis is not caused by lack of motor impulses, but by a dynamic conflict of powerful antagonistic innervations that counteract, canceling each other. This interpretation of hysterical conversion symptoms was first suggested by Otto Rank, in his pioneering book, *The Trauma of Birth* (1929). While Freud saw conversions as expressions of a psychological conflict expressed in the language of somatization, Rank believed that their real basis was physiological, reflecting the original situation that existed during birth. The problem for Freud was how a primarily psychological problem could be translated into a physical symptom, whereas Rank had to explain how an essentially somatic phenomenon could later acquire, through a secondary elaboration, psychological content and symbolic meaning.

Some serious manifestations of hysteria that border on psychosis, such as psychogenic stupor, uncontrolled daydreaming, and mistaking fantasy for reality, seem to be dynamically related to BPM I. They reflect a deep need to reinstitute the blissful emotional condition characteristic of undisturbed intrauterine existence and the symbiotic union with the mother. While the emotional component and the state of physical satisfaction involved can easily be detected as related to experiences of the desired good womb and good breast, the concrete content of daydreaming and fantasies uses themes and elements related to the individual's childhood, adolescence, and adult life.

In *anxiety hysteria* the role of perinatal dynamics is unusually obvious; it is only logical that anxiety can be traced back to an experience that involved a serious vital threat. I have already mentioned that Freud (1964) expressed early in his work the opinion that the situation of birth might be a major source and prototype of all later anxieties. However, he did not elaborate this idea any further, and when it was later articulated by his disciple Rank into a comprehensive theory (1929), he brought about Rank's excommunication from the psychoanalytic movement.

In general, free-floating anxiety can be traced back, more or less directly, to the vital anxiety of birth. In the various phobias that involve anxiety, crystallized as specific fears attached to persons, animals, or situations, the original birth anxiety is modified and mitigated by later biographical events. While the intensity of the affect reveals the deep perinatal source, the general type of the phobia reflects a particular stage or facet of birth, and the specific choice of persons, objects, and situations is determined by later biographical events.

The relation of phobias to the birth trauma is most evident in the *fear of closed and narrow places (claustrophobia)*. It occurs in confined situations, such as elevators, small rooms without windows, or in subways, and the emotional distress is strictly limited to the duration of the stay in these places. It seems to be related more specifically to the initial phase of BPM II wherein the child experiences the sense of the entire world's closing in, crushing, and choking. The experience of this aspect of BPM II in a pure and unmitigated form involves feelings of overwhelming, undifferentiated and undefined vital anxiety and generalized paranoia. The observations from deep experiential work thus unexpectedly put into deep dynamic relationship claustrophobia and paranoia, or at least one major form of paranoia that has perinatal roots. Claustrophobia is a more superficial disorder and its symptoms are bound to specific situational factors, while paranoia is deep and generalized and relatively independent of circumstances. On the biographical level, the COEX systems related to paranoia include situations of generalized threat in the very early stages of infancy, whereas claustrophobia is related to traumas that occurred later, at a time when the personality was already to some extent organized. Situations that combine physical confinement and suffocation are particularly relevant here.

Pathological fear of death (thanatophobia) has its roots in the vital anxiety and sense of impending biological catastrophe associated with birth. In this neurosis, the original feelings of perinatal emergency are only minimally modified by later biographical events, since the COEX systems involved are typically related to situations that represented a threat to survival or body integrity, such as operations, injuries, and particularly diseases that interfered with breathing. Patients suffering from thanatophobia experience episodes of vital anxiety, which they interpret as the onset of a heart attack, cerebral apoplexy, or inner choking.

The repeated medical examinations these individuals tend to seek fail to detect any organic disorder that would explain the subjective complaints, because the patients involved are not experiencing sensations and emotions related to a present physiological process, but reliving memories of past physical traumas, including that of birth. This, of course, does not make their experience less real. The only solution is to encourage an experiential confrontation of the emerging gestalts through various activating techniques; thus, thanatophobia would be resolved through the experience of death and re-birth.

A woman whose memory of perinatal events is close to the surface can suffer from a *phobia of pregnancy, delivery, and mothering*. This problem reflects the fact that the passive and active aspect of these functions are intimately connected in the dynamics of the unconscious. Women reliving their birth tend to experience themselves simultaneously, or alternately, as delivering. Similarly, memories of being a fetus in the womb are characteristically associated with an experience of being pregnant, and situations of being nursed, with those of nursing. The states that biologically involve symbiotic union between the mother and the child also represent states of experiential unity.

Clinical observations suggest that, when a woman becomes pregnant, this tends to activate in her unconscious the memory of her conception. As the child develops in her womb, the unconscious seems to replay the history of her own embryonic development. The process of delivery then reactivates the memory of ther own birth and, at the moment of giving birth to her child, she connects with her unconscious record of the time when she was born. Mothering her baby, she then replays on some level her own early infantile history.

Being close to the memory of the birth agony makes it difficult for a woman to assume her reproductive function and accept her femininity, because she associates it with inflicting pain and agony. When this occurs, it is essential to relive and work through the perinatal pain in order to embrace with enthusiasm the role of mother. An actual phobia of mothering after a child is born usually combines a variety of violent compulsions to hurt the child, panic fear of hurting it, and unreasonable concerns that something might happen to it. Whatever the biographical determinants of this problem may be, it can be traced, in the last analysis, to the delivery of that child. Its deep roots lie in the situation where the mother and child were in a state of biological antagonism, inflicting pain on each other and exchanging enormous amounts of destructive energy. This situation tends to activate the mother's own memory of birth and unleash the aggressive potential related to her perinatal matrices.

The deep connections between the experience of delivering a child and experiential access to perinatal dynamics represent an important opportunity for the woman who has just delivered to do some unusually deep psychological work. On the negative side, they seem to be responsible for postpartum depressions, neuroses, or even psychoses, if this situation is not approached with deep dynamic understanding.

Nosophobia, the pathological fear of developing or contracting a disease, is closely related to *hypochondriasis,* an unsubstantiated delusional conviction of already having a serious illness. There are smooth transitions and overlaps between nosophobia, hypochondriasis, and thanatophobia. Patients preoccupied with the issue of physical disease have a variety of strange body sensations that they cannot account for and tend to interpret them in terms of actual somatic pathology. These involve pains, pressures and cramps in different parts of the body, strange energy flows, paraesthesias and other forms of unusual phenomena. They can also show signs of dysfunction of various organs, such as breathing difficulties, dyspepsia, nausea and vomiting, constipation and diarrhea, muscular tremors, general malaise, weakness, and fatigue. Repeated medical examinations fail to detect any objective indications of actual physical disease in nosophobia or hypochondriasis. Patients with these problems often demand various clinical and laboratory tests and sooner or later become a real menace in doctors' offices and hospitals. Many end up in the care of a psychiatrist, who frequently treats them as somewhere on the continuum between malingerers and hysterics. In many instances, they continue to be seen by internists, neurologists, and specialists from other disciplines. According to some statistics and estimates, patients of this sort could represent as many as 30 percent of the clientele treated by internists.

According to my conceptual framework, the complaints of these patients should be considered very seriously despite the negative medical findings. Their physical complaints are very real; however, they do not reflect a current medical problem, but a surfacing organismic memory of serious physiological difficulties from the past, such as diseases, operations, or injuries—and particularly the trauma of birth.

Three specific forms of nosophobia deserve special attention: *pathological fear of developing or having cancer (cancerophobia), fear of microorganisms and infection (bacillophobia),* and *fear of dirt (mysophobia).* The deep roots of all these problems are perinatal, although their specific form is biographically determined. In cancerophobia, the important element is the similarity between cancer and pregnancy; it is well known from the psychonalytical literature that the malignant growth of tumors is unconsciously identified with embryonic development. This similarity is not just imaginary; it can be supported by anatomical, physiological, and biochemical studies. Another deep connection between cancer, pregnancy, and birth is the association of all these processes with death. In bacillophobia and mysophobia, the pathological fear focuses on biological material, body odors, and uncleanliness. The biographical determinants usually involve memories from the time of toilet training, but the deepest roots reach to the scatological aspect of the perinatal process. The organic link in BPM III between death, aggression, sexual excitement, and biological material is the key to understanding these phobias.

Patients suffering from these disorders are not only afraid of biological contamination for themselves, they are also frequently preoccupied by the possibility of infecting others. Their fear of biological materials is thus closely associated with aggression, oriented both inward and outward, which is precisely the situation characteristic of the final stages of birth. Deep entanglement and identification with biological contaminants are also at the basis of a particular kind of low self-esteem that involves self-degradation and a sense of disgust with oneself, referred to colloquially as "shitty self-esteem." It is frequently associated with certain behaviors that connect this problem with obsessive-compulsive neuroses. These involve rituals that represent an effort to remove or counteract the experience of biological contamination.

The most obvious of these rituals is the compulsive washing of hands or other parts of the body, although they can take many other more complex and elaborate forms. The repetitive character of these maneuvers reflects the fact that they are essentially ineffective in warding off unconscious anxiety, since they do not address it on the level on which it actually originates, that is, on the level of perinatal matrices. Instead of realizing that he or she is dealing with the memory of biological contamination, the individual believes himself or herself to be fighting actual hygienic problems in the present situation.

Similarly, the fear of death that represents a memory of actual biological emergency is misperceived as a present danger associated with an alleged infection. Thus, the failure of all the symbolic maneuvers involved is ultimately based on the individual's being trapped in a network of self-deceptions and suffering from a lack of genuine self-understanding. It should be added that, on a more superficial level, the fear of infection and bacterial growth is also unconsciously related to sperm and conception and thereby, again, to pregnancy and birth. The most important COEX systems related to the above phobias involve relevant memories from the anal-sadistic stage of libidinal development and conflicts around toilet training and cleanliness. Additional biographical material is represented by memories that depict sex and pregnancy as dirty and dangerous.

Fear of traveling by train and subway (siderodromophobia) seems to be based on certain formal and experiential similarities between the elements of the perinatal process and travel in enclosed conveyances. The most important common denominators of the two situations are the sense of enclosure or entrapment, enormous forces and energies in motion, a rapid sequence of experiences, a lack of control over the process, and the potential danger of destruction. Additional elements are fear of passing through tunnels and underground passages and the encounter with darkness. In the time of the old-fashioned steam engine, the elements of fire, the pressure of the steam, and the noisy siren seemed to be contributing factors. The lack of control is an element of particular importance; patients who suffer from the phobia of trains frequently have no problems in driving a car, where they can deliberately change or stop the motion.

Closely related phobias seem to be *fear of traveling by airplanes* and *using an elevator*. It is interesting in this connection that in some instances *seasickness* and *airsickness* are related to perinatal dynamics; they tend to disappear after the individual has completed the death-rebirth process. The essential element here seems to be the ability to give up the need to be in control and to surrender to the flow of events, no matter what they bring. Difficulties arise when the individual tries to maintain or impose his or her order on processes that are beyond human control.

The fear of heights and bridges (acrophobia) does not occur in a pure form; it is always associated with the compulsion to jump down or throw oneself from a tower, window, cliff, or bridge. The sense of falling with a simultaneous fear of destruction is a typical manifestation of the final stages of the third perinatal matrix.[12] Subjects experiencing the elements of this matrix frequently report a sense of falling, acrobatic diving, or parachuting. A compulsive interest in sports that involve falling is closely related to suicide of the second type; it reflects a need to exteriorize the feelings of impending disaster in falling, a reaction formation against the fear involved, and also the need for control that can avert the disaster (pulling on the string of the parachute) or certainty that annihilation will not occur (termination of the fall in water). The COEX systems responsible for the manifestation of this particular facet of the birth trauma involve childhood memories of being playfully tossed in the air by adults, inadvertant falls in childhood, and various forms of gymnastics and acrobatics.

In the *phobia of streets and open spaces (agoraphobia)*—the counterpart to claustrophobia—the connection with biological birth is based on the contrast between the subjective sensation of enclosure and constriction and the ensuing enormous extension of space and experiential expansion. Agoraphobia is thus related to the very end of the birth process and emerging into the world. LSD subjects reliving this moment in their psychedelic sessions characteristically describe a deep fear of impending catastrophe and annihilation associated with this final transition. The experience of ego death, one of the most demanding and difficult experiences of the transformative process, belongs psychogenetically to this category. The street phobias also typically involve an element of libidinal tension, sexual temptation, ambivalent feelings about the opportunity for promiscuous contacts, and concerns about impulsive exhibitionistic exposure in public. Most of these characteristics reflect specific biographical constituents that are connected with certain facets and aspects of the birth trauma through experiential logic. The sexual component of birth has already been discussed in detail, and the element of being seen naked by the world makes emminent sense as an anachronistic reminder of the first exposure of one's naked body to the world. If a *fear of crossing the street* is foremost, the

powerful and dangerous forces involved in the traffic are unconsciously identified with those of delivery. On a more superficial
level, this situation replays the elements of childhood dependency,
when crossing streets was not allowed without the help of the
adults.

The relationship between the *fear of various animals (zoophobia)*
and the birth trauma was discussed in detail and clearly demonstrated by Otto Rank in *The Trauma of Birth* (1929). If the object
of the phobia is a *large animal*, the most important elements seem
to be the theme of being swallowed and incorporated (wolf) or the
relation to pregnancy (cow). It was mentioned earlier that the
archetypal experience of the onset of the death-rebirth process is
that of being swallowed and incorporated. When *small animals* are
involved, the important factor seems to be their capacity to enter
narrow holes in the earth and to leave them again (mice, snakes).

In addition, certain animals have a special symbolic significance
for the birth process. Thus images of gigantic tarantulas frequently
appear in the initial phase of BPM II as symbols of the devouring
female element. This seems to reflect the fact that spiders catch
free-flying victims in their webs, immobilize them, enwrap and
constrain them, and suck the life from them. It is not difficult to
see a deep similarity between this sequence of events and the
experiences of the child during biological delivery. This connection
seems to be essential for the development of the *fear of spiders
(arachnophobia)*.

Images of snakes that, on a more superficial level, have a
clearly phallic connotation are, on the perinatal level of the unconscious, common symbols of the birth agony and thus of the
destructive and devouring female element. Poisonous vipers usually
represent the vital danger and fear of death, while large boa
constrictors symbolize the crushing and strangulation involved in
birth. The fact that, after having smothered the victim and swallowed it whole, a boa constrictor's body bulges strikingly, makes
it also a symbol of pregnancy. However, no matter how important
the perinatal component is in the development of the *phobia of
snakes*, the serpentine symbolism extends deep into the transpersonal
realms where these animals play a fundamental role in many archetypal forms, mythical themes, and cosmologies.

Phobias of small insects can frequently be traced to the dynamics
of perinatal matrices. Thus, for example, *bees* seem to be related

Fig. 40. A vision from a psychedelic session dominated by the initial phase of BPM II, reflecting the onset of biological delivery. A figure of the Devouring Mother Goddess in the form of a gigantic tarantula exposing fetuses to diabolic tortures.

to reproduction and pregnancy because of their ability to transfer pollen and fertilize plants, as well as to penetrate the skin by stinging, causing swelling. *Flies,* as a result of their affinity for excrement and their propensity to spread infection, are associated with the scatological aspect of birth. As has already been pointed out, this has a close relation to phobias of dirt and microorganisms and the compulsive washing of hands.

Since birth as a basic biological process involves a rich spectrum of physiological phenomena, it is hardly surprising that the roots of many emotional disorders with distinct somatic manifestations and psychosomatic diseases can be traced to perinatal matrices. Thus, the most common and characteristic *organ-neurotic symptoms* appear to be derivatives of the physiological processes and reactions that form a natural and understandable part of birth. This con-

Fig. 41. These two paintings of LSD subjects show the importance of snake symbolism in perinatal sessions. The first picture portrays a cluster of poisonous vipers experienced in the context of BPM ("snake pit"); they symbolize the imminent danger of sudden death. The second picture depicts another type of snake experience which occurs in the context of the death-rebirth process—crushing and strangulation by a gigantic boa constrictor-type serpent.

nection is quite obvious and requires no further explanation in the case of various forms of headaches, particularly the "belt headache," which the neurotic patient frequently describes as a tight steel band around the forehead. A subjective feeling of a lack of oxygen and of suffocation—commonly experienced by psychiatric patients under stress—is also easily accounted for. Similarly, palpitations, pain in the chest, blushing, peripheral ischemia, and other forms of cardiovascular distress, as well as muscular tensions, tremors, and twitches present no difficulty for interpretation.

Some other symptoms, for which a connection with the birth process is not immediately evident, seem to reflect the complex patterns of activation of both the sympathetic and the parasympathetic nervous systems that occur simultaneously or in an alternating fashion in various stages of delivery. Constipation or spastic diarrhea, nausea and vomiting, general irritability of the gastrointestinal system, excessive sweating, hypersalivation or dryness of the mouth, and chills alternating with flashes are examples.

A different cluster of vegetative phenomena appears in the sessions and postsession intervals of persons who have already passed the point of the death-rebirth process and are confronting various prenatal experiences. Some of these symptoms are similar to those accompanying a viral disease such as flu; they involve general weakness and malaise, feelings of inner cold, extreme nervousness, and subtle tremors of isolated muscles or muscular groups. Others are reminiscent of a hangover or food poisoning—feeling of nausea and disgust, dyspepsia, excessive intestinal gas, and general vegetative dystonia. The subjects who exhibit these symptoms during their sessions characteristically experience bad tastes in their mouths, which they describe as a mixture of a metallic or iodine taste and something organic, such as decomposed bouillon. The entire syndrome has a strange, insidious, diffuse and scarcely definable quality in contrast to the far more distinct physical phenomena of perinatal origin. Many subjects said independently that they felt this condition had a chemical basis. They related it to disturbances of intrauterine existence mediated to the fetus through changes in the chemistry of the placental blood. These physical symptoms seem to underlie some neurotic and borderline psychotic complaints of a strange and ill-defined nature. In their most extreme form they constitute a certain type of *hypochondriasis with psychotic interpretation.*

There is strong clinical evidence in the LSD literature suggesting that perinatal matrices are also involved in the pathogenesis of serious *psychosomatic diseases,* such as bronchial asthma, migraine headaches, psoriasis, peptic ulcer, ulcerous colitis, and hypertension. The material from my own psychedelic research, as well as observations from nondrug experiential work, point in the same direction. The paramount importance of emotional factors in these diseases has been generally acknowledged by traditional medicine. However, in light of deep experiential work, any of the psychoanalytically oriented theories of psychosomatic diseases that entirely explain them from biographical factors are clearly inadequate and superficial. Any therapist using experiential work is bound to develop profound respect for the elemental energies of perinatal origin underlying psychosomatic disorders.

While there can be justifiable doubts that relatively subtle biographical traumas would upset the homeostatic mechanisms of the body and cause deep functional disturbances, or even gross anatomical damage to the organs, it is obvious that this is more than a reasonable possibility in the case of the primordial and truly elemental destructive energies derived from the birth experience. It is actually not uncommon to see transient occurrence of asthmatic attacks, migraine headaches, various eczemas, and even psoriatic skin eruptions in the course of the death-rebirth process in psychedelic therapy and other types of experiential work. On the positive side, dramatic and lasting improvements have been reported in most psychosomatic diseases by therapists using psychedelic therapy and other deep experiential techniques. Wherever the reports describe the actual course of therapy, they mention reliving of the birth trauma as the most significant event of therapeutic relevance.

The connection between *psychogenic asthma* and the birth experience, which is quite obvious, has already been detailed. *Migraine headaches* are characteristically traceable to the facet of birth that involves agonizing pain and pressure on the head, together with nausea and other gastrointestinal discomfort. The frequent tendency of migraine patients to seek the womblike environment of dark places, quietude, and soft blankets and pillows can be seen as an effort to undo the birth process and return to the prenatal condition. However, it is the opposite strategy that brings resolution to migraine headaches, as indicated by many successful results of experiential therapy. Ultimately, the headache must be intensified to the extreme, even unbearable, dimensions that match the actual pains experienced at birth. This then brings a sudden explosive liberation from the migraine; characteristically, it is followed by an ecstatic state of a transcendental nature.

In *psoriasis*, the important psychogenetic element seems to be a channeling of destructive perinatal energies into the areas of skin that during birth are in immediate contact with the uterine walls or birth passageways, and thus represent the interface of the painful confrontation between the two organisms. This is borne out by the predilection sites for psoriasis, namely, the head and forehead, back, knees, and elbows. As with migraine headaches, far-reaching improvements of severe psoriasis have been reported after the reliving of biological birth.

An important component of the forces underlying *peptic ulcers* and *ulcerative colitis* is the destructive perinatal energies that have a very definite axial focus; they are typically experienced with a maximum along the longitudinal axis of the body. Conflicting innervations of both the upper part of the gastrointestinal system (oral aggression, stomach pain, nausea, and vomiting) and its lower part (intestinal pains and spasms, diarrhea, spastic constipation) are frequent concomitants of the birth process. The questions whether this aspect of the birth experience will result in manifest pathology in the future, and whether the stomach or the colon will be involved, seem to depend less on the specific mechanics of delivery than on a chain of later biographical events. The COEX systems of patients with these diseases would characteristically involve memories of events linking digestion with anxiety, aggression, or sexuality; the nature of these traumas and their timing is in general agreement with psychoanalytic theory.

Arterial hypertension is clearly related to a history of extreme emotional stress. The deep basis of this disorder is the organismic record of the prolonged emotional and physical stress of biological birth. Various later stresses in life add to this primal pool, facilitate access of perinatal elements into consciousness, connect them to specific biographical events, and provide their final elaboration and articulation. The resulting arterial hypertension is then a psycho-somatic reaction to all the unfinished gestalts of stressful situations in the life of the individual, including his or her perinatal history, rather than a reflection of only the more recent circumstances.

Neurasthenia and emotional traumatic neuroses occupy a special position among psychopathological syndromes. In a sense, they can be considered the most "normal" reactions of human beings to difficult circumstances. Symptoms of *neurasthenia* tend to develop in an individual who has been exposed for a long period of time to demanding and objectively stressful conditions, such as excess of work under conflicting pressures; lack of rest, sleep, and recreation; complex tasks to tackle; and a hectic pace of life. Neurasthenia is characterized by muscular tension, tremors, excessive sweating, cardiac distress and palpitations, free-floating anxiety, a sense of oppression, intense headaches, and *faiblesse irritable*—a feeling of general weakness and lack of energy, combined with easy irritability. It is characteristically accompanied by sexual disturbances, particularly impotence, frigidity, changes of the menstrual cycle, and precocious ejaculation.

Emotional traumatic neuroses occur in individuals who have been involved in natural catastrophies of extreme proportions, mass accidents, or war situations, or who have experienced other events that represent a potential threat to survival or to body integrity. It is important to emphasize that these conditions do not involve any physical damage to the organism, but only the psychological trauma associated with the possibility of it. And yet, the ensuing traumatic neurosis typically involves not only intense emotional symptoms but certain physical manifestations, such as pains, cramps, violent shaking, or paralysis.

Neurasthenia and emotional traumatic neuroses are closely psychogenetically related. Both represent derivatives of BPM III in relatively pure form, neither modified nor colored by later traumatic biographical events. Neurasthenia, which is a relatively normal reaction to prolonged stress of a reasonable degree, manifests the essential features of the third perinatal matrix in a somewhat mitigated form. In comparison, the acute emergency that precipitates emotional traumatic neuroses is such a close approximation to the situation encountered at birth that it overrides the defense system and connects experientially with the very core of BPM III. Thus, even after the immediate danger has passed, the individual continues to be flooded by the perinatal energies against which he or she has now lost all effective psychological protection.

This situation presents a problem, but it can also be a great opportunity for experiential confrontation of perinatal energies.

The final outcome will depend on how this condition is approached therapeutically. Efforts at psychological or pharmacological suppression of the perinatal energies unleashed in the process will be entirely futile or could result in a general impoverishment of personality.

A therapeutic strategy that frees the perinatal energies may not only resolve the symptoms of traumatic neurosis, but also mediate a process of deep healing and transformation. The best conventional approach to these conditions is hypnoanalysis or narcoanalysis which puts patients in touch with the original life-threatening situation and allows them to relive it. However, an ideal therapeutic approach should go further, to the underlying perinatal matrices that have been exposed by the emergency situation. This observations is of particular relevance in view of the fact that tens of thousands of Vietnam veterans suffering from long-term war-related emotional disorders represent a serious mental health problem for the United States.

It is not uncommon that, in situations of vital emergency, the individuals involved lose control over their bladders and bowels. This is a characteristic of the final stage of birth, or the transition between BPM III and BPM IV. It can be illustrated by the clinical observation that, in old-fashioned deliveries where no enemas or catheterization were used, the mother frequently defecated and urinated at the moment of childbirth, and so did the infant. *The neurotic loss of control over the bladder (enuresis)* and the less frequent *failure to control the bowels (encopressis)* can be, in the last analysis, traced back to the reflex urination and defecation at birth. In subjects experiencing elements of BPM III and BPM IV in their psychedelic sessions, concern about sphincters and their control frequently occurs. Urination is fairly common when a subject in experiential psychotherapy approaches the moment of total surrender and letting go. Involuntary defecation is less common, probably because of the far stronger cultural taboos, but it has occurred on several occasions. As with other disorders, later biographical events of a specific nature are necessary to change this potential, existing on the perinatal level, into an actual clinical problem. The material of the related COEX systems is in basic agreement with psychoanalytic theory. However, this is only part of the story and, ultimately, the deep roots of these disorders can be seen in the reflex release of the sphincters during the termination

of the pain, fear, and suffocation at birth and psychological re-
connection with the postnatal and prenatal condition in which there
are no impositions on unconditional biological freedom.

The Psychotic Experience:
Disease or Transpersonal Crisis?

The so-called endogenous psychoses, particularly schizophrenia,
represent one of the greatest enigmas of modern psychiatry and
medicine. In spite of extreme investment of time, energy, and
money, the problems related to nature and etiology of the psychotic
process have successfully resisted efforts of generations of scientists.
The theories of psychosis cover an extremely wide range from
strictly organic to purely psychological and even philosophical interpretations. All these extreme positions have as their representatives
brilliant, sophisticated, and respectable scientists with impressive
credentials.

According to those researchers who adhere to the medical
model, psychoses represent such a drastic distortion of the correct
perception of reality that one must postulate a serious pathology
of the organs that mediate the perception of the world and the
interpretation of the sensory data, particularly of the central nervous system. Partisans of this view insist that the cause of psychoses
must lie in some acquired or inherited biochemical, physiological,
or even anatomical anomalies of the brain. An acceptable alternative
suggests that a pathology in other organs or systems of the body
may be involved that changes the biochemistry of the body and
influences the brain indirectly. Although search for such organic
causes has so far been largely unsuccessful, all conditions involving
unusual states of consciousness continue to be treated as "diseases"
with an etiology that has yet to be discovered. Since psychiatric
research has so far failed to detect the actual causes of psychoses,
the definition of "disease" is characteristically equated with the
manifestation of symptoms, and symptomatic relief is seen as an
indicator of improvement.

The psychological theories of psychosis fall into three distinct
categories. The most extreme formulations on the opposite end of

the spectrum from the medical model see psychoses as basically problems of living or different ways of being in the world. Phenomenology, existential analysis, and Daseinsanalysis could be mentioned here as important examples of approaches that emphasize philosophical understanding rather than interpretation in terms of medical pathology. Most psychological theories see psychoses as pathological states that have psychological rather than organic roots. With a few exceptions, the orientation of these theories is biographical; this narrow focus prevents them from seeing significant psychological factors beyond the range of childhood traumas. Some of these approaches complement intrapsychic dynamics by factors of a sociological nature. The third category of psychological theories of psychosis is most interesting and promising. It involves approaches that emphasize the positive value in the psychotic process. In this view, many unusual states of consciousness traditionally considered psychotic, and thus indicative of serious mental disease, are seen as radical attempts at problem-solving. If properly understood and supported, they can result in psychosomatic healing, personality transformation, and consciousness evolution.

Clearly, then, there is no general agreement in psychiatry and psychology about the nature and etiology of the psychotic process. Most serious researchers tend to emphasize the enormous complexity of the problem and to think in terms of "multiple etiology." This term suggests that the problem of psychosis cannot be reduced to any simple chain of biological, psychological, or social causes. There is not even unanimity on the clinical diagnostic labels. For example, American psychiatrists tend to use the label of schizophrenia rather generously, whereas their European colleagues tend to reserve this diagnosis for special cases with deep "core problems" (*Kernschizophrenie*).

The situation in the therapy of psychoses is equally confusing. With the possible exception of manic-depressive disorders, where there seems to be greater unanimity, the diversity of therapeutic measures directly reflects the differences in theoretical understanding of the process. The approaches that have been used with varying degrees of success and failure range from drastic convulsive methods and psychosurgery through psychopharmacological therapy to purely psychological procedures. Some recent therapeutic methods directly contradict the medical strategy in the treatment of psychoses. Instead of aiming at reducing symptoms and inhibiting the psychotic process, they attempt to create a supportive framework and encourage the client to experience the symptoms as fully as possible. From this viewpoint, it even seems appropriate to use techniques that intensify and accelerate the process and bring it to a positive resolution, namely, psychedelics or deep experiential therapy.

It is this last approach that I would like to explore and support, since according to my experience, it is an extremely vital and promising alternative to the traditional treatment of psychosis. Strong evidence from several different fields of research shows that, among persons experiencing unusual states of consciousness and routinely labeled as psychotic, there is a substantial subgroup of individuals who are involved in an extraordinary and potentially healing process of self-discovery and consciousness evolution. If the conditions are less than optimal—which is currently the norm in this culture at its present level of psychiatric understanding—this process is frequently arrested at one of its dramatic and difficult stages.

A psychiatrist or psychologist who knows the territory both theoretically and experientially will be able to support and guide this process, instead of using an indiscriminately suppressive approach, which for these cases is inappropriate, harmful, and counterproductive. An insensitive routine administration of tranquilizers and the use of other repressive measures can freeze this potentially beneficial process and interfere with its successful resolution. Such a therapeutic strategy can lead to chronicity and the necessity of long-term maintenance medication with ensuing irreversible side effects. It remains to be seen what proportion of all psychotic states belongs to this category and how many individuals in the general population are involved in such a process. Psychiatry, with its socially stigmatizing labels and terrifying hospital milieus and therapeutic procedures, has created an atmosphere inconducive to honest feedback. Under these circumstances, it is unlikely that we will obtain reliable statistics correctly reflecting what is happening in the population until we create an atmosphere of understanding and support.

The results of anonymous polls (McCready and Greeley, 1976) indicating that 35 percent of Americans at some point in their lives have had mystical experiences show what more honest and realistic statistics about the incidence of unusual states of consciousness might look like. Until the general atmosphere changes, many individuals involved in such a process will hesitate to share their experiences, even with their closest relatives, for fear of being considered insane and subjected to the insensitive routines of psychiatric treatment.

I now turn to the question of psychosis from the viewpoint presented in this book. The first issue to consider is the problem of the current scientific paradigm. The understanding of psychosis and the approach to it are critically determined by the philosophy of Western science and by the fact that psychiatry is established as a medical discipline. All definitions of psychosis emphasize the individual's inability to discriminate between subjective experience and an objective perception of the world; the key phrase in the definition of psychosis is thus "accurate reality testing." It is therefore obvious that the concept of psychosis is critically dependent on the current scientific image of reality. As a result of its commitment to the Newtonian-Cartesian paradigm and the confusion of this model with an accurate, objective, and exhaustive description of reality, traditional psychiatry has defined sanity as perceptual and cognitive congruence with the mechanistic world view. If an individual's experience of the universe seriously deviates from this model, this will be seen as an indication of a pathological process involving the brain, or a "disease." Since the diagnosis of psychosis cannot be separated from the definition of reality, it will have to be drastically influenced when a major shift in scientific paradigms changes the image of the nature of reality.

The medical model of mental illness has been considerably weakened by overwhelming evidence from history and anthropology, indicating the relativity and culture-bound nature of the criteria for mental health and normalcy. The human behaviors that have been considered acceptable, normal, or desirable in different cultures and during various historical periods cover a very wide spectrum. They show a considerable overlap with what modern psychiatry defines as pathological and indicative of mental disease. Medical science is thus trying to establish a specific etiology for many phenomena that, in a broader cross-cultural context, appear as variations of the human condition or the collective unconscious.

Incest, which has been abhorred by most ethnic groups, was deified by such high civilizations as those of the ancient Egyptians and the Peruvian Incas. Homosexuality, exhibitionism, group sex, and prostitution have been perfectly acceptable in certain cultures and ritualized or consecrated in others. While certain ethnic groups, such as the Eskimo, have practiced the sharing of spouses and others have encouraged general promiscuity, in some cultures adultery has been punished by death. The strict endorsement of monogamy in some societies can be similarly contrasted with the social sanctioning of polygamy or polyandry in others.

Whereas some groups find nudity natural and have a casual approach to sex and/or excretory activities, others show an abhorrence of basic physiological functions and odors, or cover the entire body, including the face. Even infanticide, murder, suicide, human sacrifice and self-sacrifice, mutilation and self-mutilation, or cannibalism have been perfectly acceptable in certain cultures and glorified and ritualized by others. Many of the so-called culture-bound psychiatric syndromes—quite unusual and exotic forms of experience and behavior that occur selectively in certain ethnic groups—can hardly be interpreted as diseases in the medical sense.

Since all these extreme psychological phenomena seem to represent norms in certain cultures or at certain points of history, the determined quest for their medical causes reflects a cultural bias rather than a well-founded scientific opinion. The Jungian concept of the collective unconscious with its countless variations, offers a powerful and more promising alternative to the medical model. It is interesting to realize that even changes in the spirit of the time (Zeitgeist) and vogue can occasionally bring deviations from previous norms which, occurring in isolated individuals within the old context, would have been sufficient for a diagnosis of mental illness.

What should be seen as sane, normal, or rationally justified depends critically on circumstances and on the cultural or historical context. The experiences or behavior of shamans, Indian yogis and sadhus, or spiritual seekers in other cultures would be more than sufficient for a diagnosis of psychosis by Western psychiatric standards. Conversely, the insatiable ambitions, irrational compensatory drives, obsession with technology, the modern arms race, internecine wars, or revolutions and riots that pass for normal in the West would be seen as symptoms of utter insanity by an East Indian sage. Similarly, our mania for linear progress and "unlimited growth," our disregard for cosmic cycles, our pollution of such vital resources as water, soil, and air, and our conversion of thousands of square miles of land into the concrete and asphalt one sees in places like Los Angeles, Tokyo, or Saõ Paulo would be considered by a Native American or a Mexican Indian shaman as absolutely incomprehensible and dangerous mass madness.

But the lessons from history and anthropology go beyond the relativity of experience, appearance, and behavior. Some phenomena, seen by Western psychiatrists as symptomatic of mental disease, have been considered by ancient and non-Western cultures as healing and transformative when they occurred spontaneously. The deep appreciation of these cultures for such forms of experience and behavior is clearly reflected in the fact that they spent much time and effort in developing ingenious techniques for inducing them. The mind-altering procedures used for this purpose range from such simple techniques as fasting, sleep deprivation, social and sensory isolation (staying in high mountains, caves, or deserts), and forced restriction of oxygen supply or other respiratory maneuvers to psychedelic substances. Certain spiritual traditions have developed elaborate methods for this purpose, using visual input, sound technology, kinesthetic stimulation, or mental exercises.

Those individuals who successfully integrate their inner journeys become intimately familiar with the territories of the psyche. Such individuals are also capable of transmitting this knowledge to others and of guiding them along their path. In many cultures of Asia, Australia, Polynesia, Europe, and South and North America, this has been the traditional function of the shamans (Eliade 1964). The dramatic initiation experiences of shamans that involve powerful death-rebirth sequences are interpreted by Western psychiatrists and anthropologists as indicative of mental disease. Usually referred to as "shamanic disease," they are discussed in relation to schizophrenia, hysteria, or epilepsy.

This reflects the typical bias of Western mechanistic science and is clearly a culture-bound value judgment, rather than an objective scientific opinion. Cultures that acknowledge and venerate shamans do not apply the title of shaman to just any individual with bizarre and incomprehensible behavior, as Western scholars would like to believe. They distinguish very clearly between shamans and individuals who are sick or insane. Genuine shamans have had powerful, unusual experiences and have managed to integrate them in a creative and productive way. They have to be able to handle everyday reality as well as or even better than their fellow tribesmen. In addition, they have experiential access to other levels and realms of reality and can facilitate nonordinary states of consciousness in others for healing and transformative purposes. They thus show superior functioning and "higher sanity," rather than maladjustment and insanity. It is simply not true that every bizarre and incomprehensible behavior would pass for sacred among uneducated aboriginal people.[13]

Many ancient and aboriginal traditions have developed elaborate cartographies of unusual states of consciousness that are of inestimable value for those who are facing difficult stages of their own inner journeys. The ancient books of the dead, the traditional Hindu, Buddhist, Taoist and Sufi scriptures, the writings of Christian mystics, or Kabbalistic and alchemical texts are just a few examples of this kind. In these writings, experiences that might appear incomprehensible and bizarre to the ignorant and uninitiated are seen as predictable and lawful stages of a transformative process by the masters of the art.

Open-minded researchers willing to study the healing potential of these states will discover to their great surprise that it far exceeds any therapeutic means available to traditional psychiatry. Many cultures of the world have altogether independently developed techniques for supporting or inducing such experiences. These techniques have been used systematically in a variety of rites of passage, healing rituals, ceremonies of ecstatic sects, and mysteries of death and rebirth.

Since the ritual practices of non-Western cultures might seem too exotic to be applicable to our Western conditions, we can point to important examples from ancient Greece, which is traditionally considered the cradle of Western civilization. The sacred mysteries of death and rebirth flourished in Greece and in neighboring countries in many different forms. Among the best known were the Eleusinian and the Orphic mysteries, the Bacchanalia or Dionysian rites, the ceremonies of Attis and Adonis, and the Samothracian rituals of the Corybantes.

As a matter of fact, two giants of Greek philosophy whom Western civilization holds in great esteem have both left testimony about the healing power of the mysteries. Plato, who was himself allegedly an initiate of the Eleusinian version, gave a detailed description of the ritual experience in his dialogue, *Phaedrus* (1961), while discussing different forms of madness. He used as an example of telestic or ritual madness the Corybantic rites (1961b), in which wild orgiastic dancing to flutes and drums culminated in an explosive paroxysm. Plato considered sequence of intense activity and extreme emotions with subsequent relaxation as a powerful cathartic experience that had remarkable therapeutic potential.[14]

Another great Greek philosopher, Plato's disciple Aristotle (Croissant 1932), also saw the mysteries as powerful ritual events capable of healing emotional disorders. He believed that, through the use of wine, aphrodisiacs, and music, the initiates experienced an extraordinary arousal of passions with a subsequent catharsis. This was the first explicit statement that a full experience and release of repressed emotions is an effective mechanism in the treatment of mental illness. In agreement with the basic thesis of the Orphics, Aristotle postulated that the chaos and frenzy of the mysteries were eventually conducive to order.

The concept of psychosis presented here is also supported by important observations from traditional psychiatry. It has been known for decades that psychiatric patients can occasionally emerge from acute episodes with a level of integration and functioning higher than that before the onset of the disease. (Dabrowski 1964). It has been noted that such a positive outcome is especially likely when the content of the psychotic experience involves elements of death and rebirth or destruction and recreation of the world.

The currently routine practice of indiscriminate pharmacological suppression of psychotic symptoms is in strange conflict with the old clinical observation that dramatic psychotic states have a much better prognosis than those that develop slowly. Several controlled psychopharmacological studies have shown that certain subgroups of psychotic patients have better recovery rates when they are treated by inactive substances (placebos) than when they receive tranquilizers (Carpenter et al. 1977; Young and Meltzer 1980). This was confirmed in a controlled experiment at Agnew State Hospital in San Jose, California, conducted by Maurice Rappaport, Julian Silverman, and John Perry (1974; 1978). In some other studies, no substantial difference was found between psychotic patients treated by tranquilizers and those receiving placebos (Mosher and Menn 1978). In general, patients with paranoid symptoms exhibiting primarily the mechanism of projection seem to do better when they receive psychopharmacological treatment, whereas those who experience the process internally have a better chance without medication.

There have been other therapeutic experiments in which patients received no tranquilizers and were encouraged to experience the psychotic process. R. D. Laing's project in Great Britain (1972a; 1972b) and John Perry's Diabasis in San Francisco (1966; 1974; 1976) are examples. An even more unusual and radical approach to the psychotic process is to provide new understanding, support, and encouragement for the client and use psychedelic sessions or nondrug experiential techniques to expedite the process and facilitate good resolution. In an extensive therapeutic study of LSD psychotherapy conducted at the Psychiatric Research Institute, in Prague, I observed a dramatic improvement in several manifestly psychotic patients that transcended by far anything that can be achieved by the traditional suppressive psychopharmacological treatment. The changes in these patients involved not only the disappearance of symptoms but also a deep and significant restructuring of personality. Condensed biographies of these patients and the history of their treatment have been published elsewhere (Grof 1980). Similar results were reported by Kenneth Godfrey and Harold Voth (1971), who used LSD psychotherapy in the treatment of psychotic patients at the Veteran's Administration Hospital, in Topeka, Kansas.

Use of therapeutic strategies of this kind requires an entirely new understanding of psychosis, since it makes no sense in the context of existing theories, whether they are organically or psychologically oriented, with the exception of Jungian analytical psychology. Traditional psychiatry offers two basic options in the approach to psychoses, neither of which is particularly convincing or satisfactory. Those professionals who are organically oriented relegate all the experiences and behaviors that the mechanistic paradigm cannot explain to the realm of the bizarre and morbid. They attribute them to some pathological processes in the organism yet to be discovered and attempt to suppress them by all available means. Psychiatrists and psychologists who subscribe to psychogenic theories of psychosis are generally restricted by the conceptual straitjacket of mechanistic science and have a narrow biographical emphasis. They offer theoretical explanations that reduce the problem of psychosis to infantile regression and practice psychotherapeutic approaches that use exclusively interpretations and maneuvers related to the biographical domain.

According to the new model presented here, functional matrices that are instrumental in psychotic episodes are intrinsic and integral parts of human personality. The same perinatal and transpersonal matrices that are involved in psychotic breakdowns can, under certain circumstances, mediate the process of spiritual transformation and consciousness evolution. The critical problem in understanding psychosis is, then, to identify the factors that distinguish the psychotic process from the mystical one.

Research following the model described in this book should focus on two important issues that seem to have great theoretical and practical relevance for the understanding of psychoses. The first is the question of the triggering mechanisms that make it possible for various unconscious contents to emerge into conscious awareness. It seems important to explain why some people confront the perinatal and transpersonal elements of their psyches only when they take a psychedelic drug or use some powerful nondrug technique while others are literally bombarded by these deep unconscious contents under the circumstances of everyday life.[15]

However, this is only one part of the problem. The other issue, which is probably even more important, is the question of the individual's attitude toward the content of these experiences, his or her personal style in dealing with them, and the ability to integrate them. This can be clearly demonstrated in LSD sessions where the trigger of the experience is standard and well known, yet the style can be mystical or psychotic. Here, as in spontaneously occurring episodes of unusual experiences, the individual's capacity to keep the process internalized, "own" it as an intrapsychic happening, and complete it internally without acting on it prematurely is clearly associated with the mystical attitude and indicates basic sanity. Exteriorization of the process, excessive use of the mechanism of projection, and indiscriminate acting out are characteristic of the psychotic style in confronting one's psyche. Psychotic states thus represent an interface confusion between the inner world and consensus reality. This distinguishes them sharply from both mystical and shamanic states of consciousness where this discrimination is maintained. Obviously the choice of either the mystical or the psychotic mode not only reflects intrinsic personality factors, but can also be critically dependent on the external circumstances under which the individual experiences a dramatic confrontation with his or her unconscious.

Psychiatric research suggests that the psychotic process is a phenomenon of extreme complexity and the end result of a variety of factors operating on different levels. Careful studies have revealed significant variables related to constitutional and genetic elements, the developmental history of the individual, hormonal and biochemical changes, situational precipitating factors, environmental and social influences, and even cosmobiological determinants. However, the concept of perinatal and transpersonal matrices is still critical for the understanding of psychosis, since none of the above factors can explain the nature, content, and dynamics of psychotic phenomena. At best these factors can be seen as conditions that activate the perinatal and transpersonal matrices or weaken the defense mechanisms that prevent them from appearing under normal circumstances.

Many otherwise strange and incomprehensible aspects of psychotic states suddenly show deep experiential logic when we see them in terms of the dynamics of perinatal or transpersonal matrices. I have already discussed the specific connection between perinatal matrices and the phenomena related to depressions, manic depressive disorders, and suicide: *inhibited depressions* are psychogenetically related to BPM II, *agitated depressions* to BPM III, and *manic episodes* to an incomplete transition from BPM III to BPM IV. Similarly, the two categories of suicidal fantasies, or impulses and specific individual choice of suicide, show deep logic if approached in the context of perinatal dynamics. Any of these phenomena can reach such intensity and relevance that they will qualify for being considered psychotic. There is a smooth transition between deep depression and depressive psychosis. The latter can manifest the content of BPM II in a pure form, including hallucinations of hell, devils, and diabolic tortures. Similarly, mania frequently reaches psychotic proportions.

However, the real crux for the theory and practice of psychiatry is the multifarious and picturesque group of psychotic conditions referred to as schizophrenias. This is a rather heterogeneous group with a common denominator that seems to be our basic ignorance about the nature and etiology of the psychological states involved. It is conceivable that for some forms of this disorder we may some day be able to establish clear organic etiology and pathology. This has happened in the past, when some patients considered schizophrenic were transferred into the new diagnostic categories of general paralysis or temporal epilepsy, and successfully treated. Consequently, the following statements should not be seen as sweeping generalizations about schizophrenia, but as an interpretive framework for many conditions currently included in this category.

Since psychological traumas in the life of the individual facilitate experiential access to perinatal and transpersonal matrices, one can find distinct biographical emphasis in the symptomatology of schizophrenia. However, the presence of elements suggestive of earlier stages of psychological development does not mean that all schizophrenia can be interpreted as regression into childhood. Many aspects of schizophrenic symptomatology can be meaningfully and logically related to the dynamics of various perinatal matrices and, thus, to individual stages of the biological birth process. While in neurosis the elements of perinatal matrices appear in a mitigated form and are colored by postnatal traumatic events, in psychosis they are experienced in an unmitigated and pure form. The following discussion is based on clinical observations from LSD psychotherapy in which schizophrenialike states of various kinds not only can occur in the context of the death-rebirth process in psychedelic sessions, but also occasionally persist in postsession intervals after poorly resolved and integrated sessions that have involved perinatal elements.

The early stages of BPM II appear to be the deep basis for the undifferentiated anxiety and generalized threat characterizing paranoia. The corresponding biological situation is the very beginning of delivery mediated at first by chemical signals and changes in the organisms of the mother and child and later by the mechanical contractions of the uterus. The intrauterine cosmos of the fetus that has been its abode for the nine months of pregnancy suddenly ceases to be a safe place and becomes hostile. The nature of this assault is initially only chemical; because of the diffuse and insidious nature of the noxious influences and because of its own cognitive limitations, the fetus is unable to identify what is happening.

Reexperienced by an adult without psychological insight into its real nature, this state tends to be projected and interpreted in terms of the subject's current life situation. The most important element of this experience is a state of intense anxiety with a sense of an insidious but elemental threat and undifferentiated universal danger. The subjects involved tend to interpret these alarming feelings as the result of noxious radiation, toxic gasses, chemical poisons, evil influences from members of secret organizations, assaults of malevolent black magicians, intrigues of political adversaries, or an invasion of alien energies from extraterrestrial beings. Other experiences observed in this situation involve being drawn into a gigantic whirlpool, swallowed by a mythological monster, or descending into the underworld, where one is attacked by chthonic creatures and exposed to diabolic ordeals and trials by demonic entities.

BPM II in its fully developed form contributes to schizophrenic symptomatology the themes of inhuman torture by ingenious contraptions, an atmosphere of eternal damnation, a never-ending suffering in hell, and other types of no-exit situations. Detailed studies in early psychoanalytic literature showed that the influencing machine of the schizophrenic represents the body of the mother. Victor Tausk's paper (1933) is of particular interest in this connection, although he fails to recognize that the endangering maternal organism is the delivering mother, rather than the mother of early infancy. Here belong also the meaningless and bizarre world of cardboard figures and lifeless robots, and the grotesque atmosphere of strange and fantastic circus sideshows.

The phenomenology of BPM III adds to the clinical picture of schizophrenia a rich spectrum of experiences that characterize the various facets of this functional matrix. The titanic aspect is represented by sensations of extreme tension, powerful energy flows and discharges, and images of battles and wars. The element of warfare can be related to events in the phenomenal world or involve archetypal themes of enormous scope—angels battling devils, heros and demigods challenging gods, or fights of mythological monsters. Aggression and sadomasochistic elements of BPM III explain the occasional violence of schizophrenic patients, automutilations, murders and bloody suicides, as well as visions and experiences involving cruelties of all kinds. Strange distortions of sexuality and perverted interests seen in psychotic patients are characteristically related to the sexual aspect of the third perinatal matrix, as has been detailed earlier. And finally, interest in feces and other biological material, coprophilia and coprophagia, magical power attributed to excreta, ritual manipulation of organic substances of the body, retention of urine and feces, or refusal to control the sphincters clearly betray the involvement of the scatological facet of BPM III.

The transition between BPM III and BPM IV, then, contributes to the rich spectrum of schizophrenic phenomenology the apocalyptic images of the destruction of the world and one's own annihilation, scenes of the judgment of the dead or the Last Judgment, experiences of rebirth and recreation of the world, identification with Christ or other divine personages symbolizing death and resurrection, grandiose and messianic feelings, elements of divine epiphany, angelic and celestial visions, and a sense of redemption and salvation. The involvement of this aspect of perinatal dynamics can also contribute a manic element to schizophrenic symptomatology and create clinical pictures that represent a mixture of schizophrenic psychosis and manic-depressive disorders.

However, the entire range of schizophrenic symptomatology cannot be adequately understood without including the elements of BPM I and the wealth of transpersonal experiences. The elements of the first perinatal matrix are represented in both their positive and negative aspects. Many psychotic patients experience episodes of ecstatic union with the universe and God, sometimes in intimate connection with the feelings of symbiotic union with the maternal organism on the level of the good womb or good breast. Similar experiences have been reported by mystics, saints, and religious teachers of all ages. This naturally raises the question about the relation between psychosis and mysticism, their similarities and differences.

An experience of unity with the divine that is well completed and integrated involves a sense of deep peace, tranquility, and serenity. The individual realizes that his or her divine origin is not exclusive and personal, but applies to everyone. It seems obvious that countless people in the past and even in the present have already discovered this truth about themselves, others have that potential and will reach the insight in the future. This combination of grandiosity and utmost humility, together with a lack of ostentatiousness or demonstrativeness, seems to characterize the mystical way of dealing with experiences of this kind.

Schizophrenic patients, on the other hand, tend to interpret their experiential connection with the divine in terms of their uniqueness and their special role in the universal scheme of things. They evaluate the relevance of their new insights in terms of their identification with their everyday personalities or body-egos, which they have not surrendered. As a result, they write letters to pres-

idents ond other government officials, trying to convince the world
at large of their divine origin, they demand to be acknowledged
as prophets, and they use various means to fight their real or
imagined enemies and opponents.

It would be an obviously absurd oversimplification and reductionistic error to see states of mystical union and spiritual liberation
as being identical with undifferentiated states of consciousness experienced by the child during its embryonic existence and in the
postnatal symbiotic interaction with the maternal organism. The
regression involved is experienced by an individual who has undergone a complex development through many stages of consciousness
evolution and matured physically, emotionally, and intellectually
during the years of life following the early events in infancy. In
addition, a mystic in an ecstatic rapture is clearly tapping genuine
transcendental and archetypal dimensions that by far transcend
biology. However, the mystical and psychotic states are not always
as clearly distinguishable from each other and as far apart on a
linear scale as Ken Wilber (1980) suggests in his discussion of the
pre-egoic versus trans-egoic states.

Clinical observations suggest strongly that states of mystical
union of a certain kind are deeply connected with positive aspects
of BPM I. An individual who connects experientially with an episode
of undisturbed intrauterine existence seems to have easy access to
an experience of cosmic unity, although this in no way means an
identity of the two states. Similarly, there seems to be a definite
liaison between disturbances of embryonic life—resulting from maternal diseases during pregnancy, anxiety states and chronic emotional stress, toxic or mechanical influences, and attempted or
impending abortions—and schizophrenic distortions of spirituality
and perception of the world.

A critical and fundamental threat to embryonic existence bears
deep similarity to the onset of delivery, which represents the final
and irreversible destruction of the intrauterine state. Fetal crises
are thus experienced in a way that resembles the early stages of
BPM II; this involves a sense of universal danger, generalized
paranoid feelings, bizarre physical sensations, and perceptions of
insidious toxic influences. The archetypal images accompanying
these states take the form of demons or other metaphysical evil
forces from different cultures.

The early symbiotic union with the mother also seems to be the source of psychotic experiences in which the individual cannot distinguish between himself and other people or their various aspects, and even the elements of the nonhuman world. This can result in feelings of being influenced by telepathy or by various science fiction gadgets of thought transfer. Individuals can also believe that they are reading other people's thoughts and feelings and be convinced that their thoughts cannot be concealed and are accessible to other people or even broadcast to the entire world. The wishful delusions and elements of uncontrolled daydreaming and autistic thinking can be understood as attempts to reinstitute the original and undisturbed intrauterine condition. The same is true for certain forms of the catatonic stupor of patients who remain for hours or days in fetal positions and manifest a total disregard for the intake of food and their incontinence of bladder and bowels.

Subjects who experience in their psychedelic sessions episodes of intrauterine distress often describe or manifest perceptual and conceptual distortions that bear a close resemblance to those found in schizophrenic patients. LSD subjects who have relatives or friends suffering from schizophrenia or paranoid conditions can experience at this point a full identification with these persons and develop a deep intuitive understanding of their problems. Numerous psychiatrists and psychologists who participated in the LSD training program of professionals have reported that during such perinatal sessions they kept remembering or actually visualizing their psychotic patients and were able to gain valuable insights into their world.

Observations of this kind suggest that the reliving of undisturbed intrauterine experiences is closely related to certain types of mystical and religious states, whereas episodes of embryonic crises show association with schizophrenic experiences and paranoid conditions. This finding is obviously related to the apparent existence of a rather precarious boundary between psychosis and the process of spiritual transformation. In psychedelic sessions, a clearly psychotic state can evolve into an experience of mystical revelation. Individuals involved in spiritual search and practices occasionally confront psychotic territories within themselves, while schizophrenic patients often visit the mystical experiential realms.

A problem of great relevance for both mystical states and psychosis is the incidence of ecstatic experiences and their relation to psychopathology and to the dynamics of unconscious matrices. Observations from psychedelic therapy suggest that there is an entire spectrum of ecstatic states that differ from each other considerably, not only in the intensity of the affective component, but by their nature and the level of the psyche in which they originate. The ecstatic states associated with the biographical level are usually considerably less powerful and significant than those that originate in the perinatal or transpersonal realms. They are typically associated with positive COEX systems and reflect the individual's history of biological and psychological satisfaction. The deepest biographical sources of such ecstatic feelings are expeiences of early symbiotic union with the maternal orgnism during the period of nursing. They involve a sense of total organismic fulfillment and emotional nourishment; although they have a very strong biological emphasis, they are also characteristically accompanied by a strong feeling of the numinous.

A far more important source of ecstatic experiences is the perinatal level of the unconscious. The observations of the phenomenology of the death-rebirth process during deep experiential work offer unique insights into the psychology and psychopathology of ecstasy. Earlier in this chapter, two different types of suicide and their dynamic connections with perinatal dynamics were described. In a very similar way, it is possible to distinguish three categories of ecstasy originating on the perinatal level and to demonstrate their specific relation to basic perinatal matrices.

The first type of ecstasy can be called *oceanic* or *Apollonian ecstasy*. It is characterized by extreme peace, tranquility, serenity, and radiant joy. The individual involved is usually motionless or shows slow and flowing movements. He or she experiences a blissful, tension-free state, a loss of ego boundaries and an absolute sense of oneness with nature, with the cosmic order, and with God. A deep intuitive understanding of existence and a flood of various specific insights of cosmic relevance are characteristic for this condition. A total absence of anxiety, aggression, guilt, or any other negative emotions, and profound feelings of satisfaction, security, and transcendental love complete the picture of this type of ecstasy.

This condition is clearly related to BPM I and, thus, to the experience of symbiotic union with the mother during intrauterine existence and nursing. The associated later memories involve nourishing emotional relationships, relaxing situations with total satisfaction, and beautiful experiences with art and nature. The corresponding imagery involves beautiful natural scenery, showing nature at its best—creative, abundant, nourishing, and safe: the associated archetypal images reflecting this state are those of the great mother goddesses or Mother Nature, heaven or paradise.

Predictably, there is a very strong emphasis in this oceanic ecstasy on the element of water as the cradle of all life and on milk and circulating blood as two nourishing liquids of cosmic significance. Experiences of fetal existence, identification with various aquatic forms of life, or a consciousness of the ocean, as well as visions of the star-filled sky and a sense of cosmic consciousness are all very common in this context. The art forms related to this experience are architectural works of transcendental beauty, paintings and sculptures radiating purity and serenity, flowing, peaceful, and timeless music, and classical ballet. Monumental Hindu or Greek temples, the Taj Mahal, the paintings of Fra Angelico, Michelangelo's masterpieces, or the marble sculptures of the ancient Greeks, and Bach's music are important examples.

The second type of ecstasy is in all its aspects diametrically opposed to the first; it can best be described as *volcanic* or *Dionysian ecstasy*. It is characterized by extreme physical and emotional tension, a strong element of aggression and destructiveness oriented both inward and outward, powerful driving energies of a sexual nature, and erratic hyperactivity or rhythmic orgastic movements. From the experiential point of view, volcanic ecstasy is characterized by a unique mixture of extreme physical and/or emotional pain with wild sensual rapture. As the intensity of this peculiar amalgam of agony and ecstasy increases in intensity, various experiential polarities fuse and cannot be differentiated from each other. The experience of freezing cold appears to be indistinguishable from caustic heat, murderous hatred from passionate love, perverted sexuality from craving for trascendence, the agony of dying from the ecstasy of new birth, the apocalyptic horrors of destruction from the excitement of creation, and vital anxiety from mystical rapture.

The subject has a sense of approaching an event of world-shattering significance—spiritual liberation, revelation of the ultimate truth, or oneness with all of existence. However, no matter

Fig. 42. A painting illustrating the cycle of death and rebirth that was inspired by a psychedelic session. The fact that the little flower feeding on the remnants of the past is a carnation reflects a play on words and is an allusion to reincarnation.

how convincing the promise of physical, emotional, and meta-physical freedom may be, and no matter how close one feels to the celestial realms, the experiences connected with BPM III, to which this type of ecstasy belongs, are always just an asymptotic approach to the final goal, and they never actually reach it. To have a sense of arriving or completing the spiritual journey, one must connect with the elements of BPM IV and BPM I, and thus with the oceanic ecstasy.

The characteristic memories or visions accompanying volcanic ecstasy are related to the atmosphere of unbridled Bacchanalia and carnivals, amusement parks, red light districts and nightclubs, and fireworks, and to the excitement associated with such dangerous activities as car racing or parachuting. The religious imagery associated with this type of ecstatic rapture involves sacrificial rituals, martyr death, the Sabbath of the Witches and satanic rituals, Dionysian orgies and temple prostitution, flagellantism, and aboriginal ceremonies combining sexuality and religion, such as fertility rites and phallic worship. In everyday life, powerful elements of volcanic ecstasy can be associated with the final stages of childbirth. More mitigated forms can be encountered in various intense sport activities, rock and disco dancing, rides in amusement parks, and wild sexual parties. Related art forms involve visual arts depicting the grotesque, sensual, and instinctual aspects of life, wild rhythmic trance-inducing music, and dynamic orgiastic dance.

The third category of ecstatic rapture associated with the perinatal process is dynamically related to BPM IV. and can best be described as *illuminative* or *Promethean ecstasy.* It is typically preceded by a period of determined emotional and intellectual struggle, agonizing longing and yearning, and desperate search for answers that seem to be hopelessly out of reach. Promethean ecstasy strikes like a divine lightning that destroys all the limitations and obstructions and provides entirely unexpected solutions. The individual is flooded by light of supernatural beauty and experiences a state of devine epiphany. He or she has a deep sense of emotional, intellectual, and spiritual liberation and gains access to breathtaking realms of cosmic inspiration and insight. This type of experience is clearly responsible for great achievements in the history of humanity in the areas of science, art, religion, and philosophy.

Another interesting problem related to the dynamics of schizophrenia that should be briefly discussed in the context of perinatal matrices is the relation beween psychosis and the female reproductive functions. It is well known that various psychopathological disorders are closely connected with the menstrual cycle and particularly with pregnancy, delivery, and the postpartum period. In the past this has been interpreted almost exclusively in terms of hormonal imbalance and its effects on the psyche.

The material discussed here throws an entirely new light on this problem. Observations from deep experiential work show an important dynamic connection between the experience of being born, of giving birth, and of sexual orgasm. Women reliving their birth in psychedelic sessions frequently have a simultaneous strong feeling of delivering a child. They can actually have great difficulties distinguishing whether they are being born or giving birth, while they are at the same time experiencing orgiastic sexual feelings. This might be expressed behaviorally by switching from a fetal position to a characteristic gynecological posture with the use of abdominal press. This dilemma of giving birth versus being born is then resolved in an experience that synthetizes the two modes—that of giving birth to a new self.

These observations clearly indicate that, in addition to the hormonal imbalance emphasized by traditional psychiatry, the post partum psychopathology reflects important psychological dynamics related to perinatal matrices. The process of delivering a child seems to bring the mother close to reliving her own trauma of birth. It tends to activate not only her basic perinatal matrices, but also all the later secondary elaborations of the birth trauma involving conflicts about sex, death, biological material, pregnancy, childbirth, and pain. Under proper circumstances, with the right understanding and a sensitive approach, this period can be a great opportunity for deep psychological work. Conversely, if the dynamics involved is misunderstood and the mother is forced to repress the emerging material, it can result in the development of serious emotional and psychosomatic problems. In extreme cases, disturbances of this kind can reach psychotic proportions.

To a lesser degree, emotional problems can also be accentuated during the premenstrual period; an increased tendency to anxiety, irritability, depressions, and suicidal ideation occuring at this time has been known as the premenstrual syndrome. There are deep anatomical, physiological, and biochemical similarities between menstruation and delivery; it can be said that each menstruation is a microdelivery. It is therefore quite plausible that during each menstruation the perinatal material is experientially particularly available. This similarity between menstruation and delivery seems to suggest that the menstrual period represents a similar mixture of opportunity and problem that was discussed earlier in regard to delivery.

In the preceding discussion, considerable emphasis has been placed on the perinatal roots of various schizophrenic symptoms. However, many aspects of the phenomenology of psychosis seem to have their origins in the transpersonal realms of the human psyche. These domains contribute to schizophrenic symptomatology the interest in ontological and cosmological problems; an abundance of archetypal themes and mythological sequences; encounters with deities and demons of different cultures; ancestral, phylogenetic, and past incarnation memories; elements of the racial and the collective unconscious; the experiential world of extrasensory perception and other paranormal phenomena; and a significant participation of the principle of synchronicity in the individual's life. Also, unifying experiences of a higher order than those related to perinatal dynamics should be mentioned—identification with the Universal Mind, with the Absolute, and with the Supracosmic and Metacosmic Void.

In spite of the revolutionary developments in modern psychology represented by the contributions of Jung, Assagioli, and Maslow, all these experiences are still automatically considered symptomatic of psychosis by traditional psychiatry. In the light of LSD psychotherapy and other powerful experiential approaches, the concept of psychosis will have to be dramatically revised and reevaluated. The matrices for perinatal and transpersonal experiences seem to be normal and natural components of the human psyche, and the experiences themselves have a distinct healing potential if approached with understanding. It is therefore absurd to diagnose psychosis on the basis of the content of the individual's experience. In the future, the definition of what is pathological and what is healing or evolutionary may have to emphasize the attitude toward the experience, the style of dealing with it, and the ability to integrate it into everyday life. In this framework, it will also be necessary to distinguish clearly between a therapeutic strategy that is conducive to healing and one that is noxious and counterproductive, and ultimately causes iatrogenic damage.

CHAPTER FIVE

Dilemmas and Controversies of Traditional Psychiatry

The Medical Model in Psychiatry: Pros and Cons

As a result of its complex historical development, psychiatry became established as a branch of medicine. Mainstream conceptual thinking in psychiatry, the approach to individuals with emotional disorders and behavior problems, the strategy of research, basic education and training, and forensic measures—all are dominated by the medical model. This situation is a consequence of two important sets of circumstances: medicine has been successful in establishing etiology and finding effective therapy for a specific, relatively small group of mental abnormalities, and it has also demonstrated its ability to control symptomatically many of those disorders for which specific etiology could not be found.

The Cartesian-Newtonian world view that had a powerful impact on the development of various fields has played a crucial role in the evolution of neuropsychiatry and psychology. The renaissance of scientific interest in mental disorders culminated in a series of revolutionary discoveries in the nineteenth century that firmly defined psychiatry as a medical discipline. Rapid advances and remarkable results in anatomy, pathology, pathophysiology, chemistry, and bacteriology resulted in tendencies to find organic causes for all mental disturbances in infections, metabolic disorders, or degenerative processes in the brain.

The beginnings of this "organic orientation" were stimulated when the discovery of the etiology of several mental abnormalities led to the development of successful methods of therapy. Thus, the recognition that general paresis—a condition associated, among others, with delusions of grandeur and disturbances of intellect and memory—was the result of tertiary syphilis of the brain caused by the protozoon Spirochaeta pallida was followed by successful therapy using chemicals and fever. Similarly, once it became clear that the mental disorder accompanying pellagra was due to a vitamin B deficiency (lack of nicotinic acid or its amid), the problem could be corrected by an adequate supply of the missing vitamin. Some other types of mental dysfunction were found to be linked to brain tumors, degenerative changes in the brain, encephalitis and meningitis, various forms of malnutrition, and pernicious anemia.

Medicine has been equally successful in the symptomatic control of many emotional and behavior disorders the etiology of which it has not been able to find. Here belong the dramatic interventions using pentamethylenetetrazol (Cardiazol) shocks, electroshock therapy, insulin shock treatment, and psychosurgery. Modern psychopharmacology has been particularly effective in this regard with its rich armamentarium of specifically acting drugs—hypnotics, sedatives, myorelaxants, analgesics, psychostimulants, tranquilizers, antidepressants, and lithium salts.

These apparent triumphs of medical research and therapy served to define psychiatry as a specialized branch of medicine and committed it to the medical model. With the privilege of hindsight, this was a premature conclusion; it led to a development that was not without problems. The successes in unraveling the causes of mental disorders, however astonishing, were really isolated and limited to a small fraction of the problems that psychiatry deals with. In spite of its initial successes, the medical approach to psychiatry has failed to find specific organic etiology for problems vexing the absolute majority of its clients—depressions, psychoneuroses, and psychosomatic disorders. Moreover, it has had very limited and problematic success in unraveling the medical causes underlying the so-called endogenous psychoses, particularly schizophrenia and manic-depressive psychosis. The failure of the medical approach and the systematic clinical study of emotional disorders gave rise to an alternative movement—the psychological approach to psychiatry, which led to the development of dynamic schools of psychotherapy.

In general, psychological research provided better explanatory models for the majority of emotional disorders than the medical approach; it developed significant alternatives to biological treatment and in many ways brought psychiatry close to the social sciences and philosophy. However, this did not influence the status of psychiatry as a medical discipline. In a way, the position of medicine became self-perpetuating, because many of the symptom-relieving drugs discovered by medical research have distinct side effects and require a physician to prescribe and administer them. The symbiotic liaison between medicine and the rich pharmaceutical industry, vitally interested in selling its products and offering support to medical endeavors, then sealed the vicious circle. The hegemony of the medical model was further reinforced by the nature and structure of psychiatric training and the legal aspects of mental health policies.

Most psychiatrists are physicians with postgraduate training in psychiatry—and a very inadequate background in psychology. In most instances, individuals who suffer from emotional disorders are treated in medical facilities with the psychiatrist legally responsible for the therapeutic procedures. In this situation, the clinical psychologist frequently has the function of ancillary personnel, subordinate to the psychiatrist, a role not dissimilar to that of the biochemist or laboratory technician. Traditional assignments of clinical psychologists are assessment of intelligence, personality, and organicity, assistance with differential diagnosis, evaluation of treatment, and vocational guidance. These tasks cover many of the activities of those psychologists who are not involved in research or psychotherapy. The problem to what extent psychologists are qualified and entitled to conduct therapy with psychiatric patients has been subject to much controversy.

The hegemony of the medical model in psychiatry has resulted in a mechanical transplantation of medical concepts and methods of proven usefulness into the field of emotional disorders. The application of medical thinking to the majority of psychiatric problems and to the treatment of emotional disorders, particularly various forms of neuroses, has been widely criticized in recent years. There are strong indications that this strategy has created at least as many problems as it solved.

Disorders for which no specific etiology has been found are loosely referred to as "mental diseases."[1] Individuals who suffer from such disorders receive socially stigmatizing labels and are routinely called "patients." They are treated in medical facilities where the per diem expenses for hospitalization amount to several hundred dollars. Much of this cost reflects enormous overhead directly related to the medical model, such as costs for examinations and services that are of questionable value in the effective treatment of the disorder in question. Much research money is dedicated to refining medically oriented research that will eventually discover the etiology of "mental diseases" and thus confirm the medical nature of psychiatry.

There has been increasing dissatisfaction with the application of the medical model in psychiatry. Probably the best known and most eloquent representative of this movement is Thomas Szasz. In a series of books, including his *Myth of Mental Illness* (1961), Szasz has adduced strong evidence that most cases of so-called mental illness should be regarded as expressions and reflections of the individual's struggles with the problems of living. They represent social, ethical, and legal problems, rather than "diseases" in the medical sense. The doctor-patient relationship as defined by the medical model also reinforces the passive and dependent role of the client. It implies that the solution of the problem depends critically on the resources of the person in the role of scientific authority, rather than on the inner resources of the client.

The consequences of the medical model for the theory and practice of psychiatry are far reaching. As a result of the mechanical application of medical thinking, all disorders that a psychiatrist deals with are seen in principle as diseases for which the etiology will eventually be found in the form of an anatomical, physiological, or biochemical abnormality. That such causes have not yet been discovered is not seen as a reason to exclude the problem from the context of the medical model. Instead, it serves as an incentive for more determined and refined research along medical lines.

Thus, the hopes of organically-minded psychiatrists were recently rekindled by the successes of molecular biology.

Another important consequence of the medical model is a great emphasis on establishing the correct diagnosis of an individual patient and creating an accurate diagnostic or classificatory system. This approach is of critical importance in medicine, where proper diagnosis reflects a specific etiology and has clear, distinct, and agreed-upon consequences for therapy and for prognostication. It is essential to diagnose properly the type of an infectious disease, because each of them requires quite different management and the infectious agents involved respond differently to specific antibiotic treatments. Similarly, the type of tumor determines the nature of the therapeutic intervention, approximate prognosis, or danger of metastases. It is critical to diagnose properly the type of anemia, because one kind will respond to medication with iron, another requires cobalt treatment, and so on.

A good deal of wasted effort has been poured into refining and standardizing psychiatric diagnosis, simply because the concept of diagnosis appropriate for medicine is not applicable to most psychiatric disorders. The lack of agreement can be illustrated clearly by comparing the systems of psychiatric classification used in different countries, for example in the United States, Great Britain, France, and Australia. Used indiscriminately in psychiatry, the medical concept of diagnosis is vexed by the problems of unreliability, lack of validity, and questionable value and usefulness. A diagnosis depends critically on the school to which the psychiatrist adheres, on his or her individual preferences, on the amount of data available for evaluation, and on many other factors.

Some psychiatrists arrive at a diagnosis only on the basis of the presenting complex of symptoms, others on the basis of psychodynamic speculations, still others on a combination of both. The psychiatrist's subjective evaluation of the psychological relevance of an existing physical disorder—such as thyroid problems, viral disease, or diabetes—or of certain biographical events in the past or present life of the patient can have a significant influence on the diagnosis. There is also considerable disagreement concerning the interpretation of certain diagnostic terms; for example, there are great differences between the American and European schools about the diagnosis of schizophrenia.

Another factor that can influence the psychiatric diagnosis is the nature of the interaction between the psychiatrist and the patient. While the diagnosis of appendicitis or a hypophyseal tumor will not be appreciably affected by the personality of the doctor, a psychiatric diagnosis could be influenced by the behavior of the patient toward the psychiatrist who establishes the diagnosis. Thus, specific transference-countertransference dynamics, or even the interpersonal ineptness of a psychiatrist, can become significant factors. It is a well-known clinical fact that the experience and behavior of a patient changes during interaction with different persons and can also be influenced significantly by circumstances and situational factors. Certain aspects of current psychiatric routines tend to reinforce or even provoke various behavioral maladjustments.

Because of the lack of objective criteria, which are so essential for the medical approach to physical diseases, there is a tendency among psychiatrists to rely on clinical experience and judgment as self-validating processes. In addition, classificatory systems and concerns are frequently products of medical sociology, reflecting specific pressures on physicians in the task imposed on them. A psychiatric diagnostic label is sufficiently flexible to be affected by the purpose for which it is given—whether for an employer, an insurance company, or forensic purposes. Even without such special considerations, different psychiatrists or psychiatric teams will frequently disagree about the diagnosis of a particular patient.

A considerable lack of clarity can be found even regarding such a seemingly important question as differential diagnosis between neurosis and psychosis. This issue is usually approached with great seriousness, although it is not even clearly established whether there is a single dimension of psychopathology. If psychosis and neurosis are orthogonal and independent, then the patient can suffer from both. If they are on the same continuum and the difference between them is only quantitative, then a psychotic individual would have to pass through a neurotic stage on the way to psychosis and return to it again during recovery.

Even if psychiatric diagnosis could be made both reliable and valid, there is the question of its practical relevance and usefulness. It is quite clear that with a few exceptions the search for accurate diagnosis is ultimately futile because it has no agreed-upon relevance for etiology, therapy, and prognosis. Establishing the diagnosis consumes much time and energy on the part of the psychiatrist, and particularly the psychologist, who must sometimes spend hours of testing to make the final decision.

Ultimately, the therapeutic choice will reflect the psychiatrist's orientation rather than a clinical diagnosis. Organically-minded psychiatrists will routinely use biological treatment with neurotics, and a psychologically-oriented psychiatrist may rely on psychotherapy even with psychotic patients. During psychotherapeutic work, the therapist will be responding to events during sessions rather than following a preconceived psychotherapeutic plan determined by the diagnosis. Similarly, specific pharmacological procedures do not show a generally agreed-upon relation between diagnosis and choice of the psychopharmacon. Frequently the choice is determined by the therapist's subjective preferences, the clinical response of the patient, the incidence of side effects, and similar concerns.

Another important legacy of the medical model is the interpretation of the function of the psychopathological symptoms. In medicine, there is generally a linear relationship between the intensity of symptoms and the seriousness of the disease. Alleviation of symptoms is thus seen as a sign of improvement of the underlying conditions. Therapy in physical medicine is causal whenever possible, and symptomatic therapy is used only for incurable diseases or in addition to causal therapy.

Applying this principle to psychiatry causes considerable confusion. Although it is common to consider the alleviation of symptoms as an improvement, dynamic psychiatry has introduced a distinction between causal and symptomatic treatment. It is thus clear that symptomatic treatment does not solve the underlying problem but, in a way, masks it. Observations from psychoanalysis show that intensification of symptoms is frequently an indication of significant work on the underlying problem. The new experiential approaches view the intensification of symptoms as a major therapeutic tool and use powerful techniques to activate them. Observations from work of this kind strongly suggest that symptoms represent an incomplete effort of the organism to get rid of an old problem—and that this effort should be encouraged and supported.[2]

From this point of view, much of the symptomatic treatment in contemporary psychiatry is essentially antitherapeutic, since it interferes with the spontaneous healing activity of the organism. It should thus be used not as a method of choice but as a compromise when the patient explicitly refuses a more appropriate alternative, or if such an alternative is not possible or available for financial or other reasons.

In conclusion, the hegemony of the medical model in psychiatry should be viewed as a situation created by specific historical circumstances and maintained at present by a powerful combination of philosophical, political, economical, administrative, and legal factors. Rather than reflecting the scientific knowledge about the nature of emotional disorders and their optimal treatment, it is at best a mixed blessing.

In the future, patients with psychiatric disorders having a clear organic basis may be treated in medical units especially equipped to handle behavior problems. Those in whom repeated physical checkups detect no medical problems could then use the service of special facilities where the emphasis would be psychological, sociological, philosophical, and spiritual, rather than medical. Powerful and effective techniques of healing and personality transformation addressing both the psychological and physical aspects of human beings have already been developed by humanistic and transpersonal therapists.

Disagreements about Theory and Therapeutic Measures

Conflicting theories and alternative interpretations of data can be found in most scientific disciplines. Even the so-called exact sciences have their share of disagreements, as exemplified by the differences of opinion on how to interpret the mathematical formalism of quantum theory. However, there are very few scientific fields where the lack of unanimity is so great and the body of agreed-upon knowledge so limited as in psychiatry and psychology. There is a broad spectrum of competing theories of personality, offering a number of mutually exclusive explanations about how the psyche functions, why and how psychopathology develops, and what constitutes a truly scientific approach to therapy.

The degree of disagreement about the most fundamental assumptions is so phenomenal that it is not surprising that psychology and psychiatry are frequently denied the status of science. Thus, psychiatrists and psychologists with impeccable academic training, superior intelligence, and great talent for scientific observation frequently formulate and defend concepts that are theoretically absolutely incompatible and offer exactly opposite practical measures.

Thus, there are schools of psychopathology that have a purely organic emphasis. They consider the Newtonian-Cartesian model of the universe to be an accurate description of reality and believe that an organism that is structurally and functionally normal should correctly reflect the surrounding material world and function adequately within it. According to this view, every departure from this ideal must have some basis in the anatomical, physiological, or biochemical abnormality of the central nervous system or some other part of the body that can influence its functioning.

Scientists who share this view are involved in a determined search for hereditary factors, cellular pathology, hormonal imbalance, biochemical deviations, and other physical causes. They do not consider an explanation of an emotional disorder to be truly scientific unless it can be meaningfully related to, and derived from, specific material causes. The extreme of this approach is the German organic school of thought with its credo that "for every deranged thought there is a deranged brain cell," and that one-to-one correlates will ultimately be found between various aspects of psychopathology and brain anatomy.

Another extreme example at the same end of the spectrum is behaviorism, whose proponents like to claim that it is the only truly scientific approach to psychology. It sees the organism as a complex biological machine the functioning of which, including the higher mental functions, can be explained from complex reflex activity based on the stimulus-response principle. As indicated by its name, behaviorism emphasizes the study of behavior and in its extreme form refuses to take into consideration introspective data of any kind, and even the notion of consciousness.

Although it definitely has its place in psychology as a fruitful approach to a certain kind of laboratory experimentation, behaviorism cannot be considered a serious candidate for a mandatory explanatory system of the human psyche. An attempt to formulate a psychological theory without mentioning consciousness is a strange endeavor at a time when many physicists believe that consciousness may have to be included explicitly in future theories of matter. While organic schools look for medical causes for mental abnormalities, behaviorism tends to see them as assemblies of faulty habits that can be traced back to conditioning.

The middle band of the spectrum of the theories explaining psychopathology is occupied by the speculations of depth psychology. Besides being in fundamental conceptual conflict with the organic schools and behaviorism, they also have serious disagreements with each other. Some of the theoretical arguments within this group have already been described in connection with the renegades of the psychoanalytic movement. In many instances, the disagreements within the group of depth psychologies are quite serious and fundamental.

On the opposite end of the spectrum, we find approaches that disagree with the organic, behaviorist, or psychological interpretations of psychopathology. As a matter of fact, they refuse to talk about pathology altogether. So, for phenomenology or daseinsanalysis, most of the states that psychiatry deals with represent philosophical problems, since they reflect only variations of existence, different forms of being in the world.

Many psychiatrists refuse these days to subscribe to the narrow and linear approaches described above and instead talk about multiple etiology. They see emotional disorders as end results of a complex multidimensional interaction of factors, some of which might be biological, while others are of a psychological, sociological, or philosophical nature. Psychedelic research certainly supports this understanding of psychiatric problems. Although psychedelic states are induced by a clearly defined chemical stimulus, this surely does not mean that the study of biochemical and pharmacological interactions in the human body following the ingestion can provide a complete and comprehensive explanation of the entire spectrum of psychedelic phenomena. The drug can be seen only as a trigger and catalyst of the psychedelic state that releases certain intrinsic potential of the psyche. The psychological, philosophical, and spiritual dimensions of the experience cannot be reduced to anatomy, physiology, biochemistry, or behavior study; they must be explored by means that are appropriate for such phenomena.

The situation in psychiatric therapy is as unsatisfactory as the one just outlined in regard to the theory of psychopathological problems. It is not surprising, since the two are closely related.

Thus, organically-minded psychiatrists frequently advocate extreme biological measures, not only for the treatment of severe disorders such as schizophrenia and manic-depressive psychosis, but for neurosis and psychosomatic diseases as well. Until the early 1950s, most of the common psychiatric biological treatments were of a radical nature—Cardiazol shocks, electroshock therapy, insulin shock treatment, and lobotomy.[3]

Even the modern psychopharmacopeia that has all but replaced these drastic measures, although far more subtle, is not without problems. It is generally understood that in psychiatry drugs do not solve the problem, but control the symptoms. In many instances, the period of active treatment is followed by an indefinite period during which the patient is obliged to take maintenance dosages. Many of the major tranquilizers are used quite routinely and usually for a long period of time. This can lead to such problems as irreversible neurological or retinal damage, and even true addiction.

The psychological schools favor psychotherapy, not only for neuroses, but also for many psychotic states. As mentioned earlier, there are ultimately no agreed-upon diagnostic criteria, except for well-established organic causations of particular disorders (encephalitis, tumor, arteriosclerosis), which would clearly assign the patient to organic therapy or psychotherapy. In addition, there is considerable disagreement as to the rules of combining biological therapy and psychotherapy. Although psychopharmacological treatment may occasionally be necessary for psychotic patients who receive psychotherapy and is generally compatible with its superficial, supportive forms, many psychotherapists feel that it is incompatible with a systematic depth-psychological approach. While the uncovering strategy aims to get to the roots of the problem and uses the symptoms for this purpose, symptomatic therapy masks the symptoms and obscures the problem.

The situation is now further complicated by the increasing popularity of the new experiential approaches. These not only use symptoms specifically as the entry point for therapy and self-exploration, but see them as an expression of the self-healing effort of the organism and try to develop powerful techniques that accentuate them. While one segment of the psychiatric profession focuses all its efforts on developing more and more effective ways of controlling symptoms, another segment is trying equally hard to design more effective methods of exteriorizing them. While many psychiatrists understand that symptomatic treatment is a compromise when a more effective treatment is not known or feasible, others insist that a failure to administer tranquilizers represents a serious neglect.

In view of the lack of unanimity regarding psychiatric therapy—with the exception of those situations that, strictly speaking, belong to the domain of neurology or some other branch of medicine, such as general paresis, brain tumors, or arteriosclerosis—one can suggest new therapeutic concepts and strategies without violating any principles considered absolute and mandatory by the entire psychiatric profession.

Criteria of Mental Health and Therapeutic Results

Since the majority of clinical problems psychiatrists deal with are not diseases in the true sense of the word, application of the medical model in psychiatry runs into considerable difficulty. Although psychiatrists have tried very hard for over a century to develop a "comprehensive" diagnostic system, they have largely failed in their effort. The reason for this is that they lack the disease-specific pathogenesis on which all good diagnostic systems are based.[4] Thomas Scheff (1974) has described this situation succinctly: "For major mental illness classifications, none of the components of the medical model has been demonstrated: cause, lesion, uniform and invariate symptoms, course, and treatment of choice." There are so many points of view, so many schools, and so many national differences that very few diagnostic concepts mean one and the same thing to all psychiatrists.

However, this has not discouraged psychiatrists from producing more and more extensive and detailed official nomenclatures. Mental health professionals continue to use the established terms despite overwhelming evidence that large numbers of patients do not have the symptoms to fit the diagnostic categories used to describe them. In general, psychiatric health care is based on unreliable and unsubstantiated diagnostic criteria and guidelines for treatment. To determine who is "mentally ill" and who is "mentally healthy," and what the nature of this "disease" is, is a far more difficult and complicated problem than it seems, and the process through which such decisions are made is considerably less rational than traditional psychiatry would like us to believe.

Considering the large number of people with serious symptoms and problems and the lack of agreed-upon diagnostic criteria, the critical issue seems to be why and how some of them are labeled as mentally ill and receive psychiatric treatment. Research shows that this depends more on various social characteristics than on the nature of the primary deviance (Light 1980). Thus, a factor of great importance is the degree to which the symptoms are manifest. It makes a great difference whether they are noticeable to everybody involved or relatively invisible. Another significant variable is the cultural context in which symptoms occur; concepts of what is normal and acceptable vary widely by social class, ethnic group, religious community, geographical region, and historical period. Also, measures of status, such as age, race, income, and education tend to correlate with diagnosis. The preconception of the psychiatrist is a critical factor; Rosenhan's remarkable study (1973) shows that, once a person has been designated as mentally ill—even if actually normal—the professional staff tends to interpret ordinary daily behavior as pathological.

The psychiatric diagnosis is sufficiently vague and flexible to be adjusted to a variety of circumstances. It can be applied and defended with relative ease when the psychiatrist needs to justify involuntary commitment or prove in court that a client was not legally responsible. This situation is in sharp contrast with the strict criteria applied by the psychiatrist for the prosecution, or by a military psychiatrist whose psychiatric diagnosis would justify discharge from military service. Similarly flexible can be psychiatric diagnostic reasoning in malpractice and insurance suits; the professional argumentation might vary considerably depending on which side the psychiatrist stands.

Because of the lack of precise and objective criteria, psychiatry is always deeply influenced by the social, cultural, and political structure of the community in which it is practiced. In the nineteenth century, masturbation was considered pathological, and many professionals wrote cautionary books, papers, and pamphlets about its deleterious effects. Modern psychiatrists consider it harmless and endorse it as a safety valve for excessive sexual tension. During the Stalinist era, psychiatrists in Russia declared neuroses and sexual deviations to be products of class conflicts and the deteriorated morals of bourgeois society. They claimed that problems of this kind had practically disappeared with the change in their social order. Patients exhibiting such symptoms were seen as partisans of the old order and "enemies of the people." Conversely, in more recent years it has become common in Soviet psychiatry to view political dissidence as a sign of insanity requiring psychiatric hospitalization and treatment. In the United States, homosexuality was defined as mental illness, until 1973 when the American Psychiatric Association decided by vote that it was not. The members of the hippie movement in the sixties were seen by traditional professionals as emotionally unstable, mentally ill, and possibly brain-damaged by drug use, while the New Age psychiatrists and psychologists considered them to be the emotionally liberated avant-gard of humanity. We have already discussed the cultural differences in concepts of normalcy and mental health. Many of the phenomena that Western psychiatry considers symptomatic of mental disease seem to represent variations of the collective unconscious, which have been considered perfectly normal and acceptable by some cultures and at some times in human history.

Psychiatric classification and emphasis on presenting symptoms, although problematic, is somewhat justifiable in the context of the current therapeutic practices. Verbal orientation in psychotherapy offers little opportunity for dramatic changes in the clinical condition, and suppressive medication actively interferes with further development of the clinical picture, tending to freeze the process in a stationary condition. However, the relativity of such an approach becomes obvious when therapy involves psychedelics or some powerful experiential nondrug techniques. This results in such a flux of symptoms that on occasion the client can move within a matter of hours into an entirely different diagnostic category. It becomes obvious that what psychiatry describes as distinct diagnostic categories are stages of a transformative process in which the client has become arrested.

The situation is scarcely more encouraging when we turn from the problem of psychiatric diagnosis to psychiatric treatment and evaluation of the results. Different psychiatrists have their own therapeutic styles, which they use on a wide range of problems, although there is no good evidence that one technique is more

effective than another. Critics of psychotherapy have found it easy
to argue that there is no convincing evidence that patients treated
by professionals improve more than those who are not treated at
all or who are supported by nonprofessionals (Eysenck and Rachman
1965). When improvement occurs in the course of psychotherapy,
it is difficult to demonstrate that it was directly related either to
the process of therapy or to the theoretical beliefs of the therapist.

The evidence for the efficacy of psychopharmacological agents
and their ability to control symptoms is somewhat more encouraging. However, the critical issue here is to determine whether
symptomatic relief means true improvement or whether administration of pharmacological agents merely masks the underlying
problems and prevents their resolution. There seems to be increasing evidence that in many instances tranquilizing medication
actually interferes with the healing and transformative process, and
that it should be administered only if it is the patient's choice or
if the circumstances do not allow pursuit of the uncovering process.

Since the criteria of mental health are unclear, psychiatric
labels are problematic, and since there is no agreement as to what
constitutes effective treatment, one should not expect much clarity
in assessing therapeutic results. In everyday clinical practice, the
measure of the patient's condition is the nature and intensity of
the presenting symptoms. Intensification of symptoms is referred
to as a worsening of the clinical condition, and alleviation of
symptoms is called improvement. This approach conflicts with dynamic psychiatry, where the emphasis is on resolution of conflicts
and improvement of interpersonal adjustment. In dynamic psychiatry, the activation of symptoms frequently precedes or accompanies major therapeutic progress. The therapeutic philosophy based
primarily on evaluation of symptoms is also in sharp conflict with
the view presented in this book, according to which an intensity
of symptoms indicates the activity of the healing process, and
symptoms represent an opportunity as much as they are a problem.

Whereas some psychiatrists rely exclusively on the changes in
symptoms when they assess therapeutic results, others include in
their criteria the quality of interpersonal relationships and social
adjustment. Moreover, it is not uncommon to use such obviously
culture-bound criteria as professional and residential adjustment.
An increase in income or moving into a more prestigious residential
area can thus become important measures of mental health. The

absurdity of such criteria becomes immediately obvious when one considers the emotional stability and mental health of some individuals who might rank very high by such standards, say, Howard Hughes or Elvis Presley. It shows the degree of conceptual confusion when criteria of this kind can enter clinical considerations. It would be easy to demonstrate that an increase of ambition, competitiveness, and a need to impress reflect an increase of pathology rather than improvement. In the present state of the world, voluntary simplicity might well be an expression of basic sanity.

Since the theoretical system presented in this book puts much emphasis on the spiritual dimension in human life, it seems appropriate to mention spirituality at this point. In traditional psychiatry, spiritual inclinations and interests have clear pathological connotations. Although not clearly spelled out, it is somehow implicit in the current psychiatric system of thought that mental health is associated with atheism, materialism, and the world view of mechanistic science. Thus, spiritual experiences, religious beliefs, and involvement in spiritual practices would generally support a psychopathological diagnosis.

I can illustrate this with a personal experience from the time when I arrived in the United States and began lecturing about my European LSD research. In 1967, I gave a presentation at the Psychiatric Department of Harvard University, describing the results achieved in a group of patients with severe psychiatric problems treated by LSD psychotherapy. During the discussion, one of the psychiatrists offered his interpretation of what I considered therapeutic successes. According to his opinion, the patients' neurotic symptoms were actually replaced by psychotic phenomena. I had said that many of them showed major improvement after undergoing powerful death-rebirth experiences and states of cosmic unity. As a result, they became spiritual and showed a deep interest in ancient and Oriental philosophies. Some became open to the idea of reincarnation; others became involved in meditation, yoga, and other forms of spiritual practices. These manifestations were, according to him, clear indications of a psychotic process. Such a conclusion would be more difficult today than it was in the late sixties, in light of the current widespread interest in spiritual practice. However, this remains a good example of the general orientation of current psychiatric thinking.

The situation in Western psychiatry concerning the definition of mental health and disease, clinical diagnosis, general strategy of treatment, and evaluation of therapeutic results is rather confusing and leaves much to be desired. Sanity and healthy mental functioning are defined by the absence of psychopathology and there is no positive description of a normal human being. Such concepts as the active enjoyment of existence, the capacity to love, altruism, reverence for life, creativity, and self-actualization hardly ever enter psychiatric considerations. The currently available psychiatric techniques can hardly achieve even the therapeutic goal defined by Freud: "to change the excessive suffering of the neurotic into the normal misery of everyday life." More ambitious results are inconceivable without introducing spirituality and the transpersonal perspective into the practice of psychiatry, psychology, and psychotherapy.

Psychiatry and Religion: Role of Spirituality in Human Life

The attitude of traditional psychiatry and psychology toward religion and mysticism is determined by the mechanistic and materialistic orientation of Western science. In a universe where matter is primary and life and consciousness its accidental products, there can be no genuine recognition of the spiritual dimension of existence. A truly enlightened scientific attitude means acceptance of one's own insignificance as an inhabitant of one of the countless celestial bodies in a universe that has millions of galaxies. It also requires the recognition that we are nothing but highly developed animals and biological machines composed of cells, tissues, and organs. And finally, a scientific understanding of one's existence includes acceptance of the view that consciousness is a physiological function of the brain and that the psyche is governed by unconscious forces of an instinctual nature.

It is frequently emphasized that three major revolutions in the history of science have shown human beings their proper place in the universe. The first was the Copernican revolution, which destroyed the belief that the earth was the center of the universe and humanity had a special place within it. The second was the Darwinian revolution, bringing to an end the concept that humans occupied a unique and privileged place among animals. Finally, the Freudian revolution reduced the psyche to a derivative of base instincts.

Psychiatry and psychology governed by a mechanistic world view are incapable of making any distinction between the narrow-minded and superficial religious beliefs characterizing mainstream interpretations of many religions and the depth of genuine mystical traditions or the great spiritual philosophies, such as the various schools of yoga, Kashmir Shaivism, Vajrayana, Zen, Taoism, Kabbalah, Gnosticism, or Sufism. Western science is blind to the fact that these traditions are the result of centuries of research into the human mind that combines systematic observation, experiment, and the construction of theories in a manner resembling the scientific method.

Western psychology and psychiatry thus tend to discard globally any form of spirituality, no matter how sophisticated and well-founded, as unscientific. In the context of mechanistic science, spirituality is equated with primitive superstition, lack of education, or clinical psychopathology. When a religious belief is shared by a large group within which it is perpetuated by cultural programming, it is more or less tolerated by psychiatrists. Under these circumstances, the usual clinical criteria are not applied, and sharing such a belief is seen as not necessarily indicative of psychopathology.

When deep spiritual convictions are found in non-Western cultures with inadequate educational systems, this is usually attributed to ignorance, childlike gullibility, and superstition. In our own society, such an interpretation of spirituality obviously will not do, particularly when it occurs among well-educated and highly intelligent individuals. Consequently, psychiatry resorts to the findings of psychoanalysis, suggesting that the origins of religion are found in unresolved conflicts from infancy and childhood: the concept of deities reflects the infantile image of parental figures, the attitudes of believers toward them are signs of immaturity and childlike dependency, and ritual activities indicate a struggle with threatening psychosexual impulses, comparable to that of an obsessive compulsive neurotic.

Direct spiritual experiences, such as feelings of cosmic unity, a sense of divine energy streaming through the body, death-rebirth sequences, visions of light of supernatural beauty, past incarnation memories, or encounters with archetypal personages, are then seen as gross psychotic distortions of objective reality indicative of a serious pathological process or mental disease. Until the publication of Maslow's research, there was no recognition in academic psychology that any of these phenomena could be interpreted in any other way. The theories of Jung and Assagioli pointing in the same direction were too remote from mainstream academic psychology to make a serious impact.

In principle, Western mechanistic science tends to see spiritual experiences of any kind as pathological phenomena. Mainstream psychoanalysis, following Freud's example, interprets the unifying and oceanic states of mystics as regression to primary narcissism and infantile helplessness (Freud 1961) and sees religion as a collective obsessive-compulsive neurosis (Freud 1924). Franz Alexander (1931), a very well-known psychoanalyst, wrote a special paper describing the states achieved by Buddhist meditation as self-induced catatonia. The great shamans of various aboriginal traditions have been described as schizophrenic or epileptic, and various psychiatric labels have been put on all major saints, prophets, and religious teachers. While many scientific studies describe the similarities between mysticism and mental disease, there is very little genuine appreciation of mysticism or awareness of the differences between the mystical world view and psychosis. A recent report of the Group for the Advancement of Psychiatry described mysticism as an intermediate phenomenon between normalcy and psychosis (1976). In other sources, these differences tend to be discussed in terms of ambulant versus florid psychosis, or with emphasis on the cultural context that allowed integration of a particular psychosis into the social and historical fabric. These psychiatric criteria are applied routinely and without distinction even to great religious teachers of the scope of Buddha, Jesus, Mohammed, Sri Ramana Maharishi, or Ramakrishna.

This results in a peculiar situation in our culture. In many communities considerable psychological, social, and even political pressure persists, forcing people into regular attendance at church. The Bible can be found in the drawers of many motels and hotels, and lip service is paid to God and religion in the speeches of many prominent politicians and other public figures. Yet, if a member of a typical congregation were to have a profound religious experience, its minister would very likely send him or her to a psychiatrist for medical treatment.

CHAPTER SIX

A New Understanding of the Psychotherapeutic Process

The understanding of the nature, origin, and dynamics of psychogenic disorders is a factor of critical importance for the theory and practice of psychotherapy. It has direct implications for the concept of the healing process, the definition of the effective mechanisms of psychotherapy and personality transformation, and the choice of therapeutic strategies. Unfortunately, the existing schools of psychotherapy differ as greatly in their interpretation of psychogenic symptoms and their therapeutic strategies as they do in their descriptions of the basic dynamics of human personality.

I will not here touch on behaviorism, which sees psychogenic symptoms as isolated collections of faulty habits with no deeper meaning, rather than manifestations of a more complex underlying personality disorder. I will also omit supportive methods of psychotherapy and other forms of psychological work that refrain from in-depth probing for practical rather than theoretical reasons. However, even when we deliberately narrow our focus to the schools of so-called depth psychology, we find far-reaching differences of opinion about these issues.

In classical Freudian analysis, symptoms are viewed as the result of a conflict between instinctual demands and defensive forces of the ego, or compromise formations between the id impulses and prohibitions and injunctions of the superego. In his original formulations, Freud put exclusive emphasis on sexual wishes and saw the opposing countersexual forces as manifestations of the "ego instincts," serving the purpose of self-preservation. In his later drastic theoretical revision, he considered various mental phenomena to be products of conflict between Eros, the love instinct striving for union and the creation of higher units, and Thanatos, the death instinct, the purpose of which is destruction and return to the original inorganic condition. In any case, the Freudian interpretation is strictly biographical, operating within the confines of the individual organism. The goal of therapy is to free the instinctual energies bound in symptoms and find for them socially acceptable channels of expression.

In Adler's interpretation, the neurotic disposition stems from childhood programming, which is characterized by overprotection, neglect, or a confusing mixture of both. This results in a negative self-image and neurotic striving for superiority to compensate for exaggerated feelings of insecurity and anxiety. As a result of this self-centered life strategy, the neurotic is incapable of coping with problems and of enjoying social life. Neurotic symptoms are, then, integral aspects of the only adaptive system the individual has been able to construct from the misleading clues from the environment. While in Freud's conceptual framework everything is explained from antecedent circumstances, following rigorous linear causality, Adler emphasizes the teleological principle. The neurotic's plan is artificial and parts of it must remain unconscious because they contradict reality. The goal of therapy is to prevent the patient from living in this fiction and to help him or her recognize the one-sidedness, sterility, and ultimately self-defeating nature of his or her attitudes. In spite of some fundamental theoretical differences, Adler's individual psychology shares with psychoanalysis its strictly biographical focus.

Wilhelm Reich contributed to depth psychology a unique understanding of the dynamics of sexual energy and the role of energetic economy in psychopathological symptoms. He believed that the repression of the original trauma is maintained by the suppression of sexual feelings and by blocking of the sexual orgasm. According to him, this sexual suppression, together with the corresponding muscular armoring and specific characterological attitudes, represents the real neurosis; the psychopathological symptoms, then, are only its secondary overt expressions. The critical factor determining emotional health or disease is one's economy of sexual energy, or the balance between charge and discharge that one maintains. Therapy consists in releasing stored and pent-up sexual energies and freeing the muscular armor through a system of exercises utilizing breathing and direct body work. Although Reich's approach represented a far-reaching theoretical departure from classical psychoanalysis and a revolutionary innovation of the practice of psychotherapy, he never transcended the narrow sexual emphasis of his former teacher and his biographical orientation.

Otto Rank challenged Freud's sexual theory of neurosis by shifting the etiological focus to the trauma of birth. According to him, neurotic symptoms represent attempts to exteriorize and integrate this fundamental emotional and biological shock of human life. As a result of it, no real cure of neurosis should be expected until the client confronts this event in the therapeutic situation. In view of the nature of this trauma, talking therapy is of little value and must be replaced by direct experience.

The recognition of the primary and independent significance of spiritual aspects of the psyche, or of what would these days be called the transpersonal dimension, was extremely rare among Freud's followers. Only Jung was able to penetrate really deeply into the transpersonal domain and formulate a system of psychology radically different from any of Freud's followers. During years of systematic probing into the human unconscious, Jung realized that the psychopathology of neuroses and psychoses cannot be adequately explained from forgotten and repressed biographical material. He complemented Freud's concept of the individual unconscious with that of the racial and collective unconscious and emphasized the role of "myth-forming" structural elements in the psyche. Another major Jungian contribution was the definition of archetypes, transcultural primordial ordering principles in the psyche.

Jung's understanding of psychopathology and psychotherapy was altogether unique. According to him, when drives, archetypal urges, creative impulses, talents, or other qualities of the psyche are repressed or not allowed to develop, they remain primitive and undifferentiated. As a result, they exert a potentially destructive influence on the personality, interfere with adaptation to reality, and manifest themselves as psychopathological symptoms. Once the conscious ego is able to confront these previously unconscious or repressed components, they can be integrated in a constructive way into the individual's life. Jung's therapeutic approach does not emphasize rational understanding and sublimation, but active transformation of one's innermost being through direct symbolic experiencing of the psyche as an autonomous "other personality." The guidance in this process is beyond the capacity of any individual therapist or school. For this purpose, it is essential to mediate for the client a connection with the collective unconscious and utilize the wisdom of untold ages that lies dormant in it.

This discussion of the conceptual differences and disagreements between the major schools of depth psychology regarding the nature and origin of emotional disorders and effective therapeutic mechanisms could be continued to include the views of Sandor Ferenczi, Melanie Klein, Karen Horney, Erich Fromm, Harry Stack Sullivan, Roberto Assagioli, and Carl Rogers, or the innovations of Fritz Perls, Alexander Lowen, Arthur Janov, and many others. However, my main purpose is to demonstrate that there are popular and vital theories and systems of therapy with radical disagreements about the dynamics of psychopathology and therapeutic techniques. Some are limited to the biographical or analytical-recollective level, others put almost exclusive emphasis on perinatal elements or existential concerns, and a few include a transpersonal orientation.

We can now focus on the new insights from experiential psychotherapy that make it possible to reconcile and integrate many of the conflicts in contemporary psychiatry and to formulate a more comprehensive theory of psychopathology and psychotherapy.

The Nature of Psychogenic Symptoms

The data from experiential psychotherapy with or without psychedelics strongly suggest the need for the "spectrum approach" that has already been described. Clearly the model of the psyche used in serious self-exploration should be broader than any of the existing ones. In the new context, various psychotherapeutic schools offer useful ways of conceptualizing the dynamics of specific bands of consciousness (or of only specific aspects of a certain band) and should not be treated as comprehensive descriptions of the psyche.

Emotional, psychosomatic, and interpersonal problems can be associated with any of the levels of the unconscious—biographical, perinatal, and transpersonal—and occasionally have important roots in all of them. Effective therapeutic work must follow the process into the area involved and should not be limited by conceptual considerations. There are many symptoms that persist until and unless the individual confronts, experiences, and integrates the perinatal and transpersonal themes with which they are associated. For problems of this kind, biographical work of any variety and any scope or length will prove ineffective.

In view of the observations from experiential sessions, any psychotherapeutic approach restricted to verbal exchange is of limited value and cannot really reach the core of the problems involved. The emotional and psychosomatic energies underlying psychopathology are so elemental that only direct, nonverbal experiential approaches have any chance of coping with them effectively. However, verbal exchange is essential for proper intellectual preparation for the experiential sessions and also for their adequate integration. In a paradoxical way, cognitive work is probably more important in the context of experiential therapies than ever before.

The powerful humanistic and transpersonal techniques of psychotherapy originated as a reaction against the unproductive verbal and overintellectualized orientation of traditional psychotherapies. As such, they tend to stress direct experience, nonverbal interaction, and involvement of the body in the process. However, the rapid mobilization of energy and release of emotional and psychosomatic blocks that these revolutionary methods made possible tend to open the way to perinatal and transpersonal experiences. The content of these experiences is so extraordinary that it tends to shatter the individual's conceptual framework, basic belief system, and the world view shared by Western civilization.

Modern psychotherapy thus faces an interesting paradoxical situation. Whereas in the earlier stages it tried to bypass intellect and eliminate it from the process, at present a new intellectual understanding of reality is an important catalyst for therapeutic progress. While the resistances in more superficial forms of psychotherapy are of an emotional and psychosomatic nature, the ultimate obstacle for radical therapies is a cognitive and philosophical barrier. Many of the transpersonal experiences that are potentially of great therapeutic value involve such a basic challenge to the individual's world view that he or she will have serious difficulty in letting them happen unless properly intellectually prepared.

Defending intellectually the Newtonian-Cartesian definition of reality and the common-sense image of the world is a particularly difficult form of resistance that can be overcome only by the combined effort of the client and the facilitator. Therapists who do not offer cognitive expansion, together with powerful experiential approaches, put their clients into a difficult double-bind. They are asking them to give up all resistances and to surrender fully to the process, yet such a surrender would lead to experiences that their conceptual framework does not allow and does not account for. In such a situation, insisting on biographical interpretations, clinging to the mechanistic world view, and seeing the process in terms of linear causality will seriously impede therapeutic progress and serve as a powerful mechanism of defense, whether it occurs in the client or the facilitator. On the other hand, knowledge of the expanded cartography of the human mind that includes perinatal and transpersonal experiences, of the new paradigms emerging from modern science, and of the great mystical traditions of the world can become therapeutic catalysts of unusual power.

Since psychopathological symptoms have a different dynamic structure, depending on the level of the psyche with which they are connected, it would be incorrect and useless to describe them all in terms of one universal formula, unless such a formula could be unusually broad and general. On the recollective-analytical level, symptoms appear to be meaningfully related to important memories from childhood and later life. In this connection, it is useful to see them as historically determined compromise formations between instinctual tendencies and the repressive forces of the superego, or between emerging painful emotions and physical sensations and the defenses against facing them. In the last analysis, they represent elements from the past that have not been successfully integrated and are interfering with an appropriate experience of the present time and place. They typically involve situations that have interfered with the individual's feelings of basic unity and harmony with the universe and contributed to a sense of separation, isolation, antagonism, and alienation. A situation in which all the basic needs are satisfied and in which the organism feels secure is closely related to the sense of cosmic unity. A painful experience or a state of intense need creates a dichotomy that involves a differentiation and conflict between the victimized self and the noxious external agent, or between the unsatisfied subject and the desired object.

When the individual connects experientially with the perinatal realm, the Freudian framework and all the other systems limited to biography become entirely useless, and attempts to apply them serve the interests of defense. On this level, the symptoms can best be understood as compromise formations between emerging emotions and sensations related to the biological birth trauma and the forces that protect the individual against reexperiencing them. A useful biological model of this conflict of opposing tendencies is to see it in terms of simultaneous experiential identification with the infant struggling to be born and with the biological forces representing the introjected, repressive influence of the birth canal. Because of the strong hydraulic emphasis in this situation, the Reichian model stressing the release of pent-up energies, and loosening of the character armor can be extremely useful. The similarity between the pattern of sexual orgasm and the orgasm of birth explains why Reich confused pent-up perinatal energies with jammed libido stored from incomplete orgasms.

Another way of conceptualizing this dynamic clash is to see it in a longitudinal perspective in terms of a conflict between one's identification with the ego structure and the body image, on the one hand, and the need for total surrender, ego death, and transcendence, on the other. The corresponding existential alternatives are continued entrapment in a limited way of life governed by ultimately self-defeating ego strategies versus an expanded and enlightened existence with transpersonal orientation. However, an unsophisticated and uninformed subject naturally would not be aware of the second alternative until he or she actually had the experience of spiritual opening. The two basic strategies of existence related to the two extreme poles of this conflict are: approaching the world, or life, as struggle—the way it was experienced in the birth canal or, conversely, as a give-and-take exchange and a nourishing dynamic dance—comparable to the symbiotic interaction between the child and the good womb or breast.

Additional useful alternatives for conceptualizing the process underlying symptoms on the perinatal level are anxious holding on versus trusting letting go, determined clinging to the illusion of being in charge versus accepting the fact of total dependence on cosmic forces, or wanting to be something else or somewhere else than one is versus accepting the present circumstances.

The best way to describe the dynamic structure of psychogenic symptoms that are anchored in the transpersonal realm of the psyche is as compromise formations between defensive holding onto the rational, materialistic, and mechanistic image of the world and an invading realization that human existence and the universe are manifestations of a deep mystery which transcends reason. In sophisticated subjects, this philosophical battle between common sense and cultural programming on the one side and an essentially metaphysical world view on the other can take the form of a conceptual conflict between Freudian and Jungian psychology, or between the Newtonian-Cartesian approach to the universe and the new paradigms.

If the individual opens up to the experiences underlying these symptoms, new information about the universe and existence will radically transform his or her world view. It will become clear that certain events in the world that should be irreversibly buried in remote history or have not yet occurred in terms of our linear concept of time can, under certain circumstances, be experienced with the full sensory vividness otherwise reserved only for the present moment. Various aspects of the universe from which we would expect to be separated by an inpenetrable spatial barrier can suddenly become easily experientially available and in a sense appear to be parts or extensions of ourselves. Realms that are ordinarily inaccessible to the unaided human senses, such as the physical and biological microworld and astrophysical objects and processes, become available for direct experience. Our ordinary Newtonian-Cartesian consciousness can also be invaded with unusual power by various archetypal entities or mythological sequences that, according to mechanistic science, should have no independent existence. The myth-producing aspects of the human psyche will portray deities, demons, and rituals from different cultures that the subject has never studied. It will present them on the same continuum with elements of the phenomenal world and with the same accuracy of detail with which it depicts historically and geographically remote events of material reality.

Having set forth what appear to be the typical conflicts underlying psychogenic symptoms on the biographical, perinatal, and transpersonal levels of the human psyche, we can now attempt to bring all these seemingly diverse mechanisms under a common denominator and formulate a comprehensive conceptual model for psychopathology and psychotherapy. In view of what has been said earlier about the principles of spectrum psychology and the heterogeneity of the individual bands of consciousness, such a unifying umbrella must be unusually braod and encompassing. To create it we need to return to the new definition of human nature emerging from modern consciousness research.

I suggested earlier that human beings show a peculiar ambiguity which somewhat resembles the particle-wave dichotomy of light and subatomic matter. In some situations, they can be successfully described as separate material objects and biological machines, whereas in others they manifest the properties of vast fields of consciousness that transcend the limitations of space, time, and linear causality. There seems to be a fundamental dynamic tension between these two aspects of human nature, which reflects the ambiguity between the part and the whole that exists all through the cosmos on different levels of reality.

What psychiatry describes and treats as symptoms of mental disease can be seen as manifestations of interface noise between these two complementary extremes. They are experiential hybrids that represent neither one nor the other mode, nor a smooth integration of both, but their conflict and clash. On the biographical level this can be illustrated by a neurotic whose experience of the present moment is distorted by partial emergence of an experience that belongs contextually to another temporal and spatial framework. He does not have a clear and appropriate experience corresponding to the present circumstances, nor is he fully in touch with the childhood experience that would justify the emotions and physical sensations he is having. The mixture of both experiences without a discriminating insight is characteristic of a strange spatiotemporal experiential amalgam that psychiatry calls "symptoms."

On the perinatal level, the symptoms represent a similar spatiotemporal hybrid connecting the present moment with the time and space of biological birth. In a sense, the individual experiences the here and now as if it involved a confrontation with the birth canal; the emotions and physical sensations that would be fully consonant with the event of birth become, in a different context, psychopathological symptoms. As in the above example, such a person is experiencing neither the present situation nor biological birth; in some sense he or she is still stuck in the birth canal and has not yet been born.

The same general principle can be applied to symptoms that involve experiences of a transpersonal nature. The only major difference is that for most of them it is impossible to imagine a material substrate through which such phenomena could be mediated. Those that involve historical regression cannot be easily interpreted through memory mechanisms in the conventional sense. For others that involve transcendence of spatial barriers, the transfer of information through material channels is not only untraceable but frequently unimaginable from the vantage point of the mechanistic world view. On occasion, the phenomena underlying the transpersonal type of symptoms are outside the Occidental framework of objective reality altogether, such as the Jungian archetypes, specific deities and demons, discarnate entities, spirit guides, or suprahuman beings.

Thus, in the broadest sense, what is presented as psychiatric symptom can be seen as an interface conflict between two different modes in which humans can experience themselves. The first of these modes can be called *hylotropic consciousness*[1]; it involves the experience of oneself as a solid physical entity with definite boundaries and a limited sensory range, living in three-dimensional space and linear time in the world of material objects. Experiences in this mode systematically support a number of basic assumptions, such as: matter is solid; two objects cannot simultaneously occupy the same space; past events are irretrievably lost; future events are not experientially accessible; one cannot be in more than one place at a time; one can exist only in a single time framework at a time;

a whole is larger than a part; and something cannot be true and untrue at the same time.

The other experiential mode can be termed *holotropic conscious-ness*[2]; it involves identification with a field of consciousness with no definite boundaries which has unlimited experiential access to different aspects of reality without the mediation of the senses. Here there are many viable alternatives to three-dimensional space and linear time. Experiences in the holotropic mode systematically support a set of assumptions diametrically different from that characterizing the hylotropic mode: the solidity and discontinuity of matter is an illusion generated by a particular orchestration of events in consciousness; time and space are ultimately arbitrary; the same space can be simultaneously occupied by many objects; the past and the future can be brought experientially into the present moment; one can experience oneself in several places at the same time; one can experience several temporal frameworks simultaneously; being a part is not incompatible with being the whole; something can be true and untrue at the same time; form and emptiness are interchangeable; and others.

Thus, an individual can take LSD in the Maryland Psychiatric Research Center on a particular day, month and year. While remaining in one sense in Baltimore, he can experience himself in a specific situation in his childhood, in the birth canal and/or in ancient Egypt in a previous incarnation. While aware of his everyday identity, he can identify experientially with another person, another life form, or a mythological being. He can also experience himself in a different location in the world or in a mythical reality, e.g. the Sumerian underworld or Aztec heaven. None of these identities and temporo-spatial coordinates compete with each other or with the basic identity of the subject and the space and time of the psychedelic session.

A life experience focusing exclusively on the hylotropic mode and systematically denying the holotropic one is ultimately unfulfilling and fraught with lack of meaning, but can be practiced without any major emotional difficulties. A selective and exclusive focus on the holotropic mode is incompatible with adequate functioning in the material world for the time it lasts. Like the hylotropic mode, it can be difficult or pleasant, but it presents no major problems as long as the external situation of the experiencer is covered. Psychopathological problems result from a clash and disharmonic mixture of the two modes when neither of them is experienced in pure form nor integrated with the other into an experience of a higher order.

Under these circumstances the elements of the emerging holotropic mode are too strong not to interfere with the hylotropic mode, but at the same time the individual fights the emerging experience because it seems to disturb mental equilibrium or even to challenge the existing world view, and its acceptance would require a drastic redefinition of the nature of reality. It is the mixture of both modes interpreted as a distortion of the consensual Cartesian-Newtonian image of reality that constitutes a psychopathological disorder.[3] The milder forms that have a biographical emphasis and do not involve serious questioning of the nature of reality are referred to as neuroses or psychosomatic disorders. Major experiential and cognitive departures from the mandatory "objective reality" that usually herald the emergence of perinatal or transpersonal experiences tend to be diagnosed as psychoses. It should be mentioned in this connection that traditional psychiatry also treats all pure experiences of the holotropic mode as pathological phenomena. Such an approach, still predominant among professionals, must be considered obsolete in view of the theoretical contributions of Jung, Assagioli, and Maslow.

Not only psychopathological symptoms, but many otherwise puzzling observations from psychedelic therapy, laboratory consciousness research, experiential psychotherapies, and spiritual practices appear in a new light if we use a model of human beings that reflects the basic duality and dynamic tension between the experience of separate existence as material object and that of limitless existence as an undifferentiated field of consciousness. From this point of view, psychogenic disorders can be seen as indications of a fundamental imbalance between these complementary aspects of human nature. They appear to be dynamic nodal points suggesting the areas in which it has become impossible to maintain a distorted, one-sided image of one's existence. For a modern psychiatrist, they are also the points of least resistance where he or she can start facilitating the process of self-exploration and personality transformation.

Effective Mechanisms of Psychotherapy
and Personality Transformation

The extraordinary and often dramatic effects of psychedelic therapy and other experiential approaches naturally raise the question about the therapeutic mechanisms involved in these changes. Although the dynamics of some of the powerful symptomatic changes and personality transformations observed after experiential sessions can be explained along conventional lines, the majority of them involves processes as yet undiscovered and unacknowledged by traditional academic psychiatry and psychology.

This does not mean that phenomena of this kind have never been encountered and discussed before. Some of the descriptions occur in anthropological literature focusing on shamanic practices, rites of passage, and healing ceremonies of various aboriginal cultures. Historical sources and religious literature abound with descriptions of the effects of spiritual healing practices and meetings of various ecstatic sects on emotional and psychosomatic disorders. However, reports of this sort have not been seriously studied because of their obvious incompatibility with the existing scientific paradigms. The material accumulated in the last several decades by modern consciousness research suggests strongly that data of this kind should be critically reevaluated. Obviously there are many extremely effective mechanisms of healing and personality transformation that greatly exceed the biographical manipulations of mainstream psychotherapy.

Some of the therapeutic mechanisms operating in the initial stages and more superficial forms of experiential psychotherapy are identical with those known from traditional handbooks of psychotherapy. However, their intensity characteristically transcends that of the corresponding phenomena in verbal approaches. Experiential techniques of psychotherapy weaken the defense system and decrease psychological resistance. The emotional responses of the subject are dramatically enhanced, and one can observe powerful abreaction and catharsis. Repressed unconscious material from childhood and infancy becomes easily available. This may result not only in great facilitation of recall, but also genuine age regression and a complex, vivid reliving of emotionally relevant memories. The emergence of this material and its integration are associated with emotional and intellectual insights into the psychodynamics of the client's symptoms and maladjusted interpersonal patterns.

The mechanisms of transference and transference analysis that are considered critical in psychoanalytically oriented psychotherapy deserve special notice here. Reenactment of the original pathogenic constellations and the development of transference neurosis is traditionally considered to be an absolutely necessary condition of successful therapy. In experiential therapy, with or without psychedelic drugs, transference is considered an unnecessary complication that must be discouraged. When one uses an approach so powerful that it can take the client, frequently in one session, to the actual source of various emotions and physical sensations, transference to the therapist or sitter must be seen as an indication of resistance and defense against confronting the real issue. While in the experiential session the sitter may actually play the parental role, even to the point of offering nourishing physical contact, it is essential that minimum carry-over occurs during the free intervals between sessions. Experiential techniques should cultivate independence and personal responsibility for one's own process, rather than dependency of any kind.

In contrast to what might generally be expected, a direct fulfillment of anaclitic needs[4] during experiential sessions tends to foster independence, rather than cultivate dependency. This seems to be parallel to observations from developmental psychology suggesting that adequate emotional satisfaction in childhood makes it easy for the child to become independent from the mother. It is those children who experience chronic emotional deprivation who never resolve the bond and continue to search for the rest of their lives for the fulfillment they missed in their childhood. Similarly, it seems to be the chronic frustration in the psychoanalytic situation that foments transference, whereas the direct fulfillment of the anaclitic needs of an individual in a deeply regressed state facilitates its resolution.

Many sudden and dramatic changes on deeper levels can be explained in terms of an interplay of unconscious constellations that have the function of dynamic governing systems. The most important of these are the *systems of condensed experience* (COEX systems), which organize the material of a biographical nature, and the *basic perinatal matrices* (BPM's), which have a similar role in relation to the experiential repositories related to birth and the death-rebirth process. The essential characteristics of these two categories of functional governing systems have already been described in detail. We could also mention *transpersonal dynamic matrices*; however, because of the extraordinary richness and looser organization of transpersonal realms, it would be more difficult to describe them in a comprehensive manner. The system of perennial philosophy, which assigns various transpersonal phenomena to different levels of the subtle and causal realms could be used as an important lead for such future classifications.

According to the nature of the emotional charge, we can distinguish *negative governing systems* (negative COEX systems, BPM II, BPM III, negative aspects of BPM I, and negative transpersonal matrices) from *positive governing systems* (positive COEX systems, BPM IV, positive aspects of BPM I, and positive transpersonal matrices). The general strategy of experiential therapy is reduction of the emotional charge attached to negative systems and facilitation of experiential access to positive ones. A more specific tactical rule is to structure the termination period of each individual session in such a way that it facilitates completion and integration of the unconscious material which was made available on that particular day.

The manifest clinical condition of an individual is not a global reflection of the nature and over-all amount of that person's unconscious material (if this term is at all relevant to, and appropriate for, the events in the world of consciousness). How the individual experiences himself and the world is much more dependent on a specific, selective focus and tuning, which makes certain aspects of unconscious material readily experientially available. Individuals who are tuned in to various levels of negative biographical, perinatal, or transpersonal governing systems perceive themselves and the world in a generally pessimistic way and experience emotional and psychosomatic distress. Conversely, those persons who are under the influence of positive dynamic governing systems are in a state of emotional well-being and optimal psychosomatic functioning. The specific qualities of the resulting states depend in both instances on the nature of the activated material.[5]

Changes in the governing influence of dynamic matrices can occur as a result of various biochemical or physiological processes within the organism or be induced by a number of external influences of a physical or psychological nature. Experiential sessions seem to represent a deep intervention in the dynamics of governing systems in the psyche and their functional interplay. Detailed analysis of the phenomenology of deep experiential sessions indicates that in many instances sudden and dramatic improvement during therapy can be explained as a shift from the psychological dominance of a negative governing system to a state in which the individual is under the selective influence of a positive constellation. Such a change does not necessarily mean that all the unconscious material underlying the psychopathology involved has been worked through. It simply indicates an inner dynamic shift from one governing system to another. This situation, which can be termed *transmodulation,* can occur on several different levels.

A shift involving biographical constellations can be called *COEX transmodulation.* A comparable dynamic shift from one dominant perinatal matrix to another would be called *BPM transmodulation.* A *transpersonal transmodulation,* then, involves governing functional systems in the transindividual realms of the unconscious.

A typical *positive transmodulation* has a biphasic course. It involves intensification of the dominant negative system and a sudden shift to the positive one. However, if a strong positive system is readily available, it can dominate the experiential session from the very beginning, while the negative system recedes into the background. A shift from one dynamic constellation to another does not necessarily lead to clinical improvement. There is a possibility that a poorly resolved and inadequately integrated session will result in a *negative transmodulation*—a shift from a positive system to a negative one. This situation is characterized by a sudden occurrence of psychopathological symptoms that were not manifest before the session. This should be a rare event in experiential work conducted by a knowledgeable and well-trained therapist. It should be seen as an indication that another session should be scheduled in the near future to complete the gestalt.

Another interesting possibility is a shift from one negative system to another system also negative in nature. The external manifestation of this intrapsychic event is a remarkable qualitative change in psychopathology from one clinical syndrome to another. Occasionally, this transformation can be so dramatic that the client moves within hours into a completely different clinical category.[6] Although the resulting condition may appear on the surface to be entirely new, all its essential elements existed in a potential form in the patient's unconscious before the dynamic shift occurred. It is important to realize that experiential therapy, in addition to actual thorough working through of unconscious material, can also involve dramatic shifts of focus that change its experiential relevance.

The therapeutic changes associated with biographical material are of relatively minor significance, with the exception of those related to reliving of memories of major physical traumas and life-threatening situations. The therapeutic power of the experiential process increases considerably when self-exploration reaches the perinatal level.[7] Experiential sequences of dying and being born can result in a dramatic alleviation, or even disappearance, of a broad spectrum of emotional and psychosomatic problems.

As already discussed in detail, the negative perinatal matrices represent an important repository of emotions and physical sensations of extraordinary intensity—a truly universal matrix for many different forms of psychopathology. Such crucial symptoms as anxiety, aggression, depression, the fear of death, feelings of guilt, a sense of inferiority, helplessness, and general emotional and physical tension have deep roots on the perinatal level. The perinatal model also provides a natural explanation for a variety of psychosomatic symptoms and disorders. Many aspects of these phenomena and their interrelations make profound sense when considered in the context of the birth trauma.

It is, therefore, not surprising that powerful experiential death-rebirth sequences can be associated with clinical improvement of a wide variety of emotional and psychosomatic disorders, ranging from depression, claustrophobia, and sadomasochism through alcoholism and narcotic drug addiction to asthma, psoriasis, and migraine headaches. Even new strategies in relation to some forms of psychosis can be logically derived from the involvement of perinatal matrices in these psychopathological manifestations.

However, probably most interesting and challenging are the observations from experiential therapy related to the therapeutic potential of the transpersonal domain of the psyche. In many instances, specific clinical symptoms are anchored in dynamic structures of a transpersonal nature and cannot be resolved on the level of biographical, or even perinatal, experiences. In order to resolve a specific emotional, psychosomatic, or interpersonal problem, the client must sometimes experience dramatic sequences of a clearly

Fig. 43.   The identification with the fetus during undisturbed intrauterine existence has typically a strong numinous quality. A painting showing the insight into the relationship between embryonic bliss and the Buddha nature achieved in a high-dose LSD session.

transpersonal nature. Many extraordinary and most interesting observations from experiential therapy indicate an urgent need to incorporate the transpersonal dimension and perspective into everyday psychotherapeutic practice.

In some instances, difficult emotional and psychosomatic symptoms that could not be resolved on the biographical or perinatal level disappear or are considerably mitigated when the subject confronts various embryonic traumas. The reliving of attempted abortions, maternal diseases or emotional crises during pregnancy, and fetal experiences of being unwanted ("rejecting womb"), can be of great therapeutic value. Particularly dramatic instances of therapeutic change can be observed in connection with experiences of a past incarnation. These sometimes occur simultaneously with the perinatal phenomena, at other times as independent experiential gestalts. Occasionally, ancestral experiences can play a similar role; in this case, symptoms disappear after clients allow themselves to have experiences that seem to involve memories of events from the lives of their close or remote ancestors. I have also seen individuals who identified some of their problems as internalized conflicts between the families of their ancestors and resolved them on this level.

Some psychopathological and psychosomatic symptoms can be identified as reflections of emerging animal or plant consciousness. When this occurs, full experiential identification with an animal or plant form will be necessary to resolve the problems involved. In some instances, individuals discover in their experiential sessions that some of their symptoms, attitudes, and behaviors are manifestations of an underlying archetypal pattern. Occasionally, the energy forms involved can have such an alien quality that their manifestation resembles what has been described as "spirit possession," and the therapeutic procedure can have many characteristics of exorcism, as practiced by the medieval church, or of the expulsion of evil spirits in aboriginal cultures. The sense of cosmic unity, identification with the Universal Mind, or experience of the Supracosmic and Metacosmic Void deserve special notice in this context. They have an enormous therapeutic potential that cannot be accounted for by any of the existing theories based on the Newtonian-Cartesian paradigm.

It is a great irony and one of the paradoxes of modern science that transpersonal experiences, which until recently were indiscriminately labeled as psychotic, have a great healing potential that transcends most of what the armamentarium of contemporary psychiatry has to offer. Whatever the therapist's professional and philosophical opinion may be about the nature of transpersonal experiences, he or she should be aware of their therapeutic potential and support clients if their voluntary or involuntary self-exploration takes them into transpersonal realms.

In the most general sense, emotional and psychosomatic symptoms indicate a blockage of the flow of energy and ultimately represent potential experiences in a condensed form that are trying to emerge. Their content can consist of specific childhood memories, difficult emotions accumulated in a lifetime, birth sequences, karmic constellations, archetypal patterns, phylogenetic episodes, animal or plant identifications, manifestations of demonic energy, or many other phenomena. Effective therapeutic mechanisms in the broadest sense, then, involve release of the blocked energy and facilitation of its experiential and behavioral expression with no commitment as to which form it will take.

Completion of the experiential gestalt brings therapeutic results whether or not the processes involved have been intellectually understood. We have seen, both in psychedelic therapy and in the experiential sessions using the technique of holonomic integration, dramatic resolution of problems with long-lasting effects even when the mechanisms involved transcended any rational comprehension. The following example is a useful illustration:

> Several years ago, we had in one of our five-day workshops a woman—call her Gladys—who for many years had had serious daily attacks of depression. They usually started after four o'clock every morning and lasted several hours. It was extremely difficult for her to mobilize her resources to face the new day.
>
> In the workshop, she participated in a session of holonomic integration (see pp. 387–9). This technique combines controlled breathing, evocative music, and focused body work and is, in my opinion, the most powerful experiential approach with the exception of psychedelic therapy.
>
> Gladys responded to the breathing session with an extraordinary mobilization of body energies, but did not reach a resolution; this situation was quite exceptional in the work we are doing. The next morning the depression came as usual,

but was much more profound than at any previous time. Gladys came to the group in a state of great tension, depression, and anxiety. It was necessary to change our program for the morning and do experiential work with her without delay.

We asked her to lie down with her eyes closed, breathe faster, listen to music we were playing, and surrender to any experience that wanted to surface. For about fifty minutes Gladys showed violent tremors and other signs of strong psychomotor excitement; she was screaming loudly and fighting invisible enemies. Retrospectively, she reported that this part of her experience involved the reliving of her birth. At a certain point, her screams became more articulate and started to resemble words in an unknown language. We asked her to let the sounds come out in whatever form they took, without intellectually judging them. Her movements suddenly became extremely stylized and emphatic, and she chanted what appeared to be a powerful prayer.

The impact of this event on the group was extremely strong. Without understanding the words, most members of the group felt deeply moved and started crying. When Gladys completed her chant, she quieted down and moved into a state of ecstasy and bliss in which she stayed, entirely motionless, for more than an hour. Retrospectively, she could not explain what had happened and indicated that she had absolutely no idea what language she was using in her chant.

An Argentinian psychoanalyst present in the group recognized that Gladys had chanted in perfect Sephardic, a language he happened to know. He translated her words as: "I am suffering and I will always suffer. I am crying and I will always cry. I am praying and I will always pray." Gladys herself did not speak even modern Spanish, not to say Sephardic, and did not know what the Sephardic language was.

In some other instances we have seen a shamanic chant, speaking in tongues, or authentic animal sounds of various species expressed with similar beneficial consequences. Since no therapeutic system can possibly predict events of this kind, implicit trust in the intrinsic wisdom of the process seems to be the only intelligent strategy possible in situations of this kind.

Frequently psychopathological symptoms are related to more than one level of the psyche, or band of consciousness. I will conclude this section on effective mechanism of psychotherapy and personality transformation by describing our experience with a participant of one of our five-day groups who has since become a close friend.

Norbert, a psychologist and minister by profession, had suffered for years from severe pains in his shoulder and pectoral muscles. Repeated medical examinations, including x-rays, did not detect any organic basis for his problem and all therapeutic attempts remained unsuccessful. During the session of holonomic integration, he had great difficulty tolerating music and had to be encouraged to stay with the process in spite of severe discomfort. For about an hour and a half, he experienced severe pains in his breast and shoulder, struggled violently as if his life were seriously threatened, choked and coughed, and let out a variety of loud screams. Later he quieted down and was relaxed and peaceful. With great surprise, he reported that the experience had released the tension in his shoulder and that he was free of pain. This relief turned out to be permanent; it is now over five years since that session and the symptoms have not returned.

Retrospectively, Norbert reported that there were three different layers in his experience, all related to the pain in his shoulder. On the most superficial level he relived a frightening situation from his childhood in which he almost lost his life. He and his friends were digging a tunnel on a sandy beach. When Norbert was inside it, the tunnel collapsed and he almost choked to death before being rescued.

When the experience deepened, he relived several sequences of the struggle in the birth canal, which also involved choking and severe pain in the shoulder that was stuck behind the pubic bone of his mother.

In the last part of the session, the experience changed dramatically. Norbert started seeing military uniforms and horses and recognized that he was involved in a battle. He was even able to identify it as one of the battles in Cromwell's England. At one point, he felt a sharp pain and realized that his chest had been pierced by a lance. He fell off the horse and experienced himself as dying, trampled by the horses.

Whether or not experiences of this kind reflect "objective reality," their therapeutic value is unquestionable. A therapist who is unwilling to support them because of intellectual skepticism is giving up a therapeutic tool of extraordinary power.

Spontaneity and Autonomy of Healing

The general therapeutic strategy in psychiatry and psychotherapy is critically dependent on the medical model previously discussed at some length. In this strategy, all emotional, psychosomatic, and interpersonal problems are viewed as manifestations of disease. Similarly, the nature of the therapeutic relationship, the general context of the interaction between the client and the helper, and the understanding of the healing process are all modeled after physical medicine.

In medicine, therapists have a long and specialized training and experience, and their understanding of what is wrong with patients by far exceeds that of the patients themselves. Patients are thus expected to assume a passive and dependent role and to do as they are told. Their contribution to therapy is limited to providing subjective data about their symptoms and feedback about the effects of therapy. The emphasis in healing is on medical interventions, such as pills, injections, radiation, or surgery; the enormous contribution to healing that comes from the inner restitutive processes of the organism is taken for granted and not specifically mentioned. The extreme is the surgical model whereby the patient is treated under general anesthesia and the help with the problem is seen as coming entirely from outside the organism.

The medical model continues to rule psychiatry despite increasing evidence that it is inappropriate and, possibly, harmful when applied as the exclusive and dominant approach to all the problems with which psychiatry deals. It has a powerful influence not only on those professionals who have an explicitly organic orientation, but also on the practitioners of dynamic psychotherapy. As in medicine, the professional is considered an expert who has a better understanding of the psyche of his patients than the patients themselves, and who will give them interpretations of their experiences. The patient contributes introspective data to the therapeutic situation, but the activity of the therapist is seen as instrumental in the therapeutic process. There are many explicit and implicit aspects of the medical model that establish and maintain the patient's passive and dependent role. The general strategy of each form of psychotherapy is based on a concept of how the psyche functions, why and how symptoms develop, and what has to be done to change the situation. The therapist is thus seen as an active agent who possesses the necessary know-how and who influences the therapeutic process in a critical and decisive way.

Although various schools of depth psychotherapy emphasize in theory the need to penetrate behind the symptoms to the deeper underlying conditions, in everyday clinical practice, alleviation of symptoms is commonly confused with improvement, and their intensification, with a worsening of emotional disorders. The idea that the intensity of symptoms is a linear and reliable indicator of the seriousness of the pathological process has some justification in physical medicine. But even there it is appropriate only in those cases where healing takes place spontaneously, or where therapeutic intervention is directed toward the primary causes and not toward the presenting symptoms.

It would not be considered good medical practice to limit one's activities and efforts to an alleviation of the external manifestations of a disease if the underlying process were known and could be directly influenced.[8] Yet, this is precisely the strategy that dominates much of contemporary psychiatry. Evidence from modern consciousness research suggests that the routine medical and symptomatic orientation is not only a superficial compromise, as is usually recognized by more enlightened psychiatrists, but in many cases directly antitherapeutic, because it intereferes with the dynamics of a spontaneous process that has an intrinsic healing potential.

When a person suffering from emotional or psychosomatic symptoms confronts these problems during psychedelic therapy or with one of the new experiential techniques, it is characteristic that these symptoms become activated and intensified as the client approaches the biographical, perinatal, or transpersonal material underlying them. A full conscious manifestation and integration of the theme that underlies them then results in elimination or modification of the problem. The change of the external manifestations, then, represents a dynamic, not a mere symptomatic, solution.

Typically, confronting the underlying experience is considerably more difficult and painful than is the discomfort of the symptoms in everyday life, although it involves many of the same elements. However, this strategy offers the possibility of a radical and permanent solution, not merely a repression and masking of the real issues. This approach is quite different from the allopathic strategies of the medical model. It has its parallel in homeopathic medicine, where the general effort is to accentuate the existing symptoms to mobilize the intrinsic healing forces within the organism.

Psychological understanding of this kind is characteristic of some of the humanistic experiential approaches, particularly gestalt practice. Deep respect for the intrinsic wisdom of the healing process is also essential for Jungian psychotherapy. Healing strategies of this kind have important precedents and parallels in various ancient and aboriginal cultures—in shamanic procedures, spiritual healing ceremonies, temple mysteries, and meetings of ecstatic religious groups. The testimony of Plato and Aristotle about the powerful healing effects of the Greek mysteries are important examples. All these therapeutic strategies share the belief that, if the process behind the symptom is supported, it will result in self-healing and consciousness expansion after a temporary accentuation of the discomfort. Effective eradication of psychopathological problems does not come through alleviation of the emotional and psychosomatic symptoms involved, but through their temporary intensification, full experience, and conscious integration.

As suggested in the preceding chapter, the driving force behind the symptoms seems to be, in the last analysis, the tendency of the organism to overcome its sense of separateness, or its exclusive identification with the body ego and the limitations of matter, three-dimensional space, and linear time. Although its ultimate objective is to connect with the cosmic field of consciousness and with a holonomic perception of the world, in a systematic process of self-exploration this final goal can take more limited forms: working through one's biographical traumas and connecting with the positive and uniting aspects of one's life history; reliving the birth trauma and tuning in to the oceanic state of fetal existence or the symbiotic fusion with the mother during nursing; or partially transcending the limitations of time and space and experiencing various aspects of reality that are inaccessible in the ordinary state of consciousness.

The major obstacle in the process of healing so understood is the resistance of the ego, which shows a tendency to defend its limited self-concept and world view, clings to the familiar and dreads the unknown, and resists the increase of emotional and physical pain. It is this determined effort of the ego to preserve the status quo that interferes with the spontaneous healing process and freezes it into a relatively stable form that we know as psychopathological symptoms.

From this point of view, any attempt to cover up or artificially alleviate the symptoms should be seen not only as a denial and avoidance of the problem, but as interference with the spontaneous restitutive tendencies of the organism.[9] It should, therefore, be done only if the patient who has been informed about the nature of the problems and the alternatives, explicitly refuses to enter the process of ongoing self-exploration, or if lack of time, human resources, and adequate facilities make the uncovering process impossible. In any case, a professional using a symptomatic approach, such as tranquilizers and supportive psychotherapy, should be fully aware that it is a palliative measure and a sad compromise, rather than a method of choice reflecting a scientific understanding of the problems involved.

The obvious objections regarding the feasibility of the approach recommended here are, of course, lack of human resources and the expensive nature of depth-psychological therapy. As long as we think in terms of the Freudian norms, where a single analyst treats on average eighty patients in a lifetime, such concerns might seem appropriate. The new experiential techniques have changed this prospect drastically. Psychedelic therapy offers a substantial acceleration of the therapeutic process and makes it possible to extend indications of psychotherapy to categories of persons who were previously excluded, such as alcoholics, drug addicts, and criminal psychopaths. Since the future of psychedelic therapy is problematic in view of the administrative, political, and legal obstacles, it seems more reasonable to think in terms of the new experiential nondrug approaches. Some of them offer therapeutic possibilities that far surpass those of the verbal techniques. However, a truly realistic approach to emotional disorders would have to take much of the exclusive responsibility from the hands of professionals and utilize the enormous resources of the general population.

In the technique of holotropic therapy, developed by my wife Christina and myself, as many as twenty persons can make considerable progress in their self-exploration and healing within a session that lasts two to three hours. An additional twenty persons who function as sitters are meanwhile developing confidence in assisting other human beings in such a process. Two to three specially trained individuals are usually present to help where necessary. In

many instances, sitters develop considerable benefit from helping
others. Such situations not only can enhance self-confidence and
provide satisfaction, but may be a source of important insights into
one's own process. Once the spell of the medical model is removed
from the system, it is conceivable that the science and art of self-
exploration and assistance in the emotional process of others can
be included in basic education. Many techniques already in existence
combine self-exploration and psychological learning with art and
entertainment in a way that makes them unusually suitable for use
in an educational context.

The insights from modern consciousness research also have
far-reaching consequences for the definition of the role of the
therapist. The idea that basic medical and specialized psychiatric
training is an adequate preparation for dealing with psychiatric
problems was frequently criticized even in traditional practice.
While emotional problems do not interfere with the therapeutic
abilities of a surgeon or a cardiologist, unless they become excessive,
they do significantly affect the work of a psychiatrist. This is why,
ideally, the psychiatrist should undergo a process of deep self-
exploration.

However, several years of psychoanalytic training involving free
association on the couch and supervised work with patients, barely
scratch the surface of the psyche. The method of free association
is a very weak tool for effective self-exploration. In addition, the
narrow theoretical focus keeps the process within the biographical
realm. Even years of analytic training (with the exception of Jungian
analysis) will not bring the analysand in touch with the perinatal
or transpersonal elements in the psyche. The use of the new
experiential techniques thus requires training that involves a personal experience of the states that they facilitate. In addition, such
a process is never complete; therapeutic work with others, or even
everyday life, will always confront the therapist with new issues.
When he or she has successfully worked through and integrated
the material on the biographical and perinatal levels, the scope of
transpersonal issues that can emerge is commensurate with existence
itself.

For the same reason, the therapist will never become the
authority interpreting for the clients what their experiences mean.
Even with much of a therapist's clinical experience, it is not always
possible to predict correctly what the theme underlying a particular

symptom is. The credit for this discovery belongs to Jung, who was the first to realize that the process of self-exploration is a journey into the unknown that involves constant learning. This recognition changes the doctor-patient relationship into a shared adventure of two fellow seekers.

There is, of course, seniority in this procedure; the therapist offers techniques for the activation of the unconscious, creates a supportive setting for self-exploration, teaches the basic strategies, and instills trust in the process. However, the client is ultimately the authority as far as his or her own inner experience is concerned. An experience that has been successfully completed does not require interpretation. Thus, much interpretive work is replaced by a sharing of what happened. One of the important tasks of the therapist is to insure that the experiences are completed internally and to discourage acting out, which is probably the most serious problem in this kind of work. In many instances, the difference between disciplined internalization of the process and projective acting out is a critical factor distinguishing mystical quest from serious psychopathology.

There are indications that even many of the acute psychotic conditions, for which the application of the medical model might seem most indicated and justifiable, are dramatic attempts on the part of the organism at problem solving, self-healing, and achieving a new level of integration. As I mentioned earlier, it has been reported in the literature that a certain number of acute psychotic breakdowns—even under the current circumstances that are far from ideal—result in a better adjustment that the patient had before the episode.

It is also well known that acute and dramatic psychotic states have a much better prognosis than those that develop slowly and insidiously. Observations of this kind seem to support the material from modern consciousness research suggesting that the major problem in many psychotic episodes is not the upsurge of the unconscious material, but the remaining elements of ego control that interfere with successful completion of the gestalt involved. If this is the case, the strategy of choice should not be to put a psychopathological label on the process and try to interfere with it by suppressing the symptoms, but to facilitate and expedite it in a supportive atmosphere.

Thus, the experiences of psychotic patients should be validated, not in terms of their relevance in regard to the material world, but as important steps in the process of personality transformation. Support and encouragement of this process, therefore, does not mean agreement with perceptual distortions and delusional interpretations of consensual reality. The facilitating strategy involves a systematic effort to internalize and deepen the process by diverting it from the phenomenal world to the inner realities. Attaching the inner experiences to external persons and events frequently serves as powerful resistence to the process of inner transformation.

The few alternative approaches to psychosis that have been used in the past were based on the principle of support and noninterference. My own observations from psychedelic therapy with psychotic patients and from nondrug experiential work clearly suggest that a more effective approach to psychotic episodes involves acceleration and intensification of the process by chemicals or nondrug means. This therapeutic strategy is so effective and promising that it should be tried routinely wherever possible, before the patient is admitted to a psychiatric hospital and assigned to prolonged and potentially dangerous medication with large doses of tranquilizers.

On several occasions in our workshops, I have seen that individuals whose momentary emotional condition was approaching psychotic proportions were able to reach (after an hour or two of in-depth individual work using hyperventilation, music, and body work) an entirely symptom-free state or even an ecstatic condition. The experiences that mediated such dramatic changes typically involved perinatal or transpersonal themes. Although such a transmodulation should not be confused with a "cure" or a deep restructuring of personality, systematic use of this approach whenever difficult symptoms appear represents an exciting alternative to psychiatric hospitalization and the chronic use of tranquilizers. In addition, consequential use of the uncovering strategy has a potential for actually solving the problems instead of masking them and is conducive to self-actualization, personality transformation, and consciousness expansion.

The use of the approach outlined above represents a viable alternative to the traditional treatment of nonparanoid patients with acute psychotic symptoms. It involves acknowledging and validating the process as a "spiritual emergency" or a "transpersonal crisis," instead of labeling it as "mental disease." The patient is encouraged to go deeper into the inner experience with the assistance of the therapist. It is absolutely essential for the therapist to be familiar with the extended cartography of the psyche, to feel comfortable with its entire experiential spectrum, including the perinatal and transpersonal phenomena, and to have a deep trust in the intrinsic wisdom and healing power of the human psyche. This makes it possible to help the client to overcome the fears, blocks, and resistances that interfere with the intrinsic trajectory of the process, and support a variety of phenomena that conventional psychiatry would try to suppress at all costs.

The degree and nature of the therapist's involvement depend on the stage of the process, on the attitude of the client, and also on the nature of the therapeutic relationship. There are two categories of patients for whom the above approach runs into considerable difficulty and might not be applicable. As a rule, patients with strong paranoid tendencies are very poor candidates; for the most part they are experiencing the early stages of BPM II. Any attempt at deep self-exploration under these circumstances is equivalent to an invitation for a ride to hell, and the therapist who makes it automatically becomes an enemy. An excessive use of projections, an unwillingness to own the inner process, a tendency to hang onto the elements of external reality, and an inability to form a trusting relationship is a combination that represents a serious obstacle for effective psychological work. Until the development of techniques that can successfully overcome this difficult set of circumstances, paranoid patients may continue to be candidates for tranquilizing therapy.

Manic patients are difficult to reach for a different set of reasons. Their condition reflects an incomplete transition from BPM III to BPM IV. A therapist attempting experiential psychotherapy with manic patients has the difficult task of convincing them that they must abandon defensive clinging to their precarious new freedom and do more serious work on the remaining elements of BPM III. For many manic patients the current treatment with Lithium salts might remain the therapy of choice, even when skilled experiential guidance is available. Paranoid and manic patients are thus poor candidates for the experiential approach, and utilizing the intrinsic healing potential of the psyche with them is an extremely tedious task. On occasion, patients from other diagnostic categories may prove unwilling or unable to confront their problems experientially; the best answer for them could be a suppressive psychopharmacological approach. Yet, others can best benefit from simple support and noninterference with the process. However, when the circumstances are favorable, active facilitation and a deepening of the process seems to be the method of choice.

Once the symptoms are mobilized and begin their transformation into a flow of emotions and physical feelings or vivid and complex experiences, it is important to encourage full experiential surrender and peripheral channelling of pent-up energies without censoring or blocking the process because of cognitive reservations. With this strategy, the symptoms will be literally transmuted into various experiential sequences and consumed in the process. It is important to know that some symptoms and syndromes are more resistant to change than others. The situation seems to be similar to the sensitivity and responsiveness to psychedelic drugs. In the spectrum of differential responses, one extreme position is occupied by obsessive-compulsive patients with their excessive rigidity and strong defenses, the other by hysterical patients who show dramatic responses to minimal interventions. A high level of resistance represents a serious obstacle in experiential therapy and requires special modifications of technique.

Whatever the nature and power of the technique used to activate the unconscious, the basic therapeutic strategy is the same: both the therapist and the client should trust the wisdom of the client's organism more than their own intellectual judgement. If they support the natural unfolding of the process and cooperate with it intelligently—without restrictions dictated by conventional conceptual, emotional, aesthetic, or ethical concerns—the resulting experience will automatically be healing in nature.

Psychotherapy and Spiritual Development

As has already been mentioned, Western schools of psychotherapy, with the exception of psychosynthesis and Jungian psychology, have not acknowledged spirituality as a genuine and authentic force of the psyche. Most theoretical speculations have not taken into consideration the wealth of knowledge about consciousness and the human mind that has been accumulated through the ages by the great spiritual traditions of the world. The profound messages of these systems have been either entirely ignored or discarded and explained away as primitive superstition, an elaboration of infantile conflicts, or cultural equivalents of neurosis and psychosis.

In any case, spirituality and religion have been treated by Western psychiatry as something that the human psyche generates as a reaction to external influences—the overwhelming impact of the surrounding world, threat of death, fear of the unknown, conflict-ridden relationship with parents, and the like. The only framework available for a direct experience of alternative realities of a spiritual nature has been, until recently, that of mental disease. In concrete clinical work with patients, religious beliefs have usually been tolerated as long as they were shared by large groups of people. Idiosyncratic belief systems deviating from codified and culturally accepted forms, or direct experiences of spiritual realities, tend to be interpreted as pathological and indicative of a psychotic process.

Several exceptional researchers have found this situation untenable and challenged the traditional psychiatric view of spirituality and religion. Roberto Assagioli, the Italian-born founder of psychosynthesis, saw spirituality as a vital force in human life and an essential aspect of the psyche. He interpreted many of the phenomena that mainstream psychiatry treats as psychopathological manifestations to be concomitants of spiritual opening (1977). Carl Gustav Jung also attributed great significance to the spiritual dimensions and impulses of the psyche and created a conceptual system that bridges and integrates psychology and religion. Another important contribution to a new understanding of the relationship between mysticism and human personality came from Abraham Maslow. On the basis of extensive studies of individuals who had had spontaneous mystical, or "peak," experiences, he challenged the traditional psychiatric view that equated them with psychosis and formulated a radically new psychology. According to him, mystical experiences should not be considered pathological; it seems more appropriate to view them as supernormal, since they are conducive to self-actualization and can occur in otherwise normal and well-adjusted individuals.

The observations from psychedelic therapy and other forms
of deep experiential work fully confirm the views of these three
researchers and suggest an even more radical formulation of the
relationship between human personality and spirituality. According
to the new data, spirituality is an intrinsic property of the psyche
that emerges quite spontaneously when the process of self-exploration reaches sufficient depth. Direct experiential confrontation
with the perinatal and transpersonal levels of the unconscious is
always associated with a spontaneous awakening of a spirituality
that is quite independent of the individual's childhood experiences,
religious programming, church affiliation, and even cultural and
racial background. The individual who connects with these levels
of his or her psyche automatically develops a new world view within
which spirituality represents a natural, essential, and absolutely vital
element of existence. In my experience, a transformation of this
kind has occurred without exception in a wide range of individuals,
including stubborn atheists, skeptics, cynics, Marxist philosophers,
and positivistically oriented scientists.

In view of these facts, an atheistic, mechanistic, and materialistic
approach to the world and to existence reflects deep alienation
from the core of one's being, a lack of genuine self-understanding,
and psychological repression of the perinatal and transpersonal
realms of one's psyche. It also means that the individual in question
identifies one-sidedly with only one partial aspect of his or her
nature, that characterized by the body-ego and the hylotropic mode
of consciousness. Such a truncated attitude toward oneself and
toward existence is, in the last analysis, fraught with a sense of the
futility of life, with alienation from the cosmic process, and with
insatiable needs, competitive drives, and ambitions that no achievement can satisfy. On a collective scale, such a human condition
leads to alienation from nature, an orientation toward "unlimited
growth," and an obsession with objective and quantitative parameters of existence. This way of being in the world is ultimately
destructive and self-destructive on both the individual and the
collective planes.

In a process of systematic in-depth self-exploration, death-
rebirth sequences and transpersonal phenomena occur on the same
experiential continuum as biographical material, the analysis of
which is considered therapeutically useful in traditional psychiatry.
It is therefore interesting to examine how conventional recollective-

analytical psychotherapeutic work is related to the process of spiritual opening. Clinical observations suggest that biographically oriented analysis and transpersonal experiences are two complementary aspects of the process of systematic self-exploration.

A gradual working through of the traumatic aspects of one's early history tends to open the way to the perinatal and transpersonal experiences that mediate the spiritual opening. Conversely, individuals who have deep spiritual experiences early in the process of self-exploration, with psychedelics or other powerful experiential techniques, find subsequent work on the remaining biographical issues much easier and faster.

Particularly those who have experienced states of cosmic unity have an entirely new attitude toward the psychotherapeutic process. They have discovered a new, unexpected source of strength and their true identity. They now see their current life problems and past biographical material from a completely new perspective. From this new perspective, the events of their present existence do not seem to have the same overwhelming relevance that they had before. In addition, the goal of the psychological work is now clear; further self-exploration resembles the broadening and clearing of a road to a known destination, rather than blind digging in a dark tunnel.

The therapeutic potential of the experiences that have a spiritual quality by far surpasses anything available in connection with manipulations focusing on biographical material. Any conceptual system and technique of psychotherapy that does not acknowledge and utilize the perinatal and transpersonal domains of the psyche not only offers a superficial and incomplete image of human beings, but deprives itself and its clients of powerful mechanisms of healing and personality transformation.

Dependence on a narrow conceptual framework can prevent scientists from discovering, recognizing, or even imagining undreamed-of possibilities in the realm of natural phenomena. This can be illustrated by two examples from modern physics. A scientist rigidly clinging onto the Newtonian-Cartesian model of the universe that implies the indestructibility of matter could not conceive of utilizing atomic energy, which requires fission of the atom. Similarly, the system of mechanical optics that views light as particles (photons) offers no theoretical access to holography, which utilizes interference of light waves. Projected into the future, a physicist who would treat Einstein's theory of relativity as an accurate description of reality, rather than a useful but ultimately limited model, could never conceive of travel and communication faster than light. For the same reason, psychiatrists adhering to strictly biographical models of human beings cannot imagine the transformative power associated with perinatal experiences or transpersonal states of consciousness.

A strictly personal concept of the unconscious limited to biographically explainable elements is not only less effective and of limited value, but ultimately antitherapeutic. A logical consequence of such a theoretical orientation is to put psychopathological labels on perinatal and transpersonal phenomena that cannot be explained or accounted for in such a limited context. This then creates an unsurmountable obstacle for the recognition of the healing and transformative power of the process that involves the perinatal and transpersonal domain. In the context of traditional thinking, healing and spiritual opening is thus interpreted as pathology, which must be suppressed at all costs through the use of various drastic measures. As a result of this therapeutic strategy, contemporary psychiatry faces a strange situation: much of the combined efforts of psychiatrists, psychologists, neurophysiologists, biochemists, and other related professionals is one-sidedly directed toward interfering with processes that have unique therapeutic and transformative potential.

On the positive side, it should be acknowledged that in light of the present limited understanding of the nature of psychopathology and the lack of a truly healing strategy in psychiatry, the use of tranquilizers has had great historical significance. It did humanize the medieval atmosphere of psychiatric wards; it has prevented and alleviated much suffering; and it has probably saved many thousands of human lives.

CHAPTER SEVEN

New Perspectives in Psychotherapy and Self-Exploration

The new insights into the structure of psychogenic symptoms, the dynamics of therapeutic mechanisms, and the nature of the healing process are of great relevance for the practice of psychotherapy. Before discussing the implications of modern consciousness research for the future of psychotherapy, it may be useful to summarize briefly the current situation as outlined in preceding chapters.

The application of the medical model to psychiatry has had serious consequences for the theory and practice of therapy in general and for psychotherapy in particular. It deeply influenced the understanding of psychopathological phenomena, the basic therapeutic strategies, and the role of the therapist. By extrapolation from somatic medicine, the terms "symptom," "syndrome," and "disease" are quite routinely applied not only to psychosomatic manifestations, but also to a variety of unusual phenomena that involve changes in perception, emotions, and thought processes. The intensity of such phenomena and the degree to which they are incompatible with the leading paradigms of science are seen as measures of the seriousness of the clinical condition.

In consonance with the allopathic orientation of Western medicine, therapy consists in some external intervention aimed at counteracting the pathogenic process. The psychiatrist assumes the role of an active agent who decides which aspects of the patient's mental functioning are pathological and combats them with a variety of techniques. In some extreme forms of its therapeutic methods, psychiatry has reached, or at least approached, the ideal of Western mechanistic medicine represented by the surgeon. In such approaches as psychosurgery, electroshock treatment, Cardiazol, insulin, or atropine shock, and other forms of convulsive therapy, medical intervention occurs without the patient's cooperation or even conscious participation. Less extreme forms of medical treatment involve the administration of psychopharmacological agents designed to change the individual's mental functioning in the desirable direction. During procedures of this kind, the patient is entirely passive and expects help from the scientific authority who takes all the credit and all the blame.

In psychotherapy, the influence of the medical model has been more subtle, yet significant. This holds true even for Freudian psychoanalysis and its derivatives, which specifically advocate a passive and nondirective approach by the therapist. Ultimately, therapeutic change depends critically on the therapist's intervention, such as relevant insights into historical and dynamic connections in the material presented by the patient, correct and well-timed interpretations, an analysis of resistance and transference, the control of countertransference, and other therapeutic maneuvers, including the proper use of silence. Both the theory and practice of psychoanalysis offer the possibility of relegating much of the responsibility for the process to the patient and attributing the failure of treatment, or lack of progress, to the sabotaging effect of resistance. Yet, in the last analysis, clinical success reflects the skill of the therapist; it depends on the appropriateness of his or her verbal and nonverbal reactions during the therapeutic sessions.

Since the theoretical constructs of the individual schools of psychotherapy and their techniques differ considerably from each other, the appropriateness of the therapist's interventions can be evaluated only in relation to his or her particular orientation. In any case, the conceptual framework of the therapist will confine the client explicitly or implicitly to a certain thematic area and a limited range of experiences. As a result, the therapist will not be able to help those patients whose problems are critically related to realms or aspects of the psyche that his or her system does not acknowledge.

Until recently, most psychotherapeutic approaches were limited almost exclusively to verbal interaction. Powerful emotional or behavioral reactions of clients were therefore seen as undesirable acting out and violations of the basic rules of therapy. In addition, traditional psychotherapies focused exclusively on manipulations of mental processes, neglecting the physical manifestations of emotional disorders. Direct physical contact was thought to be contraindicated and was discouraged. As a result of this strict taboo, body work was not practiced even in neuroses with intense muscular tensions or spasms and other forms of dramatic involvement of the physiological and psychosomatic processes.

Principles of Psychotherapeutic Assistance

The new comprehensive approach to self-exploration and psychotherapy, based on observations from modern consciousness research, differs from the traditional systems and strategies in many important aspects. I have developed this approach with my wife, Christina, and we have been practicing it in our seminars under the name of *holonomic integration* or holotropic therapy. Altogether it represents a unique package, although many of its constituent parts appear in various existing schools of psychotherapy.

It uses the extended cartography derived from psychedelic research that has already been described. This map of the psyche is broader and more encompassing than those used in any of the Western schools of psychotherapy. In the spirit of spectrum psychology and the "bootstrap" philosophy of nature, it integrates in a comprehensive way the Freudian, Adlerian, Reichian, Rankian, and Jungian perspectives, as well as important aspects of the work of Ferenczi, Fodor, Peerbolte, Perls, the existential psychologists, and many others. Instead of seeing these schools as accurate and exhaustive descriptions of the psyche, it includes their concepts as useful ways of organizing the observations of phenomena related to specific levels of the psyche, or bands of consciousness. By including the archetypal and transcendental realms of the psyche, the new system also bridges the gap between Western psychotherapies and perennial philosophy.

An important feature of the theoretical model associated with the new therapeutic approach is the recognition that human beings show a strange paradoxical nature, sometimes manifesting properties of complex Newtonian-Cartesian objects, at other times those of fields of consciousness unlimited by time, space, and linear causality. From this vantage point, emotional and psychosomatic disorders of psychogenic origin are seen as expressions of a conflict between these two aspects of human nature. This conflict seems to reflect dynamic tension between two opposite universal forces: the tendency of undifferentiated, unified, and encompassing forms of consciousness toward division, separation, and plurality, and that of isolated units of consciousness to return to the original wholeness and unity.

While the movement toward experiencing the world in terms of separation is associated with increasing conflict and alienation, experiences of holotropic consciousness have intrinsic healing potential. From this point of view, an individual experiencing psychogenic symptoms is involved in an ultimately self-defeating struggle to defend his or her identity as a separate being existing in a limited spatiotemporal context against an emerging experience that would undermine such a restricted self-image.

From the practical point of view, an emotional or psychosomatic symptom can be seen as a blocked and repressed experience of a holotropic nature. When the resistances are reduced and the blockage released, the symptom will be transformed into an emotionally highly charged experience and consumed in the process. Since some symptoms contain experiences of a biographical nature and others perinatal sequences or transpersonal themes, any conceptual restrictions will ultimately function as limitations of the power of the psychotherapeutic process. A therapist operating in the framework described in this book seldom knows what kind of material is contained in the symptoms, although with sufficient clinical experience in this area a certain degree of general anticipation or prediction is possible.

Under these circumstances, the application of the medical model is inappropriate and not justifiable. An honest therapist should do anything possible to undermine the "surgical ideal" of psychiatric help that the client might bring into therapy, no matter how flattering the role of the all-knowing expert might appear. It should be made clear that in its very nature the psychotherapeutic process is not the treatment of a disease, but an adventure of self-exploration and self-discovery. Thus, from the beginning to the end, the client is the main protagonist with full responsibility. The therapist functions as a facilitator, creates a supportive context for self-exploration, and occasionally offers an opinion or advice based on his or her past experience. The essential attribute of the therapist is not the knowledge of specific techniques; although these represent a necessary prerequisite, they are quite simple and can be learned in a relatively short time. The critical factors are his or her own stage of consciousness development, degree of self-knowledge, ability to participate without fear in the intense and extraordinary experiences of another person, and willingness to face new observations and situations that may not fit any conventional theoretical framework.

The medical model is thus useful only in the initial stages of therapy before the nature of the problem is sufficiently known. It is important to conduct a careful psychiatric and medical examination to exclude any serious organic problems that require medical treatment. Patients with underlying physical diseases should be treated in medical facilities equipped to handle behavior problems. Those clients with negative medical diagnosis who prefer the path of serious self-exploration to symptomatic control should be referred for psychotherapy to special facilities outside of the medical context. This strategy would apply not only to neurotic patients and people with psychosomatic disorders, but also to many of those patients who in the traditional context would be labeled as psychotic. Patients dangerous to themselves or others would require special arrangements, which would have to be determined from situation to situation.

Every professional who has conducted psychedelic therapy or experiential nondrug sessions is well aware of the enormous emotional and psychosomatic energies underlying psychopathology. In view of these observations, any exclusively verbal technique of psychotherapy is of limited value. A verbal approach to the elemental forces and energy reservoirs of the psyche can be likened to an attempt to empty an ocean with a sieve. The approach recommended here has a distinct experiential emphasis; talking is used primarily for preparing clients for experiential sessions and for retrospective sharing and integration of the experience. As far as the actual therapeutic procedure is concerned, the therapist offers the client a technique or a combination of techniques capable of activating the unconscious, mobilizing blocked energies, and transforming the stagnant state of emotional and psychosomatic symptoms into a flow of dynamic experiences. Some of the techniques that are most suitable for this purpose will be described in detail later.

The next step, then, is to support and facilitate the emerging experiences and assist the client in overcoming resistances. On occasion, a full unleashing of the unconscious material can be quite challenging and taxing, not only for the subject, but also for the therapist. The dramatic reliving of various biographical episodes and sequences of death and rebirth are becoming increasingly common in modern experiential therapies and should not present any major problems for a professional who has been adequately trained in this area. It is important to emphasize that the therapist should encourage and support the process, no matter what form or intensity it assumes. The only mandatory limits should be physical danger to the subject or to others. Major therapeutic breakthroughs can frequently be seen after episodes of complete loss of control, blackout, excessive suffocation, violent seizurelike activity, profuse vomiting, loss of bladder control, emitting of inarticulate sounds, or bizarre grimacing, postures, and sounds that resemble those described for exorcist seances. Many of these manifestations can be logically related to the biological birth process.

Although reliving early childhood memories and the trauma of birth are being accepted these days even by rather conservative professionals, a major philosophical reorientation and fundamental paradigm shift will be required when the process moves into the transpersonal realms. Many of the experiences that occur in this process are so extraordinary and seemingly absurd that an average therapist feels uncomfortable with them, finds it difficult to see how they could be of any therapeutic value, and tends to discourage them explicitly or implicitly. There is a strong tendency among professionals to interpret transpersonal phenomena as manifestations of biographical material in symbolic disguise, as expressions of resistance against painful traumatic memories, as experiential oddities without any deeper significance, or even as indications of a psychotic area in the psyche that the client should shy away from.

Yet, transpersonal experiences often have an unusual healing potential, and repressing them or not supporting them critically reduces the power of the therapeutic process. Important emotional, psychosomatic, or interpersonal difficulties that have plagued the client for many years and have resisted conventional therapeutic approaches can sometimes disappear after a full experience of a transpersonal nature, such as an authentic identification with an animal or plant form, surrender to the dynamic power of an archetype, experiential reenactment of a historical event, dramatic sequence from another culture, or reliving what appears to be a scene of a past incarnation.

The basic strategy leading to the best therapeutic results requires that the therapist and the client temporarily suspend any conceptual frameworks, as well as any anticipations and expectations as to where the process should go. They must become open and adventurous and simply follow the flow of energy and experience wherever it goes, with a deep sense of trust that the process will find its own way to the benefit of the client. Any intellectual analysis during the experience usually turns out to be a sign of resistance and seriously impedes the progress. This is because transcendence of the usual conceptual limits is an integral part of the adventure of in-depth self-exploration. Since none of the transpersonal experiences makes sense in the context of the mechanistic world view and linear determinism, intellectual processing during transpersonal sessions usually reflects an unwillingness to experience what cannot be understood, what is incomprehensible within the conceptual framework available to the client. Seeing oneself and the world in a particular way is an integral part of a subject's problems and in a certain sense is responsible for them. Determined reliance on the old conceptual frameworks is thus an antitherapeutic factor of prime importance.

If the therapist is willing to encourage and support the process, even if he or she does not understand it, and the client is open to an experiential venture into unknown territories, they will be rewarded by extraordinary therapeutic achievements and conceptual breakthroughs. Some of the experiences that occur in this process will be understood later within vastly expanded or entirely new frameworks. However, on occasion, a far-reaching emotional breakthrough and personality transformation may be achieved with no adequate, rational understanding. This situation sharply contrasts with the one so painfully common in Freudian analysis—a sense of detailed understanding of the problems in terms of one's biography, but therapeutic stagnation or very limited progress.

In the procedure I have been suggesting, the therapist supports the experience no matter what it is, and the client lets it happen without analyzing it. After the experience is completed, they may try to conceptualize what happened if they feel inclined to do so. However, they should be fully aware that it is more or less an academic exercise with little therapeutic value. Each of the explanatory frameworks they will come up with has to be treated as a temporary auxiliary structure, since the basic assumptions about the universe and about oneself change radically as one moves from one level of consciousness to another. Generally, the more complete the experience, the less analysis and interpretation it requires, since it is self-evident and self-validating. Ideally, talk following the therapeutic session takes the form of sharing the excitement of discovery, rather than a painful struggle to understand what has happened. A tendency to analyze and interpret the experience in Newtonian-Cartesian terms is quite exceptional under these circumstances. It becomes too obvious that such a narrow approach to existence has been shattered and transcended. If philosophical discussion occurs at all, it tends to take the form of considering the implications of the experience for the nature of reality.

In view of the rich spectra of experiences characterizing the different bands of consciousness available in psychedelic therapy or through nondrug experiential techniques, it is useful to conduct systematic self-exploration in the spirit of the "bootstrap philosophy of nature." Many of the existing theoretical systems can occasionally prove adequate for conceptualizing some of the experiences and organizing one's thinking about them. However, it is important to realize that they are only models and not accurate descriptions of reality. In addition, they are applicable only to the phenomenology of certain limited sectors of human experience, not to the psyche as a whole. It is, therefore, essential to proceed eclectically and creatively in each individual case, rather than trying to squeeze all clients into the conceptual confines of one's favorite theory or psychotherapeutic school.

Freud's psychoanalysis or, occasionally, Adler's individual psychology seem to be the most convenient frameworks for discussing experiences that focus predominantly on biographical issues. However, both of these systems become utterly useless when the process moves to the perinatal level. For some of the experiences observed in the context of the birth process, the therapist and the client may be able to apply the conceptual framework of Otto Rank. At the same time, the powerful energies manifesting themselves on this level might be described and understood in Reichian terms. However, both Rank's and Reich's systems require substantial modifications in order to reflect correctly the perinatal process. Rank conceives of the birth trauma in terms of the difference between the intrauterine state and the existence in the external world and does not take into consideration the specific traumatic impact of the second and third perinatal matrix. Reich correctly describes the energetic aspects of the perinatal process, but in terms of jammed sexual energy instead of birth energy.

For experiences on the transpersonal level, only Jungian psychology, Assagioli's psychosynthesis, and to some extent Hubbard's scientology, seem to provide valuable guidelines. Also a knowledge of mythology and of the great religions of the world can prove of invaluable help in the process of in-depth self-exploration, since many clients will experience sequences that make sense only in a particular historically, geographically, and culturally determined symbolic system. On occasion, experiences will be understandable in the framework of such systems as Gnosticism, Kabbalah, alchemy, tantra, or astrology. In any case, the application of these systems should follow the experiences that justify it; none of them should be used a priori as an exclusive context for guiding the process.

Although the dynamics of the intrapsychic process is of fundamental importance, any psychotherapy that would focus exclusively on the individual and treat him or her in isolation would be of limited value. An effective and comprehensive approach must consider the client in a broad interpersonal, cultural, socioeconomic, and political context. It is important to analyze the life situation of the client from a holistic point of view and be aware of the relationship between his or her inner dynamics and the elements of the external world. Obviously, in some instances environmental conditions, cultural or political pressures, and an unhealthful life regime might play an important role in the development of emotional disorders. Such factors should be identified and dealt with if the circumstances allow it. However, in general, self-exploration and personality transformation should be the primary concern as the critical and most easily available aspect of any therapeutic program.

Techniques of Psychotherapy and Self-Exploration

The main objective of the techniques used in experiential psychotherapy is to activate the unconscious, unblock the energy bound in emotional and psychosomatic symptoms, and convert a stationary energetic balance into a stream of experience. In many instances, this balance is so precarious that it is maintained only by great subjective effort on the part of the subject. In psychotic states, such equilibrium comes from the client's residual resistances, fear of social pressures and measures, therapeutic and institutional deterrents, and tranquilizing medication. Even in less profound dynamic disturbances, such as depressions, psychosomatic disorders, and neurotic states, it is frequently more difficult to suppress the emerging experiences than to allow them to surface. Under such circumstances, no powerful techniques are necessary to initiate the process. It is usually sufficient to provide a new understanding of the process, establish a good relationship and an atmosphere of trust, and create a supportive and permissive environment in which the client can fully surrender to the process. Focusing attention on the emotions and sensations, a few deep breaths, and evocative music are usually enough to mediate a deep therapeutic experience.

When resistances are strong, it is necessary to use specific techniques to mobilize the blocked energy and transform symptoms into experiences. The most effective way of achieving this is without doubt the use of psychedelic substances. However, this approach is associated with many potential dangers and requires special precautions and observance of a set of strict rules. Since I have described the therapeutic use of psychedelics in several books and since this treatment modality is not easily available, I will focus here on nondrug approaches that I find particularly useful, powerful, and effective.[1] Because they all follow the same general uncovering strategy, they are mutually compatible and can be used in various combinations and sequential patterns.

The first of these techniques was actually developed gradually during the years of my LSD research, originally as a method of clearing residual problems persisting after incompletely resolved psychedelic sessions. Since I started using it apart from psychedelic therapy about ten years ago, I have been repeatedly impressed by its efficacy as an independent therapeutic tool. The major emphasis in this approach is on a release of pent-up energies by maneuvers focusing on the physical symptoms as points of least resistance. Traditional psychotherapists may have serious doubts about the usefulness of this technique because of its strong emphasis on abreaction. In psychiatric literature, the value of abreaction has been seriously questioned outside of the realm of traumatic emotional neuroses. An important precedent in this sense was Freud's rejection of his early concepts attributing great importance to abreaction of affect as a major therapeutic mechanism and his shift of emphasis to the analysis of transference.

The work with psychedelics and the new experiential techniques have rehabilitated to a great extent the principles of abreaction and catharsis as important aspects of psychotherapy. My experience has been that the seeming failure of abreaction described in psychiatric literature was the result of its not having been carried far enough or used in a systematic way. It was kept on the relatively superficial level of biographical traumas and was not encouraged or allowed to go to the experiential extremes that usually lead to successful resolution. On the perinatal level, these can involve alarming suffocation, loss of control, blackout, projectile vomiting, and other quite dramatic manifestations. It is also important to emphasize that mechanical abreaction is of no use; it must come in a rather specific form reflecting the nature of the experiential gestalt and the type of energy blockage involved.

If the subject systematically avoids one particular aspect of the experiential complex, mechanical repetition of all the other facets brings no resolution. It is absolutely essential that the emotional and motor discharge be experienced in connection with the corresponding unconscious content. Thus, abreactive approaches that do not give the client unlimited freedom for the entire experiential spectrum, including the perinatal and transpersonal phenomena, cannot expect dramatic therapeutic success. In spite of all I have said in defense of abreaction, it would be a mistake to reduce the technique I am about to describe to abreaction alone, since it involves many other important elements.

A person who wants to use this nondrug technique is asked to assume a reclining position on a comfortable large couch, on a mattress, or on a floor that is padded or covered with a rug. He or she is asked to focus on breathing and on the process in the body and to turn off the intellectual analysis as far as possible. As the breathing gradually becomes deeper and faster, it is useful to imagine it as a cloud of light traveling down through the body and filling all the organs and cells. A short period of this initial hyperventilation with focused attention will usually amplify the pre-existing physical sensations and emotions, or induce some new ones. Once the pattern is clearly manifested, the experiential work can begin.

The basic principle is to encourage the client to surrender fully to the emerging sensations and emotions and find appropriate ways of expressing them—by sounds, movements, postures, grimaces, or shaking— without judging or analyzing them. At an appropriate moment, the facilitator offers assistance to the client. The facilitating work can be done by one person, although the ideal situation seems to be a male-female dyad. Prior to the experience, the client is instructed to indicate all through the process with as few words as possible what the energy is doing in his or her body—the location of blockages, excessive charges of certain areas, pressures, pains, or cramps. It is also important for the client to communicate the quality of emotions and various physiological sensations, such as anxiety, guilt feelings, anger, suffocation, nausea, or pressure in the bladder.

The function of the facilitators is to follow the energy flow, amplify the existing processes and sensations, and encourage their full experience and expression. When the client reports pressure on the head or chest, they produce more pressure in exactly those areas by mechanically laying on their hands. Similarly, various muscular pains should be amplified by deep massage, sometimes approaching Rolfing. The facilitators provide resistance if the client feels like pushing against something. By rhythmical pressure or massage they can encourage gagging and coughing spasms to the point of breakthrough vomiting or discharge of mucus. Feelings of suffocation and strangulation in the throat, which are very common in experiential therapy, can be worked through by asking the client to engage in forceful twisting of a towel while projecting the choking sensations into the hands and the wringing of the fabric. It is also possible to produce pressure on some hard spot near the throat, such as the mandible, the scalenus muscles, or the clavicle; for obvious reasons, the larynx is one of the places where one cannot apply direct pressure.

For working on certain areas of blockage, one can use eclectically various bioenergetic exercises and maneuvers, or elements of Rolfing and polarity massage. The basic principle is to support the existing process rather than impose an external scheme reflecting a particular theory or the ideas of the facilitators. However, within these limits there is ample opportunity for creative improvisation. This can be quite specific when the facilitators know the nature and the content of the experience that is unfolding. In that case their intervention can reflect very concrete details of the theme involved. They can enact mechanically a convincing replica of a particular birth mechanism, offer comforting physical contact during reliving of an early symbiotic situation with the mother, or enhance by localized finger pressure the pain experienced in the context of a past incarnation sequence that involves a wound inflicted by a sword, lance, or dagger.

The behavior of the assisting persons should sensitively follow the nature of the experience. Ideally, it should reflect the intrinsic trajectory of the process unfolding from within the client rather than therapeutic concepts and convictions of the facilitators. Individuals who have experienced this technique as protagonists, assistants, or participant observers frequently liken it to biological delivery. The process unfolds in an elemental fashion; it has its own trajectory and intrinsic wisdom. The role of the facilitator, like that of a good obstetrician, is to remove the obstacles, not to impose his or her own alternative pattern on the natural process unless absolutely necessary.

In congruence with this basic strategy, it is clearly communicated to the client that it is his or her own process and that the facilitators represent only "supporting cast." If assistance seems appropriate, it is offered to the client, not imposed or enforced. In each stage of the process, the client has the option to interrupt all the external intervention by a specific agreed-upon signal. We ourselves use the word "stop"; this is considered to be an absolutely mandatory and imperative message for the facilitators to stop any activity, no matter how convinced they might be that continuation of what they are doing is indicated and would be beneficial. Any other reactions of the subject are then ignored and are considered part of the experience. Such statements as "You are killing me," "It hurts," "Don't do this to me," unless they come in connnection with the word "stop," are taken as reactions the the symbolic protagonists, whether they be parental figures, archetypal entities, or persons from a past incarnation sequence.

This work requires observance of fundamental principles of ethics and the facilitators should under all circumstances respect the physiological and psychological tolerance of the subject. It is important to use one's judgment as to what constitutes a reasonable amount of pressure or pain. Since it is applied in places of the original trauma, it is frequently experienced by the client as far more intense than it actually is. Even so, the client will typically ask the facilitators to increase the discomfort beyond the level they might feel is appropriate. This seems to reflect the fact that the original amount of pain by far surpasses that which is imposed externally, and the client senses that, in order to complete the gestalt, he or she must experience consciously the full extent of the emotions and sensations that are involved in the emerging theme.

The facilitators should follow the movement of energy and encourage full experience and expression of whatever is happening until the subject reaches a tension-free, pleasant, and clear state of mind. At this time, suportive physical contact might be appropriate, especially if the experience involved early childhood memories. Enough time should be allowed for the subject to integrate the experience and to return to everyday consciousness. An average duration of this work is between half an hour and an hour and a half. If it is not possible to reach full completion of the gestalt, the rule is to deal with the emotions and sensations that are easily available without forceful maneuvers on the part of the facilitators. The work then should continue whenever the tensions build up again to a sufficient degree; this can be a matter of hours or days.

The client is encouraged to keep the experiential channels open and not to let the situation develop to the point where extreme effort has to be exerted to control the emerging emotions and sensations.

The above technique is very effective in bringing fast relief from emotional and psychosomatic distress. I have repeatedly seen individuals whose emotional condition would, from a conventional psychiatric point of view, justify hospitalization, reach within an hour or two not only symptomatic relief but a state of active well-being or even ecstasy. The potential of this approach to resolve acute emotional and psychosomatic distress is so striking that I would never consider psychiatric hospitalization or tranquilizing medication without first trying it. However, the value of this technique seems to go beyond the momentary relief. Continued on a systematic basis, it becomes a powerful means of self-exploration and therapy. Whereas, in traditional psychoanalysis and related forms of verbal therapy, it can take months or years to reach memories from early stages of childhood development, here clients can frequently not only recall but fully relive events from early postnatal life and even birth sequences within minutes or hours.

An important byproduct of this therapeutic strategy is the development of the sense of mastery in the clients. They realize very quickly that they can help themselves and that they are the only ones who can do it. This insight tends to cut down very drastically the belief in and reliance on some magic external intervention of the therapist, brilliant interpretation, revealing intellectual or emotional insight, advice, or guidance. Even one experiential session of this kind may show clearly where the problems are and what has to be done to work them through. In this connection, clients are not asked to believe anything that they have not directly experienced. The connections discovered in this way are not a matter of opinion or conjecture; they are usually so self-evident and convincing that the client would defend them against the facilitators, should they disagree.

This process can be further intensified and deepened by an appropriate use of music. High-fidelity, stereophonic music selected and combined in a particular way can in itself be a powerful tool for self-exploration and therapy. The principles of using acoustic input for consciousness expansion have been developed by Helen Bonny (1973), a former member of the team at the Maryland

Psychiatric Research Center, in Catonsville, Maryland, where she participated in psychedelic research as a music therapist. During her work with psychedelics, she recognized the mind-altering potential of music and created a technique call Guided Imagery with Music, or GIM.

If used with special preparation and in an introspective mannner, music tends to evoke powerful experiences and facilitates a deep emotional and psychosomatic release. It provides a meaningful dynamic structure for the experience and creates a continuous carrying wave that helps the subject move through difficult sequences and impasses, overcome psychological defenses, and surrender to the flow of the experience. It tends to convey a sense of continuity and connection in the course of various states of consciousness. On occasion, a skillful use of music can also facilitate the emergence of specific contents, such as aggression, sensual or sexual feelings, emotional or physical pain, ecstatic rapture, cosmic expansion, or an oceanic atmosphere of the womb.

To use music for self-exploration as a catalyst of deep experiences, it is essential to abandon the Occidental ways of listening to music, such as the disciplined and intellectualized approach of the concert hall, the irrelevance of the acoustic input characteristic of piped, recorded light music (Muzak), or of background music at cocktail parties, as well as the dynamic and elemental but extroverted style of rock concerts. The clients are asked to assume a relaxed reclining position on the floor or a couch and open themselves completely to the flow of music. They should let it resonate in the entire body and allow themselves to react in any way that seems appropriate—cry or laugh, make sounds, move the pelvis, grow tense, go through contortions, or be seized by violent tremors and shakes.

Used in this way, music becomes a very powerful means of inducing unusual states of consciousness that can be used either independently or in combination with other experiential techniques like the body work described earlier. For this purpose, the music must be of high technical quality and of sufficient volume to have a driving effect on the listener. The most important rule is to respect the intrinsic dynamics of the experience and select the pieces accordingly, rather than trying to influence the situation by a specific choice of music.

Another powerful and extremely interesting technique for self-exploration and healing uses the activating effect of fast breathing on the unconscious. It is based on entirely different principles than the technique of focused abreactive body work described above. However, in spite of their differences, these two techniques seem to be mutually compatible and complementary. The approach through body work and music stems from the therapeutic tradition and was developed in the context of experiential work with psychiatric patients. At the same time it has the potential for taking the individual through the biographical realm and the death-rebirth level to the transpersonal domain.

In contrast, the following method is by its very nature primarily a spiritual procedure. It has the power to open very quickly the transcendental experiential domain. In this process of spiritual opening many individuals must confront various traumatic areas of a biographical nature and experience the encounter with birth and death. Although there is no specific therapeutic emphasis, healing and personality transformation occur as the side-effects of this process. Various procedures using breathing maneuvers have played an all-important role in certain ancient Indian practices and in many other spiritual traditions. The approach was rediscovered by Orr and Ray (1977), and one of its varieties is currently being used in the context of Orr's "rebirthing" programs.

Our own approach is based on a combination of intense breathing and an introspective orientation. The client is asked to assume a reclining position with the eyes closed, focus on breathing, and maintain a respiratory pattern that is faster and more effective than usual. In this context, abreaction and external manipulation are explicitly discouraged. After an interval that varies from individual to individual, usually between forty-five minutes and an hour, the tensions in the body tend to collect into a stereotyped pattern of muscular armoring and are eventually released as the hyperventilation continues. The bands of intense constriction that tend to develop occur approximately where the Indian system of Kundalini Yoga places the centers of psychic energy, or the chakras. They take the form of an intense belt pressure, or even pain, in the forehead or the eyes, constriction of the throat with tension and strange sensations around the mouth and locking of the jaws, and of tight belts in the areas of the chest, the navel, and the lower abdomen. In addition, the arms and hands, as well as the legs and feet, tend to develop characteristic contractions that can reach painful dimensions. In actual clinical work, subjects do not usually undergo the whole spectrum of constrictions and tensions, but show individual patterns of distribution in which certain areas are dramatically represented, others not involved at all.

In the context of the medical model, this reaction to hyperventilation, particularly the famous carpopedal spasms—contractions of the hands and feet—has been considered a mandatory physiological response to fast and intense breathing and referred to as the "hyperventilation syndrome." It has been associated with an aura of alarm and is usually treated with tranquilizers, injections of calcium, and a paper bag placed over the face when it occasionally occurs in neurotic patients, particularly hysterical persons. The use of hyperventilation for self-exploration and therapy proves this view to be incorrect. With continued breathing, the bands of tight constriction, as well as the carpopedal spasm, tend to relax instead of increasing, and the individual eventually reaches an extremely peaceful and serene condition associated with visions of light and feelings of love and connectedness.

Frequently, the final outcome is a deep mystical state that can be of lasting benefit and personal significance for the subject. Ironically, the routine psychiatric approach to occasional episodes of spontaneous hyperventilation thus interferes with a potentially therapeutic reaction of neurotic patients. It is interesting to mention in this connection individuals whose Kundalini became activated either spontaneously or as a result of shaktipat—direct transmission of energy from an accomplished spiritual teacher. In Kundalini Yoga and in Siddha Yoga, in contrast with contemporary psychiatry, these episodes of hyperventilation and the concomitant motor and emotional manifestations, or kriyas, are seen as a purging and healing process.

During the hyperventilation, as the tensions build up and gradually disappear, it seems useful to assume a mental set that involves imagining an increase of pressure with each inhalation and its release with each exhalation. While this is happening, the individual can have a variety of powerful eperiences—reliving important biographical events from childhood or later life, confronting different aspects of the memory of biological birth and, quite commonly, also encountering various phenomena from the broad spectrum of transpersonal experiences. In the holotropic therapy we use in our work, the already powerful effect of hyperventilation is further enhanced by the use of evocative music and other sound technology. If administered in a supportive context and after proper preparation, these two methods potentiate each other to what is undoubtedly the most dramatic means of changing consciousness with the exception of psychedelic drugs.

The efficacy of this technique can be increased even further if it is used in a group context, where the participants form working dyads and alternate in the roles of sitters and experiencers. Here the experiences in both roles tend to be very profound and meaningful. In addition, they seem to have a mutually catalyzing influence and tend to create an atmosphere that breeds chain reactions. In a group of randomly selected individuals under these circumstances, at least one out of three can reach transpersonal states of consciousness within an hour of the first session. It is quite common for participants to report authentic experiences of the embryonal state or even conception, elements of the collective or racial unconscious, identification with human or animal ancestors, or reliving of past incarnation memories. Equally frequent are encounters with archetypal images of deities or demons and complex mythological sequences. The spectrum of experiences that are available for an average participant include telepathic flashes, experiences of leaving the body, and astral projection.

Ideally, the individuals need do nothing but maintain a certain pattern of breathing and be entirely open to whatever happens. With this approach, many subjects end in a totally resolved and relaxed state of a deeply spiritual nature, or at least with mystical overtones. Occasionally, deep breathing will trigger elements of abreaction, such as screaming, gagging, or coughing; this is particularly common in those persons who have previously been involved in such abreactive therapies as primal treatment or some neo-Reichian approaches. It is important to let the abreactive response pass and return the individual to controlled breathing as soon as possible. Occasionally, the hyperventilation activates an experiential sequence, but does not bring it to a successful resolution. In that case, it is useful to apply the abreactive approach to complete the gestalt, rather than to leave the experience unfinished. The combination of deep breathing, evocative music, focused body work, and an open-minded approach with an extended cartography of the psyche, in my experience, surpasses the efficacy of any other existing nondrug technique and deserves a prominent place in the psychiatric armamentarium.

Another technique that should be mentioned is a particular use of the mandala drawing. Although perhaps of limited value as an independent therapeutic tool, it is extremely useful if combined with various experiential approaches. Developed by Joan Kellogg (1977; 1978) a psychologist and art therapist from Baltimore, it was used with success during psychedelic therapy at the Maryland Psychiatric Research Center. The subject is given crayons or magic markers and a large piece of paper with the outline of a circle, and is asked to fill the circle in any way that seems appropriate. It can be simply a combination of colors, a design composed of geometrical patterns, or complex figurative drawing.

The resulting "mandala" can be subjected to formal analysis according to the criteria developed by Kellogg on the basis of her work with large groups of psychiatric patients. However, it can also be used as a unique device facilitating interaction and sharing of experiences in small groups. In addition, certain mandalas lend themselves to further experiential work with the use of Gestalt practice, expressive dancing, or other techniques. The mandala method can be used to document an experience with psychedelics or with the experiential approaches described above. In our workshops and during four-week seminars, it became very popular among participants to keep a "mandala log," illustrating the ongoing process of self-exploration.

This graphic form of documenting one's experience is also extremely useful as a tool for sharing one's inner states with other group members and working on them with their help. My wife and I have been using a three-step process of mandala work that seems particularly effective. It is done with groups of six to eight people who bring together into a small circle their mandalas, reflecting their experiences with hyperventilation and music. Each is asked to choose a mandala painted by another group member to which he or she has a particularly powerful emotional response, either positive or negative. After the mandalas are distributed, the group members proceed working successively on each of them.

The first step is a discussion of the mandala by the person who has selected it on the basis of his or her strong emotional reaction to it. After this person finishes an account of his or her subjective reaction, the other members of the group add their

Fig. 44. Two paintings from an advanced stage of psychedelic therapy, providing interesting insights into the dynamics of mandalas. When the process of LSD self-exploration was moving from the personal to the transpersonal stage, the patient felt a strong need to draw a synoptic diagram that would contain the most important events from her life in a condensed and stylized way.

The first version of this diagram is shown on the first picture. Although all the individual elements had personal biographical meaning for the patient, she chose unbeknownst many symbols with deep transpersonal connotation to depict them (svastika, Star of David, Eye of God, rainbow, cardinal points). The second picture shows a further simplification of the diagram. On about twenty typewritten pages, the patient was able to explain, how this diagram was applicable not only to her personal problems, but also to such general problems as life and death, origin of cancer, birth, and the relationship between matter and consciousness.

observations. The third step then is an account of the experience that was expressed in the mandala by its creator. This process requires full awareness that in the comments of the group members their personal projections are inextricably mixed with what might be accurate and valuable insights into the mental processes of the creator.

The aim of this exercise is not to arrive at an "objective" assessment and diagnostic evaluation, but to facilitate the personal process of all the participants. Approached this way, the mandala work represents a unique catalyst of self-exploration and interpersonal interaction. It is also extremely useful and productive for those who have chosen each other's mandalas to spend some time together exploring the psychodynamic factors underlying the affinity or aversion expressed by their choice.

Another powerful uncovering method is the therapeutic sand play developed by the Swiss psychologist, Dora Kalff (1971) who was Jung's former disciple. The client undergoing therapy with this technique has at his or her disposal a rectangular box filled with sand and several thousand little figures and objects representing people, animals, trees, and houses from different countries and cultures. The task is to create an individual symbolic scene—shape the sand in the form of mountains, valleys or plains; expose the light blue bottom of the box to create rivers, lakes, and ponds and complete the scenery by adding figures and objects of one's own selection. Unless one has tried this technique personally, it is difficult to imagine the unique power it possesses to mobilize the archetypal dynamics of the psyche. The transpersonal nature of the process is well illustrated by the fact that it tends to create an experiential field conducive to the occurrence of extraordinary synchronicities. Through the sand play, deep unconscious material is exteriorized and concretized to such an extent that it can be fully experienced, analyzed, and integrated. A series of sand-play sessions provides an opportunity to develop the themes involved in fine detail, resolve the underlying conflicts, and simplify one's unconscious dynamics.

There is a variety of other approaches that are compatible with, and complementary to, those described above. Unlike the traditional techniques of psychotherapy, the process of holotropic therapy focuses much attention on the psychosomatic aspects of self-exploration. Although the emphasis on the body's processes is implicit in both the abreactive technique and the breathing method, various procedures involving the body can and should be used in connection with them. Experimentation with such techniques as Esalen and polarity massage (Gordon 1978), Rolfing (Rolf 1977), acupuncture (Mann 1973), Feldenkrais (Feldenkrais 1972), Trager psychophysical integration (Trager 1982), tai chi, aikido, or various forms of dance therapy can make valuable contributions to the process of self-exploration. A useful complement is also physical exercise, particularly hiking, jogging, and swimming, or garden work. However, integration of all these body-oriented approaches into a comprehensive program of personality transformation requires a consistent introspective focus and a broad conceptual framework allowing the entire spectrum of experiences that might occur in the context of procedures that are seemingly strictly physical.

Gestalt practice (Perls 1976a; 1976b) deserves special notice since its basic principles are very similar to those outlined above. Gestalt work is a particularly suitable complement to the technique of holotropic therapy. It can be very useful in completing or further exploring the themes and issues that have surfaced in sessions using a combination of breathing, music, and body work. We have already mentioned (p. 000) the modifications necessary to make Gestalt practice fully compatible with the strategies advocated here. Additional uncovering approaches that can be useful are Assagioli's psychosynthesis (1976) and Leuner's Guided Affective Imagery (GAI). (1977; 1978).

It should also be emphasized that various techniques of meditation and other forms of spiritual practice are not in conflict with the general approach described here. Once a psychotherapeutic system acknowledges the perinatal and transpersonal levels of the psyche, it has bridged the gap between psychology and mysticism and has become compatible with, and complementary to, spiritual practice. I have observed in such diverse frameworks as the Brazilian umbanda, rituals of the Native American Church, ceremonies of the Mexican Huichol and Mazatec Indians, and the weekend intensives of the late master of Siddha Yoga, Swami Muktananda, that primarily spiritual or religious events can have a powerful healing impact and can be easily integrated with in-depth self-exploration and therapy as described here.

In addition, transit astrology, a discipline rejected and ridiculed by Newtonian-Cartesian science, can prove of unusual value as a source of information about personality development and transformation. It would require a long discussion to explain why and how astrology can function as a remarkable referential system. This possibility seems quite absurd from the point of view of mechanistic science, which treats consciousness as an epiphenomenon of matter. However, for an approach that sees consciousness as a primary element of the universe that is woven into the very fabric of existence, and that recognizes archetypal structures as something that precedes and determines phenomena in the material world, the function of astrology would appear quite logical and comprehensible. This topic is so complex that it requires a separate presentation.[2]

Advocating such a long list of approaches might at first seem to be therapeutic anarchy. Apparently there is an increasing number of individuals in the human potential movement who move from one therapy to another and do not stay long enough with any of them to derive any benefit. They certainly represent deterrent examples of therapeutic eclecticism. However, what may be wrong with this "therapeutic promiscuity" is not the experimentation with various approaches, but the failure to treat them as partial elements or steps in the process of self-exploration, rather than magic panaceas. It is thus the unrealistic expectation and uncritical reliance, followed by an equally strong disappointment, that is unhealthy, not the interest in, and experimentation with, different approaches. If one expects no more than a small piece of the overall jigsaw puzzle and sees the entire life as an ongoing adventure of self-exploration and search for knowledge, they can become extremely useful and synergistic.

To illustrate this point, I would like to mention our observations from four-week experimental educational programs that my wife Christina and I have been coordinating and conducting at the Esalen Institute, in Big Sur. I conceived the idea of these seminars more than ten years ago, originally as an opportunity for professionals and students from across the United States and from other countries to gain exposure to a wide variety of humanistic and transpersonal leaders, concepts and techniques in a relatively short time. These workshops combine information, experiential exercises, group process, body work, experimentation with various mind-altering devices, slide shows, and film performances. Each of these seminars has a different topic related to modern consciousness research, the psychotherapeutic revolution, and the paradigm shift in science. They use the resources of the Esalen staff, as well as those of a wide range of guest faculty members, specifically selected to deal with particular topics. The general orientation of these workshops can be illustrated by a few past titles: Schizophrenia and the Visionary Mind; Holistic Medicine and Healing Practices; Maps of Consciousness; New Approaches to Birth, Sex, and Death; Realms of the Human Unconscious; Energy: Physical, Emotional and Spiritual; Alternative Futures; Frontiers of Science; Paranormal Intelligence; The Mystical Quest; and Evolution of Consciouness: Perspectives of Inner and Outer Space Research.

In these workshops the participants have been exposed in various unpredictable patterns to lectures expanding and stretching their conceptual horizons, emotionally evocative slide shows and movies, holonomic integration and other powerful experiential techniques, intense body work, group process, and occasional aboriginal rituals with visiting shamans. It should be emphasized that all this took place in the relaxing and aesthetically exquisite atmosphere of the Esalen Institute with its famous mineral hot springs. The guest faculty members ranged from scholars such as Gregory Bateson, Joseph Campbell, Fritjof Capra, Michael Harner, Jean Houston, Stanley Krippner, Ralph Metzner, Ajit Mookerjee, Karl Pribram, Rupert Sheldrake, Huston Smith, Russel Targ, Charles Tart, and Gordon Wasson, through human potential leaders of the stature of John Heider, Michael Murphy, Richard Price, and Will Schutz, to famous psychics, Western and oriental spiritual teachers, and North American and Mexican shamans.

This seminar format, which was originally conceived as an innovative educational tool, turned out to be the most powerful instrument of personality transformation I have ever experienced or witnessed, with the exception of psychedelic sessions. In systematic therapeutic work, limited to one particular technique, the client soon learns the language and the codes; after a while it becomes possible to play the therapy game and move through the process essentially untouched. In the Esalen format that combines a variety of approaches in random patterns, people are suddenly influenced in many different ways, and from unexpected angles, in a supportive environment that explicitly encourages deep experience and self-exploration.

Under these circumstances, powerful transformative processes tend to occur at any hour of day or night. This full-time commitment to self-exploration for a certain limited period of time seems far superior to the usual, externally imposed psychotherapeutic schedule of short appointments. The latter are unlikely to coincide with the times when the psychological defenses are particularly low and, in addition, their format does not allow a process of sufficient depth and duration. In our Esalen monthlong seminars, we have systematically used the techniques and strategies described in this chapter. Numerous letters from former participants indicate

that a four-week experience of this kind can initiate a deep process
of transformation and have a lasting influence on one's life.

Goals and Results of Psychotherapy

The traditional definition of sanity and mental health involves
as a fundamental postulate a perceptual, emotional, and cognitive
congruence with the Newtonian-Cartesian image of the world,
which is seen not only as an important pragmatic framework of
reference, but also as the only accurate description of reality. More
specifically, this means experiential identification with one's physical
body or the so-called body image, acceptance of three-dimensional
space and irreversible linear time as objective and mandatory coordinates of existence, and the limitation of one's sources of information to sensory channels and records in the material substrate
of the central nervous system.

Another important criterion of the accuracy of all data about
reality is the possibility of consensual validation by other persons
who are mentally healthy or functioning normally by the above
definition. Thus, if the data agreed upon by two or more individuals
should represent a major departure from the conventional image
of reality, the shared perception would still be described in pathological terms, such as *folie à deux, folie à famille,* superstition, mass
suggestion, group delusion, or hallucination. Minor individual distortions of self-perception and the perception of other people in
this sense would be referred to as neuroses, if they did not seriously
challenge the essential Newtonian-Cartesian postulates. Substantial
and critical deviations from the agreed-upon description of reality
would be labeled psychoses.

Mental health is defined in terms of absence of psychopathology
or psychiatric "disease"; it does not require active enjoyment or
appreciation of existence and the life process. This can best be
illustrated by Freud's famous description of the goal of psychoanalytic therapy: to change the extreme neurotic suffering of the
patient into the normal misery of everyday life. In this sense, an
individual leading an alienated, unhappy, and driven existence,
dominated by excessive power needs, competitive urge, and insa-

tiable ambition could still fall within the broad definition of mental health, if he did not suffer from manifest clinical symptoms. In addition, in the general lack of clarity about the criteria of mental health, some authors would include such value-laden external indicators as fluctuation of income, changes of professional and social status, and "residential adjustment."

Modern consciousness research has now generated abundant data indicating an urgent need for a revision of this approach. A new definition of healthy functioning would include as a critical factor the recognition and cultivation of the two complementary aspects of human nature—one's existence as a separate material entity and as a potentially unlimited field of consciousness. I have already described the two corresponding experiential modes, the *hylotropic* and *holotropic* modes of consciousness (p. 345–6). According to this concept, a "mentally healthy" person functioning exclusively in the hylotropic mode, even though free from manifest clinical symptoms, is cut off from a vital aspect of his or her nature and does not function in a balanced and harmonious way. An individual with this orientation has a linear concept of existence dominated by survival programs and sees life in terms of exclusive priorities— myself, my children, my family, my company, my religion, my country, my race—unable to see and experience a unifying holistic context.

Such a person has a limited ability to draw satisfaction from the ordinary activities of everyday life and is obliged to resort to complicated schemes involving future plans. This results in an approach to life based on a sense of deficiency, an inability to enjoy fully what is available, and being painfully aware of what is missing. Such a general strategy of life is used in relation to concrete persons and circumstances of life, but in the last analysis represents a driving pattern devoid of specific content. Consequently, it can be practiced on extreme levels of wealth, power, and fame and continue changing its specific form as conditions change. For a person whose life is dominated by this mechanism, nothing is enough and no possessions and achievements bring genuine satisfaction.

Under these circumstances, if goals are not attained, the continuing dissatisfaction is rationalized as reflecting the failure to create a more desirable set of conditions. However, if a project succeeds, it typically does not bring the expected desirable emotional result. This is then attributed to wrong choice or the insufficient scope of the original goal, and the latter is replaced by a more ambitious one. This leads to what the subjects themselves refer to as a "rat race" or a "treadmill" existence: living emotionally in fantasies about the future and pursuing projected goals, although their achievement does not bring fulfillment. In the existentialist literature, this is called "auto-projecting." The life of such an individual is infused with a sense of meaninglessness, futility, or even absurdity, which no amount of seeming success can dispel. It is not uncommon that under these circumstances a great success will trigger a profound depression—a direct opposite of what was expected. Joseph Campbell describes this situation as "reaching the top of the ladder and finding it was against the wrong wall."

The existence of a person whose experiential world is limited to the hylotropic mode has, thus, a quality of inauthenticity. It is characterized by selective focus on, and pursuit of, goals and an inability to appreciate the process of life. Typical characteristics of this way of being in the world are a preoccupation with the past and future, a limited awareness of the present moment, and the exclusive emphasis on manipulation of the external world associated with critical alienation from the inner psychological process. A painful awareness of the limited life span available for all the projects that should be accomplished, an excessive need for control, an inability to tolerate impermanence and the process of aging, and a deep underlying fear of death are additional important attributes.

Projected on a social and global scale, this experiential mode focuses on external indexes and objective parameters as indicators of the standard of living and well-being. It tends to measure the quality of life by the quantity of material products and possessions, rather than by the nature of the life experience and a subjective sense of satisfaction. Moreover, it tends to consider this life philosophy and strategy as natural and logical. The characteristic features of this approach—short-sighted emphasis on unlimited growth, egotistical and competitive orientation, and disregard for cyclical patterns and holistic interdependencies in nature—reinforce and potentiate each other. Together, they create a fatal global trajectory with nuclear holocaust or total ecological disaster as the logical alternatives for the future of the planet.

In comparison, the individual in the holotropic mode of consciousness is incapable of relating adequately to the material world as a mandatory and all-important frame of reference. The pragmatic reality of everyday life, the world of solid material objects and separate beings appears to be an illusion. The inability to identify with the body ego and experience oneself as a separate entity clearly distinguishable from the totality of the cosmic web leads to neglect of the basic rules that must be observed if the individual organism is to continue to exist. It can result in a disregard for personal safety, elementary hygiene, supply of food and water, or even oxygen. The loss of individual boundaries, temporal and spatial coordinates, and adequate reality testing represent a serious survival threat. The extreme forms of the holotropic mode, such as identification with the Universal Mind or the Supracosmic Void represent the exact opposite of matter-related ego-body consciousness. The underlying unity of all existence transcending time and space is the only reality. Everything appears to be perfect as it is, and there is nothing to do and nowhere to go. Needs of any kind are nonexistent or are totally satisfied; an individual immersed in the holotropic experiential mode has to be attended by other people who take care of his or her basic needs, as illustrated by many stories about disciples providing basic care for their masters during their samadhi or satori experience.

We can now return to the problem of mental health. In contrast to traditional psychiatry with its simple dichotomy of mental health-mental disease, we have several important criteria to consider. The first step should be to exclude organic diseases that might be the causes, contributing factors, or triggers of the emotional and behavioral disorder. If the examination detects a disease in the medical sense of the word, such as inflammation, tumor, or circulatory disturbance of the brain, uremia, severe hormonal imbalance, and the like, the patient should receive specific medical treatment.

After having considered the health-disease dimension, we are left with the problem of evaluating the two modes of consciousness described above and their combinations. Within the conceptual framework presented in this book, an individual functioning exclusively in the hylotropic mode would at best qualify for "lower sanity," even if he or she manifested no psychopathological symptoms in the conventional sense. This mode of consciousness in its extreme form, associated with a materialistic and atheistic attitude toward existence, involves repression of vital and nourishing aspects of one's being and is ultimately unfulfilling, destructive, and self-destructive.

The experience of holotropic consciousness should be treated as a manifestation of a potential intrinsic to human nature and does not in itself constitute psychopathology. When it occurs in a pure form and under the proper circumstances, it can be healing, evolutionary, and transformative. While it can be extremely valuable as a transitional state followed by good integration, it can not be reconciled with the demands of everyday reality. Its value depends critically on the situation, the style of the subject in approaching it, and his or her ability to integrate it in a constructive way.

The two modes can interact in ways that disrupt everyday existence or blend harmoniously to enhance the life experience. Neurotic and psychotic phenomena can be seen as resulting from an unresolved conflict between the two modes; they represent compromise formations and interface noise. Their various aspects—perceptual, emotional, ideational, and psychosomatic—which appear as incomprehensible distortions of the logical and appropriate way of reacting to current material circumstances, are perfectly understandable as integral parts of the holotropic gestalt that is trying to emerge.

This becomes clear to the subject as soon as the theme underlying the symptoms is fully experienced and integrated. Sometimes the intruding element is an experience from another temporal context, such as childhood, biological birth, intrauterine existence, ancestral or evolutionary history, or a previous incarnation. At other times it involves transcendence of the usual spatial barriers; it takes the form of conscious identification with other people, various animal forms, plant life, or inorganic materials and processes.

In some instances, the emerging theme has no connection with the phenomenal world and the usual temporal and geographical coordinates, but represents various transitional products characterizing levels of reality that lie between the undifferentiated cosmic consciousness and the separate existence of the individual material form. Vivid encounters or full identification with archetypal entities in the Jungian sense, or participation in dramatic mythological sequences would belong to this category.

The basic principle of symptom resolution is a full experiential shift into the corresponding holotropic theme; this requires a special context with unconditioned therapeutic support for as long as the unusual experience continues. When this process is completed, the subject returns automatically to everyday consciousness. A full experience of the holotropic mode will alleviate or eliminate the symptom, but as a result of it the philosophical commitment of the subject to the hylotropic mode will become looser and more tentative. When the underlying gestalt is a powerful perinatal or transpersonal experience, this typically leads to a process of spiritual opening.

This new approach to the problem of psychogenic emotional disorders, based on an expanded concept of the human personality, abandons the practice of using psychopathological labels for people on the basis of the content of their experience. This emerges from the observation that many of the experiences that used to be considered psychotic can be easily induced in a random sample of the population, not only by psychedelic drugs but by such simple methods as meditation practices and hyperventilation.

In addition, it has become quite clear that the spontaneous occurrence of these phenomena is far higher than has been suspected by mainstreaim psychiatry. The use of stigmatizing diagnoses, forced hospitalization in locked wards, and deterrent forms of therapy have discouraged large numbers of people from admitting even to their close friends and relatives that they have had perinatal or transpersonal experiences. Under these circumstances, psychiatry has obtained a distorted image of the nature of the human experience.

A harmonious blending of the two modes does not distort external reality, but gives it a mystical flavor. The person involved in such a process is capable of responding to the world as if it were made of solid discrete objects, but does not confuse this pragmatic notion with the ultimate truth about reality. He or she experiences many additional dimensions operating behind the scenes and is philosophically fully aware of various alternatives to ordinary reality. This situation seems to occur when the individual is in touch with the holonomic aspects of reality but no specific holotropic gestalts are competing for the experiential field.

The concept of "higher sanity," or genuine mental health, should be reserved for individuals who have achieved a balanced interplay of both complementary modes of consciousness. They should feel comfortable and familiar with both modes, give them appropriate recognition, and be able to use them with flexibility and appropriate discrimination, depending on circumstances. For a full and healthy functioning in this sense, it is absolutely necessary to transcend philosophically dualisms, particularly the dualism between the part and the whole. The individual approaches everyday reality with utmost seriousness and full personal and social responsibility, while being simultaneously aware of the relative value of this perspective. The identification with the ego and body is playful and deliberate, rather than unconditional, absolute, and mandatory. It is not fraught with fear, need for control, and irrational survival programs; the acceptance of material reality and existence is pragmatic, not philosophical. There is deep awareness of the significance of the spiritual dimension in the universal scheme.

The individual who has experienced and integrated a considerable amount of holotropic material has an opportunity to see human life and existence from a perspective that exceeds that of an average Westerner who is "normal" by the standards of traditional psychiatry. Balanced integration of the two complemetary aspects of human experience tends to be associated with an affirmative attitude toward existence—not the status quo or any particular aspects of life, but the cosmic process in its totality, the general flow of life. An integral part of healthy functioning is the ability to enjoy simple and ordinary aspects of everyday life, such as elements of nature, people, and human relations or activities, as well as eating, sleeping, sex, and other physiological processes of one's body. This capacity to appreciate life is elemental and organismic; it is essentially independent of the external conditions of life, with the exception of some drastic extremes. It can be almost reduced to the joy of existing or being conscious. If an individual is in this frame of mind, any additional assets of life—nourishing relationships, availability of money or material possessions, good working conditions, or opportunity to travel—will be experienced as extra luxuries. However, when this orientation toward life or this experiential tuning is missing, no amount of external success or material achievements can provide it.

A good integration of the hylotropic and holotropic modes makes it possible to be fully in touch with the events in the material world, but see them as processes to participate in rather than as means to achieve specific goals. The emphasis on the present moment outweighs the preoccupation with the past or concern about the future. The awareness of the goal is present in the fully experienced successive activities, but it does not become dominant until the task is completed. Then the celebration and enjoyment of the achievement constitutes the content of the present moment.

The generally affirmative attitude toward existence creates a metaframework that makes it possible to integrate in a positive way even the difficult aspects of life. In this connection, the attitude toward what conventional psychiatry considers symptoms of mental disease is more important than the presence or absence of these symptoms. A healthy attitude would view them as integral aspects of the cosmic process that can represent a great opportunity for personality growth and spiritual opening, provided they are properly approached, handled, and integrated. In a sense they indicate an opportunity to liberate oneself from the unfulfilling and crippling hegemony of the hylotropic mode of consciousness.

The occurrence of psychogenic forms of psychopathology can be considered an indication that the individual has reached a point where the continuation of a one-sided existence in the hylotropic mode has become untenable. They herald the emergence of specific holotropic elements and reflect resistance against them. Psychiatry oriented toward suppressing the symptoms and returning the individual to the straitjacket of inauthentic existence is thus essentially antitherapeutic. It interferes with a process that, supported and brought to completion, could lead to a fuller and more satisfying way of existing in the world.

The new definition of what is normal and what is pathological is not based on the content and the nature of the experience, but on the style of approaching it in the context of genuine support based on an understanding of the process; the most important criterion, then, would be the quality of the integration of the experience into the person's life. Abraham Maslow's great contribution to psychology was to demonstrate that certain mystical or "peak" experiences need not be considered pathological but can be approached positively (1964). This notion can now be extended to all perinatal and transpersonal phenomena.

However, it is absolutely essential to create for this purpose special circumstances and milieus for confronting such experiences, where the conditions and set of rules differ from those of everyday life. Full confrontation with the emerging material in a supportive framework, with the possible help of the facilitating techniques

described above, will free the subject's day-to-day existence from
the agony of the interface turmoil between competing experiential
modes. In the new approach, psychogenic disorders reflect the
confusion between the hylotropic mode and the holotropic mode
of consciousness, or the inability of the subject to confront the
emerging holotropic material and integrate it into the everyday
experience of the material world. The general strategy to be pursued is full experiential immersion in the surfacing theme and,
after its completion, return to an uncomplicated and full experience
of the present time and place. The systematic application of this
principle in one's life and openness to a dialectic and harmonious
interplay between the two basic modes of consciousness seem to
be necessary prerequisites to genuine sanity and mental health.

CHAPTER EIGHT

Epilogue:
The Current Global Crisis
and the Future of
Consciousness Evolution

The relevance of observations from LSD psychotherapy, experiential approaches to self-exploration, and various forms of spiritual practice exceeds the narrow limits of psychiatry, psychology, and psychotherapy. Many of the new insights are related to phenomena of critical importance that may be relevant for the future of the human race and life on this planet. They involve a new understanding of the forces that influence history, that contribute to the dynamics of sociopolitical movements, and that participate in creative achievements of the human spirit in art, philosophy, and science. This material also throws new light on many obscure chapters of the history of religion by allowing a clear distinction between genuine mysticism and true spirituality, on the one hand, and mainstream religions and the established church, on the other.

These are obviously topics of enormous scope and an adequate treatment of all the areas involved would require a separate volume. Here I would like to offer a very general outline of the new insights into a problem that is of critical importance for all of us—the current global crisis. For this purpose, I will first review some of the new material related to the perinatal and transpersonal dimensions of human history and then focus more specifically on the issues concerning the present situation in the world and the future of consciousness evolution.

One of the central themes of human history is that of aggression and murder, directed toward other races, nations, religious or social groups, clans, families, individuals, and even close relatives. We have discussed the new insights into the perinatal and transpersonal roots of malignant aggression. The relevance of the material from deep experiential work becomes even more obvious when we move from individual psychopathology into the world of mass psychology and social pathology. Many subjects involved in deep self-exploration frequently experience scenes related to wars, bloody revolutions, totalitarian systems, concentration camps, and genocide.

The *theme of war* is an important standard and characteristic aspect of experiential sessions on the perinatal level. The historical time period, geographical location, nature of weapons and gadgets used, and the specific features of the combat vary within a wide range. Many subjects have reported primitive and brutal fights of cavemen and savages using stone tools and wooden clubs, ancient battles with chariots and war elephants, medieval combats of armored knights on horses, wars involving such twentieth century technology as lasers and nuclear weapons, and futuristic internecine encounters of spaceships representing different stellar systems and galaxies. The intensity and scale of these war scenes and of the experiences involved usually exceed what the subject had previously considered humanly possible. While the general context of these experiences is provided by the perinatal matrices, their specific content frequently includes transpersonal phenomena.

In those individuals who have actually participated in a war as soldiers, or experienced it as civilians, reliving of memories from that time frequently occurs simultaneously with scenes of war from different historical periods in which they have not been personally involved. On occasion, the imagery can be drawn from mythology of various cultures and from the archetypal realms; the destructive potential unleashed in such scenes can surpass anything known in the phenomenal world. The revolt of the Titans against the Olympian gods, the battle of Ahura-Mazda's forces of light against the dark forces of Ahriman, the twilight of the Nordic gods during Ragnarok, and the archetypal scenes of the ultimate destruction characterizing the Apocalypse and Armaggedon are typical.

The two perinatal matrices from which most of the war symbolism is drawn are BPM II and BPM III. For our purpose, it is important to define the basic difference between these two matrices. Both are closely related to the theme of horror, agony, and death and both are typically associated with the imagery of war and concentration camps. However, they differ in the experiential emphasis and in the nature of the roles available to the subject. An individual under the influence of BPM II is involved in scenes of violence in the position of the helpless victim, whereas the aggressors are always identified as the others. Such individuals experience endless tortures by assuming the roles of civilians subjected to air-raids, persons trapped under the debris of collapsed houses, villagers whose settlements are being burned by vicious invaders, mothers and children attacked by napalm, soldiers exposed to poisonous gases, or prisoners in concentration camps. The general atmosphere of these scenes is that of desolation, despair, anguish, hopelessness, and the absurdity of human existence.

The nature of the war experiences associated with BPM III is very different. Although the actual imagery may be similar, the subject does not identify exclusively with the victim, the oppressed, and the down-trodden. He or she also has experiential access to the emotions and physical sensations of the aggressor and tyrant, and at the same time can assume the role of an observer. In this matrix, all the roles can be experientially explored, but the actual emphasis seems to be on the relationship of the protagonists and their interaction with each other. The predominant emotional atmosphere is that of wild instinctual arousal involving aggression, anxiety, sexual excitement, a strange fascination, a peculiar mixture of pain and pleasure, and a scatological component.

It is interesting to relate the experiential characteristics of these two matrices to the biological situations with which they are associated—the first and second stage of biological delivery. The second matrix, which is related to the first stage of delivery, represents a situation of blockage and energetic stagnation. It seems that the subject reliving it has experiential access only to the emotions and sensations of the victimized child and their psychological correlates and derivatives.

BPM III, which involves elements of propulsion through the birth canal, is associated with a certain degree of energy flow. The subject confronting this phase of the birth process can experientially identify not only with the child, but also with the feelings of the delivering mother, and with the constricting birth canal, including all the related and analogous roles and themes. It is fascinating to realize that all the major experiential facets of BPM III find an ideal expression in the context of the war scenes in psychedelic sessions; it is not necessary to emphasize that the same is true in the case of actual war situations. It is hard to imagine that this connection is purely accidental and does not have a deep psychological significance.

The *titanic aspect* is represented by the monumental military technology using and unleashing phenomenal energies—from gigantic stone-throwers and ramming devices of ancient armies to colossal tanks, amphibian vehicles, battleships, flying fortresses, and missiles. Here, atomic bombs and thermonuclear weapons seem to have special symbolic significance, as will be discussed later.

The *sadomasochistic aspect* of BPM III is certainly characteristic for any kind of war situation; however, it is most clearly manifested in close hand-to-hand combat in which hurting and being hurt is equally possible and can even occur simultaneously, for example, scenes of wrestling, boxing, gladiator combats with men or animals, Neanderthal warfare, primitive aboriginal battles, medieval sword and shield encounters, jousting tournaments, and bayonet attacks during the First World War. There seems to be a close parallel between two warriors involved in this intimate, internecine encounter and the symbiotic involvement of the mother and child in the process of delivery. In both situations, the protagonists are locked in a situation of life and death that they must face; each also simultaneously inflicts pain and is hurt by the other. It seems especially significant that the blood spilled on both sides can mix, fuse, and merge.

On occasion, LSD subjects mention other forms of internecine dyadic interlocks that seem to be related to the dynamics of BPM

Fig. 45. A picture showing the ritual practices of the Aztecs. According to the Aztec belief, the sun god Huitzilopochtli had to be nourished with offerings of the "red cactus fruit"—human hearts and blood.

III. The relationship and interaction between the partners in sadomasochistic practices has already been discussed. Another interesting example is the relationship between the pre-Columbian high priests and their victims. Among the Aztecs this relationship had an explicitly filial nature and involved a close emotional tie. On the frescoes in the ancient Mayan center, Bonampak, representing a sacrificial festival, the priests are shown injuring their tongues so that their own blood can mix with that of the ritually killed captives. We have already discussed the deep psychological similarity between the Inquisitors and the satanists or witches whom they persecuted. The sadistic methods of the Inquisition, their torture chambers, bestial intruments of torture, *autos-da-fé*, as well as their interest in the sexual and scatological behavior of their victims, reflect essentially the same deep motivational structure as the performance of the Black Mass or participation in the Witches' Sabbath.

In recent years, reports of murderous riots in several American prisons have brought into focus another characteristic dyad of this kind, namely that of the prisoner and the prison guard. The bestial nature of these riots might be incomprehensible and puzzling for psychiatrists and psychologists with Freudian or behaviorist training who are trying to explain such extreme behavior from biographical material. They are not at all surprising to one who has even a superficial knowledge of the perinatal dynamics. Such riots are obviously induced by prison conditions that activate perinatal material—including cruel treatment and overcrowding—and the behavior of the rioting inmates has classical perinatal features. Recent investigations of the behavior of police officers and their frequent abuse of power also provide interesting insights into the dyadic interlock existing between policemen and criminals.

There are two additional examples that have great social and historical relevance—the autocratic tyrant and the revolutionary, and the ultrarightist politician and the radical leftist. (Both dyads are discussed later in the context of social upheavals and revolutions.) In all these instances, the protagonists in the interlock are trapped in destructive interaction and both are psychologically enslaved by it regardless of their role as victim or aggressor. One can say that, in a certain sense, they actually create each other by feeding each other's behavior. The ultimate solution for such situations, offered by many of the spiritual paths and by transpersonal psychology, is not to win or get on top, but to step out of the psychological bondage of "us and them" thinking and move toward synergistic strategies.

The *sexual aspect* of the third perinatal matrix is expressed in many different ways during wartime. The general population usually shows a vast moral and sexual slackening and increased interest in erotic activities. A similar effect is also observed in situations that involve major natural catastrophies and epidemics. It has been referred to as *avant deluge* or *carpe diem* psychology and is usually interpreted as a reaction to impending death. It has been emphasized that a heightened interest in sex increases the rate of conception and is nature's compensation for the mass killing that will occur. The alternative suggested here is that it reflects the powerful sexual component of perinatal dynamics and is thus an inherent aspect of the unleashed elemental instinctual forces.

The explicit promises of military leaders before important battles frequently include that of sexual access to women of the conquered villages and towns. It would be superfluous to emphasize the high incidence of rape in the wars throughout human history and the number of illegitimate children conceived both in voluntary and involuntary sexual interactions during the time of war. Also, the sexual crimes committed in concentration camps have been widely publicized and are well known.

The *scatological aspect* is a characteristic concomitant of the war scenes of all times. It is one of the most typical features of war to destroy order and beauty and leave debris, chaos, and decay. Total disarray, piles of rubble and garbage, generally unhygienic conditions, colossal pollution of many different kinds, massacred and disemboweled bodies, and panoramas of putrefying corpses and carcasses represent a mandatory aftermath of the wars in all ages.

Further, the *pyrocathartic aspect* of BPM III is a standard and important element of most of the scenes of war destruction. The concrete situations involving this element can take many different forms, from pouring burning resin from the ramparts of fortresses and destroying conquered villages and towns by fire, to bombs exploding in air raids, the mass rocket flames of "Stalin's organ," and nuclear warfare. The element of fire can be seen as ominous and destructive, but more frequently the subject experiences it with the fascination of a pyromaniac and draws satisfaction from its power and purging action. Many individuals who have experienced war recall that they could not resist the pull of its archetypal power when they actually got involved in a life-and-death confrontation. This feeling usually sharply contrasts with one's attitudes and standards in everyday life. Freud (1955a; 1955b) described the psychological changes that occur under such circumstances in terms of mob psychology and the development of "war superego."

The visions accompanying the experience of birth in the context of BPM IV frequently include scenes symbolizing the end of war, or the victory in a revolution. Celebration of a military triumph, cheering processions, waving banners, dancing in the streets, and fraternizing between soldiers and civilians belong to common images reported by subjects who have relived the moment of birth. This period of carefree jubilation before the call of new duty following a major war or revolution seems, thus, to be psychologically equivalent to the short period after birth before the newborn encounters the difficulties and vicissitudes of his or her new existence.

All these observations can be summed up in the surprising conclusion that the human personality structure contains, in the unconscious repertoire of the perinatal level, functional matrices the activation of which can result in a complex and realistic reproduction of all the experiences of horror, agony, polymorphous instinctual arousal, and strange fascination associated with the various forms of war.

On many occasions, subjects experiencing perinatal elements in their sessions have also reported many interesting insights into other sociopolitical situations closely related to the theme of war. These involve the problems of *totalitarian systems, autocracy, dictatorship, police states,* and *bloody revolutions.* Deep experiential confrontation with the elements of BPM II is typically associated with images of, and identification with, the population of countries oppressed by a dictator, subjected to a police state, or living in a totalitarian regime, such as Czarist Russia, Nazi Germany, or one of the Communist or Latin American countries. Such empathic identification can also involve a severely persecuted minority group, or a category of people in a particularly difficult predicament.

Examples of such experiences are sequences involving Christians at the time of the emperor Nero, serfs and slaves, Jewish groups at various historical periods and geographical locations, prisoners in medieval dungeons and concentration camps, or inmates of insane asylums. Some Czech patients who had had painful experiences with either the Nazi occupants during the Second World War or with the Communist regime, frequently relived their memories of actual political traumas, such as scenes from a concentration or labor camp, brutal investigations, imprisonments, or episodes of brainwashing. According to the insights from psychedelic sessions, there is a deep psychological connection and similarity between the atmosphere in an oppressed country, or the experience of a persecuted group, and the experience of the fetus in the clutch of the birth canal.

Experiences associated with BPM III characteristically include images and symbols of the oppressive forces, aggressors, and tyrants. The dynamics of this matrix is related to the politics of power, tyranny, exploitation, and subjugation of others, dirty tricks and intrigues, cloak-and-dagger diplomacy, secret police, betrayal, and treason. Many LSD subjects have experienced—in the terminal phases of the birth agony—identification with despotic rulers and dictators of all times, such as Nero, Genghis Khan, Hitler, or Stalin. As a result of this profound experiential identification they stopped seeing dictatorship as a manifestation of genuine strength and power. They realized that the mental set of a dictator has a deep similarity to that of a child struggling in the birth canal. He is torn by a strange mixture of chaotic and incompatible feelings and energies: impulsive aggression intolerant of any obstacles, abysmal self-doubts, inflated megalomaniac feelings, insatiable ambitions, primitive childlike anxiety, generalized paranoia, and great physical discomfort, particularly a sense of choking and strangulation.

Subjects who had first-hand experience of this state realized how disastrous it can be when somebody in this psychological condition manages to get into a position of power instead of therapy, where he belongs. Conversely, they realized that the mass support that a dictator requires at the different stages along his way to power reflects the fact that similar elements are bound to be a standard part of the makeup of the human personality. It becomes obvious that anybody could be capable of committing the same crimes if the corresponding level of his or her unconscious were unleashed and the external circumstances played into it.

The real problem does not consist in isolated individuals or political parties and factions. The task is to create safe and socially sanctioned situations in which certain toxic and potentially dangerous elements of the human personality structure can be confronted and worked through without any harm or damage to others, or society as a whole. Externally oriented radical programs and political power struggles, although of vital importance if challenging a murderous regime of a Hitler or Stalin, cannot solve the problems of humanity without a simultaneous inner transformation. They typically create a pendulum effect whereby yesterday's underdog becomes tomorrow's ruler and vice versa. Although the roles change, the amount of malignant aggression remains the same, and humanity as a whole is not helped. The prisons, concentration camps, and labor camps continue to function; they just change their inmates.

Genuine strength does not need ostentatious display ad demogogic rhetoric; its presence is self-evident and obvious. What is experienced by a dictator is not strength, but an agonizing inferiority complex, an insatiable hunger for recognition, an excruciating loneliness, and consuming mistrust. In the course of deep experiential therapy, the "dictator complex" is resolved when the death-rebirth process is completed. The experiential connection with the elements of BPM IV moves one out of the realm of fear and agony and opens up channels for entirely new feelings—a sense of fulfillment, belonging, and security, a respect for life and creation, understanding, tolerance, a live-and-let-live attitude, and an awareness of one's cosmic significance associated with humility.

The tyrant and the rebel represent an internecine dyadic interlock; their deep psychological motivations come from the same source and are of a similar kind. The state of mind of the angry dictator and that of the infuriated revolutionary do not, at the time of their murderous encounter, differ from each other in their deepest nature. There are obvious differences in their ideologies and moral justifications for their actions. Occasionally, there can be significant difference in the ethical and social value of the systems they represent. However, they have in common a fundamental lack of genuine psychological insight into the real motives of their behavior. It is therefore a situation with no gain, only loss; no matter who wins or what the moral judgment of history may be, a real solution escapes both parties.

Both sides are under the influence of a basic confusion, trying to solve an intrapsychic problem by manipulations of the external world. This is clearly documented by the fact that visions of bloody revolutions inspired by utopian ideals and alternating identification with the oppressors and the revolutionaries are characteristic of the dynamics of BPM III. They become psychologically irrelevant and disappear from the picture when the individual reaches BPM IV. The concrete images characteristic of the third perinatal matrix cover a wide range from the revolt of Roman slaves led by Spartacus through the conquest of the Bastille in the French Revolution to such recent events as the Bolshevik takeover of the Winter Palace of the Czars and the victory of Fidel Castro in Cuba.

Subjects involved in LSD therapy and other forms of deep experiential self-exploration quite independently report their insights into the reasons for the tragicomical chronic failure of all violent revolutions, despite their high ideals and the general appeal of the radical philosophies on which they are based. It should be mentioned that all the LSD subjects in Prague had a first-hand experience with communism and Marxism-Leninism, in theory and practice, and many of them had also experienced nazism. Essentially, the external situation of oppression—real or imaginary—becomes confused and identified with the inner psychological imprisonment from the unconscious pressure of the memory of the birth trauma. The intuited possibility of liberation by the instinctual unleashing characteristic of BPM III is then projected and translated into a concrete plan for overthrowing the tyrant. Thus, the actual motive and driving force behind violent revolutions and plans for social utopias is an unconscious need for freeing oneself from the repressive and constricting influence of the birth trauma and connecting experientially to the nourishing feelings associated with BPM IV and BPM I.

What makes communism a particularly powerful and problematic force in today's world is that it presents a program that is true psychologically when applied to the process of inner transformation, but is deceptively false as a recipe for social reform. The basic notion that a violent and stormy upheaval of a revolutionary nature is necessary to terminate the condition of oppression and institute a situation of harmony and satisfaction reflects correctly the dynamics of the inner transformation associated with the death-rebirth process. For this reason, it seems to communicate some fundamental truth and has the widespred appeal of a plausible and promising political program.

The basic fallacy lies in the fact that the stages of archetypal unfolding of a spiritual process are projected onto the material reality and camouflaged as an atheistic recipe for a social transformation of the world; it is quite obvious that in this form it cannot possibly work. One need only look at the present fragmentation of the communist world, at the hostility among the nations pursuing the ideals of Marxism-Leninism, or at the walls, mine fields, barbed wire, and trained dogs that these nations are obliged to use to keep their populations within the confines of their social paradises, to judge the success of this fascinating experiment.

The study of history indicates that violent revolutions are unusually powerful and successful in their destructive phase, when they are using the unleashed perinatal forces to destroy the old corrupted regime. They tend to fail inevitably in the following stage, when they try to create the paradisean condition that they had promised and the image of which was the driving moral force of the revolution. The perinatal forces that are instrumental in such sociopolitical upheavals are not consumed or worked through, they are simply activated and acted out. Thus, the elemental forces that were so useful during the destructive phase of the revolution become the seed of corruption of the new system and continue to operate after victory within the camp of the architects of the new order. These are, in a nutshell, the insights from experiential work explaining the frequently stunning military successes of radical revolutions and their equally astonishing failure to deliver the utopia, the vision of which the leaders use as the carrot for the masses.

It seems obvious that individuals who have not been able to solve their own intrapsychic problems and reach inner peace and harmony are not the best judges as to what is wrong in the world and what should be the means to correct it. The basis for a real solution would be to connect experientially with the feelings of BPM IV, BPM I, and the transpersonal dimension of one's own psyche before venturing on a crusade to transform the world. This is essentially identical with Krishnamurti's statement that the only revolution is the inner one. Military revolutions, although they frequently represent some degree of historical progress, are bound to fail in their utopian efforts, because their external accomplishments are not matched by the inner psychological transformation that would neutralize the powerful destructive forces inherent in human nature.

This point can be illustrated by insights of LSD subjects who saw a parallel between the situation of the revolutionary overjoyed by his victory on the barricades and that of a newborn child overwhelmed by the explosive liberation from the oppressive grip of the birth canal. The neonate's feelings of triumph are soon replaced by distress brought on by the newly discovered and quite unexpected sensations of cold, wetness, hunger, and emotional starvation. The revolutionary, instead of attaining and enjoying the promised paradise, must now cope with the vicissitudes of his new situation, including a modified version of the old repressive system insidiously developing on the ruins of the utopia.

As the newborn goes through life, he or she will be increasingly harrassed by the shadow of the perinatal energies that have not been confronted and integrated. In a similar way, the perinatal energies that were instrumental in the revolution will continue to emerge within the political structure of the new regime. Unable to comprehend the fundamental fallacy of their approach to reality, the revolutionaries have to find explanations for the failure of utopia, as well as culprits—their comrades who contaminated the true doctrine by deviating too far to the right or to the left, indulging in some obnoxious leftovers of the old regime's ideology, or manifesting some other of the many children's diseases of the revolutionary movement.

This does not mean that we should give up our attempts at just political and social reforms or stop challenging tyrants and totalitarian regimes. It suggests that ideally leaders of such movements should be those who have done sufficient inner work and reached emotional maturity. Politicians who convert their inner emotional turmoil into a program of a bloody revolutionary massacre are dangerous and should not be trusted or supported. The real problem is to raise the consciousness of the general public so that it is capable of recognizing and ignoring public figures who belong to this category.

Another area into which observations from experiential psychotherapy offer revealing insights is that of *concentration camps, mass murder,* and *genocide.* It has already been mentioned that experiences of BPM II typically involve identification with the inmates of prisons and concentration camps, including feelings of despair, hopelessness, helplessness, extreme anguish, starvation, physical pain, and suffocation in gas chambers. This is usually associated with a profound existential crisis. The sense of meaninglessness and absurdity of human existence alternates here with an excruciating desire and need to find meaning in life against the background of this apocalyptic reality. In view of this fact, it does not seem accidental that Victor Frankl (1956), the father of logotherapy or existential analysis, developed his insights into the importance of the sense of meaning in human life during his long stay in a Nazi concentration camp. When the images of concentration camps occur in the context of the third perinatal matrix, subjects experience not only identification with the tortured helpless victims, but also with the devious, cruel, and bestial Nazi officers, or red commissars of the Gulag Archipelago.

Closer examination of the general atmosphere and specific living conditions in concentration camps reveals that they are a vivid, literal, and realistic enactment of the nightmarish symbolism of negative perinatal matrices in the material world. The pictures from these camps of death show scenes of insanity and sheer horror. Emaciated naked bodies can be seen piled up in gigantic heaps, strewn all over the roads, and hanging half-burned in the barbed wire fences—anonymous skeletons stripped of all human dignity and identity. Among the specters of watchtowers equipped with fast submachine guns and high-voltage electric fences, sounds of shots are heard almost incessantly and the fiendish Kapos with their trained half-wild Alsatian dogs walk around looking for victims.

Violence and sadism, so typical for perinatal experiences, was manifested here on a scale that is hard to imagine. The unbridled fury and pathological rage of the SS officers, their capricious cruelty and boundless desire to ridicule, humiliate, and torture, went far beyond what was necessary for the alleged goal of the camp system, which was to deter the enemies of the Third Reich, to provide slaves, and to liquidate individual adversaries of the Nazi regime and "racially inferior groups."

This is particularly clear in regard to the scatological dimension, which presented a striking aspect of life in the Nazi concentration camps. In many instances, prisoners were forced to urinate in each other's face or into each other's mouths. They were allowed to go to the latrines only twice a day and those who tried to get to them at night risked being shot by the guards; this forced some prisoners to use their eating bowls as chamber pots. In Birkenau, soup bowls were periodically taken from the prisoners and thrown into the latrines, from which the prisoners had to retrieve them.

The inmates in the Nazi camps were literally drowning in their own waste, and death in and by excrement was quite common. One of the favorite games of the SS was to catch men during the act of relieving themselves and throw them into the pit; in Buchenwald, ten prisoners suffocated in feces in a single month as a result of this perverted entertainment. These practices obviously represented a severe hygienic risk and health hazard and were thus directly contrary to the usual meticulous concerns about epidemic control in prisons, armies, or any situation of communal living. Thus, they must be interpreted in psychopathological terms, and viewing them in the context of perinatal dynamics seems to provide a plausible explanation.

The sexual aspect of perinatal experiences was also amply displayed in the conditions of concentration camps. The sexual abuse of prisoners, both heterosexual and homosexual, including rape and manifest sadistic practices, were perpetrated on a mass scale. In some instances, SS officers forced prisoners to engage each other in sexual activities to provide entertainment. Selected women and girls, including those in their early teens, were assigned to houses of prostitution to satisfy the sexual needs of soldiers durig their furloughs. A shattering description of the sexual practices in German concentration camps can be found in *House of Dolls*, by the legendary Israeli writer who uses as his pseudonym the index name he carried as a concentration camp inmate, Ka-Tzetnik 135633 (1955).

The perinatal experience of ego death commonly involves feelings of complete humiliation, degradation, debasement, and defilement. What the psyche of LSD subjects retrieves from the rich repositories of unconscious matrices, in the form of inner experience and symbolic imagery, was enacted in the concentration camps with frightening realism. Prisoners were stripped of all their possessions, clothes, hair, and name—anything that they could have associated with their identity. In the conditions of camp life, an absolute lack of privacy, unimaginable dirt, and the inexorable dictates of biological functions were amplified to grotesque proportions. This then became the baseline for a more specific program of dehumanization and total debasement carried out by the SS in as methodical and systematic a way in its general strategy as it was capricious, erratic, and unpredictable in its daily manifestations.

The series of uncanny parallels between the experiential elements related to perinatal matrices and concentration camp practices also includes the element of suffocation. The Nazi program of systematic extermination was carried out in the infamous gas chambers where the victims choked to death in overcrowded, confined spaces by inhaling toxic gases. The element of fire has an important role in the symbolism of both the second and the third perinatal matrix. In BPM II it is part of the atmosphere of the archetypal infernal scenes in which condemned souls undergo inhuman tortures. In BPM III it appears in the final pyrocathartic stage of the death-rebirth process, characterizing termination of agony and heralding transcendence. The glowing furnaces of the crematoria were both part of the hellish scenery of the camps and places for the disposal of dead bodies, where the last biological remnants of the tortured victims were eliminated without a trace. This aspect of perinatal symbolism was expounded with frightening power in another book by Ka-Tzetnik 135633, *Sunrise Over Hell* (1977).

It must also be mentioned here that the Nazis seemed to focus their perverse fury especially on pregnant women and little children, which further supports the perinatal hypothesis. The most powerful passage from Terrence des Près's *The Survivor* (1976), is without doubt the description of a truck full of babies dumped into fire; it is closely followed by a scene in which pregnant women are beaten with clubs and whips, torn by dogs, dragged around by the hair, kicked in the stomach, and finally thrown into the crematorium while still alive.

Professor Bastians, from Leyden, Holland, has had extensive experience in the treatment of the so-called concentration camp syndrome—a complex of emotional and psychosomatic disturbances that develops in former inmates after a delay of several decades following their incarceration. He has been conducting a unique program for individuals suffering from these belated psychological consequences of an ordeal that ended a long time ago. Under the influence of LSD, former inmates are encouraged to relive, abreact, and integrate various traumatic experiences from the camp the memory of which still holds them in thrall. In his paper describing this program, Bastians came to a conclusion very similar to the one presented here, although in a far less specific form. He pointed to the fact that the idea of a concentration camp is a product of the human mind. No matter how unacceptable this may sound, it must therefore represent a manifestation of a certain aspect of human personality and the dynamics of the unconscious. This was succinctly expressed in the title of his paper, "Man in the Concentration Camp and the Concentration Camp in Man" (n.d.).

These observations reveal a surprising fact about the psyche and the human personality structure. As with wars and revolutions, the unconscious also has functional matrices that can, under certain circumstances, generate the entire gamut of both passive and active experiences related to concentration camps, reflecting their general atmosphere, as well as specific details. In addition, many other powerful images and experiences involving mass extermination and genocide in different cultures and historical periods are extremely common in perinatal sessions. They represent an important channel for the extraordinary amount of aggression that is associated with the dynamics of the third perinatal matrix.

In recent years, an unexpected confirmation of the relationship between perinatal dynamics and important sociopolitical phenomena came from a completely independent source. Lloyd de Mause (1975; 1982)—journalist, psychoanalyst, and foremost proponent of psychohistory[1]—has analyzed speeches of important military and political leaders and other material from periods of history immediately preceding and associated with major wars and revolutions. His fascinating data bring convincing support for the thesis that regressive infantile material, particularly that related to the process of biological birth, plays an important role in a variety of serious political crises. His analytical method is altogether unique, imaginative, and creative. In addition to traditional historical sources, de Mause draws data of great psychological relevance from jokes, anecdotes, caricatures, dreams, personal imagery, slips of the tongue, side comments of speakers, and even scribbles and doodles on the edges of documents.

The results of de Mause's study of a wide variety of historical crises suggest that political and military leaders, rather than being strong oedipal figures, seem to function as "garbage collectors" for various repressed feelings of individuals, groups, and entire nations. They provide socially sanctioned channels for the projection and acting out of emotions that cannot be kept under control by the usual systems of intrapsychic defenses. According to de Mause, in the psychology of large groups the psyche regresses to archaic modes of relating that are characteristic of the preverbal stages of infancy. The infantile emotions and sensations emerge from all levels of psychic organization, not only the oedipal and phallic, but also the anal, urethral, and oral.

In analyzing the historical material from the times immediately preceding the outbreak of wars or revolutions, de Mause was struck by an extraordinary abundance of figures of speech and images related to biological birth. Thus, politicians of all ages, when declaring war or describing a critical situation, typically refer to strangulation, choking, a life-and-death struggle for breath or living space, and feelings of being crushed by the enemy. Equally frequent are allusions to dark caves and confusing labyrinths, tunnels, descents into an abyss, or, conversely, the need to break through and find the way to light out of darkness. Additional images include feeling small and helpless, drowning, hanging, fire, falling, or jumping from a tower. Although the last three images seem to have no immediately obvious relation to birth, they are common perinatal symbols that occur in the context of BPM III, as indicated by observations from psychedelic therapy and from Nandor Fodor's analytical work with dreams (1949). The fact that pregnant women and children are the center of the war fantasy deserves special attention.

Lloyd de Mause's psychohistorical illustrations are drawn from many historical periods and different geographical regions. Examples from world history, involving such famous personages as Alexander the Great, Napoleon, Kaiser Wilhelm II, and Hitler are complemented by those taken from remote, recent, and contemporary history of the United States. Thus de Mause analyzed the psychohistorical roots of the American Revolution and discussed its relation to birth practices and the specifics of child rearing. He was able to find striking elements of birth symbolism in the statements of Admiral Shimada and Ambassador Kurasa before the attack on Pearl Harbor. Particularly chilling was the use of perinatal symbolism in connection with the explosion of the second atomic bomb. The airplane that carried the bomb was given the name of the pilot's mother as a nickname; the bomb itself bore the written title "The Little Boy," and the code wired to Washington after successful detonation was: "The baby was born."

In the correspondence between John Kennedy and Khrushchev around the Cuban crisis, there is a reference to a situation that these two statesmen wanted to avoid; it is symbolized by an image of two blind moles who meet in a dark underground passage and get entangled in a life-and-death struggle. Henry Kissinger, when asked if the United States would consider military intervention in the Middle East, touched his throat and answered: "Only if another strangulation occurs. . . ."

Many additional examples could be mentioned in support of de Mause's thesis. A striking finding in his own studies is the fact that references to strangulation and oppression occurred only in speeches preceding a war, but not during war situations that involved actual encirclement. In addition, the accusations of choking, strangling, and crushing were occasionally made in regard to nations who were not even immediate neighbors. The fact that masses respond emotionally to speeches of this kind, unable to see their obvious irrationality and absurdity, betrays the existence of a universally present blind spot and vulnerability in the area of perinatal dynamics.

Lloyd de Mause has produced ample evidence for the hypothesis that in wars and revolutions nations act out a group fantasy of birth. It is clear from these examples that his findings and ideas are closely related to the observations from psychedelic research. His psychohistorical research represents a continuation of the tradition of depth-psychological analysis of social upheavals initiated by Gustav le Bon (1977) and Sigmund Freud (1955b). Although generally compatible with the conclusions of these two authors, the new data present important specific insights of great theoretical and practical relevance. The shift of emphasis by de Mause from the Freudian individual unconscious to the dynamics of the birth trauma represents a quantum leap in the understanding of elemental social events.

According to the new interpretation, supported jointly by psychedelic observations and de Mause's psychohistory, powerful energies and emotions derived from, or related to, the birth trauma are a standard component of the makeup of the human personality. Their activation in individuals by factors of a psychological nature, by biochemical changes, or by other influences results in either individual psychopathology or a process of spiritual transformation, depending on circumstances. It seems that, for reasons insufficiently understood at this time,[2] the psychological defenses that normally prevent the perinatal energies from surfacing into consciousness can start breaking down simultaneously in a large number of individuals belonging to a social, political, or national group. This creates a general atmosphere of tension, anxiety, and anticipation. The person who becomes the leader of the masses under these circumstances is an individual whose awareness of the perinatal forces is greater than average, and who has the ability to disown them and attach them projectively to events in the external world. He then clearly formulates his own perception for the group or nation, giving an acceptable explanation for the existing emotional climate in terms of political problems.

The pressures, tensions, and choking feelings are blamed on a group of enemies, the sense of danger is exteriorized, and a military intervention is offered as a remedy. The final outcome of the bloody confrontation is then described metaphorically in terms of images related to biological birth and spiritual rebirth. The use of this symbolic language makes it possible to exploit the psychological power associated with the transformation process for political purposes. In view of these facts, it seems extremely important that the findings of psychohistory be publicized and the symbolism of the perinatal process become generally known. It should be possible to create a situation in which demagogic statements about choking, crushing, and a lack of living space would be taken as indications that the person making them needs depth-psychological work, rather than accepted as a valid incentive to start a war. With a little training, the public can learn to decipher and understand the symbolic language of birth and death, just as it has successfully mastered the Freudian sexual symbolism.

Lloyd de Mause's speculations have been, up to this point, in far-reaching agreement with the conclusions I have drawn from my psychedelic observations. The only major conceptual difference I have found between the general theses of these two interpretations of historical crises involves the explanations of the psychological dynamics at the time of the onset of wars or revolutions. It has been repeatedly stated that, when a war is declared after a period of general tension and anticipation, this paradoxically results in feelings of relief and extraordinary clarity. Lloyd de Mause attributes this psychologically to leaders and nations connecting at this point with the memory of the moment of birth. My own interpretation of the atmosphere preceding a war emphasizes the element of a strong emotional-cognitive dissonance between the existing emotional tension and the lack of a concrete external situation to which it can be attached. When war erupts, the preexisting feelings of the leaders and nations are suddenly in general congruence with the external circumstances. The emotions appear to be justified, and the only thing required is to deal in the best possible way with the dismal reality of the situation. In the course of the war, the nightmarish content of the perinatal matrices then turns into the reality of everyday life, as we have shown. Despite its absurdity, monstrosity, and insanity, the new situation displays a peculiar logic, because there is no major disparity between the events and the emotional reactions of the people involved.

This mechanism has its parallels in individual psychopathology. Persons who are under the strong influence of a negative dynamic matrix of the unconscious show intolerance of emotional-cognitive dissonance. They tend to seek situations that are congruent with their inner feelings, or even become instrumental in unconsciously creating such situations. It has also been repeatedly observed that a wide variety of emotional disorders tends to disappear under certain extreme and drastic circumstances, the infamous examples being the concentration camp, the Foreign Legion, and the old-time whaling ship. The emotional-cognitive dissonance disappears when the external circumstances match or surpass the preexisting neurotic feelings.

This description of the perinatal roots of wars, revolutions, and totalitarian systems reflects only one important aspect of a very complex problem area. The strong emphasis on perinatal dynamics that it entails reflects the purpose of this discussion, which was to communicate new and fascinating material that, in the past, has not been taken into consideration. It was by no means my intention to reduce the problems involved to intrapsychic dynamics and deny or disregard its significant historical, racial, national, political, and economic determinants. The new data should thus be seen as a contribution to a future comprehensive understanding of these phenomena, rather than an adequate explanation replacing all others.

Even from a psychological point of view, this description covers only one important dimension or aspect of the problem. The view that sociopolitical phenomena are meaningfully related to perinatal dynamics is not incompatible with the view that history has also important transpersonal dimensions. Jung and his followers have demonstrated that powerful archetypal constellations do not influence only individuals; they are also instrumental in shaping events in the phenomenal world, and in human history. Jung's interpretation of the Nazi movement as a mass spell of the Ragnarok, or Götterdämmerung, archetype is an important example (1961). Jung's understanding of history is compatible with the approach of archetypal astrology, which studies correlations of historical events with planetary transits. I have already mentioned the fascinating research in this area conducted by Richard Tarnas.

A discussion of the transpersonal dimensions of human history would be incomplete without mentioning Wilber's systematic and comprehensive transpersonal reinterpretation of history and anthropology, described in his book *Up From Eden* (1981). In his unique way, Wilber was able to introduce unusual clarity into the seemingly impenetrable and unmanageable jungle of historical facts and theories, reducing them to a few common denominators. Wilber basically portrays human evolution as a history of the love affair between humanity and the divine. He analyzes each of the consecutive periods in terms of three key questions: (1) What are the major forms of transcendence available at this time? (2) What substitutes for transcendence are created when these fail—in other words, what are the forms of the Atman project, both subjective for the self and objective for the culture? (3) What are the costs of these substitutes?

As has been pointed out, my own observations differ in certain details from Wilber's views, and I cannot provide at present a smooth integration between the model presented in this book and his exciting vision. However, the similarities between the two approaches are so far-reaching that such a synthesis should be possible sometime in the near future. I believe that eventually the insights from Jungian psychology, archetypal astrology, psychedelic research, and Wilber's spectrum psychology will merge into a comprehensive interpretation of the psychological aspects of human history and the evolution of consciousness.

We turn now to the present world situation to explore the practical relevance of the new insights. In recent years, many authors have tried to explain the catastrophic situation humanity has created for itself. The dangerous schism that underlies it has been described in many different ways—as an imbalance between the intellectual development and emotional maturation of the human race, a disproportionate evolution of the neocortex in relation to the archaic parts of the brain, an interference of instinctual and irrational forces of the unconscious with conscious processes, and the like.

Whatever metaphor we use, the situation seems very clear. Over the centuries, humanity has attained incredible achievements. It has been able to release nuclear energy, send spaceships to the moon and the planets, and transmit sound and color pictures all over the globe and across cosmic space. At the same time, it has been incapable of harnessing certain primitive emotions and instinctual impulses—its legacy from the Stone Age. As a result, surrounded by technology approaching science fiction, mankind now lives in chronic anguish, on the verge of a nuclear and ecological catastrophy.

Modern science has developed technologies that could solve most of the urgent problems in to-day's world—combat diseases, starvation, and poverty, and develop renewable forms of energy. The problems that stand in the way are neither technological nor economical; they are forces intrinsic to human nature and the human personality. Because of them, unimaginable resources are wasted in the insanity of the arms race, power struggle, and pursuit of "unlimited growth." These forces also prevent a more appropriate division of wealth among individuals and nations, as well as a reorientation of ecological priorities that are vital for survival of life. For this reason, it seems of great interest to look more closely at the relevant material from deep self-exploration.

The psychological death-rebirth process and its symbolic language can be applied to our condition. Even a cursory look at the world situation reveals that we have exteriorized in our present life all the essential aspects of BPM III that an individual involved in a tranformative and evolutionary process must face internally. The third perinatal matrix has a number of important facets—the titanic, aggressive and sadomasochistic, sexual, demonic, messianic, scatological, and pyrocathartic.

Technological progress has provided the means of modern warfare with a destructive potential beyond the imagination. The aggressive impulse has been unleashed all over the world in the form of internecine wars, bloody revolutions, totalitarian regimes, race riots, concentration camps, brutality of police and secret police, student unrest, and increasing criminality.

Similarly, sexual repression is being lifted and erotic impulses are being manifested in a variety of straightforward and distorted ways. The sexual freedom of youngsters, promiscuity, open marriage, overtly sexual plays and movies, gay liberation, pornographic literature, sadomasochistic parlors, sexual slave markets, and the popularity of "fist-fucking" are just a few examples of this trend.

The demonic element finds expression in increasing interest in books and movies with occult themes, such terroristic organizations as Charles Manson's gang and the Symbionese Liberation Army acting out distorted mystical impulses, and the renaissance of witchcraft and satanic cults. The messianic impulse is prominent in many of the new age religious movements, such as the "Jesus freaks" or the cults expecting salvation from UFOs and extraterrestrial intervention. The fact that extremes of spiritual pathology involving a perinatal mixture of sadomasochism, deviant sexuality, scatology, and self-destructive tendencies today attract thousands of followers can best be illustrated by the tragedy of Jonestown.

The scatological dimension is evident in increasing industrial pollution, the rapidly deteriorating quality of air and water, the accumulation of waste products on a global scale, degenerating hygienic conditions in large cities and, in a more abstract and metaphorical sense, the alarming rise of political, social, and economic corruption. The visions of thermonuclear reactions, atomic explosions, and the launching of missiles are typical images of the transition from BPM III to BPM IV. The perspective of a sudden unleashing of this doomsday technology has become in recent decades a calculated risk of everyday life.

An individual undergoing the death-rebirth process would confront such themes internally as mandatory stages of the process of inner transformation. He or she would have to experience them and integrate them to reach "higher sanity" and a new level of consciousness. Observations from experiential work strongly suggest that the success of this process depends critically on consistent internalization of the experiences involved and their completion on the inner plane. If this condition is not met and the individual begins to act out, confusing the inner process with external reality, he or she faces grave dangers. Instead of being confronted and integrated internally, the instinctual impulses lead to destructive and self-destructive actions. The critical turning point in the process of inner transformation is ego death and the conceptual destruction of the individual's old world. The extreme end result of the exteriorization of the death-rebirth process and an acting out of its archetypal themes can bring suicide, murder, and destruction. In contrast, the internalized approach leads to ego death and transcendence, which involves a philosophical destruction of the old world view and an emergence of a saner and more enlightened way of being.

Individuals involved in systematic in-depth self-exploration frequently develop, quite independently from each other, convincing insights that humanity at large is facing these days a serious dilemma fully comparable to that described for the process of individual transformation. The alternatives involved seem to be continuation of the present trend toward exteriorization, acting out, and external manipulation of the world, or turning within and undergoing a process of radical transformation to an entirely new level of consciousness and awareness. While the easily predictable end result of the former strategy is death in an atomic war or in technological waste products, the latter alternative could result in evolutionary perspectives described in the writings of Sri Aurobindo, Teilhard de Chardin, Ken Wilber, and many others.

It seems appropriate to review from this standpoint the characteristic changes that tend to occur in individuals who have successfully completed such a transformative process and integrated the material from the perinatal level of the unconscious. This will provide a more concrete basis for the discussion of whether the resulting human type and the corresponding level of consciousness offer a promising and hopeful alternative to the present situation.

Numerous observations suggest that an individual who is under a strong influence of the negative perinatal matrices approaches life and its problems in a way that is not only unfulfilling, but in its long-term consequences destructive and self-destructive. We have discussed earlier the "treadmill" and "rat-race" type of existence and life strategy that characterizes to various degrees those individuals who have not confronted experientially the issue of death or completed the gestalt of birth.

The dynamics of negative perinatal matrices imposes on life a linear trajectory and creates a strong and unrelenting drive toward the pursuit of future goals. Since the psyche of such a person is dominated by the memory of the painful confinement in the birth canal, he or she never experiences the present moment and circumstances as fully satisfying. Like the fetus who is trying to escape from the uncomfortable constriction into a more acceptable situation, such a person will always strive for something other than what the present circumstances offer. The goals the mind will construct in this circumstance can easily be identified as substitutes for biological birth and postnatal care. Since these goals are mere psychological surrogates and unreal mirages, their achievement can never bring true satisfaction. The resulting frustration will then generate new plans or more ambitious ones of the same kind. In this frame of mind, nature and the world are seen in general as a potential threat and something that must be conquered and controled.

On the collective and global scale, this frame of mind generates a philosophy of life that emphasizes strength, competition, and self-assertion and glorifies linear progress and unlimited growth. It considers material profit and an increase of the gross national product to be the main criteria of well-being and measures of one's living standard. This ideology and the resulting strategies bring humans into a serious conflict with their nature as biological systems and with basic universal laws. Although biological organisms in general depend critically on optimal values, this strategy introduces the artificial and dangerous imperative of maximizing pursuits.[3] In a universe the very nature of which is cyclical, it advocates and recommends linearity and unlimited growth. A further complication is that this approach to existence cannot recognize and acknowledge the urgent and absolutely vital need for synergy, complementarity, cooperation, and ecological concerns.

The individual who has completed the perinatal process and connected experientially with the memories of the positive intra-uterine state (and to positive transpersonal matrices) presents a very different picture. The experience with the maternal organism on the fetal level is equivalent to the experience of the adult in relation to the entire world and all of humanity. The former in a sense represents a prototypical model and template for the latter. The nature and quality of the perinatal matrix that influences the psyche of the individual will thus have a very profound influence not only on the subjective experience of this person, but also on his or her attitude and approach to other people, to nature, and to existence in general.

When one experiences the shift from negative to positive perinatal matrices, the general degree of zest in life and the ability to enjoy life increases considerably. It becomes possible to draw satisfaction from the present moment and from many ordinary situations and functions, such as eating, sex, simple human inter-actions, work activities, art, music, play, or walks in nature. This reduces considerably the emotional investment in the pursuit of various complicated schemes from which satisfaction is expected in the future and which fail to bring it whether or not the goals are attained. In this state of mind, it becomes obvious that the ultimate measure of one's standard of living is the quality of the experience of life and not the quantity of achievements and material possessions.

Together with these changes, the individual develops a deep sense of the critical importance of synergy, cooperation, and harmony, as well as natural ecological concerns. The attitude toward nature ("Mother Nature") described earlier was modeled after the precarious and conflictful experience of the fetus with the maternal organism in the process of biological delivery. The new values and attitudes reflect the experience of the fetus with the womb during prenatal existence. Mutually nourishing, symbiotic, and complementary aspects of this situation (in the case of a predominantly good womb) tend to replace quite automatically the competitive and exploitative emphasis of the old value system. The concept of human existence as a life-and-death struggle for survival gives way to a new image of life as a manifestation of the cosmic dance or divine play.

It becomes quite clear that ultimately we cannot do anything to other people and nature without simultaneously doing it to ourselves. Any attempt to divide the unity of existence philosophically, ideologically, sociopolitically, and spiritually into independent separate units with conflicting interests—individuals, families, religious and social groups, political parties, commercial alliances, and nations—if taken seriously as ultimate reality, appears as superficial, short-sighted, and in the last analysis self-defeating. From this new point of view, it is hard to imagine, how anybody could be blind to the suicidal perspectives of an increasing dependence on the fast vanishing fossil fuels and would not see as absolutely critical the task of reorienting the world toward cyclical and renewable sources of energy.

As a result of these changes, the consumer strategy naturally shifts from conspicuous consumption and a waste-making psychology toward conservation and "voluntary simplicity," in Duane Elgin's sense (1981). It becomes obvious that the only hope for a political and social solution can come from a transpersonal perspective that transcends the hopeless "us versus them" psychology, producing at best occasional pendulumlike changes in which the protagonists exchange their roles of oppressors and oppressed.

The only genuine solution must acknowledge the collective nature of the problem and offer satisfactory perspectives to everybody involved. The deeply felt unity with the rest of the world tends to open the way to a genuine appreciation of diversity and a tolerance of differences. Sexual, racial, cultural, and other prejudices appear absurd and childish in light of the vastly expanded world view and understanding of reality that includes the transcendental dimension.

Having researched the potential of unusual states of consciousness for more than a quarter of a century, I have no doubts that the transformation I have here described can be achieved on an individual scale. I myself have witnessed over the years many dramatic examples of such an evolution while assisting other people in psychedelic therapy and experiential self-exploration without the use of drugs, particularly holotropic therapy. It remains to be seen to what extent the same approach is applicable on a larger scale. Certainly the increasing popularity of various forms of meditation and other spiritual practices, as well as various experiential forms of psychotherapy, represents an encouraging trend.

Whatever questions one may have about the feasibility of this strategy as a world-changing force, it could well be our only real chance under present circumstances. The currently available means and channels for solving the global crisis do not leave a critical observer with much hope. In practical terms the new approach means to complement whatever one is doing in the external world with a systematic process of in-depth self-exploration. In this way the pragmatic technical knowledge of each of us can be complemented and guided by the wisdom of the collective unconscious.

Inner transformation can be achieved only through individual determination, focused effort, and personal responsibility. Any plans to change the situation in the world are of problematic value, unless they include a systematic effort to change the human condition that has created the crisis. To the extent to which evolutionary change in consciousness is a vital prerequisite for the future of the world, the outcome of this process depends on the initiative of each of us.

I have written this book with the hope that the concepts, techniques, and strategies that it describes could be of value to those involved in the transformation process or those interested in pursuing this route. It is an expression of my deep belief and trust in the evolutionary process in which we are all involved.

Notes

Notes to Chapter One

1. In his later work, Thomas Kuhn has begun differentiating more specific constituents and elements of what he originally referred to by the global term *paradigm*. He thus distinguished, for example, *symbolic generalizations* (the practice of expressing certain fixed relations in succinct equations, such as $f=ma$, $I=V/R$, or $E=mc^2$); *beliefs in particular models* (planetary model of the atom, particle or wave model of light, model of gas as tiny billiard balls of matter in random motion, etc.); *sharing of values* (importance of prediction, testability, replicability, logical consistence, plausibility, visualizability, or acceptable margin of error); and *exemplars* (examples of concrete problem solutions in which agreed-upon principles are applied to various areas).

2. Examples of these are the basic axioms of Euclid's geometry (only one straight line connects two points; two parallel lines never meet), Newton's postulate of the indestructibility of matter or his laws of motion, and Einstein's principles of constancy, or relativity.

3. According to Frank, the goal of science is to set up a system of relations between symbols and operational definitions of these symbols in such a way that the logical conclusions drawn from these

statements become statements about observable facts that are confirmed by actual observations of the senses.

4. The following discussion of the Newtonian-Cartesian paradigm follows to some extent the formulations of Fritjof Capra in his books, *The Tao of Physics* (1975) and *The Turning Point* (1982). I gratefully acknowledge the influence he has had on my thinking on this subject.

5. The Greek name *atomos* is derived from the verb *temnein*, meaning "to cut"; with the negating prefix *a-*, it means "indivisible"—that which cannot be cut any further.

6. This concept was expressed in the most succinct form by "vulgar materialists." They refused to accept consciousness as being in any way different from other physiological functions and maintained that the brain produces consciousness in much the same way the kidneys produce urine.

7. A similar point of view was recently expressed by R. D. Laing, in his articulate and well-documented book, *The Voice of Experience* (1982).

8. A good example of this experience is the vision of Charlotte analyzed in my book, *Realms of the Human Unconscious: Observations from LSD Research* (1975, pp. 227 ff).

9. A detailed description of the various types of psychedelic experience, with clinical examples, can be found in my book, *Realms of the Human Unconscious* (1975). A condensed version of this material constitutes chapter 2 of the present book.

10. The term *perinatal* is a Greek-Latin composite word; the prefix *peri-* means literally "around" or "near," and *natalis* translates as "pertaining to delivery." It suggests events that immediately precede, are associated with, or follow biological birth.

11. Occasional experiences of historical progression, precognition flashes, or complex clairvoyant visions of the future present a special problem in this context.

12. Examples of these are Fritjof Capra's *The Tao of Physics* (1975) and *The Turning Point* (1982); Lawrence LeShan's *The Medium, the Mystic, and the Physicist* (1974); Arthur Young's *The Reflexive Universe* (1976b) and *Geometry of Meaning* (1976a); Gary Zukav's *The Dancing Wu-Li Masters* (1979); Nick Herbert's *Mind Science: A Physics of Consciousness Primer* (1979); Fred Wolf's *Taking A Quantum Leap* (1981); and Itzak Bentov's *Stalking the Wild Pendulum* (1977). There are many others.

13. This concept of the dynamic vacuum shows a striking similarity to the concept of the metacosmic and supracosmic void found in many systems of perennial philosophy.

14.   Most important aspects of this criticism of mechanistic science can be found in Gregory Bateson's *Steps to an Ecology of Mind* (1972) and *Mind and Nature: A Necessary Unity* (1979).

15.   This conceptual conflict between mechanistic science and modern revolutionary developments represents a replica of the ancient conflict among the major schools of Greek philosophy. The Ionian school in Miletos—Thales, Anaximenes, Anaximander and others—considered the basic philosophical question to be: "What is the world made of?" "What is its basic substance?" In contrast, Plato and Pythagoras believed that the critical issue was the world's form, patterning, and order. Modern science is distinctly neo-Platonic and neo-Pythagorean.

16.   "Dissipative structures" derive their name from the fact that they maintain continuous entropy production and dissipate the accruing entropy by exchange with the environment. The most famous example is the so-called Belousov-Zhabotinski reaction, which involves oxidation of malonic acid by bromate in a sulphuric acid solution in the presence of cerium, iron, or manganese ions.

17.   Erich Jantsch's books, *Design For Evolution* (1975) and *The Self-Organizing Universe* (1980), can serve as unique sources of further information about the developments discussed above.

18.   The most famous example is the anecdotal observation reported by Lyall Watson, in *Lifetide* (1980), and referred to as the "hundredth monkey phenomenon." When a young female Japanese monkey (Macaca fuscata), on the island of Koshima, learned an entirely new behavior—washing raw sweet potatoes covered with sand and grit—this behavior was not only transmitted to her immediate peers, but appeared in monkeys on neighboring islands when the number of monkeys who had learned the trick reached a certain critical number.

19.   In recent years, physics has been rapidly approaching the point at which it will have to deal explicitly with consciousness. There are prominent physicists who believe that a future comprehensive theory of matter will have to incorporate consciousness as an integral and crucial constituent. Different versions of this view have been expressed by Eugene Wigner (1967), David Bohm (1980), Geoffrey Chew (1968), Fritjof Capra (1982), Arthur Young (1976b), Saul-Paul Sirag, and Nick Herbert (1979).

20.   The clinical data on which this assumption was based and the logical errors involved in their interpretation have been discussed (p. 00).

21.   The sages of the Hwa Yen tradition (Japanese Kegon and Sanskrit Avatamsaka), see the whole embracing all universes as a single living organism of mutually interdependent and interpenetrating processes

of becoming and un-becoming. Hwa Yen expresses this situation by the formula: "ONE IN ALL; ALL IN ONE; ONE IN ONE; ALL IN ALL."

22. This means that exploring the holographic image from different angles unfolds and reveals aspects previously hidden; this is not the case in conventional photography or cinematography, where inspection from additional angles simply distorts the image.

23. David Bohm's theories have been described in a number of articles in professional journals and in his book, *Wholeness and the Implicate Order* (1980).

24. The interested reader will find a popular explanation of these new avenues of brain research in Paul Pietsch, *Shufflebrain: The Quest for the Hologramic Mind* (1981).

25. A recent attempt of the Soviet scientist V. V. Nalimov to formulate a theory of the unconscious based on semantics and probability theory is of particular interest here. He explored this idea in *Realms of the Unconscious: The Enchanted Frontier* (1982).

Notes to Chapter Two

1. An important task of the therapist in traditional forms of psychotherapy is to distinguish the relevant material from the irrelevant, detect psychological defenses, and provide interpretations. The crux of such an endeavor is that it is paradigm bound. What is relevant is not a matter of general agreement; it depends on whether one is Freudian, Adlerian, Rankian, Kleinian, Sullivanian or an exponent of yet other schools of dynamic psychotherapy. When we add to this the distortion produced by countertransference, the advantage of experiential approaches becomes immediately obvious.

2. For the etymology of the word *perinatal*, see note 10, chapter 1.

3. Ego death and rebirth is not a one-time experience. During systematic deep self-exploration, the unconscious presents it repeatedly with varying dimensions and emphasis until the process is completed.

4. This description reflects the ideal situation of a normal and uncomplicated birth. A prolonged and debilitating course of delivery, the use of forceps or general anesthesia, and other complications would introduce specific experiential distortions into this matrix.

5. In the symbiotic state of union with the maternal organism, there is no dichotomy between subject and object as long as there is no

interference. Disturbances of the intrauterine state or the pain and distress of birth seem to create the first distinction between "the suffering me" and "the hurtful other."

Notes to Chapter Three

1. Many ideas discussed in this chapter were part of a background paper written for Fritjof Capra at the time when we were jointly exploring the relationships between psychology and modern physics. This explains a certain conceptual overlap with two chapters of his book, *The Turning Point* (1982).
2. The genetic proposition of psychoanalysis refers to psychogenesis and should not be confused with heredity. It deals with developmental logic, showing how past events have determined the history of the individual and how the past is contained in the present.
3. Defense mechanisms emerge as a result of the struggle between the pressures of the id and the demands of external reality. They show specific association with the individual phases of libidinal development and have a fundamental relationship to the etiology of various kinds of psychopathology. The most important defense mechanisms found in psychoanalytic literature are repression, displacement, reaction formation, isolation, undoing, rationalization, intellectualization, denial, regression, counterphobic mechanisms, withdrawal and avoidance, introjection, identification, acting out, sublimation, and creative elaboration. The best source of further information on defense mechanisms is Anna Freud's pioneering book on the subject, *The Ego and the Mechanisms of Defense* (1937).
4. Jay Haley presented a brilliant and humorous analysis of this frustrating situation in his paper, "The Art of Psychoanalysis" (1958).
5. According to Sullivan's description, the "good nipple" gives milk and also a sense of comfort and security. An "evil nipple" provides nourishment, but in an unsatisfactory emotional context, as in the case with an anxious, tense, or unloving mother. A "wrong nipple," such as the infant's own thumb, feels like a nipple, but fails to provide nourishment or security.
6. Freud's biographer, Ernest Jones (1961), gives a fascinating description of Freud's reaction to Rank's publication of *The Trauma of Birth* (1929). According to Jones, Freud experienced a deep emotional shock on reading the book. He was deeply concerned that Rank's discoveries might overshadow his own contributions to

psychology. In spite of this, his approach to the matter was initially very fair; he referred to Rank's ideas as "the most important progress since the discovery of psychoanalysis," and suggested that they should be given proper scientific attention. It was not Freud's scientific disagreement but his deep political concerns that prompted him to excommunicate Rank. They were triggered by disquieting letters from Berlin warning Freud that Rank's heretical views would cause an incurable schism in the psychoanalytic movement.

7. It deserves special notice in this connection that Jean Paul Satre's philosophy and literary work were deeply influenced by a poorly resolved mescaline session that was dominated by elements of BPM II. This matter has been explored in detail in a special paper by Thomas Riedlinger (1982).

8. It was Einstein who during a personal meeting encouraged Jung to pursue the concept of synchronicity (1973b). Particularly close was Jung's friendship with Wolfgang Pauli, one of the founders of the quantum theory, which found its expression in a joint publication of Jung's essay on synchronicity and Pauli's study of the archetypes in the work of Johannes Kepler (Pauli 1955).

Notes to Chapter Four

1. It should be clear from the context that we are limiting our discussion to problems caused by psychological factors and are excluding conditions that have an obvious organic cause, such as total exhaustion by a severe physical disease, paraplegia, or serious chemical dysfunction of the autonomic nervous system.

2. The Latin saying, *Inter feces and urinas nascimur* ("We are born among feces and urine") is thus not a philosopohical metaphor, but a realistic description of a typical human delivery, unless specific provisions are made to modify it.

3. Regular observations of reliving the pain associated with the cutting of the umbilical cord contradict the medical claims that this procedure cannot be painful since the umbilical cord has no nerves. Careful study of newborns during the cutting of the cord clearly reveals the presence of behavioral reaction to pain.

4. This was, according to the CIA reports quoted in the book, the sexual preference of Adolf Hitler. A dictator aspiring to become the absolute ruler of the entire world wanted in his private sexual life to be bound, tortured, humiliated, and defecated on.

5.   The use of all these ingredients makes good sense from the point
      of view of modern psychopharmacology. The plants from the night-
      shade family contain powerful psychoactive alkaloids *atropine, sco-
      polamine,* and *hyoscyamine,* while the toad skin is the source of the
      psychedelic *dimethylserotonin* or *bufotenin.*

6.   Strong, irrational, and incomprehensible feelings of guilt can be
      absolutely unbearable and actually drive the individual to commit
      crime. The ability to link this guilt to a concrete situation usually
      brings a certain degree of relief. This condition, in which guilt
      precedes and actually generates crime, is known in psychiatry as
      pseudodelinquency. A typical criminal usually does not suffer from
      guilt and his conflict is with society and justice, not of an intrapsychic
      nature.

7.   Jane English (1982), who has been systematically studying the im-
      plications of elective Caesarean birth, describes some additional
      characteristics, such as bonding with the obstetrician and subsequent
      specific distortions of relationships with persons of the same sex,
      different body tension patterns, defensiveness in relation to physical
      approach, and others.

8.   The new technique of underwater birth introduced by the Soviet
      physician, Igor Charkovsky, of Moscow's Scientific Research Insti-
      tute, deserves special attention in this context.

9.   The anatomical structure of the uterus involves a very complex
      arrangement of muscular fibers combining longitudinal, circular,
      and spiral elements. The uterine arteries have a winding course
      woven into this complex muscular fabric. As a result, every con-
      traction compresses the vessels and interrupts internally the contact
      between the mother and the child mediated by the placental blood
      supply.

10.   A former colleague of mine who committed suicide can be men-
      tioned here as an example. He was a prominent university professor
      specializing in psychiatry and toxicology. In one of his attacks of
      periodic depression, he killed himself at the institute where he
      worked, opening his throat wide by several deep cuts of a razor
      blade. If he had just wanted to end his life, he knew of many
      poisons that would have served the purpose in a clean, elegant,
      and painless way. Yet, something in him drove him to choose a
      drastic and bloody way to do it.

11.   According to popular lore and the descriptions of persons who
      have been rescued from death in snow and ice, the initial period
      of agonizing cold and freezing is followed by an experience of
      soothing warmth, pleasant melting, and a condition that resembles
      sleep or a stay in a nourishing womb.

12. The origins of this phenomenon are not altogether clear. There seems to be some connection to the birth practices of certain ethnic groups in which women deliver in a standing position, or to phylogenetic memories of the delivery of some mammalian species in which birth actually involves a fall.

13. For a most interesting discussion of the relationship between shamanism and psychosis, see the paper by Julian Silverman, "Shamans and Acute Schizophrenia" (1967). The shamanic state of consciousness and shamanic techniques have been explored from a modern point of view in Michael Harner's excellent book, *The Way of the Shaman* (1980) and in Mircea Eliade's classic study, *Shamanism: The Archaic Techniques of Ecstasy* (1964).

14. It seems appropriate here to mention a scholarly and well-documented book by Wasson, Hofmann and Ruck, *The Road to Eleusis* (1978). The authors bring strong evidence that an ergot preparation with ingredients chemically close to LSD-25 was used as a sacrament in the death-rebirth mysteries in Eleusis for almost 2000 years.

15. Observations from the practice of holotropic therapy (described on pp. 387–9) are relevant from this point of view. It does not require a powerful psychoactive drug like LSD to confront experientially the perinatal or transpersonal levels of the psyche. A supportive environment, faster breathing, and evocative music will in a matter of minutes induce in a group of randomly selected individuals unusual experiences that would be traditionally labeled as psychotic. Yet, this phenomenon is short-term, fully reversible, and conducive to psychosomatic healing and personality growth.

Notes to Chapter Five

1. The term *disease,* or *nosological unit* (from the Greek *nosos,* "disease"), has a very specific meaning in medicine. It implies a disorder that has a specific cause, or etiology, from which one should be able to derive its pathogenesis, or the development of symptoms. An understanding of the disorder in these terms should lead one to specific therapeutic strategies and measures, and to prognostic conclusions.

2. The principle of the intensification of symptoms is essential for psychedelic therapy, holonomic integration, and Gestalt practice. The same emphasis also governs the practice of homeopathic med-

icine and can be found in Victor Frankl's technique of paradoxical intention.

3. *Lobotomy* is a psychosurgical procedure that in its crudest form involves severing the connections between the frontal lobe and the rest of the brain. This technique, for which the Portuguese surgeon Egas Moniz received the 1949 Nobel prize, was initially used widely in schizophrenics and severe obsessive-compulsive neurotics. Later, it was abandoned and replaced by more subtle microsurgical interventions. The significance of irrational motifs for psychiatry can be illustrated by the fact that some of the psychiatrists who did not hesitate to recommend this operation for their patients later resisted the use of LSD on the premise that it might cause brain damage not detectable by present methods.

4. A detailed discussion of the problems related to psychiatric diagnosis, definition of normalcy, classification, assessment of therapeutic results, and related issues is not possible here. The interested reader will find more relevant information in the works of Donald Light (1980), Thomas Scheff (1974), R. L. Spitzer and P. T. Wilson (1975), Thomas Szasz (1961), and others.

Notes to Chapter Six

1. *Hylotropic* (derived from the Greek *hylé*, "matter" and *trepein*, "to move toward") means matter-oriented.

2. *Holotropic* (derived from the Greek *holos*, "whole" and *trepein*, "to move toward") means aiming for wholeness or totality.

3. In a personal discussion about the application of the holonomic theory to psychopathology, Karl Pribram offered a very interesting simile. He pointed to the fact that neither the solid shore nor the waves in the open ocean present any problem or danger and can be easily handled by a human being. It is the interface between the sea and the solid ground, the water line where these two modes conflict with each other, that is the site of dangerous turmoil.

4. *Anaclitic needs* (from the Greek *anaklinein*, "to lean upon") are primitive needs of an infantile nature, such as the needs for being held, rocked, cuddled, and fed.

5. For a detailed discussion of the influence of COEX systems, basic perinatal matrices, and transpersonal governing systems, see Grof, *LSD Psychotherapy* (1980, pp. 218–227).

6.   A dramatic clinical illustration of this phenomenon appears in my book, *LSD Psychotherapy* (1980, p. 219).

7.   Experiences involving perinatal elements have a therapeutic power and potential that is beyond comprehension for psychotherapists used to never-ending and tedious analytical work within the biographical realm. The therapeutic and transformative impact of near-death experiences and experiences of psychological death is illustrated by David Rosen's study (1975) of ten survivors of suicidal jumps off the Golden Gate and Oakland Bay Bridges, in San Francisco. All of them showed signs of a profound personality transformation, although the fall from the railing to the surface of the water lasted only three seconds of clock time, and the successful rescue operations took a matter of minutes. Similar changes can often be observed in survivors of serious diseases, accidents, and operations. I mention these extreme examples to illustrate the extraordinary transformative potential of certain powerful experiences. Utilization of these healing mechanisms in a safe and supportive set and setting offers new, revolutionary possibilities for psychotherapy.

8.   Fritjof Capra, in a lecture on holistic medicine and modern physics, once used a poignant example from everyday life to illustrate the absurdity of the symptomatic orientation in therapy. He asked the audience to imagine a driver who responded to the red light on the dashboard of his car, indicating a critical oil shortage, by disconnecting the cables leading to the warning signal system. Satisfied that he had adequately handled the problem, he would then continue driving his car.

9.   Parallels to this situation in physical medicine would be suppressing vomiting that would free the stomach from its toxic content, interfering with the process of inflammation that is trying to eliminate a foreign body, or prescribing sedatives for sexual tension instead of endorsing sexual activity.

Notes to Chapter Seven

1.   The reader interested in the therapeutic use of psychedelics can find more information in my books *Realms of the Human Unconscious* (1975), *The Human Encounter with Death* (1977), and *LSD Psychotherapy* (1980).

2.   Richard Tarnas' forthcoming book available at present only in
      mimeographed form is a unique source of information about the
      understanding of transit astrology I am talking about. An excellent
      basic handbook on transit astrology is Robert Hand's *Planets in
      Transit* (1976).

Notes to Chapter Eight

1.   Psychohistory is a new social science that studies historical moti-
      vation. It applies the method of depth-psychological analysis to
      historical events with special emphasis on child-rearing practices of
      various periods and the childhood dynamics of important historical
      figures.
2.   The most fascinating and promising explanatory system for the
      dynamics of historical events of large scope is, in my opinion, transit
      astrology, based on archetypal symbolism. A demonstration of its
      power and relentless logic would by far transcend the scope of this
      book. A scholarly and extremely well-documented discussion of this
      approach can be found in the manuscript by Richard Tarnas men-
      tioned in note 2, chapter 7.
3.   If maximum rather than optimum body size were the goal and
      ideal of evolution, the dinosaurs would still be around today and
      would represent the dominant species; there is a most interesting
      discussion of this topic in the fable about the "polyploid horse,"
      in Gregory Bateson's *Mind and Nature* (1979). Higher and lower
      blood pressure or temperature, increase and decrease in the number
      of blood cells, deficit and surplus of hormones—all these extremes
      in both directions are associated with specific problems. Similarly,
      more food, water, vitamins, and minerals are not necessarily better
      for the organism than a lesser supply of these items; for all of
      them there are certain optimal values.

Bibliography

Adler, A. 1932. *The Practice and Theory of Individual Psychology.* New York: Harcourt, Brace & Co.

Alexander, F. 1931. "Buddhist Training as Artificial Catatonia." *Psychoanalyt. Rev.* 18: 129.

Ardrey, R 1961. *African Genesis.* New York: Atheneum.

Ardrey, R. 1966. *The Territorial Imperative.* New York: Atheneum.

Assagioli, R. 1976. *Psychosynthesis.* New York: Penguin Books.

———. 1977. "Self-Realization and Psychological Disturbances." *Synthesis* 3–4.

Bache, C.M. n.d. "A Reappraisal of Teresa of Avila's Hysteria from the Perspective of LSD Psychotherapy." Mimeographed.

———. n.d. "On the Emergence of Perinatal Symptoms in Buddhist Meditation." Mimeographed.

Bastians, A. n.d. "Man in the Concentration Camp and the Concentration Camp in Man." Mimeographed.

Bateson, G. 1972. *Steps to An Ecology of Mind.* San Francisco: Chandler Publ.

———. 1979. *Mind and Nature: A Necessary Unity.* New York: E.P. Dutton.

Bell, J.S. 1966. "On the Problem of Hidden Variables in Quantum Physics." *Review of Modern Physics* 38:447.

Bentov, I. 1977. *Stalking the Wild Pendulum.* New York: E.P. Dutton.

Bentov, I. and Bentov, M. 1982. *A Cosmic Book: On the Mechanics of Creation.* New York: E.P. Dutton.

Bindrim, P. 1969. "Peak-Oriented Psychotherapy." Paper presented at the Annual Convention of the American Psychological Association, Washington, D.C., September 2.

————. n.d. Aqua-Energetics. Mimeographed.

Blanck, G. and Blanck, R. 1965. *Ego Psychology: Theory and Practice.* New York: Columbia University Press.

Bohm, D. 1980. *Wholeness and the Implicate Order.* London: Routledge & Kegan Paul.

Bohr., N. 1934. *Atomic Physics and the Description of Nature.* Cambridge: Cambridge University Press.

————. 1958. *Atomic Physics and Human Knowledge.* New York: John Wiley & Sons.

Boisen, A.T. 1936. *The Exploration of the Inner World.* New York: Harper.

Bonaparte, M. 1934. *Edgar Poe: Eine psychoanalytische Studie.* Vienna: Internationaler Psychoanalytischer Verlag.

Bonny, H., and Savary, L.M. 1973. *Music and Your Mind.* New York: Harper & Row.

Brun,A. 1953. "Ueber Freuds Hypothese vom Todestrieb." *Psyche* 17:81.

Capra, F. 1975. *The Tao of Physics.* Berkeley: Shambhala Publ.

Capra, F. 1982. *The Turning Point.* New York: Simon & Schuster.

Carpenter, W.T., et al. 1977. "The Treatment of Acute Schizophrenia without Drugs: An Investigation of Some Current Assumptions." *Amer. J. Psychiat.* 134:14.

Chew, G. 1968. "Bootstrap: A Scientific Idea?" *Science* 161: 762.

Croissant, J. 1932. *Aristôte et les mystères.* Liege: Faculté de Philosophie et Lettres.

Dabrowski, K. 1964. *Positive Disintegration.* Boston: Little, Brown.

Darwin, C. 1859. *Origin of Species.* London: John Murray.

Elgin, D. 1981. *Voluntary Simplicity.* New York: William Morrow & Co.

————. n.d. "The First Miracle and the Fifth Dimension: Exploring the Holodynamic View of Reality." Mimeographed.

Eliade, M. 1964. *Shamanism: Archaic Techniques of Ecstasy.* Bollingen Series, vol. 76. New York: Pantheon Books.

Eliot, C. 1969. *Japanese Buddhism.* New York: Barnes & Noble.

English, J. 1982. "Caesarean Birth and Psychotherapy." *Newsletter of the Association for Transpersonal Psychology (fall),* p. 5.

Eysenck, H.J., and Rachman, S. 1965. *The Causes and Cures of Neurosis.* San Diego: R.R. Knapp.

Feher, E. 1980. *The Psychology of Birth.* London: Souvenir Press.

Feldenkrais, M. 1972. *Awareness Through Movement.* New York: Harper & Row.

Fenichel, O. 1945. *The Psychoanalytic Theory of Neurosis.* New York: W. W. Norton.

Ferenczi, S. 1938. *Thalassa.* New York: Psychoanalytic Q., Inc.

Feyerabend, P. 1978. *Against Method: Outline of an Anarchistic Theory of Knowledge.* London: Verso Press.

Fodor, N. 1949. *The Search for the Beloved: A Clinical Investigation of the Trauma of Birth and Prenatal Condition.* New Hyde Park, N.Y.: University Books.

———. 1971. *Freud, Jung and Occultism.* New Hyde Park, N.Y.: University Books.

Franck, F. 1976. *Book of Angelus Silesius.* New York: Random House.

Frank, P. 1974. *Philosophy of Science: The Link Between Science and Philosophy.* Westport, Conn.: Greenwood Press.

Frankl, V.E. 1956. *Theorie und Therapie der Neurosen: Einfuehrung in Logotherapie und Existenzanalyse.* Vienna: Urban & Schwarzenberg.

———. 1962. *Man's Search for Meaning: An Introduction to Logotherapy.* Boston: Beacon Press.

Franz, M.-L. von. 1974. *Number and Time: Reflections Leading toward a Unification of Depth Psychology and Physics.* Evanston: Northwestern University Press.

———. 1980. *Projection and Recollection in Jungian Psychology: Reflections of the Soul.* LaSalle, Ill.: Open Court.

Freud, A. 1937. *The Ego and the Mechanisms of Defense.* London: Hogarth Press.

Freud, S. 1924. "Obsessive Acts and Religious Practices." *Collected Papers* vol. 6, Institute of Psychoanalysis. London: The Hogarth Press and the Institute of Psychoanalysis, 1952.

———. 1953a. *Three Essays on the Theory of Sexuality.* Standard Edition, vol. 7. London: The Hogarth Press.

———. 1953b. *The Interpretation of Dreams.* Standard Edition, vols. 4 and 5. London: The Hogarth Press.

———. 1955a. *Introduction to Psychoanalysis and the War Neuroses.* Standard Edition, vol. 17. London: The Hogarth Press.

———. 1955b. *Group Psychology and the Analysis of the Ego.* Standard Edition, vol. 18. London: The Hogarth Press.

———. 1961. *Civilization and Its Discontents.* Standard Edition, vol. 21. London: The Hogarth Press.

———. 1964. *An Outline of Psychoanalysis.* Standard Edition, vol. 23. London: The Hogarth Press.

Freud, S., and Breuer, J. 1936. *Studies on Hysteria.* New York: Nervous and Mental Diseases Publ. Co.

Fromm, E. 1962. *Beyond the Chains of Illusion.* London: ABACUS.

————. 1973. *Anatomy of Human Destructiveness*. New York: Holt, Rinehart & Winson.

Godfrey, K.D., and Voth, H.M. 1971. "LSD As an Adjunct to Psychoanalytically Oriented Psychotherapy." *Ztschr. dynam. Psychiat.* (Journal of Dynamic Psychiatry) Berlin: Sonderheft (special issue).

Gordon, R. 1978. *Your Healing Hands: The Polarity Experience*. Santa Cruz, Cal.: Unity Press.

Gormsen, K., and Lumbye, J. 1979. "A Comparative Study of Stanislav Grof's and L. Ron Hubbard's Models of Consciousness." Presented at the Fifth International Transpersonal Conference, Boston, Mass., November, 1979.

Grof, S. 1966. Tentative Theoretical Framework for Understanding Dynamics of LSD Psychotherapy. Preprint for the European Conference on LSD Psychotherapy, Amsterdam, Holland.

————. 1970. Beyond Psychoanalysis 1. Implications of LSD Research for Understanding Dimensions of Human Personality. *Darshana International* 10: 55.

————. 1975. *Realms of the Human Unconscious: Observations from LSD Research*. New York: Viking Press.

————. 1980. *LSD Psychotherapy*. Pomona, Cal.: Hunter House.

Grof, S., and Grof, C. 1980. *Beyond Death*. London: Thames & Hudson.

Grof, S., and Halifax, J. 1977. *The Human Encounter with Death*. New York: E.P. Dutton.

Group for the Advancement of Psychiatry, Committee on Psychiatry and Religion. 1976. "Mysticism: Spiritual Quest or Psychic Disorder?" Washington, D.C.

Haley, J. 1958. "The Art of Psychoanalysis." *ETC*.

Hand, R. 1976. *Planets in Transit: Life Cycles for Living*. Gloucester, Mass.: Para Research.

Harner, M. 1980. *The Way of the Shaman: A Guide to Power and Healing*. New York: Harper & Row.

Hastings, A. 1978. "The Oakland Poltergeist." *J. Amer. Soc. for Psychic Res.* 72:233.

Heidegger, M. 1927. *Sein und Zeit*. Halle, East Germany: Max Niemager.

Heisenberg, W. 1971. *Physics and Beyond: Encounters and Conversations*. New York: Harper & Row.

Herbert, N. 1979. *Mind Science: A Physics of Consciousness Primer*. Boulder Creek, Cal.: C-Life Institute.

Hubbard, L.R. 1950. *Dianetics: The Modern Science of Mental Health*. East Grinstead, Sussex, England: Hubbard College of Scientology.

Jammer, M. 1974. *The Philosophy of Quantum Mechanics: The Interpretation of Quantum Mechanics in Historical Perspective*. New York: J. Wiley & Sons.

Janov, A. 1970. *The Primal Scream: Primal Therapy—The Cure for Neurosis.* New York: G.P. Putnam's Sons.

——. 1972a. *The Primal Revolution: Toward A Real World.* New York: Simon & Schuster.

——. 1972b. *The Anatomy of Mental Illness.* New York: G.P. Putnam's Sons.

Jantsch, E. 1975. *Design for Evolution: Self-Organization and Planning in the Life of Human Systems.* New York: Braziller.

——. 1980. *The Self-Organizing Universe.* New York: Pergamon Press.

Janus, S., Bess, B., and Saltus, C. 1977. *A Sexual Profile of Men in Power.* Englewood Cliffs, N.J.: Prentice-Hall.

Jeans, J. 1930. *The Mysterious Universe.* New York: Macmillan.

Jones, E. 1961. *The Life and Work of Sigmund Freud.* Garden City, N.Y.: Doubleday.

Jung, C.G. 1956. *Symbols of Transformation.* Collected Works, vol. 5, Bollingen Series XX, Princeton: Princeton University Press.

——. 1960a. *On the Nature of the Psyche.* Collected Works, vol. 8, Bollingen Series XX. Princeton: Princeton University Press.

——. 1960b. *Synchronicity: An Acausal Connecting Principle.* Collected Works, vol. 8, Bollingen Series XX. Princeton: Princeton University Press.

——. 1961. *Memories, Dreams, Reflections.* New York: Pantheon Books.

——. 1973a. *Experimental Researches.* Collected Works, vol. 2, Bollingen Series XX. Princeton: Princeton University Press.

——. 1973b. Letter to Carl Seeling, February 25, 1953. *C.G. Jung's Letters,* vol. 2, Bollingen Series XCV. Princeton: Princeton University Press.

Kalff, D. 1971. *Sandplay: Mirror of a Child's Psyche.* San Francisco: Hendra & Howard.

Ka-Tzetnik 135633 1955. *The House of Dolls.* New York: Pyramid Books.

——. 1977. *Sunrise over Hell.* London: W.A. Allen.

Kellogg, J. 1977. "The Use of the Mandala in Psychological Evaluation and Treatment." *Amer. J. of Art Therapy* 16:123.

——. 1978. *Mandala: The Path of Beauty.* Baltimore: Mandala Assessment & Research Institute.

Keynes, J.M. 1951. "Newton the Man." In *Essays in Biography.* London: Hart-Davis.

Klaus, M.H., and Kennell, J.H. 1976. *Maternal-Infant Bonding.* Saint Louis: Mosby.

Kornfield, J. 1979. "Intensive Insight Meditation: A Phenomenological Study." *J. Transpersonal Psychol.* 11: 11.

Korzybski, A. 1933. *Science and Sanity: An Introduction to Non-Aristotelian Systems and General Semantics.* Lakeville, Conn.: The International Non-Aristotelian Library Publ. Co.

Kučera, O. 1959. "On Teething." *Dig. Neurol. Psychiat.* 27:296.

Kuhn, T. 1962. *The Structure of Scientific Revolutions.* Chicago: University of Chicago Press.

Laing, R.D. 1972a. "Metanoia: Some Experiences at Kingsley Hall." In *Going Crazy: The Radical Therapy of R.D. Laing and Others,* ed. H.M. Ruitenbeek. New York: Bantam Books.

———. 1972b. *Politics of Experience.* New York: Ballantine Books.

———. 1976. *Facts of Life: An Essay in Feelings, Facts and Fantasy.* New York: Pantheon Books.

———. 1982. *The Voice of Experience.* New York: Pantheon Books.

Lashley, K.S. 1929. *Brain Mechanisms and Intelligence.* Chicago: University of Chicago Press.

LeBon, G. 1977. *The Crowd.* New York: Penguin Books.

Leboyer, F. 1975. *Birth Without Violence.* London: Wildwood House.

Leibnitz, G.W. von 1951. *Monadology.* In *Leibnitz Selection,* ed. P.P. Wiener. New York: C. Scribner's Sons.

LeShan, L. 1974. *The Medium, the Mystic, and the Physicist: Toward a General Theory of the Paranormal.* New York: Viking Press.

Leuner, H. 1977. "Guided Affective Imagery: An Account of Its Development." *J. of Mental Imagery* 1:73.

———. 1978. "Basic Principles and Therapeutic Efficacy of Guided Affective Imagery (GAI)." In *The Power of Human Imagination,* ed. J.L. Singer and K.S. Pope. Plenum Publ.

Light, D. 1980. *Becoming Psychiatrists.* New York: W.W. Norton & Co.

Lilly, J.C. 1974. *The Human Biocomputer: Theory and Experiments.* London: ABACUS.

———. 1972. *The Center of the Cyclone.* New York: Julian Press.

Locke, J. 1823. *Essay Concerning Human Understanding.* In *The Works of John Locke.* London: T. Tegg.

Lorenz, K. 1963. *On Aggression.* New York: Bantam Books.

Lovelock, J. 1979. *Gaia: A New Look at Life on Earth.* New York and London: Oxford University Press.

Lowen, A. 1976. *Bioenergetics.* New York: Penguin Books.

Mann, F. 1973. *Acupuncture: The Ancient Chinese Art of Healing and How It Works Scientifically.* New York: Vintage Books.

Maslow, A. 1962. *Toward A Psychology of Being.* Princeton: VanNostrand.

———. 1964. *Religions, Values, and Peak Experiences.* Columbus: Ohio State University Press.

————. 1969. "A Theory of Metamotivation: The Biological Rooting of the Value of Life." In *Readings in Humanistic Psychology*, ed. A.J. Sutich and M.A. Vich. New York: The Free Press.

Mause, L. de 1975. The Independence of Psychohistory. In *The New Psychohistory*, ed. L. de Mause. New York: The Psychohistory Press.

————. 1982. *Foundations of Psychohistory*. New York: Creative Roots, Inc.

May, R., Angel, E., and Ellenberg, E., ed. 1958. *Existence: A New Dimension in Psychology and Psychiatry*. New York: Basic Books.

McCready, W.C., and Greeley, A.M. 1976. *The Ultimate Values of the American Population*. Beverly Hills, Cal.: Sage.

Mettrie, J.O. de la. 1912. *Man A Machine*. LaSalle, Ill.: Open Court.

Mookerjee, A. 1982. *Kundalini: The Arousal of the Inner Energy*. New York: Destiny Books.

Morris, D. 1967. *The Naked Ape*. New York: McGraw-Hill.

Mosher, L.R., and Menn, A.Z. 1978. "Community Residential Treatment for Schizophrenia: A Two-Year Follow-Up." *Hosp. & Commun. Psychiat.* 29: 715.

Mott, F.J. 1948. *The Universal Design of Birth*. Philadelphia: David McKay.

Mott, F.J. 1959. *The Nature of the Self*. London: Allen Wingate.

Murphy, M., and White, R.A. 1978. *The Psychic Side of Sports*. Menlo Park, Cal.: Addison-Wesley.

Nalimov, V.V. 1982. *Realms of the Unconscious: The Enchanted Frontier*. Philadelphia: ISI Press.

Orr, L., and Ray, S. 1977. *Rebirthing in the New Age*. Millbrae, Cal.: Celestial Arts.

Pagels, H.R. 1982. *The Cosmic Code: Quantum Physics as the Language of Nature*. New York: Simon & Schuster.

Pauli, W. 1955. "The Influence of Archetypal Ideas on the Scientific Theories of Kepler." In *The Interpretation of Nature and the Psyche*. Bollingen Series LI. New York: Pantheon.

Peerbolte, L. 1975. *Prenatal Dynamics*. In: *Psychic Energy*. Amsterdam, Holland: Servire Publ.

Penfield, W. 1976. *The Mystery of the Mind*. Princeton: Princeton University Press.

Perls, F. 1976a. *Gestalt Therapy Verbatim*. New York: Bantam Books.

Perls, F. 1976b. *The Gestalt Approach and Eye-Witness to Therapy*. New York: Bantam Books.

Perry, J. 1966. *Lord of the Four Quarters*. New York: Braziller.

————. 1974. *The Far Side of Madness*. Englewood Cliffs, N.J.: Prentice-Hall.

————. 1976. *Roots of Renewal in Myth and Madness*. San Francisco, Cal.: Jossey-Bass Publ.

Pietsch, P. 1981. *Shufflebrain: The Quest for the Hologramic Mind.* Boston: Houghton Mifflin.

Planck, M. 1968. *Scientific Autobiography and Other Papers.* Westport, Conn.: Greenwood Press.

Plato. 1961a. *Phaedrus.* In *The Collected Dialogues of Plato.* Bollingen Series LXXI. Princeton: Princeton University Press.

———. 1961b. *Laws.* In *The Collected Dialogues of Plato.* Bollingen Series LXXI. Princeton: Princeton University Press.

Popper, K.R. 1963. *Conjectures and Refutations: The Growth of Scientific Knowledge.* New York: Harper & Row.

———. 1965. *The Logic of Scientific Discovery.* London: Hutchinson.

Près, T. des 1976. *The Survivor: An Anatomy of Life in the Death Camp.* Oxford: Oxford University Press.

Pribram, K. 1971. *Languages of the Brain.* Englewood Cliffs, N.J.: Prentice-Hall.

———. 1976. "Problems Concerning the Structure of Consciousness." In *Consciousness and the Brain,* ed. G. Globus. New York: Plenum.

———. n.d. "Holonomy and Structure in the Organization of Perception." Mimeographed. Department of Psychology, Stanford University, Stanford, Cal.

———. 1981. "Non-Locality and Localization: A Review of the Place of the Holographic Hypothesis of Brain Function in Perception and Memory." Preprint for the Tenth ICUS, November.

Prigogine, I. 1980. *From Being to Becoming: Time and Complexity in the Physical Sciences.* San Francisco: W.H. Freeman.

Prigogine, I., and Stengers, I. 1984. *Order out of Chaos: Man's Dialogue with Nature.* New York: Bantam Books.

Quinn, S. 1982. "The Competence of Babies." *The Atlantic Monthly* (January): 74.

Rank, O. 1929. *The Trauma of Birth.* New York: Harcourt Brace.

Rappaport, M. et al. 1974. *Selective Drug Utilization in the Management of Psychosis.* NIMH Grant Report, MH-16445, March.

———. 1978. "Are There Schizophrenics for Whom Drugs May be Unnecessary or Contraindicated?" *Internat. Pharmacopsychiat.* 13:100.

Reich, W. 1949. *Character Analysis.* New York: Noonday Press.

———. 1953. *The Murder of Christ.* New York: Noonday Press.

———. 1961. *The Function of the Orgasm: Sex-Economic Problems of Biological Energy.* New York: Farrar, Strauss & Giroux.

———. 1970. *The Mass Psychology of Fascism.* New York: Simon & Schuster.

———. 1972. *Ether; God and Devil; and Cosmic Superimposition.* New York: Farrar, Straus & Giroux.

———. 1973. *Selected Writings: Introduction to Orgonomy.* New York: Farrar, Strauss & Giroux.

Riedlinger, T. 1982. "Sartre's Rite of Passage." *Journal of Transpersonal Psychol.* 14:105.

Rogers, C. 1951. *Client-Centered Therapy: Its Current Practice, Implications and Theory.* Boston: Houghton Mifflin.

————. 1961. *On Becoming a Person.* Boston: Houghton Mifflin.

Rolf, I. 1977. *Rolfing: The Integration of Human Structures.* New York: Harper & Row.

Rosen, D. 1973. "Suicide Survivors: A Follow-Up Study of Persons Who Survived Jumping from the Golden Gate and San Francisco-Oakland Bay Bridges." *West. J. Med.* 122:289.

Rosenhan, D. 1973. "On Being Sane in Insane Places." *Science* 179:250.

Sagan, C. 1974. *Broca's Brain.* New York: Random House.

Sargant, W. 1957. *Battle for the Mind.* London: Pan Books.

Scheff, T.J. 1974. The Labeling Theory of Mental Illness. *Amer. Sociol. Rev.* 39: 444.

Schroedinger, E. 1967. *What Is Life?* and *Mind and Matter.* Cambridge: Cambridge University Press.

Schutz, W., and Turner, E. 1982. *Body Fantasy.* New York: Irvington.

Sheldrake, R. 1981. *A New Science of Life: The Hypothesis of Formative Causation.* Los Angeles, Cal.: J.P. Tarcher.

Silverman, J. 1967. "Shamans and Acute Schizophrenia." *Amer. Anthropol.* 69:21.

Singer, J. 1972. *Boundaries of the Soul: The Practice of Jung's Psychology.* Garden City, N.Y.: Doubleday/Anchor Press.

Spitzer, R.L., and Wilson, P.T. 1975. "Nosology and the Official Psychiatric Nomenclature." In *Comprehensive Textbook of Psychiatry,* ed. H.I. Kaplan and B.J. Sadock. Baltimore: Williams & Wilkins.

Stapp, H.P. 1971. "S-Matrix Interpretation of Quantum Theory." *Physical Rev. D* (March 15).

————. 1979. "Whiteheadian Approach to Quantum Theory and the Generalized Bell's Theorem." *Foundations of Physics* 9:1.

Sullivan, H.S. 1955. *The Interpersonal Theory of Psychiatry.* London: Tavistock.

Sutich, A. 1976. "The Emergence of the Transpersonal Orientation: A Personal Account." *J. Transpersonal Psychol.* 8:5.

Szasz, T. 1961. *The Myth of Mental Illness.* New York: Hoeber-Harper.

Tarnas, R. in press. Title to be announced. Dallas: Spring.

Tart, C. 1975. *States of Consciousness.* New York: E.P. Dutton.

————. 1977. *PSI: Scientific Studies of the Psychic Realm.* New York: E.P. Dutton.

Tausk, V. 1933. "On the Origin of the Influencing Machine in Schizophrenia." *Psychoanalyt. Quart.* 11.

Thom, R. 1975. *Structural Stability and Morphogenesis.* Reading, Mass.: Benjamin.

Toben, B. 1975. *Space-Time and Beyond* (with J. Sarfatti and F. Wolf). New York: E.P. Dutton.

Trager, M. 1982. "Psychophysical Integration and Mentastic." *Journal of Holistic Health* 7:15.

Vaughan, F. 1980. "Transpersonal Psychotherapy: Context, Content and Process." In *Beyond Ego*, ed. R.N. Walsh and F. Vaughan. Los Angeles, Cal.: J.P. Tarcher.

Walsh, R.N., and Vaughan, F., eds. 1980. *Beyond Ego*. Los Angeles, Cal.: J.P. Tarcher.

Walsh, R.N. 1980. "The Consciousness Disciplines and the Behavioral Sciences: Questions of Comparison and Assessment." *Amer. J. Psychiat.* 137: 663.

Wasson, R.G.; Hofmann, A.; and Ruck, C.A.P. 1978. *The Road to Eleusis: Unveiling the Secret of the Mysteries*. New York: Harcourt, Brace Jovanovich.

Watson, L. 1980. *Lifetide*. New York: Bantam Books.

Wheeler, J.A. 1962. *Geometrodynamics*. New York: Academic Press.

Whitehead, A.N. 1929. *Process and Reality*. New York: Macmillan.

Wigner, E. 1967. *Symmetries and Reflections*. Bloomington, Ind.: Indiana University Press.

Wilber, K. 1977. *The Spectrum of Consciousness*. Wheaton, Ill.: The Theosophical Publ. House.

―――. 1979. "Physics, Mysticism, and the New Holographic Paradigm: A Critical Appraisal." *Re-Vision J.* 2:43.

―――. 1980. *The Atman Project: A Transpersonal View of Human Development*. Wheaton, Ill.: The Theosophical Publ. House.

―――. 1981. *Up From Eden: A Transpersonal View of Human Evolution*. Garden City, N.Y.: Doubleday/Anchor Press.

―――, ed. 1982. *The Holographic Paradigm and Other Paradoxes: Exploring the Leading Edge of Science*. Boulder, Colo.: Shambala.

Wolf, F.A. 1981. *Taking the Quantum Leap*. San Francisco: Harper & Row.

Young, A.M. 1976a. *The Geometry of Meaning*. New York: Delacorte Press.

―――. 1976b. *The Reflexive Universe: Evolution of Consciousness*. New York: Delacorte Press.

Young, M.A., and Meltzer, H.Y. 1980. "The Relationship of Demographic, Clinical, and Outcome Variables to Neuroleptic Treatment Requirements." *Schizophrenia Bull.* 6: 88.

Zukav, G. 1979. *The Dancing Wu Li Masters*. New York: W. Morrow.

Index

Italicized page numbers indicate references to illustrations.